MISS CAVELL WAS SHOT

Also by Monica Kendall:

The Duchess of Malfi (ed.) by John Webster (Pearson/Longman, 2004)

The Brontës and My Family: In Search of the Jenkinses (forthcoming)

Miss Cavell Was Shot

The Diaries of
Amy Hodson,
1914–1920

Ed. Monica Kendall

Published in 2015 by SilverWood Books

SilverWood Books Ltd
14 Small Street, Bristol, BS1 1DE
www.silverwoodbooks.co.uk

Copyright © Monica Eve Kendall 2015

The right of Monica Eve Kendall to be identified as the author
of this work has been asserted by her in accordance with
the Copyright, Designs and Patents Act 1988.

All rights reserved. No part of this publication may be reproduced,
stored in a retrieval system, or transmitted in any form or by any means,
electronic, mechanical, photocopying, recording or otherwise,
without prior permission of the copyright holder.

ISBN 978-1-78132-367-0 (paperback)
ISBN 978-1-78132-368-7 (ebook)

British Library Cataloguing in Publication Data
A CIP catalogue record for this book is available from
the British Library

Set in Bembo by SilverWood Books
Printed on responsibly sourced paper

*To my great-aunt Amy, with admiration,
and to her brother Charlie – no longer missing*

Fine day, cold. Went to church this morning and to Children's Service this afternoon. Several more people been shot.
— Amy Hodson, 7 November 1915 (aged fourteen)

Lucky are those who have a mother, a real one! May they never love anybody more than her.
— 16 July 1919

The sea is so calm at the moment and the sun shoots its luminous rays on this page of stupidities that I write.
— 13 August 1919

Contents

List of Figures	ix
Preface and Acknowledgements	xi
Family Who's Who	xvi
Non-Family Who's Who	xxi
Textual Note and Note on Churches	xxv
Map of Belgium	xxvii
Map of Brussels	xxviii
Hodson Family Tree	xxix
Introduction	1
My Experience on the Belgian Sea-Coast During the Year 1914	37
1914	45
1915	47
1916	107
1917	152
1918	201
1919	227
1920	287
Coda	292
Bibliography	295
Index	298

List of Figures

Cover
Amy Hodson in her school class photo, July 1919

1.	Amy and her son-in-law Jack Davidson in Canada, 1940s	xii
2.	'My Adventures with Nurse Cavell by Madame Bodart', *The Sunday Post*, 22 April 1923, p. 6. Credit: *Sunday Post*/British Library	4
3.	Ernest Rust Hodson, c. 1898. Credit: Tania Swift	14
4.	Margaret Maria Hodson née Kendall, c. 1880, Ernest's first wife	17
5.	43 rue Saint-Bernard (previously 27/29), St Gilles, Brussels: St Bernard's School. Photo: Monica Kendall	19
6.	Annie de Salis Hodson née Mourilyan, c. 1898. Credit: Conrad Walker	21
7.	Charlie Hodson and his half-sister Connie Jenkins, London, 1915	25
8.	Wedding of Constance Agnes Hodson and John Card Jenkins, 23 December 1913	32
9.	Amy in Canada, 1945	36
10.	Doris Walker née Hodson, with two of her children, Rhodesia, 1938	49
11.	Ada Bodart, 1928. Credit: Ernest Fawbert Collection	53
12.	Charlie, Connie and her son Desmond, and Tommy, London, 1915	64
13.	27 rue Africaine, St Gilles, Brussels, the Hodson home. Photo: Monica Kendall	69
14.	Tommy, Jack and son Desmond, and Charlie, London, 1915	75
15.	Charlie and Tommy, London, 1915	87
16.	Two pages from Amy's diary, 11–13 October 1915	92
17.	Garden party at the Brussels Lawn Tennis Club, 18 June 1890	135
18.	Arthur in Coquitlam, BC, Canada, 1972	176
19.	Amy's boarding-school timetable, 30 July 1917	179
20.	Lieut. Jack Jenkins, Royal Army Service Corps, probably Boulogne, c. 1918	193
21.	Newspaper photo of 'Representatives of the British Colony in	

	Brussels' presented to King Albert, c. 1919	207
22.	Charlie, Jack and Tommy, London, 1915	211
23.	Ernest and his daughter Connie, Broadstairs, Kent, 1932	217
24.	Church of the Resurrection, rue de Stassart, Ixelles, Brussels. Photo: Monica Kendall	221
25.	Review of the 55th (West Lancashire) Division, Brussels, 3 January 1919 © IWM. Imperial War Museum Q 3505	228
26.	Review of the 3rd British army corps outside the Palace, Brussels, 26 January 1919 © IWM. Imperial War Museum Q 7305	234
27.	Lieut. Jack Jenkins with his men, Royal Army Service Corps, probably Boulogne, c. 1918	235
28.	Henry and his father Ernest, and Jack's three children, Broadstairs, Kent, 1932	241
29.	Nurse Cavell's coffin at the Gare du Nord, 13 May 1919 © IWM. Imperial War Museum Q 70081	249
30.	Charlie, probably in London, c. 1919	255
31.	Amy's school photo, 2 July 1919	258
32.	Ernest with his granddaughter Doris and grandson Desmond, Siasconset, Nantucket island, 1920	264
33.	Rev. C.E. (Edward) Jenkins, 1914	275
34.	Tommy, Connie and family in Edgware, Middlesex, 1956	283
35.	Henry in Broadstairs, Kent, with Connie's children and Jack, 1932	286
36.	Amy in Lowestoft, Suffolk, 1921	293
37.	Amy and her daughter Mimi, Broadstairs, Kent, 1929	294

Maps

1.	Belgium under occupation, 1914–18. Credit: Wikimedia	xxvii
2.	Brussels and environs, 1904. Credit: Discusmedia.com/ Historical Antique Maps	xxviii

Unless otherwise noted, all photographs © Monica Eve Kendall

Preface and Acknowledgements

In June 2000, my great-aunt Amy's son-in-law, John R. Davidson, came on a visit from Canada to London and saw my mother Dorice and myself. He had heard I was interested in family history – I had written an article, 'My Grandfather Jack', about John Card Jenkins for the St Bernard's School magazine in New York. (Grandfather founded the school in 1904.) 'Jack' Jenkins was Amy's brother-in-law and is mentioned in her diaries. John R. Davidson (also a Jack!) gave me Amy's diaries. I read them with huge interest but didn't know what to do with them until the centenary of the outbreak of the Great War: I saw that the Imperial War Museum was interested in acquiring first-hand accounts. I contacted them and they were delighted to be given Amy's typewritten account of the outbreak of the war, 'My Experience on the Belgian Sea-Coast During the Year 1914' (transcribed below), together with her notebook containing drafts of it. Finding out that what Amy had experienced and written was of such interest, I woke up in the middle of the night, determined to start typing out her diaries and publish them. My sincere thanks go to Jack Davidson.

The most enormous debt of thanks goes to my research colleague and sounding board, my cousin Marcia Watson in Australia. Marcia is not related to the Hodsons or Jenkinses, so her online research has been stunning, generous and often unprompted – whether shipping registers, wills, birth and death certificates, or Brussels almanacs. While I slept, Marcia would sit at her computer (well, not all day!), and in the morning goodies would arrive in my email box. One of my favourite 'goodies' was when I told Marcia that Amy kept mentioning a Miss Mellin, who had a father called Mr Mellin (not much to go on, I thought). In the morning I found that Marcia had sent me almost their entire family tree (I exaggerate, but it felt like that)! One of the most spectacular finds

1. Amy and her son-in-law Jack Davidson in Canada, 1940s

was Ada Bodart's birth and death certificates (Amy's Mrs B.) since the latter was in her maiden name, and she wasn't christened Ada. She is the most elusive of 'Miss Cavell's network', as you will read below. But the most shocking of Marcia's discoveries was about Amy's half-brother Tommy (see the Introduction).

Marcia and I were first in contact in 2000 – because of my article for the St Bernard's School magazine. She sought permission to include my article in the Dalwood Restoration newsletter of New South Wales. The house and vineyard were created by the Wyndhams, sister and brother-in-law of my great-great-grandmother Eliza Jenkins, née Jay. I lost contact with Marcia until 2014, when I wrote an article online about looking for my ancestors, 'Brussels, Brontë, Jenkins: My Great-great-grandparents Rev. Evan and Eliza Jenkins and the Brontës'. Helen MacEwan of the Brussels Brontë Group passed on to me an email that Marcia had written to the Group, since Marcia seemed to be a cousin of mine. So my thanks go to Helen, too. Marcia and I are both descended from John Jay – father of Eliza Jenkins and Marcia's ancestor Margaret Wyndham. John Jay had a school in Brussels in the first decades of the nineteenth century (my family seems to consist entirely of schoolteachers and vicars!).

Thanks so much also to Hodson cousins in South Africa – Henry's daughter Shirley Swift, and granddaughters Melinda and Tania Swift – for their interest and for sending me Henry's memoirs and the photo of Ernest; and to Doris's grandson Conrad Walker for his help and information on his grandmother, Amy's half-sister, and for the photo that we think is Annie. Thanks to cousin Suzie Walker (née Jenkins) for lunches, support and chats. There are also marvellous people not related to me that I must thank: Linda Overton and staff at Beckenham Crematorium and Cemetery, Kent, were not only outstandingly efficient and kind in tracing Annie Hodson's grave, and sending me a map, but also quickly found the location of some Jay graves (who will make an appearance in my next book about the Brontës). Jane Horton gave me advice on indexing that I hugely appreciate: I edit and 'improve' numerous indexes as an editor, but I haven't compiled one from scratch for years (although I sometimes find myself doing it with the really hopeless!). I hope that the index is not only useful, but thanks to the Society of Indexers booklet she sent me that it is also interesting to consult. And because I have included as many names as possible, I hope descendants of those living in Brussels during the Great War will find it of value.

    I also want to give huge thanks to Anthony Richards, Head of Documents and Sound at the Imperial War Museum, for meeting me and finding Amy's account of her experiences on the Belgian seacoast in 1914 'exceptionally interesting' and 'full of historical value'. His first expression of interest inspired me to spend the long hours on transcribing and publishing this book, and I am so pleased Amy's account will be preserved properly. Thanks to the Imperial War Museum for permission to use three photographs. Thanks also to Barry Sullivan, Archives Assistant at D.C. Thomson & Co Ltd, Dundee, for sending me those extraordinary articles by Ada Bodart published in *The Sunday Post* in 1923, totally unsolicited (I had resigned myself to a long sitting in the British Library), which made my jaw drop. As far as I can see no biographer of Edith Cavell has seen or mentioned the articles. Thanks also to M. Emmanuel Debruyne of the Université catholique de Louvain who contacted me after I mentioned my book on the Edith Cavell website. He kindly sent me the essay on Ada Bodart written and researched by his student Clothilde de Brabant; I in turn sent him the *Sunday Post* articles and Amy's mentions of Ada Bodart – that's the way research works wonderfully, whether one holds an academic post or not, and I look forward very much to reading his forthcoming book about the network. Thanks also to staff at the British Library and National Archives, Kew for being so patient and guiding me through the new high-tech wonders of their libraries, especially when I muddle up passwords. And I would also like to thank the staff member at Amy's school – Institut des Filles de Marie – for showing me the courtyards and refectory that Amy frequented. Although another storey has been added to the school, the balcony may be the same. It is at 8 rue Théodore Verhaegen; no. 6 is now separate and partly occupied by nuns. Alas, I wasn't allowed to see the chapel. Thanks also to the staff at the Cimetière de Saint-Gilles for locating the site of Ernest's grave.

    I did wonder when I got to 1919 whether I should just give extracts from then on, or stop at some point after the reviews of troops that Amy watched and the demobilization of her brothers, but Marcia encouraged me to type up all the diaries I had been given (I presume these are all that survived), as she said people would be interested in what happened to Amy, and I certainly was. So the diary transcriptions end in 1920 when the diaries I have do (when Amy was nineteen).

I warn readers who might only be interested in occupied Brussels that these are a teenager's diaries – a feisty and troubled teenager (a sympathetic teacher might call her 'challenging') who, in 1917, is rejected by her mother. Amy longs for her love, and finds a complicated mother figure in Sister St Charles, her teacher at school, and the Virgin Mary. But for those who are interested in the occupation, there are extraordinary details about 'Mrs B.' helping the Allied soldiers escape, who is more or less forgotten by history, and Amy's reaction to her and Nurse Cavell's sentencing in 1915; 'Germs' requisitioning mattresses, kettles and bicycle tyres; and the lack of food: Amy mentioned the lack of potatoes so often that I dashed out to buy a 2.5 kilo bag. Also, her brother, half-brother and brothers-in-law joined the British army. The youngest of them, Charlie, ran away to join the army underage and was not heard of by Amy for a long time: a constant refrain of Amy is 'No news from Charlie.' Because he was for so long forgotten in the family after his early death at twenty-five, I also dedicate this book to him.

Family Who's Who

Note: The dates for the Mourilyan family have been taken from genealogy websites. The dates for the Hodson and Jenkins families are from birth, marriage and death certificates and family records.

The Hodson clan
My great-grandfather Ernest Rust Hodson (1853–1934) married twice. In order to untangle the names in Amy's diary I begin with a note here about the issue of each wife (see also the family tree, p. xxix). In 1880 he married my great-grandmother Margaret Maria Kendall in England, with surviving offspring: Connie, Doris and Lionel (known as Tommy). Margaret died in Brussels in June 1893. Ernest then married Annie de Salis Mourilyan in Brussels, in 1898, offspring: Charlie, Amy, Arthur and Henry. As far as I know, descendants of both marriages are currently living in the UK, France, Canada, South Africa and Australia. Thumbnail entries are given for those people who have longer entries in the Introduction, or, in Amy's case, throughout this book. Amy's relationship is mentioned after some of them.

Uncle Algie: Henry Algernon Hodson (uncle) (1852–1915). Ernest's elder brother. His son, Sir Arnold Wienholt Hodson (1881–1944), worked in the civil service in Africa, and was Governor of the Falkland Islands (1926–30). Among his books are *Trekking the Great Thirst* (1912) and *Seven Years in Southern Abyssinia* (1927). Wilfred Thesiger, the great explorer and writer, knew him and wrote to me in 1989, 'I always admired him and wished as a boy to lead a life like his in Abyssinia.' Amy doesn't mention her cousin Arnold, but he was close to her half-sister Connie.

Amy Victoria Hodson (the diarist) (1901–67). Born in Brussels on 23 February to British parents Ernest Rust and Annie de Salis

Family Who's Who

Hodson. Died in Canada. See Introduction, her diaries and Coda. Figures 1, 9, 31, 36, 37.

Annie de Salis Hodson, née Mourilyan (mother) (1870–1943). British, though born in Germany and living in Brussels when she married Ernest. In her old age she was cared for by her youngest son Henry. She died in London. See Introduction. Figures 6, 8.

Arthur: Arthur Robert Hodson (brother) (1904–73). He went with his younger brother Henry and mother Annie to England in 1918 and then to boarding school in Kent. He emigrated to Canada in May 1921, aged sixteen, to try farming in Quebec, his passage paid for by Uncle Fred. According to Henry, the job was poorly paid, with no prospects, and he eventually found employment with the Canadian Railways. Arthur and his wife Alma adopted two children. He died in Vancouver. Figure 18.

Auntie (1847–1916). Amy never gives her a name, and it was a Eureka moment at the National Archives when I found discussion about a Bengal pension for a woman living at 27 rue Africaine, giving the date she died. She was *Esther Hamilton Irvine*, and was the younger sister of Annie's mother Amy, née Irvine, who was born in Berhampore, Bengal, India, daughter of an army surgeon. If I had paid closer attention to the witnesses at Ernest and Annie's wedding I might have found her name a long time before. See Introduction.

Charlie: Charles Thomas Hodson (brother) (1899–1925). I had never heard of him until I was given Amy's diaries. He joined the Royal Fusiliers at fifteen and was in the trenches and later in German prisoner-of-war camps. After the war he tried to emigrate to Canada. See Introduction. Figures 7, 12, 14, 15, 22, 30.

Connie/Conn: Constance Agnes Jenkins, née Hodson (half-sister) (1881–1963). My grandmother. See Introduction. Figures 7, 8, 12, 17, 23, 34, 37.

Doris: Margaret Doris Walker, née Hodson (half-sister) (1886–1970). Emigrated to South Africa in 1904 at the age of seventeen, as it is said she didn't get on with her stepmother Annie. She first worked as a governess in Pretoria, then went to Filabusi Mine in Rhodesia in about 1907, and later to Essexvale (Esigodini). She married John Mortimer Brownlee Walker in June 1913. They had three children: Kendall (b. 1914), Kathleen (b. 1915) and Betty (b. 1919). She stayed with her sister Connie after the Second World War in Folkestone, with no doubt lengthy walks with the dogs. Figure 10.

Edward Jenkins: Rev. Charles Edward Jenkins (1873–1931). Elder brother of Jack Jenkins. Born in Brussels, sixth child of Rev. John Card Jenkins and Mary Elizabeth, née Tompson. In 1890 Edward went to Constantinople as tutor to the family of the British Ambassador and then accompanied them to Vienna. In 1896 he went to Jesus College, Cambridge, where he was a double blue in rugby football and tennis. He was ordained as a priest in 1901, and was later appointed vicar at St Paul's Church, Leicester (1911–28), serving as chaplain to the forces during the First World War. In 1928 he became chaplain at his father's church in Brussels, the Church of the Resurrection, until his death after suffering severe pneumonia. He was unmarried and lived with his sister Rosie. Figures 8, 33.

Ernest Rust Hodson (father) (1853–1934). My great-grandfather. See Introduction. Figures 3, 8, 21, 23, 28, 32.

Uncle Fred: Frederick James Mourilyan (great-uncle) (1846–1927) and *Auntie Flo*: Caroline Florence, née Gardiner (1841–1922). Fred was the younger brother of Annie's father, Thomas. Fred and Thomas's father had been a solicitor with the British colony in Paris. Fred started as a banker in Paris and then worked in Romania. In 1879 the family moved to Brussels, where Fred worked for the Imperial Continental Gas Company. In 1914 they were living at 11 rue du Châtelain. According to Amy's diary, Uncle Fred moved to England in 1914/15, and was at one point staying with his sister *Polly*.

Henry/Baby: Henry Clarence Hodson (brother) (1906–99). Henry is known as 'Baby' in the first part of the diaries. My mother met him when he came for the summer holiday in Broadstairs, Kent, in 1929. He was terrific at tennis: beating her mother (Connie's)

'French friends' satisfactorily! After working in Belgium, his job moved him to London in 1936 and he brought his mother Annie to live with him in Muswell Hill. Henry married in 1938, and Annie moved to a house nearby. He was conscripted into the army, then emigrated to Rhodesia, to join his half-sister Doris, in 1953. His daughter and granddaughters kindly sent me his memoirs, which I quote from in my Introduction. Figures 28, 35.

Jack Jenkins: John Card Jenkins (brother-in-law) (1874–1958). My grandfather. Went to Corpus Christi College, Cambridge. Founded St Bernard's School in New York in 1904. Married Constance Agnes Hodson (eldest daughter of Ernest Rust Hodson and Margaret Maria Kendall) in 1913. See Introduction. Figures 8, 14, 20, 22, 27.

'Paddy' Palmer: Major Frederick Edmund Corbett Palmer (1872–1915). Acting Lieutenant Colonel (7th York and Lancaster Regiment), husband of Janet, née Jenkins (1870–1954), the brother-in-law of Amy's half-sister Connie. He arrived in France in July 1915. A month later the battalion was at Reningheist, Belgium. He was wounded, and died on 28 August. Fred and Janet had one son, *Edward John* (1911–86), a musical prodigy, who won many prizes at the Royal Academy of Music (1929–33) and became a professional musician, as John Palmer. He was a big bear of a man, alarmingly short-sighted (I remember him offering me mouldy strawberries in his tiny sitting-room dwarfed by two grand pianos sometime in the early 1980s). Figure 8.

Aunt Polly: Mary Anna (Polly) Robinson, née Mourilyan (great-aunt) (1845–after 1915). Younger sister of Annie's father (Thomas Burton Mourilyan, 1843–79). Married to Frederick Dalgarno Robinson, a solicitor (c. 1830–1901). In the 1911 census Polly is living with her daughter at 105 Cheriton Road, Folkestone, Kent, but she was possibly only visiting her daughter, who had a son less than one month old. Polly's address in 1901 was Marshgate House, Richmond, Surrey. An address near London makes sense since Charlie joined a London regiment: the Royal Fusiliers.

Tommy: Lionel Ernest Hodson (half-brother) (1890–1964) was born in Brussels and emigrated to Canada in 1906 when he was sixteen.

Amy's diary entry of 16 December 1918 states that she hadn't seen him for twelve years; and the emigration date is confirmed by a US record of aliens in 1923. His story is complicated. See Introduction. Figures 12, 14, 15, 22.

Non-Family Who's Who

Further information is given on some people in the Introduction, as noted.

B., Mrs (1874–1936) Amy doesn't give her full name until after her trial. She is *Ada Bodart*, née Anna Maria Doherty, acquaintance of the Hodson family and part of the secret network with Edith Cavell and Philippe Baucq to get Allied soldiers safely across the Dutch frontier to prevent them from being shot. Born in Northern Ireland, Ada (or Anne/Anna/Annie) married a Belgian and had two children, both of whom Amy knew. She was on trial for treason with Miss Cavell in October 1915; the death penalty for her was commuted to fifteen years' hard labour. She played herself in a silent film about Miss Cavell, *Dawn* (1928), directed by Herbert Wilcox, with Sybil Thorndike as Nurse Cavell. She was awarded an OBE in 1928 and also honoured by the Belgians, but there are puzzles about her life. See Introduction. Figures 2, 11.

Butcher, (Mr) Alfnoth Bourchie (b. c. 1864 in Bombay), his wife *Gertrude* and their daughters *Joan* and *Meg*. Friends of the Hodsons. Alfnoth Butcher was British, manager of a lace glove factory in the heart of the old city, place Vieille Halle aux Blés, part of the premier glove producer in the world: Dent-Allcroft. His older sister *Bertha Butcher* was one of the Ladies-Superintendent of a charity, the Queen Victoria Institute for Governesses and Nurses, established in Brussels in 1815, and a colleague of Nurse Cavell.

Cavell, Edith (Miss/Nurse) (1865–1915) Born in Norfolk, she went to Brussels in 1890 as a governess. She returned to Norfolk to nurse her father in 1895 and decided to train as a nurse. In 1907 she returned to Brussels as director of a nurses' training school, the first in Belgium. In World War I her training school and clinic became part of the network to help Allied soldiers escape. She was arrested by the Germans on 5 August 1915, as Amy describes, and put on trial for treason on 7 October along with thirty-four others. On 11 October she received the death sentence. Rev. Gahan gave her final Communion that evening. She told him: 'standing as I do in view of God and Eternity: I realise that patriotism is not enough. I must have no hatred or bitterness towards anyone.' She was shot at the Tir National rifle range at Schaerbeek at dawn on 12 October with Philippe Baucq. A brave woman, but her biographers tend to give an unbalanced view of her role in the network. The American Minister Brand Whitlock in his *Journal* says that Prince Reginald de Croÿ (a leading member of the network) called her 'exceedingly imprudent' (p. 493). Figure 2.

Ehrlich, Carl (Charles Worsley Ehrlich) (1884–1957) and *Mrs Olga Ehrlich* (b. 1888). Amy set a challenge as she misspelt his name as Erlich. He was an American citizen from Chicago, student at Trinity College, Cambridge, who moved permanently to Brussels in 1905, where his father, Eugene Mortimer Ehrlich, and mother, Isabel, were living. At one stage he worked for SOFINA with Dannie Heineman (see below). An excellent tennis player, he presented the Carl Ehrlich Cup for a men's tournament to the tennis club. His wife, Olga, née Wehrhahn, was born in Chile. They married in 1913 in Kent and don't seem to have had children.

Gahan, Rev. Horace Stirling Townsend (1870–1959) Born in Donegal, Ireland, he was ordained in Coventry in 1895. In 1914 he married *Florence Buxton Muriel Marston*, and in that year took over the Anglican chaplaincy in Brussels at Christ Church, rue Crespel, where the Hodsons and Edith Cavell worshipped during the closure of the Church of the Resurrection. He administered Holy Communion to Nurse Cavell on the evening before her execution. From 1923 until his death he was the rector of Thrussington village church, Leicestershire. Figure 21.

Heineman, Mr Daniel (Dannie) (1872–1962) and his German-born wife *Mrs Hettie Heineman* (b. 1890). Amy plays with their children *Stephen* (b. 1912) and *James (Jimmy)* (b. 1917). She mentions also

Joe Heineman as dying in 1919: possibly a son born c. 1915. Daniel Heineman was an American citizen, of German Jewish descent. He went to Germany for his education, studying electrical engineering, and moved to Brussels as the managing director of the Société Financière de Transports et d'Enterprises Industrielle (SOFINA). He was involved with the Commission for Relief in Belgium (CRB), led by Herbert Hoover from October 1914, which saved those in occupied Belgium from starvation. Mrs Heineman generously sends chocolate to Amy and takes her (under duress) to see *Tosca* in 1919. Amy says mysteriously in December 1918: 'Mrs Heineman invited us three to dinner at 7 o'clock. I told Daddy that I didn't want to go for various reasons. I don't know why, or, at least, yes, I know why Daddy would like me to like this woman but I will never do it.'

J./Joséphine Lives with the Hodson family and is the family's cook.

Lecourt, Father Roman Catholic priest who helps Amy and is a friend of Miss Mellin. Amy goes with other schoolgirls to a service at his church on 16 September 1917, and meets his cousin Cécile in August 1919. He leaves Brussels in 1919, and in Amy's 1920 diary he is with her and Rita Mellin in Bognor Regis, West Sussex. On 9 July 1915 Amy writes: 'Mrs B. has again changed her house and she won't tell anybody but Father Lecourt.' I have been unable to find out anything more about him. An unnamed clergyman who helps Ada Bodart is mentioned in her *Sunday Post* article of 3 June 1923: 'I sought out one of the members of our organisation, who was a clergyman, and whose name for that reason I will not give.' It is not clear why she can't name him eight years later. Maybe it was Father Lecourt.

Mellin, Miss Rita (1870–1956) is a constant support to Amy after she is rejected by her mother; for example, Amy spends Christmas Day and New Year in 1917 with her and they go on holiday together. Detective work online has revealed she was Marguerite (Rita), daughter of Theresa and Lassen Mellin. Amy mentions her younger sister *Ethel*, who goes to England in July 1915, returning to Brussels in 1918, and she also mentions their father, *Mr Mellin*. He was living in avenue Louise at the time of his death in December 1918, aged seventy-seven. Before his retirement he was a 'négociant', according to the Brussels almanac – a merchant. Rita was born and died in England. I envisioned Rita as a stalwart member of the Anglican community but on 25 July 1919 she becomes a Roman Catholic.

poet, the According to Amy 'the poet' is Raymond Collart, and his birthday was on 18 June. Arthur, aged eleven, is constantly going places with him on his own. But on 12 April 1916 Amy writes: 'Daddy won't let Arthur go to the poet any more.' And on 11 May 1916 she writes: 'Went to tennis this afternoon and in coming back we met the poet; Arthur talked to him but we have been forbidden to talk to him, why, I don't know; so Baby and I walked on.'

St Charles, Sister/Soeur (S.S.C) A nun-teacher of huge emotional importance to Amy at her convent boarding school, in rue Théodore Verhaegen, St Gilles, Brussels, from 1917 to 1919. Amy is a boarder at the school, then a day girl, and returns as boarder and teacher because of her mother's second rejection of her. See Introduction.

Villiers, Rt Hon. Sir Francis Hyde (1852–1925) Son of the 4th Earl of Clarendon. British diplomat. Envoy Extraordinary and Minister Plenipotentiary to Belgium (1911–19), Ambassador (1919–20). Figure 25.

Watts, Ethelbert (1845–1919) Born in Philadelphia, he was an engineer and iron manufacturer. In his fifties he joined the American foreign service, serving as Consul in Prague, St Petersburg and finally Brussels (1907–17).

Whitlock, Brand (1869–1934) Born in Urbana, Ohio, he was by turns a reporter, lawyer and mayor of Toledo, Ohio, before being appointed Minister to Belgium (1913–19) and Ambassador (1919–22). He was also a novelist. His journal and letters give a fascinating and eloquent account of his time in Brussels during World War I.

Textual Note and Note on Churches

In June 2000, Amy's son-in-law, John R. Davidson, visited London from Canada and gave me five notebooks containing Amy's diaries, dated from 1914 to 1920; also her *carnet de conscience* ('conscience diary'); a typewritten account of the German invasion in 1914 that she called 'My Experience on the Belgian Sea-Coast During the Year 1914', typed up c. 1919; and her notebook of 1913–15 containing two drafts of it in English (with corrections) and one in French. I donated the invasion accounts to the Imperial War Museum, London, in October 2014.

I have transcribed all the notebooks and her account of the German invasion of 1914 in this book. I have taken her account of the invasion from her typewritten 'fair copy', adding from her notebook (which has pages missing) when the typewriter ink is too faint to be read, or the thin paper is torn, or a passage was crossed out in her notebook and interestingly not typed up.

I have also transcribed one account of a nightmare concerning her mother from her 'conscience diary'. And I have given examples from it of her 'bad conduct' in the Introduction in the section 'Amy's conscience diary'.

There are some gaps in her diaries, including a major one for 28 February to 27 November 1918 – alas, for the end of the war. Since the notebooks either side of this gap are complete, it seems a notebook went missing. But her account of 1919 is of much interest since most serving personnel weren't demobbed until that year, for many months no one was sure that the war really had ended, and there were splendid reviews of troops as King Albert led his country into a difficult peace.

Amy's spelling and punctuation are generally good, but I have corrected, modernized and regularized spellings, except for numbers. Spellings of towns follow her main usage, such as Westend, Knocke or Berghem; when they were obviously misspelled I have corrected them. The various spellings of people's names was harder to tackle; I have usually used her most frequent spellings (when I could decipher her handwriting), comparing them to names used in Belgium today. Sometimes it is not clear on which day her entry is intended for: I have used common sense, that is, a schoolgirl would probably know the day of the week rather than the date. I have noted on the few occasions when I can't read her words, shown as [...]. The long ellipses are Amy's. I have italicized names of ships, films and newspapers, for example the 'Times' I have changed to *The Times*, but have kept her underlinings which she uses for emphasis. Amy copies out several extracts from newspapers, including some poems, which I haven't compared with the originals, apart from the Hansard extract (26 October 1915): it seemed more useful to the reader to substitute the fairly accurate summary in French with the original. From the end of 1918 Amy often writes in French. I have translated these diary entries and have placed asterisks at the start and end of the translated sections. As she was bilingual in French and English, her English often has French syntax, which I have not altered.

Churches

Until her move to a Roman Catholic boarding school ('pensionnat'), Amy usually means by going to church the Anglican Christ Church in rue Crespel, consecrated in 1902. My Jenkins ancestors had built the Anglican Church of the Resurrection nearby, in rue de Stassart, consecrated in 1874, but the latter was closed during World War I. It was High Church. Edith Cavell worshipped there before the war and then at Christ Church. In one of her *Sunday Post* articles (22 April 1923), Ada Bodart says she first met Edith Cavell at the Church of the Resurrection. Rev. Gahan, British Chaplain in Brussels, took over the Anglican chaplaincy at the start of the war. Later, in 1958, the congregation of the Church of the Resurrection joined Christ Church at the latter's church, which was renamed Holy Trinity, at rue Capitaine Crespel, 29. Once Amy started boarding in 1917 she went to Catholic churches, including St Jacques-sur-Coudenberg in Place Royale, St Gudule (now the Cathedral of St Michael and St Gudula) and St Gilles. The Church of the Resurrection – the building of which was a huge, almost impossible effort that contributed to the death of one of my Jenkins ancestors – was destroyed by fire in 1927, restored, became a shop, and is currently a nightclub.

Map of Belgium

Belgium under occupation, 1914–18

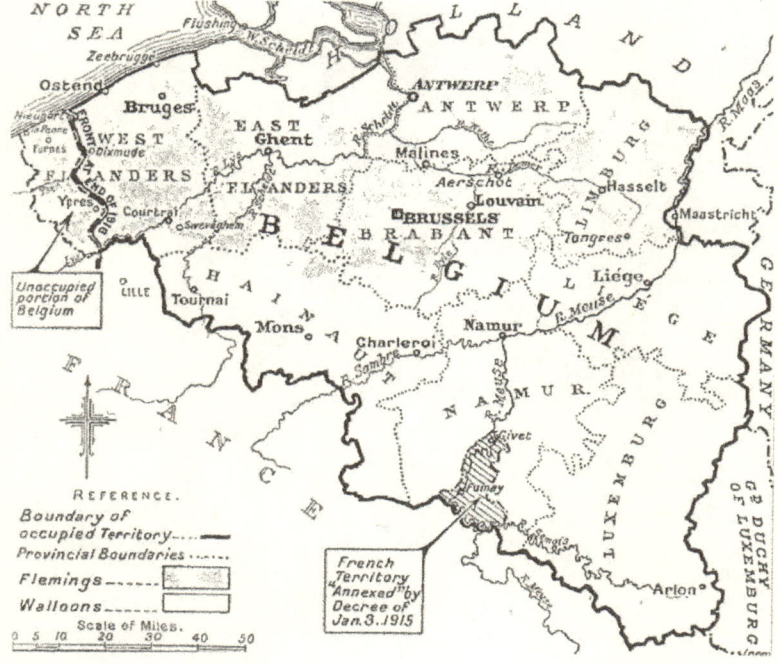

'Miss Cavell Was Shot': The Diaries of Amy Hodson, 1914–1920

Brussels and environs, 1904

Hodson Family Tree

Ernest's First Marriage

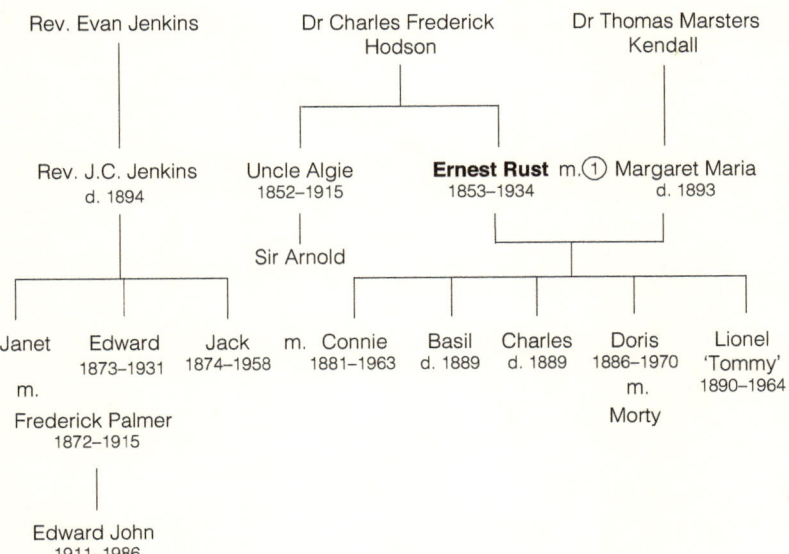

Ernest's Second Marriage

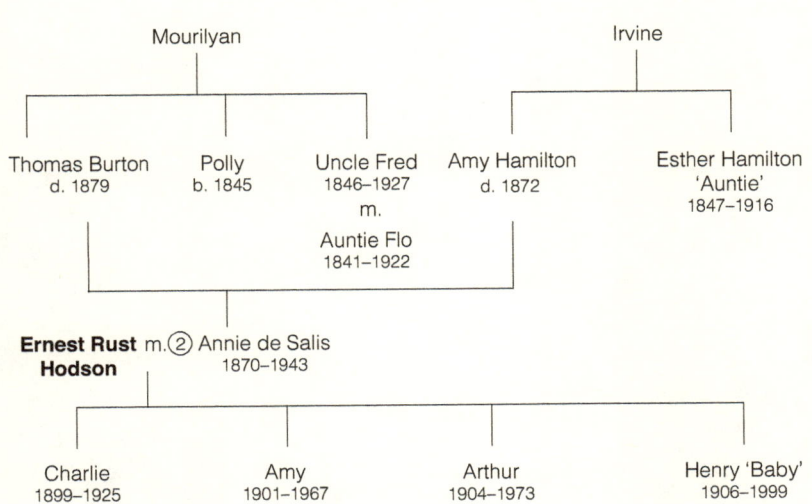

Simplified family tree of the Hodson family. Full dates are given
for those mentioned in Amy's diary

Introduction

> Miss Cavell, Princesse de Croÿ, Mr Severin etc. were shot this morning by those fiends! Outrageous thing! Several people who saw Miss Cavell yesterday said that she was perfectly calm and dignified. She has died like a martyr. Heaven punish those demons who judged and sentenced her to death. She, who did such a lot of good.

Amy Hodson, my great-aunt, wrote this on 12 October 1915 in her diary as the rumours spread through Brussels. She corrects it later; we now know that only two people were shot on that occasion: Edith Cavell and Philippe Baucq. Amy was a British teenager living in occupied Brussels. She had been born there; her father had come to Brussels from Bishop's Stortford, England, to take over the Jenkins school (founded by my British ancestors) in the St Gilles area of Brussels (south of the city centre). Everyone knew everyone among the British and American community in the city, so of course Amy knew Nurse Cavell and Father Gahan – who gave Edith Cavell her final Communion before she was shot. Amy survived the food shortages – 'no potatoes' runs through much of her text – endured occupation, the continuous sound of the guns, the zeppelins, the news of people taken or shot, spies everywhere, and also knew some of those who helped the Allies, especially 'Mrs B.'

Mrs B. and Miss Cavell
On 10 October 1915, Amy writes:

> Met Mrs B.'s children coming back from the Kommandantur, and they said that they spoke of Miss Cavell being shot, and as she has not had half so many Tommy Atkins as Mrs B. they are very much frightened of their mother being shot too.

'Miss Cavell Was Shot': The Diaries of Amy Hodson, 1914–1920

Many times in her diary Amy refers to Mrs B. – hiding Allied soldiers in the cellar of her home, changing house to keep from detection, brave when confronted by Germans at the Kommandantur (the German headquarters). Amy doesn't give her full name until after her trial, wary of her diaries being taken: she is Mme Ada Bodart. Some months before the Germans arrested Mme Bodart, Amy wrote on 9 May 1915:

> Beautiful day. I went to see the English soldiers at Mrs B.'s. One of them picked a big bunch of white lilac for Mother, and Hilda, Mrs B.'s girl, puts a forget-me-not in their button-holes every morning. There are eleven of them and they each signed their names on a handkerchief.

This account is different in her younger brother Henry's memoirs 'This Is My Life' (written about sixty years later):

> We had some interesting experiences in War-time Brussels, and notably we met Nurse Cavell at the nearby hospital, whom we found so very nice and kind. We had the wonderful experience of meeting some wounded British soldiers, whom she was treating there. My sister produced a silk handkerchief, and obtained all their signatures on it. Unfortunately, she lost this somewhere.

I think it is likely that, so many years later, Amy's brother Henry confused meeting Miss Cavell with the signing of Amy's handkerchief – and, by then, Ada Bodart was forgotten. Edith Cavell's story is well known, but little if anything is written about Mme Bodart. In the British Library I browsed through seven books about Edith Cavell, dating between 1941 and 2007: most had just a few mentions of her (one didn't mention her at all). A few said she was 'Irish' (possibly copying this from Princess Marie de Croÿ's book *War Memories* of 1932). One called her Mme Ida [*sic*] Doherty Bodart and said she was thirty-four at her trial (she was forty-one). The most recent one couldn't even provide her with a first name – just calling her 'Mrs Bodart' in her one mention in the text and index.

Newspaper obituaries tell a conflicting story. *The Times* of 8 February 1936 states:

> Mme. Ada Bodart, a companion of the late Nurse Cavell, has died in Brussels after a long illness, telegraphs our Brussels Correspondent. She was sentenced by a German military court on August 6, 1915, to 15 years' penal servitude and interned in Silesia. Mme. Bodart, formerly Miss Doherty, was born at Richmond, Surrey. She rendered great services to the Allied soldiers in the Great War, and whenever in post-War years the 'Old Contemptibles' made a pilgrimage to Belgium they never failed to visit their benefactress.

The date of the sentencing is totally wrong and I don't think Ada Bodart went anywhere near Richmond in Surrey. The *Dundee Evening Telegraph*, 7 February 1936 states:

> Many a British prisoner of war has cause to remember with gratitude Madame Ada Bodart.
> With Nurse Cavell and the young Belgian architect, M. Baucq, this gallant Irishwoman led many convoys of fugitives to the Dutch Frontier before discovery put an end to her efforts and resulted in the death of her two heroic colleagues.
> Born of Irish parents in 1882, Madame Bodart adopted Belgium as her home. She married a Belgian architect who died before the outbreak of the Great War in 1914, leaving her with two children – Philippe born in April, 1904 and Ada born in December, 1906. Even before war broke out in 1914 she was a close friend of Nurse Cavell.

Confusing even further is the *Dundee Courier* on 8 February 1936 which says she was half-Scottish and half-English and that she lived in Edinburgh before going to Belgium, and that her husband was in 'a high position in the Belgian Foreign Office'. It also states that among the Bodarts' friends was the Graux family, with whom Miss Cavell was a governess. However, on the marriage certificate of 1898, Louis-Joseph Bodart is a 'cocher' – a coachman or cabby. According to official documents and Ada's own account, he died in 1909. It was also his second marriage.

The only points of agreement in the obituaries were that Ada Bodart's maiden name was Doherty and that she was born in the UK. Then my research colleague Marcia found Mme Bodart's death certificate, witnessed by her son Philippe (mentioned in Amy's diary). It states that she was born 'Anne Marie' Doherty on 22 July 1874 in Newry, County Down, Ireland, United Kingdom of Great Britain and Ireland, to Richard James Doherty and Elizabeth née Kelly. She died aged sixty-one on 6 February 1936 in rue de Pascale, Brussels (now near the European Parliament). After her name it reads: 'Chevalier de l'Ordre de La Couronne avec rayures d'Or'. This was a high Belgian honour for civilians.

But it was at this point in my research that I discovered ten articles published by the Dundee *Sunday Post* in 1923, called 'My Adventures with Nurse Cavell by Madame Bodart (formerly Miss Ada Doherty)'. This is not the book to discuss these articles (over 40,000 words) or who wrote them – my instinct is that a journalist interviewed her, wrote them and mangled some of what she told him (the D.C. Thomson archivist told me that the business archives for 1923 are not available for research). Ada Bodart declares in them that she is Scottish, born in Edinburgh in 1881. Obviously there are many fascinating details, but it seems that a fine sieve is needed to distinguish between the truths and non-truths or journalist invention. For a moment I was swayed by this Scottish-born story. However, my research colleague Marcia then unearthed

2. 'My Adventures with Nurse Cavell by Madame Bodart',
The Sunday Post, 22 April 1923, p. 6

a christening document for Anna Maria Doherty, born in Newry on 22 July 1874 to Richard James Doherty and Elizabeth Kelly. The date and parentage matched the death certificate. Whatever the reason for the untruths in the newspaper, the difficult job of separating fact from fiction in the articles in the Scottish *Sunday Post* will be helped by the fact that Amy knew Mme Bodart; knew that she was sheltering Allied soldiers; thought that she had sheltered far more than Nurse Cavell.

Amy calls Ada's daughter Hilda in the diary, and indeed *The British Journal of Nursing* in November 1924 also calls her by that name:

'Edith Cavell'

The 12th of October was the Anniversary of the Martyrdom of Edith Cavell and was solemnly celebrated at the Prison of Saint Gilles in a suburb of Brussels.

The cell which she had occupied was decorated with flowers, the gift of her devoted collaborator, Mme. Bodart, and Mme. de Leu de Cecil and others. In the Prison Chapel an address was delivered recalling Miss Cavell's heroic action, and beautiful music, concluding with a patriotic hymn sung by Mlle. Hilda Bodart, was performed.

Hilda was born in 1900, and therefore was almost the same age as Amy. On Ada Bodart's death certificate in 1936, one of the witnesses is Robert Recour, 'gendre' (son-in-law), who must be Hilda's husband. On it, Ada's son Philippe states he is a 'technicien', aged thirty-six. Amy says he was thirteen when he was arrested by the Germans in August 1915 for not disclosing who was the editor of the resistance newspaper *La Libre Belgique*, and some court documents from 1915 say he was twelve. Philippe was actually born in 1899 and was sixteen at the time. It is probable that Mme Bodart dropped three years off his age to save him from being taken by the Germans.

Uncovering the network of those who helped Allied soldiers and young men to escape from German-occupied territory is a complex issue. But it is clear from Amy's accounts in her diary that the Hodson family were also involved – even if it was only visiting the Allied soldiers in hiding, or Amy taking letters to Mme Bodart. Though on one occasion Hilda brings a French soldier on the run to them (22 July 1915); perhaps the Hodsons sheltered others. The shock of M. Baucq and Miss Cavell being shot was huge – as Amy's reaction above shows. If Ada Bodart was as involved as Miss Cavell, and maybe even more than her, why was she sentenced to hard labour and not shot as well? The accounts suggest that she either went mad, or pretended to be, and that the Spanish Minister helped get her sentence commuted. Indeed, Ada Bodart says that she feigned illness before the trial (*Sunday Post*, 17 June 1923, p. 6). In an earlier *Sunday Post* article Ada (or the ghostwriter journalist) says:

> It was [Edith Cavell's] great love of truth that sent her to her doom, and I am afraid that I cannot hope to be judged by her standard, for while she continued to implicate herself, I was strenuously denying that I had ever done anything against what the Germans called the 'enemy'.
>
> It was necessary for me to do this, even at the expense of truth, for, while by telling the truth I might have escaped with my own life, I would most certainly have been responsible in some measure for the shooting not only of Philip Baucq, but for half a dozen other prisoners who, along with us, were lying under suspicion in the prison of St Gilles. (*Sunday Post*, 10 June 1923, p. 7)

However kindly put, that seems to be a criticism of Edith Cavell. Ada Bodart writes about the night when Miss Cavell and M. Baucq were shot:

> It was not till three years afterwards, when I came out of prison, that I learned that the Spanish Minister, the Marquis de Villalobar, had pleaded all night at the German Headquarters for my life, and the Germans, not knowing that I was British like Edith Cavell, but thinking I was a Belgian woman, gave in to his pleas. (*Sunday Post*, 17 June 1923, p. 6)

It is probable that Miss Cavell's confession was irrelevant: she was shot because she was English.

Mme Bodart's reaction to being summoned to the Kommandantur, a few months before she was arrested, shows the character of a person determined to survive. Amy writes in her diary on 17 May 1915:

The other day Mrs B. was told to go to the Kommandantur: she went, and by clever tricks she managed to get round the Germans by pretending she was helping them, or else they would have kept her prisoner. She has now got rid of all the English but one and has gone back to her old house and she has made the Germans sign a paper that they must not be allowed to go into her house.

One conundrum is where Ada Bodart was living. For some of 1915 it must have been near rue Africaine in St Gilles, where Amy lived, in order for Amy to meet her and her children so often, and indeed visit the soldiers and get her handkerchief signed. But the addresses normally given in biographies of Miss Cavell are all to the east of the city, such as rue Emile Wittmann. In the *Sunday Post* articles and Foreign Office papers Ada Bodart says she was indeed at that address. But it is unlikely that Amy, then aged fourteen, would have been sent with letters to her an hour's walk away. In Ada Bodart's account in the *Sunday Post* she mentions that she also had a house in rue Washington: it is only nine minutes' walk from rue Africaine. It is the only address that makes sense of Amy meeting Philippe and Hilda coming back from the Kommandantur, as quoted above, which was in the rue de la Loi. But another puzzle is that in her diary Amy says that Mrs B. goes back to her 'old house' and changes her house twice (17 May, 2 June, 9 July 1915). Different addresses are not mentioned in the *Sunday Post* nor in the National Archives papers. One wonders if she was concealing something, and wonders how the widow of a 'cocher' could afford it. Perhaps her father-in-law left her money, but after release from prison she was destitute.

Returning to Amy's declaration that Miss Cavell 'has not had half so many Tommy Atkins as Mrs B.' one has only to look at the Foreign Office file 'Germany: Prisoners', in the National Archives at Kew, which extraordinarily no writer on Miss Cavell seems to have done. The summary of the file includes 'Ada Bodart, asking for 4425 francs'. The file consists entirely of the correspondence of Belgian and French nationals requesting compensation from the British government for the cost of aiding Allied soldiers during the war. It seems Mme Bodart first requested expenses in January 1919, not long after her release from a German prison. She writes a letter on 14 May 1919 from 106 rue Goffart (the spelling is hers or the typist's):

Your Excellency,

There are four months, since I gave my reports, to the General Lyon, English militaire attache to the Legation to Bruselles, till this present date, there is not an answer which I think is very unkind, considering all I have done and suffered in a German Prison, during three years for having kept, fed clothed and conducted into Holland, the English soldiers. The circumstances in I and my two children at present is very sad, as we have lost all, of course as I am Belgium by marriage, the Belgium Government will restore the value of my furniture, and etc. but when in waiting this promised time I am obliged to live in a very small furnished flat, almost starving. I feel quite sure that the rich English Goverment will not leave a poor widow and her two children without help. Useless I go into detail, the Belgium press has spoken enough of my devotement, I am Ada Bodart condemned with Miss Cavell, in 1915 as we worked together, my home was 19 Rue Emile Wittmann, as this address I suppose is on all the reports. I simply reclaim my money I spent during my nine months of work, which amounts only to a few thousand francs. Had I reflected such a time to the soldiers into my home, caused my present ruin and risk of my life (as the ministre of Spain Le Marquis de Villalobar svaed my head, othewise to day I should be side by side with Miss Cavell as we were condemned to the same fate) I may state what a different result might have been on both sides. Your Excellency will think as I do, this does not give courage to my decendants.

Your Excellency, I beg of you, to refer to where my reports have been sent, and this letter to, if it is not for your Department. Your Excellency may refer to the English Ministre Sir Francis Villers, The Spanish Ministre Le Marquis de Villalobar and the Prince R. de Croy, who is to the Legation de Belgique, 59 Sloane Gardens S.W. Your Excellency I have all my confidences in you, and hope it is not in vain, as we are now in great want of our money.

I remain,
Yours respectfully,
(Sgd.) Ada Bodart née Doherty

She had to write again on 23 June when no money was forthcoming:

> Have been three years and four months in Germany in Prison. Money could never pay my awful sufferings I had to endure there, loss of health etc. treated as a criminal. Worked from November 1914 until August 1915 during which time I sent into Holland eight hundred and fifty British soldiers, hid, fed, lodged, clothed and conducted them into Holland, at the risk, you already know ... I simply ask five francs per day for each man, although I kept a great number more than two months, who were ill or wounded; so the small sum is four thousand two hundred and twenty five francs.
>
> It is not <u>a recompense</u> I beg but my own money spent for the British troops.

On 19 July Sir Francis Villiers wrote to the Earl Curzon of Kedleston at the Foreign Office that 'Mrs. Ada Bodart has been carefully investigated by Captain Landau of the Military Intelligence Commission at Brussels', who has recommended 'that a payment should be made to Mrs. Bodart' and that Landau also recommends her for an OBE. Sir Francis quibbles on 20 August that she should only get an MBE as 'a sufficient recognition of the services which she rendered'. Notwithstanding, Ada Bodart received the compensation she requested and an OBE. Eventually.

One final fascinating aspect of Ada Bodart is her appearance in the film *Dawn*, directed by Herbert Wilcox in 1928, with Sybil Thorndike as Edith Cavell, and Ada Bodart playing herself. It is a silent film, made in Brussels, whose scenario is necessarily simplified: the only members of the clandestine organization who appear are Nurse Cavell, Ada Bodart and her son Philippe, and a barge lady named as Julie Pitou. M. Baucq, for example, does not make an appearance, neither at the trial nor at the Tir National, where he was shot alongside Miss Cavell. The film was refused a certificate by the British Board of Film Censors – which obviously made it the most famous film of the year. The reason seems to have been that the British government didn't want to offend the Germans, and indeed the German government wanted it banned. Ada Bodart, in disgust at the 'banning' of the film, returned her OBE. She might have been a broken woman by 1928 after her prison experiences, but that action rings true with the courageous behaviour that Amy describes in her diary. Edith Cavell confessed, said she had saved 200 British soldiers, was shot and is a heroine. Ada Bodart was as courageous, maybe saved over 800 British soldiers, told a few lies and is forgotten. Ada Bodart, née Annie Doherty of Newry, Co. Down, I think deserves not to be forgotten, but nor do the hundreds of Belgians who risked their lives to rescue Allied soldiers.

Amy's war and peace

> Fine day, cold. Went to church this morning and to Children's Service this afternoon. Several more people been shot. (7 November 1915)

> A lot more people shot. The Germans were going to shoot a girl, but then they released her because they thought her too young so she is instead condemned to hard labour for life. Rosine, Raymond and Mme Tadini are leaving tonight for Italy. Many trains passed last night. We went to see *Les Trois Mousquetaires*. Windy day. New troops and mitrailleuses come in. (31 December 1915)

On 1 August 1914 Amy went from Brussels to the seaside near Ostend with her mother and younger brothers for a holiday. On 2 August Germany issued an ultimatum to Belgium asking for safe passage in order to attack France. On 3 August King Albert rejected the ultimatum. On 4 August German troops advanced into Belgium, and at 2300 hours Britain and Germany were at war. Her mother Annie dashed back to Brussels on 5 August to see their father. For Amy, aged thirteen, being trapped on the seacoast as the war started, in rented rooms in a holiday villa with her two younger brothers, it was often terrifying, but also an exciting story to tell later. It's hard to understand how their mother left the three children there, especially as the Germans did not enter Brussels until 20 August. But they were finally rescued in October by the Americans and brought back to occupied Brussels.

There were awful food and fuel shortages, but thanks to the American-led Commission for Relief in Belgium and the work, among others, of Dannie Heineman, Brand Whitlock and the future president Herbert Hoover, the Belgians didn't starve. The CRB got the food to Belgium, where it was distributed by the Comité National de Secours d'Alimentation (CNSA).

There were also constant and upsetting requisitions by the Germans: on 29 January 1918, Amy writes: 'All the wool has to be taken out of the mattresses and given to the Germans, so the girls sleep on mattresses stuffed with straw, dead leaves and horse hair.'

There were arbitrary orders. On 17 February 1917:

> Von Bissing is shutting up all schools, private, free, etc. Today we all assembled in the préau [indoor playground] and Mme Scheppers read to us the letter for shutting the schools. Lots of girls cried, you bet I didn't. Went to the last music lesson. Rain and fog.

At least Amy was happy with that German order, and there were visits to the cinema and games of tennis. But it was not just the Germans who could be violent. This is written on 28 November 1917 about a fellow pupil:

> Jeanne Hensmans came today in a pitiable state to fetch her things. Her father, so furious at her being expelled, knocked her head against a red-hot fire; the poor girl is almost blind and all her head is bandaged. She must suffer!

And of course the shooting of Nurse Cavell and Philippe Baucq was unbelievably shocking for those who thought theirs was just a brave effort to help Allied soldiers escape, and when a schoolgirl could get her handkerchief signed by eleven Allied soldiers on the run (9 May 1915).

After the Armistice, her father Ernest was invited to several significant events, and asked Amy to accompany him. Some of these events are also described (at greater length) by the American Minister Brand Whitlock. On 10 December 1918 she went to a ceremony at the Tir National rifle range where Miss Cavell and M. Baucq were shot. It is interesting to see the same event from different eyes: one a seventeen-year-old schoolgirl, one an American diplomat, troubled by different things. Whitlock writes in his *Journal* of that same ceremony:

> This afternoon at three o'clock Nell [his wife] and I drove to the services Villiers had organized in honour of Miss Cavell. What is left of the British colony there, reinforced by Lord Athlone – before whom Lady Villiers and Marjory [her daughter] curtsied there in the rainy entrance to the arsenal – and Lord Vivian. Villalobar there. A dreary procession, passing through the armory or arsenal or school or whatever it is, in and out of doors, struggling across the rifle range, across the rifle pits and targets ... in the mud and pouring rain, under a low sky of gloomy clouds, most sad and melancholy, to that distant corner, where there are forty-one graves in clay, covered with withered flowers and drenched sodden ribbons ...
>
> Villiers tried to point out the spot on the wall against which she [Miss Cavell] was stood when they shot her, but no one was quite sure. Poor Baucq's grave was beside hers ... There are forty-one such graves there, victims of the firing squad, and the grave of one German soldier who refused to fire on some one of the victims, and was himself shot. (pp. 537–8)

Incidentally, the controversy over the 1928 film *Dawn* was mainly because the Germans were unhappy about a film showing a German soldier refusing to shoot Miss Cavell. But there seems to have been one incident of this happening, though not necessarily involving Miss Cavell. On her part, Amy doesn't notice the dreariness that Whitlock felt; for her it is a solemn service.

Another occasion at which the American Minister and the schoolgirl Amy were present was the military review on 26 January 1919 (see figure 26). Whitlock writes in his journal:

> Cold, snowing – and all morning shivering at the review of the 3rd British Army Corps at the Palace, before the King. The Prince of Wales rode with him – a nice, good-looking boy, smart in the uniform of a captain – a band of crêpe on his left arm, for his brother, Prince John, who died the other day, poor little chap. The spectacle of the review was magnificent, of course, as anything the English organize would be, quite the finest looking of all the armies. Our men are bigger and

finer looking and generally more intelligent than the English, but their officers are superior to ours, and the general effect is finer because their uniforms are better, smarter, and they know how to wear them ...

For two hours it was the roll and beat of drums, the skirl of the pipes – 'The British Grenadiers,' 'The Campbells Are Coming,' and all that.

But it was terribly cold. (p. 548)

Amy agrees it was a 'fine show' – but being younger, she enjoyed the snow that day. And finally, on 13 May 1919, Ernest, Amy and this time Henry went to the ceremony at the Gare du Nord to see Miss Cavell's coffin taken to England (see figure 29). Whitlock writes:

The streets were thronged with silent crowds. The school children had all turned out with flags, tied with crêpe, the flags were everywhere at half-mast, and what I had never seen before, the street-lamps were swathed in black crêpe and lighted.

At the Gare du Nord the dear colleagues were gathered, a catafalque was set up. Gahan read some prayers, the body was put in a van of the train for Ostend, and when the band had played 'God Save the King' the train was off.

It was a moving and affecting and dignified ceremony, organized as only the English can organize such solemn occasions. And of what significance, of what immense implications! The obscure little English nurse, whom the stupid Germans thought to suppress, goes now to immortal glory and fame, in her apotheosis to Westminster Abbey, the centre of civilization on this planet. (p. 562)

Amy decides that day after watching the ceremony: 'From today I will be serious.'

Amy's father Ernest (1853–1934)
Amy's father (my great-grandfather) Ernest Rust Hodson, MA, scholar of Trinity Hall, Cambridge, was born in a house called The Chantry in Bishop's Stortford, Hertfordshire, England.

According to a genealogical site he was the eighth of ten children of his father's first wife, Elizabeth (Betsy) Conquest. His father was a surgeon – Dr Charles Frederick Hodson FRCS; Ernest's two wives were respectively the daughter and granddaughter of surgeons. Dr Hodson was the uncle of Francis Bourne, later Cardinal-Archbishop of Westminster, who visited The Chantry frequently as a young man.

One family story is that Ernest was at school with Cecil Rhodes, who asked him to come out to Africa with him. It might be true: they were the same age, and both born in Bishop's Stortford. Rhodes was sent to his father's Anglican grammar school in 1861. Ernest is recorded at the nonconformist Bishop Stortford Collegiate School in 1864, when he was eleven, but he might have attended Rev. Rhodes's school before then. Cecil Rhodes was sent by his family to Africa in 1871, when Ernest was a pupil at Felsted School in Essex. According to *The Essex Standard* of 1872, at one cricket match against Colchester and East Essex, Ernest scored an undefeated sixty-one and 'at the conclusion of the innings was carried in to the Pavilion amidst the applause of the spectators – friends and foes'. At

3. Ernest Rust Hodson, c. 1898

Introduction

the Felsted School Athletic Sports Day the next year, Ernest came first in 'putting the weight', and second at pole jump, high jump and hurdles. The article in the *Chelmsford Chronicle* ends:

> The pleasures of the day were crowned by a telegram from Cambridge in the evening announcing that an open Mathematical Scholarship at Trinity Hall had been gained by E.R. Hodson.

A few years later, Ernest's Felsted tutor wrote in his testimonial in 1879:

> he went into residence at the University with excellent promise of ultimately taking a high Mathematical degree.
>
> I believe that he would have taken a much higher degree than he actually did, if it had not been for the circumstance that much of his energy was devoted to Athletic Sports, which are so popular among the Undergraduates.

Ernest certainly played cricket for Cambridge University, and his son Henry said he was also a Rowing and Tennis Blue. After graduating in 1877 he became Mathematical Master at Loretto School, Musselburgh (Scotland's oldest boarding school, near Edinburgh). The testimonial by the headmaster says:

> His manly character and cheerful, gentlemanly bearing, are calculated to make him a favourite both among his colleagues and among boys, and I may add that he was exceedingly useful to us in the charge he took of our Athletic Sports in spring.

While there he played for the Eighteen of Edinburgh/Grange against the United South of England, unfortunately being bowled by the legendary W.G. Grace for only eight (W.G. Grace scored 109 – of course!). After six months Ernest moved on to Fauconberge School, Beccles in Suffolk to be nearer his family, teaching Latin as well as Mathematics. Then in 1879 he moved to King Edward VI Grammar School in Louth, Lincolnshire, where again he was Mathematical Master (also teaching Astronomy and Chemistry), and he was now looking for a headmastership. But it was not easy. The former headmaster of Felsted School wrote to him in November

1879 as Ernest tried to get appointed to the headmastership of the Mathematical School in Rochester, and it's not encouraging – that is, Ernest spent too much time on the cricket pitch during his days at Cambridge:

> I sincerely believe that you would fill such a position [the headship] far more efficiently than very many men, who could show much higher honours. You allowed yourself to be drawn away at Cambridge from close Mathematical Readings by your love for athletics and cricket, for music, &c., your degree was therefore far below your powers and real acquirements in Mathematics ... high degrees show well and have more weight by far than they should have, and therefore I think it probable that you will find preferred before you some high wrangler who possibly never has been, and never will be, capable of being anything else but a good Mathematician.

Ernest didn't get the post. In April 1880 he married Margaret Maria Kendall in London. She was twenty-three, an orphan, five years younger than Ernest, and, according to her daughter Connie, petite and stylish. She was the third daughter of Thomas Marsters Kendall, General Practitioner Surgeon of King's Lynn, Norfolk. At the time of his death in 1871 he was Medical Attendant to the Prince and Princess of Wales (the future Edward VII and Queen Alexandra) at Sandringham. Interestingly one of Margaret's sisters, born in 1855, the year that Charlotte Brontë died, was named Jane Eyre Kendall. Eyre was their mother's maiden name, but I wonder if 'Jane' is a nod to Brontë's heroine: my Jenkins family knew the Brontës but there is no evidence that they read their books; it would be nice to discover that my Hodson family did! In the year of his marriage, Ernest accepted the House Mastership at Queen Elizabeth's Grammar School, Barnet, Hertfordshire, with Margaret performing the duties of a housemaster's wife. Six years later, in 1886, he tried for the headship of Heath Grammar School in Halifax. His current headmaster wrote:

> He is an excellent disciplinarian, combining firmness with kindness; and his class-room always presents the spectacle of a well-ordered and efficient department of the School.

4. Margaret Maria Hodson, née Kendall, Ernest's first wife, c. 1880

> In addition to his qualifications as a teacher, Mr Hodson possesses also the valuable property of a strong physique, and is remarkably proficient in all Athletic Exercises.

He didn't get that post. And then the testimonials I have finish, because it was at that point that he must have seen an advertisement for a headmaster to take over St Bernard's School in Brussels. In *The Morning Post*, August 1887, it states that the former headmaster, Rev. J.C. Jenkins, was now 'Visitor and Lecturer' and that the Principal was Ernest Hodson, MA, 'Pupils carefully prepared for Army, Universities, Public Schools'. My Hodson great-grandfather had taken over the school, which had moved to rue Saint-Bernard in 1868, from my Jenkins great-grandfather. Ernest at last had his headship. Rev. J.C. Jenkins, the British chaplain in Brussels at the Church of the Resurrection that he and his brother had built, was a former Cambridge rower, and a cricketer, and he must have relished a Cambridge man taking over St Bernard's who was as keen on sport as on mathematics. Ernest had written in trying to get the headship in Halifax in 1886:

> I have been instrumental in instituting the various sources of recreation, cricket and football [possibly rugby] clubs, and athletic sports, which I feel necessary to the salutary welfare of a boys' school.

And no doubt he wrote the same, successfully, to Rev. J.C. Jenkins in Brussels. So Ernest moved to Brussels with his wife and four children, aged between one and six: Connie, Basil, Charles and Doris. Ernest sang in the choir at the Church of the Resurrection (alongside Frederick Mourilyan) and was one of the leaders of the Anglo-American community. But tragedy struck: in May 1889 both of his sons died, aged four and five, the elder of bronchitis.

In April 1893 the family went to the Belgian royal garden party at Laeken. The newspaper correspondent wrote:

> Emerging from our cosy retreat [in one of the greenhouses] we met Mr Hodson, the genial Principal of St Bernard's, where Eddie is going (D.V.) next September to be prepared for Sandhurst. Mr Hodson, who is both an athlete and

a disciplinarian, was resplendent in a white waistcoat with three gilt buttons. His wife was very simply attired in white *foulard* and a white straw bonnet adorned with forget-me-nots.

Two months later, his wife Margaret died, aged thirty-five. Those at the funeral service in the Church of the Resurrection included Ernest's father Dr Hodson, Mr and Mrs Mellin, and Mr and Mrs Mourilyan (the future Uncle Fred and Auntie Flo), and the Lawn Tennis Club had sent a 'splendid wreath'. This 'gentle and warm-hearted lady' (the journalist's words) had given Ernest one more son, Lionel Ernest (known as Tommy), in 1890. After the devastating deaths of two sons, dying within two days of each other, Tommy was a replacement that must have given her some happiness for a few short years.

After Margaret's death, Ernest had three children to bring up

5. 43 rue Saint-Bernard (previously 27/29), St Gilles, Brussels: St Bernard's School, 1868–c. 1904, the Jenkins then Hodson school and home, and where Amy was born in February 1901

as he managed St Bernard's School without a wife. It was not until five years later, in July 1898, that Ernest married again, in Brussels. She was Annie de Salis Mourilyan, Frederick's niece. Annie was twenty-eight, Ernest was forty-four. The witnesses were Thomas E. Jeffes (British Vice-Consul), Esther Hamilton Irvine (see 'Auntie' below; in marrying Annie it looks like Ernest also took on her aunt) and Frederick Mourilyan. They had four children: Charlie, Amy (our diarist), Arthur and Henry.

According to his son Henry's memoirs, Ernest had to abandon the school and their home at 43 rue St Bernard, St Gilles, where some of the Hodson children were born or had died, because of the Boer War (1899–1902) and the antagonism to anything British. The almanacs show that the Hodsons had moved five minutes away to a newly built house in rue Africaine by 1905 (see figure 13) and Ernest was now teaching privately. He was also the Hon. Secretary of the Brussels Cricket, Lawn Tennis and Football Club, which had conveniently opened in the same year as the Hodson family's arrival in 1886, with mostly British and American members (see figure 17).

Ernest continued to live in Brussels until his death, making solo trips to stay with his daughter Connie and son-in-law Jack when they rented a house at the English seaside in the summer.

Amy's mother Annie (1870–1943)

According to the memoirs of Amy's brother Henry, their mother was of Irish and French stock, but she was British. Her father, Thomas Burton Mourilyan, a manager of manufactures, lived in Paris, but died in Ramsgate, Kent, in 1879. Her mother, Amy, née Irvine, was born in India and died in Germany when Annie was one. Annie was living in Brussels when she became the second wife of Ernest Rust Hodson in 1898. According to Amy's diary, her relationship with her mother is normal until suddenly on 3 March 1917:

> Today everybody has to declare their copper, linen, mattresses to the Germans. A fine scene this morning with her [Mother]: she said she hated, loathed the sight of me. Dined in my room.

The juxtaposition of the German demands and her treatment of her daughter may well be linked. But there was friction before, as Amy says on 11 March that her mother took her souvenir soldier buttons

Introduction

6. Annie de Salis Hodson, née Mourilyan, c. 1898

'months ago' and 'pretends she has lost' them.

It is hard to know why Annie rejected her daughter Amy; one can only guess that she might have had mental problems and couldn't deal with a (sometimes rebellious) teenage daughter. This is Amy's entry for 13 May 1917:

> Sister Clarice let me see Daddy at the Union Club. He told me Mother is very ill, is so thin. Poor Mother. I suppose it was not her fault that she was not good to me.

Their souring relationship could well have been exacerbated by the occupation and the war: the constant sound of gunfire, news of people being shot or interned in Germany, food scarcity, shortage of money – none of that would have helped. Obviously here we have Amy's side of the sad story, but it is believed among some descendants that Ernest's daughter Doris, from his first wife, emigrated at seventeen to get away from her stepmother; and of Annie's own children, three emigrated to Canada in 1921, leaving only the youngest, Henry, to care for her after her husband Ernest died in 1934. In Henry's memoirs he seems unaware of Amy's estrangement from their mother, merely writing that Amy went to a convent in order to become a nun. Connie Jenkins's daughter Dorice (my mother) at the age of ninety-five said she had heard of an 'Auntie Annie' but didn't think she had ever met her, and was very surprised to learn that she was her grandfather Ernest's wife. She said Ernest stayed with them every summer for a month at the seaside, always on his own (in the 1920s and early 1930s), and it is clear from shipping records that Annie didn't go with Ernest to New York to visit Connie and his grandchildren in 1920.

I am descended from Ernest's first wife, but I was sad to discover that when Annie died in London in December 1943 she was buried in a common grave, at Beckenham cemetery, south London, with four other people. Her son Henry was in the army and was given quick leave to arrange it, and had no money. I think I found it eventually, by counting eleven 'plots' west from a named grave on the map I was given. It is an anonymous rectangle of grass in between stone-bordered graves. Whatever problems there were between mother and daughter, and how little help there was in the past for people with mental problems, I found it satisfying that she was buried in the same cemetery as W.G. Grace – a ball's throw from her husband's one-time foe on the cricket pitch.

'Auntie'

> At about 2.30 Auntie's death rattle was much worse, her bed shook with it. Suddenly she stopped, opened her eyes, gave three huge sighs and she was dead. Poor darling! her sufferings are all at an end. (I saw her spirit over my bed.) She never said a word. Daddy took me to the Uccle cemetery to choose a piece of ground for the darling. The undertaker came to take her measures. Arthur is 12 years old today. Lovely day.

That is on 19 July 1916. All I knew from Amy's diaries was that Auntie lived with them, I knew her birthday (not date of birth), and that she was little and often ill. Investigating Hodson, Mourilyan and Kendall family trees yielded no obvious candidate. When I received younger brother Henry's memoirs from his descendants I hoped she might receive a name, but she is not mentioned. She is much loved by Amy and her mother, and it seemed right to find her name, but, alas, Belgian law says that one cannot find out someone's name from a date of burial for one hundred years – which is 2016. But then I went to the National Archives in Kew to check on a mention of 'E.R. Hodson, and his wife Mrs Annie Hodson, in Brussels' under a heading 'Belgium: Prisoners, including: Pensions'. And within a large section of papers concerning the Hodsons (mainly Uncle Fred's attempts to send them money) was something to do with a 'Bengal Orphan Fund' and the name Esther Hamilton Irvine, the address was 27 rue Africaine, E.R. Hodson was her nephew and she had died on 19 July 1916. This was Auntie! Auntie Esther was Amy's great-aunt, born in Bengal and the daughter of an army surgeon, the younger sister of Annie's mother, who had died in 1872.

'Poor Charlie' (1899–1925)

My mother, Connie's daughter Dorice, was a great letter writer to Hodson and Jenkins cousins, especially at Christmas. So I knew their names, even if I got them confused. But when Amy's son-in-law gave me her surviving diaries in 2000 I kept coming across the name Charlie or Charley. (I've standardized to Charlie.) Who is he? I wondered. And gradually it became clear he was Amy's older brother. But it was only fourteen years later that I knew exactly when and where he had died, because my research colleague Marcia found a notice in a Canadian newspaper:

> Charles Thomas Hodson, 621 Ross avenue, died on Friday at King Edward hospital, in his 26th year. Deceased, who is survived by his widow, had been a resident of the city for the past two years. The funeral will take place at 10 a.m. today from the A.B. Gardiner funeral home to Brookside cemetery. (*Winnipeg Free Press*, 13 April 1925)

He was married? It was probably a mistake by the funeral home: we can't find any records.

But to go back to the beginning. Amy's brother Charlie disappeared, aged fifteen, in February 1915 from his school in Brussels. Amy finally finds out in 1916 that he got to England and joined the Royal Fusiliers, and was in the trenches in Flanders. In June 1917 their (great-) Uncle Fred, then staying in Worthing, Sussex, sums up Charlie's story so far in a letter to Downing Street, now in the National Archives (as F.J. Mourilyan tries to sway Foreign Office/the Treasury's intransigence to allow him to send money to his niece Annie and her husband Ernest in occupied Brussels):

> I may mention that Mr E.R. Hodson ... has two sons serving in the army: Lieut. Lionel Hodson [Tommy] – who came back from Canada to enlist – is in Lovat's Scouts, Charles Hodson, who escaped from Brussels, walked to the Dutch frontier in Feb. 1915, when only 15 ½ years old, reached England, enlisted in the Royal Fusiliers, before the end of 1915 was in the trenches in France. In 1916 he was sent back, as being underage, on the 1st June, having reached the age of 18, he joined up, is now at Rugby Camp, in the 3d training Reserve Battalion.
>
> I mention this that the Foreign Office may know that the younger members of the family are not shirking their duty. I am persuaded that the Government will be of my opinion that the father of such sons might be helped as much as possible.

The Government was not impressed.

From Amy's diary we learn that Charlie managed to get to England from German prisoner-of-war camps in 1919. He was in a bad way, with 'poisoned feet', maybe trench foot; he looks deceptively well in his photo after the war (figure 30), probably in London in 1919. If this was a novel we would have Amy's description of how her brother looked after not seeing him for four years, but, alas, she just describes Charlie going skating and staying out late. Perhaps it was too difficult to talk about. At the end of October 1919 he was on a month's leave, and Amy's last mention of him is that he is leaving for England again on 19 December.

I found from shipping records that he emigrated to Canada in May 1921, travelling steerage. His brother Arthur had emigrated

Introduction

7. Charlie Hodson and his half-sister Connie Jenkins, London, 1915

earlier that month, aged sixteen; Amy emigrated in December. Charlie was thinking of changing regiments in April 1919 – so what happened as regards the army? Was he invalided out? Both he and Arthur are heading for the same place – Sherbrooke in Quebec to do farming. In his memoirs, their younger brother Henry writes:

> My brother, Arthur, found employment on a farm in Quebec, which he had to give up, owing to very poor wages obtained, and very hard work with no future in view. He, eventually, obtained employed with the Canadian Railways, as a surveyor in the very wilds of Canada.

But Charlie, only four months later, on 10 September 1921, was deported from Canada. He is next found in February 1922 on a ship going from St John, New Brunswick to Liverpool. He noted on the shipping form that he was a scholar, and going to Belgium. Just weeks later, in March 1922, he sailed from Southampton to New York. He gives an address in West Kensington, London, says he is a clerk and intends to settle in the United States. But he wasn't allowed in: he was deported. When I visited Ellis Island a few years ago I had no idea that any member of my family had queued in that vast hall and been turned away. We don't have all the shipping records. How many times did he try to get to North America? It's not even certain that May 1921 was the first time he had gone to Canada, since on the 'Passenger's Declaration' he writes that his nearest relative in the country from where he comes is 'Sister. Connie Jordson [sic], Norman Hotel, Leicester Gds, London'. She was certainly in England at that date, but I can't find a Leicester Gardens. Even if he got the address wrong, it is odd to change Jenkins to Jordson.

    I was hoping that the death registration certificate that I ordered from Manitoba, Canada might fill in something of what happened between Charlie being deported, yet again, in 1922 and dying in Winnipeg, Manitoba in 1925. I opened it feeling quite emotional. It says he had been in Manitoba since September 1923. I know his sister Amy and her new husband Tom Field were in Winnipeg. The certificate says that he was admitted to the King Edward Memorial Hospital on Boxing Day 1924. The form also says he was Danish (British is half-erased), that he was single, born in Brussels to Ernest and Annie, and it has the right date of birth. His profession was 'Ex-Soldier'. His brother Henry is correct in his memoirs about Charlie having TB: Charlie died of Pulmonary Tuberculosis, with contributory Tuberculosis Enteritis, at the age of twenty-five on 10 April 1925. It was possibly the result of being gassed in the trenches, or the appalling conditions and diseases in the German prisoner-of-war camps. The Danish error may show Charlie's final, successful attempt to get to Canada: that he sailed from Copenhagen this time.

Charlie was so desperate to get to Canada that when he was deported (probably because of his TB) he simply turned around and tried again. Desperate to get away from Belgium? Perhaps desperate for a cure. The King Edward Memorial Hospital was founded in 1911 and considered one of the most modern hospitals in the world for people with tuberculosis.

One final thought: since the family knew Mme Bodart – did she help Charlie get across the Dutch border in February 1915? It's possible. Amy quotes Ada Bodart on 5 June 1915:

> When she heard that we had not any news from Charlie, she said: 'What not yet any news, well I will dress as a soldier and go and fetch him back.'

Even Mme Bodart couldn't do that, but I presume Amy was a constant support at Charlie's bedside before he died. And she may be the 'widow' mentioned in the funeral home's notice.

Tommy: the black sheep (1890–1964)

Lionel Ernest Hodson (Tommy), Amy's half-brother, was intended to have merely a note in Who's Who above, but only a week before I sent this book to the publisher a bombshell was dropped by my research colleague Marcia. Tommy had seemed uncomplicated: emigrated to Canada when he was sixteen; enlisted with the British army and served with Lovat's Scouts from 1914 to 1919. Married in 1928 (we had seen the marriage certificate online), and the only Hodson great-uncle I had met (see figure 34). He has a happy face in the photos, and he gave me a huge Canadian doll. Nice man: that was that.

Then we found that he had married twice – not unusual:

I rewrote the caption to figure 34 saying it was his *second* wife, Eliza. The name of Tommy's first wife had appeared on a 'Primary Inspection Memorandum' of the US Department of Labor, which states that he is going to visit his sister Connie in New York in March 1923. His wife, Gladys Kate, was given as the name of his nearest relative in the 'country whence alien came', and she was living in Winnipeg. He is 5ft 10½ inches tall, with brown hair and blue eyes, he has a mark of identification on his left thigh, and is an accountant. Although it is recorded in *The Times* that he was born in Brussels, he states he was born in Bishop's Stortford (perhaps not to muddle the Americans). He intends to stay in the United States for less than six months.

Then Marcia sent me this cutting from the *San Diego Union* for 20 August 1924:

LIONEL HODSON, BOOKKEEPER AT ARMOUR PLANT, HELD IN CITY JAIL WITHOUT BAIL

Lionel Hodson, bookkeeper of the Armour Packing company at Seventh and E streets was arrested yesterday and held at the city jail without bail while the officers of the company and the police are investigating an alleged shortage of several hundred dollars in his accounts.

The alleged shortage is believed to have existed for a period of several months, and the arrest followed an alleged suspicious chain of circumstances.

Suspicion was first directed toward the accounts when early on the morning of Aug. 10 Hodson reported that while he was working over the accounts two men tied him in the rear room while they took $35 of the company's money.

Although Hodson said he had been left in a dirty room, his clothes, according to the police who investigated, showed no signs of being dirty, and little credence was placed in his story.

PAGES MISSING

The next day it was learned several pages from two ledgers were missing.

Yesterday morning a fire of mysterious origin destroyed

office records. The blaze was reported about 6 o'clock. When the firemen arrived the fire had assumed dangerous proportions and had apparently been burning for some time. The office was badly damaged, estimates placing the amount at $3000.

Hodson, it has been learned, had been lavishly entertaining a dance hall girl. Every night for several months, it is alleged, he had been spending anywhere from $10 to $15. His salary is said to be $35 a week.

On 29 October the *Evening Tribune* of San Diego says that Lionel E. Hodson indicated that he would plead guilty to a felony embezzlement charge. Online were found mug shots and measurements of this 'Lionel E. Hodson' from St Quentin State Prison, California, for 8 November 1924. The form said he was 5ft 10 1/8 inches tall, of muscular build, with blue eyes, brown hair, born in England, aged twenty-nine. The photo shows a diagonal scar on his right cheek. Wrong age, I said to Marcia, and it certainly doesn't look like him – our Lionel doesn't have a scar, and he's not in San Diego.

Then Marcia sent me forms from California State Prison at Folsom: 'Lionel' had been moved there in May 1926; one form stated that he had been sentenced to four years for embezzlement and that he had a criminal record from Alberta in Canada – three years in April 1911 for theft. There was also another mug shot. It looked even less like my great-uncle in his photos of 1915 and 1956.

But Marcia was undeterred. She sent me a newspaper cutting from the *Evening Tribune* of San Diego for 22 September 1924:

> Two husbands and a wife were deserted by their partners in the matrimonial venture, according to their complaints, filed this morning. Lionel E. Hodson wants a divorce from Gladys Kate Hodson on those grounds. They married in England June 28, 1919, and lived together until Sept. 30, 1923, the complaint states.

It seems fairly unlikely that there were two couples called Lionel E. Hodson and Gladys Kate Hodson in North America at that time, and that both Lionels were 'clerks'. That both were the same height, with the same colour hair and eyes. The same distinguishing mark on their left leg/thigh (embezzler's prison record; our Tommy/Lionel's 1923 record) – and Amy's diary says on 27 March 1919: 'Tommy has just come out of the hospital; he had to have a piece of shrapnel, which had remained in his leg, taken out.' The embezzler married in England on 28 June 1919; our Tommy/Lionel married in England on 28 June 1919. I looked again at his photos from 1915: in figure 12 I saw that he had indeed a diagonal scar on his right cheek. The embezzler was Amy's brother.

And then an immigration record for Gladys surfaced showing that on 27 July 1923 she was going with her daughter Margaret, aged one, from Winnipeg to Los Angeles to join her husband. Tommy/Lionel had a daughter!

So when Tommy came to England in December 1914 and joined Lovat's Scouts, serving firstly in the Dardanelles, he was a discharged prisoner: a clerk who had committed theft. But there must be more to his story: Lovat's Scouts were recruited from Highland gamekeepers and gillies who were adept at stalking and shooting. Tommy surely must have been employed similarly in Canada before becoming a clerk; and he was promoted to Captain, Amy says. He was certainly a Lieutenant (medal card in the National Archives).

One can possibly understand a young man's foolish mistake, but to embezzle again after the war is harder to take in, except that for someone who had spent five years in the army – regular pay, respected, tough, promoted to officer – returning to civilian life may have been very hard. Somehow his first marriage collapsed – since he had been in hospital in Leicester in spring 1919, according to Amy, and married there in June, it sounds like a whirlwind romance. Whether he ever saw Gladys and his daughter Margaret again, I don't know. Amy had joined them in Winnipeg at the end of 1921, so maybe she and Gladys kept in touch. There might be some attics in Canada with old letters or journals.

But it seems that Tommy/Lionel turned over a new leaf. On 10 March 1928 he married Eliza Jane Payne in Montreal, and they had a son, John, known as Jack, later that year. He states on the marriage certificate that he is a bachelor. They came to visit my family in the suburbs of London in 1956 – bringing that Canadian doll!

Perhaps there is a clue to his going astray in his childhood: his mother died when he was two; and despite possibly adoring older sisters, his stepmother may not have cared for him, while Charlie arriving when he was eight may have sidelined him. But Amy's description on 16 December 1918 of Ernest's agitation as he waits to see his eldest son is touching: 'On going home at midday, Daddy told me that Tommy is in Brussels and that he's coming to see us at 12.30. We are waiting for him now so impatiently. Daddy is walking up and down in the room.'

Connie (1881–1963) and Jack (1874–1958)

These were my grandparents: Amy's eldest half-sister and her husband – Constance Agnes née Hodson and John Card Jenkins. They would have first met in 1887 when Connie's father took over St Bernard's School, though Jack was possibly at boarding school in England when the six-year-old Connie first arrived. There were no memories passed on in the family about her two younger brothers dying two years later. There is a poignant article in a newspaper in September 1889 saying that Connie had won a prize at the Bishop's Stortford Horticultural Show; she was possibly staying with her grandparents as her parents tried to get over their loss.

In 1903, aged twenty-two, Connie started to train as a nurse in Isleworth, west London; shortly afterwards her younger sister Doris emigrated to South Africa. Maybe neither could get on with their stepmother, but it is also probable that with the failure and closing of St Bernard's School by their father, and the idea of downsizing to rue Africaine, it was time for both of them to leave, and earn some money and independence, especially as their stepmother had two small children, Charlie and Amy. In 1910 Connie was registered as a midwife in London. And then in 1913 she was engaged to Jack Jenkins and they married in Leicester in December; according to her daughter Dorice, ever after she didn't like Leicester. It didn't turn out to be the most blissful of marriages – they lived apart most of the time – and what happened between Connie qualifying as a midwife and marrying Jack is unknown. The family story is that she wanted to get out of Brussels – but since she was in London, that doesn't sound correct. The families met each other often and maybe Connie preferred marriage and children of her own to delivering other people's.

Jack Jenkins's British family had been in Brussels since the

1820s, as Anglican chaplains. I will be writing about this in my book *The Brontës and my Family*. He was the seventh child of Rev. John Card Jenkins (1834–94), who, with his older brother, Rev. Charles Edward Jenkins (1826–73), had built the Church of the Resurrection in rue de Stassart. Jack's elder brother Edward became a clergyman (see Amy's entries for 16 and 19 October 1919). Jack went to school at St Bernard's and later in Devon, where the headmaster, Frederick Buckle, was Jack's brother-in-law. Fred later did a runner, leaving his wife Lellie and three children; no one knows what happened to him. After Corpus Christi College, Cambridge, Jack left for New York in 1900 to get experience of teaching in America at Mr Craigie's school in West 46th Street. It is satisfyingly neat that Jack started St Bernard's School there (now at 4 East 98th Street) in 1904, probably the same year that his father-in-law had to abandon St Bernard's School in Brussels.

The Jenkins school had moved to rue Saint-Bernard, St Gilles

8. Wedding of Constance Agnes Hodson and John Card Jenkins, 23 December 1913, Leicester. Standing, left to right: Frederick Palmer, Rev. Edward Jenkins, Ernest Hodson, Connie, Jack, Prescott Metcalf (best man). Sitting, left to right, Janet Palmer with Edward John, a young Fawcus cousin, Rosie Jenkins, Jack's niece Phyllis Buckle (maid of honour), Annie Hodson

in 1868. It had been founded by Jack's grandfather, Rev. Evan Jenkins – who knew the Brontë sisters and was honorary chaplain to King Léopold I – in Brussels in 1825. Sometime after its founding it was established in rue des Champs-Elysées, Ixelles, a short walk from rue Saint-Bernard. Later there was also a Jenkins pensionnat (boarding school) for girls in the same road, run by Rev. Evan's widow Eliza and then by her daughter Helen.

In July 1917 Jack volunteered for military service and had to risk leaving his school in New York and return to England. On 31 December 1918, a document, 'Officers Recommended for Command and Staff Appointments', says that 2nd Lieutenant J.C. Jenkins ('aged 44 years and 6 months, service of 1 year and 3 months') joined the 14th Divisional Train on 8 December 1917 and was transferred to Base Supply Depot, Boulogne on 14 December 1918. The Lieut. Colonel comments that Jack 'has shown consistent devotion to duty, has rendered all the help in his power on personnel duties in the Company offices. Lieut. Jenkins would undoubtedly make a useful Officer.' And one of the remarks states: 'This Officer's capacity and tact for training are exceptional, as he is a most successful school-master in civilian life ... he is a man with brains and wide experience ... has an unusually good knowledge of French.' It was signed by a Major, RASC (Royal Army Service Corps). Jack was demobbed on 5 April 1919, and in September he returned to his school in New York, with Connie and the children following a month later.

Connie and Jack had two sons (Desmond 1915–92 and Jack [John Chevalier] 1920–2000) and a daughter (Doris, who changed the spelling to Dorice, b. 1919 – my mother). He retired in 1949, after forty-five years as headmaster, and died in England.

Amy and Sister St Charles

In 1917 Amy's mother Annie had what seems to have been a mental breakdown, confining Amy to the house and attacking her physically. Through the intervention of a Roman Catholic priest, Father Lecourt, and another family friend, Miss Rita Mellin, Amy escaped the family home and went to a boarding school in rue Théodore Verhaegen, possibly on charity. In the almanac for 1920 it is the École professionelle, run by 'les religieuses filles de Marie'. Amy finds a mother figure in one of the nun teachers, Sister St Charles. But she is a mother figure who is as challenging as Amy is to her.

One night Amy dreams that her brother Arthur comments about the Sister (28 June 1917) '"she looked so like Mother when she was well." And true enough she did look like her, same size and stoutness.' Amy loves her but often feels rejected, and receives constant punishments. Amy is candid that she is often rebellious, but her diary entry for 1 November 1917 is troubling: 'I almost hate Soeur St Charles now. She has taken my violin, has stopped me from going to the piano. Then she said that it was through me that Mother was ill, that I was fit to be in the streets, and all sorts of things.'

On 16 July 1919 Amy seems to understand why she loves and hates Sister St Charles so much, she writes:

> Oh! if only Mother loved me I should not have searched affection anywhere but in her heart! I should not have this passionate love for a person who looks down upon me as a thief, a liar, etc., etc. Lucky are those who have a mother, a real one! May they never love anybody more than her.

Somehow, Amy eventually broke away and found a new life in Canada.

Amy's conscience diary

This is a small notebook written in French, which she refers to on 1 May 1919: 'I know M. [Mother] at least has seen my conscience book for she told Daddy.' The first date is 5 October 1916 – but under it is a blank. This is followed on other days with notes on homework, such as for 13 October (in French) 'Geography: learn about the Universe and the Earth', later: about the religion of the Egyptians, grammatical analysis, conjugations to learn, and 'Learn the 2nd stanza of Cock-a-doodle-do'. The first misdemeanour was on 18 January 1917 when she and two other girls got two conduct marks for drawing attention to themselves in the road when returning to school, and it is initialled as read by her father. As we can see from Amy's diary: they were throwing snowballs at each other! On other days she was in trouble for eating sweets or laughing in class or chapel, distracting other pupils, playing the piano when she didn't have permission, drawing caricatures on steamed-up windows, whistling, arriving late, talking in church. There is one rare comment on 10 February 1919: 'J'ai été sage aujourd'hui.' That is the only entry for that day. A sadder one is for 13 February 1919:

> Instead of writing my essay I laughed and stopped several pupils from working. I was angry and I threw my report on the stairs saying that I wanted to die, that I hated everybody, etc.

'Everything bothers me, except the piano,' she writes four days later. And in English, two days later, 'I am just sick of life, everything is against me.' But Amy continues resilient and feisty, a battler: 'During the French lesson I changed places and put myself at the back for fun' (18 February). 'I answered Mother back and finally so as not to say all that I thought I went up to my room' (4 March). And on 8 March: 'I climbed on the roof twice; once to get a ball and the second time for fun.' On 4 April: 'When the teacher rang for silence after tea, I pulled at some chairs in order to make a noise.' On 7 April: 'I said very loudly that a teacher was an imbecile.' On 14 April: 'I grumbled because Mother said that I could not go to the pensionnat. I took two biscuits without permission and I didn't tell Mother.' The next day: 'I distracted Henry while he was saying his prayers before bed.' On 25 April: 'I read fairy tales.' On 28 April: 'I went to tennis and to the fair.' On 29 April: 'I again answered Mother back.' On 1 May: 'I quarrelled with my brother.' 20 May: 'I answered my parents back really impatiently.' 30 May: 'I didn't want to repeat to Daddy what I'd said which he didn't hear; I left in tears.' 11 June: 'I arrived late in class because I stayed in the small courtyard with a bird who didn't know how to fly.' 17 June: 'I threw water onto pupils in the courtyard from the balcony.' 30 June: 'I argued.' 2 July: 'Going into the study-room I imitated the howling of a dog and I resisted leaving the study-room.' 8 July: 'I said: je m'en fiche.' 20 July: 'I jumped on the benches in the study-room and I went out through the window.'

Amy was obviously a challenging pupil for the teacher nuns to handle, and would be today. But other pupils, she tells us, were expelled; Amy wasn't, and was even kept on as a teacher for a while, though she hated it.

Finally, the following diary entry is why I admire my great-aunt Amy. Here she is on 20 December 1915, being interrogated by a German at the forbidding Kommandantur (the German headquarters, at

6 rue de la Loi, in the building of the Ministère de l'Intérieur) in Brussels about her older brother, aged sixteen, who is missing:

> Daddy took me to the Kommandantur with him, where we had to go in an awful room. The Germ said: 'Where's Charlie?' Daddy said he did not know. 'You do know,' said the Germ, 'for here is a letter which I have received to say that Charlie has been seen, and you will just stop here till he has been found.' I was shaking with fury. Then I spoke up: 'Do you think that Mother would cry so often if Charlie were here? Besides Daddy is not responsible for his son when he is in a school.' He got calmer at that. But all the time he was talking sneerely. At last he said: 'Well, it is a pity to keep you in when it is such weather (it rained two minutes after), and I suppose you would rather spend your Christmas at home than here. Scootum.' I could have shot him. Dull day.

Ernest has taken his fourteen-year-old daughter to confront the German occupying forces. And Amy wins!

9. Amy in Canada, 1945

My Experience on the Belgian Sea-Coast During the Year 1914

by Amy Victoria Hodson

[Amy's account of her experience of the start of World War I was written summer 1915, as she states in her diary: '20 July Tuesday: I have written a long story about my experience during the bombardment of Middelkerke, and am going to write them in books and sell them.' Another of her notebooks contains drafts of it in English and French. She says on 21 July: 'Sold two of my books.' Amy was thirteen at the time of the German invasion of Belgium; her brother Arthur ten; 'Baby' Henry eight.]

On the 1st of August, 1914 we all went for our summer holidays to Crocodile, a little seaside place between Westend and Middelkerke. I had a lovely time for two or three days while Mother was with us, but on the 4th the landlady of the Villa Hortensias, where we were staying, came in all of a flurry, while we were breakfasting, saying that the Germans were in Belgium. Mother immediately thought of Daddy and Auntie, who were in Brussels.

I helped her to pack, and she left us in charge of Mlle Hannah, the landlady.

But Mother promised us to come back in a few days, so we kissed her and wished her farewell: she did not come back, for the Germans came into Brussels the 20th of August. They forbade anybody going in or out of Brussels. So we got a few letters from Mother, and all went well for a month. But after the month was passed, I began to get uneasy, for Mother could not send any more letters. The weather was beginning to get colder, so we could not bathe nor catch shrimps any more. There was a small convent near our villa, Asile des Petits Lits Roses, which belonged to Mlle

Hannah's sister, and we passed the time playing there with the children.

One fine day when I woke up, my bed being near the window, I saw a great many horses and waggons going along the chaussée de Nieuport. I woke up Arthur and Baby, my brothers, dressed hurriedly and went out to see what was going on. They were the Belgian soldiers! Oh! our delight! we danced and skipped about with joy. There were heaps of them. A great many had come from Liège and Antwerp. The poor things! Some of them could scarcely walk, their boots were hurting them so.

Then Mlle Hannah asked them if they would like something to eat. Their faces beamed with delight! We managed to get twelve of them in the kitchen. They were so pleased to sit down, they had walked such a lot! I went to the cellar to fill up the jugs of beer, Arthur ground the coffee, Baby went to buy some more beer as there wasn't enough in the tap, and he smashed a bottle. Then when they had refreshed themselves they went on their way and more came in. They had posted sentinels on each side of Crocodile.

We were coming back one evening to the villa, after having talked to the soldiers, when we heard a troop of poor tired soldiers, singing the 'Brabançonne' and the 'Marseillaise': we immediately joined in. When we got closer to them we saw that, mixed with them, were some women pushing perambulators with all their goods in them: they were evidently the wives of some of the soldiers. One man got out from the troop and sat on our doorstep, he could not walk a step further, his feet were hurting so! We brought him in the kitchen and we gave him some food. He was so tired, he could scarcely eat, but he begged us to take off his boots. Three nice chaps slept in our house, in the room adjoining the dining room. They had brought their bicycles with them and they hoped to stay for a little time. [The last two sentences are added from Amy's notebook, where they are crossed out.]

The next day they were digging trenches a hundred yards from our house. I went with them and talked to them. Arthur threw off his coat and began digging while the soldiers rested a while. Baby tried to also, but the spade being as big and as heavy as himself, it was rather a difficult job for him. Every morning we helped to carry hot soup and coffee to the sentinels who were so cold.

And so it went for about a week, till one morning there came some Johnnies who did not look like Belgians, and to our great delight and surprise, we saw they were our dear Tommies. Then Arthur and I rushed home to fetch our Union Jacks, which we waved from morning till night, scarcely going home to feed. They looked so clean and jolly. The sailors then came on the tops of buses as merry as if they were going to a feast. An aeroplane came down on a field further off. I went through hedges, jumped over streams, Arthur a mile in front, Baby half a mile behind; cows came after me though I did not have a red dress on; heaps of aeroplanes flying about. Baby dropped his shoe in an eel-stream and could not get it out. Then when I thought I was hearing the machine, to my fury I saw a river which I had to cross to get to the flying-machine. I was giving it up in despair, when some Belgian soldiers called us to get in a ferry. Baby without his shoe, I, out of breath, got into it. There were some eels wriggling about and every second I thought we'd go over into the water. Anyhow we got across, and, when at last I reached their machine, I was too late to see the aviators, for they had gone off to rest at an inn close by. So I came back to the Tommies. They asked if we were British, and when we told them that we were, they shook hands with us and said: 'Why, you are the first English kiddies we have talked to on the coast.' They gave us souvenirs, such as buttons off their coats, cartridges, badges, etc. etc. But Mlle Hannah made us give them up to her to bury in case of the Germans coming. I kept four buttons: I have them still and always shall in memorial of those brave men. Some of them wanted us to go as *cantinières* with them: we were dying to go, but we could not. They asked us how far Nieuport was and they roared with laughter when we told them the name of the place where they were was Crocodile.

A few days after heaps of Belgian wounded, carried by the British, came to Westend. Several of them came to tea with us, but they were not badly hurt. Nearly everybody was leaving Ostend because the Germans were approaching. Hundreds of refugees passed on their way to France, all walking. We saw a few French soldiers in cars. All the peasants had fled and left the trenches half finished on hearing the detested Huns were approaching. So we told the Belgian soldiers that it would be safe if they went too, and they took our advice. We bade them farewell with tears in our eyes.

Well, everything went on all right till, on the 17th of October, we were all gathered in the drawing-room, when suddenly we heard an enormous bang. We jumped up and ran to the kitchen-window, from which one could see all the fields and a faint view of Ypres: we perceived nothing, but we remained in the kitchen. A quarter of an hour after we heard a similar bang. This time we did see something: a shell had burst a hundred yards or so from our house, all the earth was flying in the air and a huge hole had been made in the ground. We could not make it out. Then I ran out and, to my horror, I saw a small wood, a mill and several farms burning in the distance. I called Arthur and Baby to see it: it was dreadful: one wing after the other fell off the windmill.

That night we slept downstairs in our clothes. Next morning, we went to see if anything more was burning. The fire was worse: one thing after the other was blazing.

Just before breakfast, I went to the convent, then at eight, I left to come home and feed: as I was coming out of a hedge, I saw, galloping towards me horses, and then ... to my terror and surprise I discovered they were the German Lancers, with their long pikes in their hands. I took to my heels and fled home. Then there was a great commotion: the British men-o'-war were in the sea, the Germans rushing everywhere, hiding in the downs. I was cowardly crouching behind the window-curtain. Then the big guns were rushing up and down our street, till they made a halt at our door and three guns were placed there.

We took chairs and the ladies their valuables, and we all hid in the cellar. The noise was deafening: one lady fainted, another was praying. Baby and I were sitting on a box, and I thought every minute we would fall through the lid. It wasn't very cheerful. Suddenly there was a tap at the front: my heart leapt in my mouth. Nobody dared to open. Then another louder tap came: summoning courage, Mlle Hannah went to the door: it was a German officer who wanted to look through our top-window to see where the English ships were. He did not remain long. With a sigh of relief, Mlle Hannah came back. At about 3 p.m. we heard queer noises. One after the other we crept upstairs and we saw, through the window, that the 'Chien-Vert', our favourite tuck-shop in front of our villa, had been smashed by a shell. We were nearly all crazy.

Hatless and stockingless, with Baby and Arthur, I rushed to the convent: the Huns were everywhere. The nuns and the children were in a frenzied state. I sent my brothers on with some ladies and

My Experience on the Belgian Sea-Coast

I stayed behind to help carry a child or two. The rain came pouring down in torrents. With a right hand I was holding a lame girl, and with my left I had a screeching baby. How I blessed that kid! So, in the rain, all the seventy children of the convent and we were escaping across the downs, bombs flying over our heads and Allied aeroplanes going about, which at any moment could have thrown bombs on us thinking we were Germans. In every little spot of the downs there were those horrible creatures, some with such evil-looking faces. One, with awful spectacles, came up to me and asked me if I was English: then he gave me some chocolate, which came in very usefully for the screeching baby to make him shut his mouth for a while. We did not know where to go: an idea struck Mlle Hannah to go to the 'Bourgmestre' at Middelkerke. We were received by his wife, who ushered us all into a large room.

I looked like a drowned rat. The lady gave us a few biscuits and then the children were sent to a kind of Children's Hospital called Roger de Grimbergen. My brothers and I slept with a lady in a flat, which we were able to get to with great difficulty. As we opened one of the windows (it was dark now), we saw from afar, people praying round a burning farm, nothing but farms and woods burning wherever we looked and nearly every minute bombs were exploding.

Arthur nearly fainted when we saw that awful sight, so we took him up to bed. Our life was in constant danger: any moment a bomb could have fallen on the house, which we had requisitioned, Villa Clairette, on the avenue Léopold. All night long there was incessant firing from the Germans, and they were singing and dancing, making a terrible noise. One night we slept in one place, and another night in the other.

Next morning, as I was in the street, an English aeroplane came flying over: from right and left Germans came with their rifles to shoot after it. As I was looking at it, I suddenly got an awful shock: a German next to me had let off his gun, not knowing I was near him: I never shall forget the bangs. I rushed into the house like a mad thing, my ears were hurting and buzzing all day long. They did not capture the aeroplane though it came back twice. After it had disappeared there were a great many cartridges in the streets. All day long the Germans came in our house, luckily I did not have my Union Jack: I had given it to a poor Belgian soldier who stuck it in his rifle. I must allow that the Germans were kind to us: we had nothing to eat, so they gave us food. On the 25th of October Baby and I were buying peppermints in a shop close by the Villa Clairette, when suddenly there was a terrific bang. The woman of the shop came tearing out, screaming: 'Oh! my husband, my husband!' A shell had fallen close to us and as her husband was in the street she thought he had been hurt. Luckily the shell had fallen through the chimney of a big villa, and nobody was hurt. So as we saw bombs were beginning to fall so near to us we thought it was high time to take our belongings and get away. But where were we to go to? Some of the children were sent to Mariakerke near Ostend, and we stayed on at Roger de Grimbergen, in the cellars. The Germans told us that the coast was going to be bombarded, and then we were sure we should be killed. What were we to do? I was frightened about Arthur and Baby because we were forbidden to speak English, for we might have been shot.

We slept part of the night on mattresses which were so low I bumped my head on the ground, six or eight children on each mattress. I had an awful headache. All the time there was loud firing and suddenly it ceased; so we begged Mlle Hannah to let us go up to bed, and she let some of us go. I went in the girls' dormitory and the boys in their own. I could not sleep, so I began to sing with the girls until the nun came in the room to turn off the light and to tell us to keep quiet.

Our window overlooked a big garden in which the German Red Cross vans were. In the middle of the night there was a lot of running about. I crept noiselessly out of bed and I saw all the boys had come out of their dormitory and were arranging their mattresses in the hall. I caught sight of Arthur and asked him what it meant, he told me the Germans had requisitioned their dormitory and were bringing in a great number of wounded. As I spied the nun approaching, I scooted back to bed and slept till the morrow. Then in the morning we all got up, said our prayers and did the little toilette we had to do. There was scarcely any water to wash with. I did not belong to that convent, nor did my brothers, but as we had to go somewhere we went there though the children were not over clean. The Germans then took our dormitory, so we had to go to the Villa Clairette.

To get out of the building we had to cross the room where

My Experience on the Belgian Sea-Coast

the wounded were, and we saw on one side the French and on the other the Germans. One poor French soldier had been burnt by a shell and his face was horrible to look at, all black. As one of the nuns was approaching the bed of a Frenchman, he begged her for a glass of water: a German said she was not to give him any, and the poor man died that night. We saw several dead soldiers going to be buried and also some French prisoners.

Nobody was allowed to go in the downs, but a young lady who was with us managed to and she saw from the top of a high hill great numbers of Germans firing near the Villa Hortensias at the English ships. A lot of them were killed and that day the Germans had a great loss. That same lady went to try and get some of our clothes for us from the Villa Hortensias: the doors of every room had been pulled off to make bridges, and in the yard of the convent the Germans were roasting chickens and drinking coffee. They took all the sheets and blankets from off the beds.

Next day our villa and the convent, as well as a large brewery on the chaussée de Nieuport, were smashed and burnt. Westend was blazing so, the flames seemed to touch the sky. From every street that we passed we saw nothing but dreadful fires.

All this time Mother, Auntie and Daddy were in Brussels, not knowing what was happening. How I was longing to get home! The noise was enough to make one go mad, and there was no bread to be had.

At last, on the 29th of October, a gentleman came to fetch my brothers and myself. The American Consul-General of Brussels, Mr Watts, had lent us his car and we were at last going home. But a tyre burst, so we had to remain one night in Ostend. There were German officers sleeping in that hotel [in Amy's diary, crossed out, she continues: I was in a funk that we should be murdered in our beds]. Anyhow the night passed all right and the next day we jumped into the car to come home. All went well till we got to Ghent: there, a beastly sentry stopped us and asked us for our passports. The gentleman gave it to him: the sentinel said it was a wrong one, that a notice had just been put up that nobody could come in or go out of the town. We were in despair. Then we were sent to the American Consulate, and after two hours' explanation we were allowed to start off. We went at a rapid pace. When we got quite near Brussels, Berghem, the car began to play us some dirty tricks: we were nearly dashed into a stream on one side, and on the other, we were nearly knocked against some trees. After all was right again, I roared with laughter, for we had left the seaside to escape from being killed, and now we were to break our necks near home. At 7 p.m. we got home and we were hugged in our parents' arms. How happy we were to see our house again! Instead of having spent one month at the seaside, we had stayed three months. Thanks to Mr Watts we got back for the other children did it not until long after, and they had to walk.

Soon after that I caught blood-poisoning [in her notebook draft but not in her typed account she continues: evidently caught it from one of the children]. Anyhow, my brothers and I are now safe and sound, and we are jolly glad, now that we are back, to have seen something of the War.

Arthur was then ten years old, Baby, eight, and I thirteen.
GOD SAVE THE KING AND THE ALLIES!!!!!

[signed] Amy Victoria Hodson

1914

3 August Monday The Germans have declared war to the Belgians. Mother, Baby and I are at Crocodile so we don't know what is happening in Brussels.

4 August Tuesday Mother took us to the Kursaal at Middelkerke to hear a speech about girls wanting to join for the Red Cross. Great enthusiasm. We all had a big Union Jack given to us and we were singing merrily on the *digue* [sea wall]. The policemen were breaking in a house where some Germans were supposed to be hidden. Great excitements everywhere.

5 August Wednesday Took Mother to the Ostend station to get back to Brussels. Walked back by the beach. Got lost on the docks. Met Kitty and Eileen Bowen and Dorothy Larking .... About a month after the English and Belgian troops passed on their way to Nieuport. All day I stood there with my Union Jack asking them if they would like a whiskey and soda. Belgian sentinels at both ends of Crocodile. A French aeroplane came down near our villa. Heaps of them flying everywhere.

18 October Sunday The Germans have come to Crocodile. Terrified we stood watching them behind the curtain. Shells bursting here and there. Awful fight between sea and land. Had to hide in the cellars for eight hours and then escaped from the villa to Middelkerke. Pouring with rain, no hat or stockings on, holding two kids by the hand, Germans by hundred everywhere in dunes, shells flying over our heads we at last reached Middelkerke. No home to go to. 70 children to look after. We all got separated. Arthur nearly fainted when he watched from the window farms burning. It was a pitiable sight. Germans making an awful noise.

19 October Monday Still fighting. The Germans have brought us sweets, toys and clothes which they stole, thankful to get them. Everything shaking, the Germans behind the house firing at the sea. Had dinner at Roger de Grimbergen.

20 October Tuesday Still fighting. No news.

21 October Wednesday The cannons as loud as ever. English aeroplane.

22 October Thursday A shell burst a few yards from our villa.

23 October Friday A German invited us in one villa for some music.

24 October Saturday Terrible noise. All night and all day firing.

25 October Sunday Had to go in one of the enormous cellars of Roger G.

26 October Monday Scarcely had any sleep. Saw the ships firing.

27 October Tuesday Mr and Mme Michot came to Ostend. Firing terribly.

28 October Wednesday Incessant cannonading.

29 October Thursday Mr and Mme Michot came to fetch us. Slept one night at Ostend. Beastly lonely in that hotel.

30 October Friday Had a walk round Ostend, then got inside Mr Watts's motor car and at last off we are for Brussels. Had lunch at Ghent. Rotten German stopped us, he must have been tipsy. Wasted 3 hours there. Nearly had our necks broken at Berghem. Got home safely and huddled in our parents' arm. Had a good feed and we related our story.

18 November Wednesday Mr Butcher taken prisoner.

19 November Thursday Mr Gahan. [Rev. Gahan was arrested by the Germans on 17 November and released by 24 November, according to Brand Whitlock's journal.]

1915

13 February Saturday Rainy day. Charlie disappeared on the 3rd of February, no news. The Germans as usual going out for their morning ride. Daddy dining at Mr Jarvis's.

16 February Tuesday Fine day. Captive balloons up. Saw the German motor cars with American officers in them. No news from Charlie. Bigwood taken.

17 February Wednesday Rainy day. No news from Charlie. Lost my purse. Daddy gone out for dinner. The Germans have taken Mr Bigwood. Rosine had tea with us.

18 February Thursday Went to the police station with Daddy to see if my purse was found. No. But later a policeman fetched me to get it. Went to make toffee at Miss Mellin's house. Rainy day.

20 February Saturday Fine day but very windy. Went to tea with Miss Jemmett. No news from Charlie.

21 February Sunday Captive balloons up. The cannons are faintly heard. Captain Tannero gone back to fight after having wounded his wrist. Uncle Fred and Auntie Flo both well in England. No news from Charlie.

22 February Monday Lovely day. Went to the Banque nationale with Daddy to see if they would change my torn tickets. They did.

23 February Tuesday My birthday [fourteen]. Fine day. Went downtown with Mother in the morning and to the cinema after dinner. Captive balloons up.

24 February Wednesday Fine day. Captive balloons up. A little snow.

25 February Thursday Captive balloons up. Heard a few cannons. Heaps of Germans everywhere. Went down with Miss Mellin in the afternoon. Arthur in bed with a bad cold.

26 February Friday Fine day, rather cold.

27 February Saturday Fine day. Heaps of mitrailleuses [machine guns/gunners], mules carrying packets of cartridges and Austrian mitrailleuses on their backs, Germans singing, great excitement.

28 February Sunday Sunny day, very windy. Went to Children's Service in the afternoon.

1 March Monday Mother and Daddy gone to sign at the [École Militaire] rue du Méridien 10.

2 March Tuesday Fine day. Nothing new.

3 March Wednesday Got a letter from the Germans asking why Charlie did not turn up on Monday. Order that all the American flags must be pulled down not to tease the Germans.

4 March Thursday Lovely day. The cannons are rather loud. Went to see the trenches and the cemetery at Ixelles. Saw the tombs of the English, French and Belgian soldiers killed for their country. The names of five English soldiers: James Brackie, Cameron Highlanders; John Hulse, Kur Royal Reserve; Hubert Williams, Welsh Regiment; Albert Richards, 9th R.L.V.; Orielly, 1st Regiment of Lancers.

5 March Friday Lovely day. No news about Charlie. A zeppelin taken or smashed. Arthur better and gone back to school.

6 March Saturday Changeable weather. No news.

7 March Sunday Nasty day. The Germans actually allow that the English have sunk a German submarine. Went to the Children's Service.

8 March Monday Very cold day. Went to tea at Miss Doyle's. The cannons are going.

9 March Tuesday Fine day but very cold. The cannons are distinctly heard in the afternoon. Daddy had letter from Jack.

10 March Wednesday Went to the dentist in the morning. Saw a poor French woman carrying a little tiny baby and four children she had left in a house. She had been walking from Liège to Brussels, and her face had wounds and her eyelashes were half burnt. She said the Germans had done that to her.

11 March Thursday The captive balloon up for a little time. Many Germans about. Had a card from my great friend Henriette Hetjen. Daddy got two letters from Doris.

12 March Friday Dull day. Three English men'o-war sunk.

13 March Saturday Lovely warm day. A zeppelin passed over Arthur's school at dinner-time. English taken Capelle Neuve.

10. Doris Walker, née Hodson, with two of her children: Betty and Kendall, Rhodesia, 1938

14 March Sunday Went to church with Mother and to Children's Service with Arthur. Mrs May came to fetch Baby in the pony-cart to go to Boitsfort.

15 March Monday Lovely warm day. No news.

16 March Tuesday Captive balloon up. Cannons heard in the afternoon. Saw three Austrian mitrailleuse rushing down the avenue Louise. New Germans came into Brussels.

17 March Wednesday Captive balloons up. Another German ship, the *Dresden*, sunk. Saw the old spy of a crippled woman talking outside the club to a German soldier. She was evidently talking about the club, for he called me and showed me a paper on which was written 'Mr Maerken'. I said I never heard of the name and off I went. Three prison vans with either English or Belgian prisoners in them. Cannons in the afternoon. Had a card from Auntie.

18 March Thursday No news. Could not stay at Rita's, she has a cold.

19 March Friday Snow, sleet and rain. An Italian father at Father Lecourt's taken up; two criminal-looking Germans shook the two little children who opened the door to them. One fainted. Father Lecourt and the other father had to go off with the Germans.

20 March Saturday Captive balloon up. Guns are heard. The new mode for Brussels children and women is to wear Belgian soldier hats. No tea to be had, been in several shops, tea all sold out and can't get any more. At half past eight in the evening Arthur heard a funny noise. He jumped out of bed, looked out of the window and saw an enormous zeppelin. We rushed up. The first zeppelin I had ever seen; a little red light was hanging from it. Auntie not well, is in bed.

21 March Sunday Beautiful day. Got a bad foot, so could not go to church. Captive balloon up.

22 March Monday Beautiful day. Saw an English aeroplane. Mr Butcher has come back from Ruhleben [internment camp]; great excitement. Miss Doyle invited us to tea. Captive balloon up.

23 March Tuesday Beautiful weather. No news.

24 March Wednesday Saw the German Uhlans from the club window. François said that if a German was to only touch his flesh he would not come away alive; he was furious with rage. Colonel Prower is dead. Cyril Crawford is in Germany in solitary confinement.

25 March Thursday Horrible rainy day, but not cold. Daddy had a long talk with Mr Butcher. He says that five men have to sleep on four sacks [in Ruhleben] which they have to make themselves, they have a horrid soup, etc. Cyril Crawford is with them now, it was false about saying he was in prison.

26 March Friday Saw Mr Butcher. Captive balloon up. Changeable day. The Russians have made 120 thousand German prisoners: 9 generals included at Przemyśl in Galicia; great victory on the Allied side.

27 March Saturday Fine day, rather cold. Captive balloons up. Went shopping with Mother in the morning. Daddy dined with the family Jeffes: they have been told to quit Brussels, or else the Germans will put them in prison.

28 March Sunday Fine day, but cold. Went to Christ Church in the morning with Mother and Baby. After lunch went to pick anemones in the Bois. Saw a funny thing in the sky, could not make out what it was.

29 March Monday Fine day, cold. Captive balloon up but very soon came down again. The Belgians have a new idea of telling if the news is good or bad. As the Germans won't allow them to put the news in the *Belgique*, so now they put stars, four if good news, three for bad news. Today there are four.

30 March Tuesday Went to the dentist after tea with Mother and Baby. When we came back we saw in the chaussée de Louvain scattered crowds: a woman told us that the Germans were bringing in their wounded from the Gare du Nord. Then we saw the big red + omnibuses rushing to and fro, heaps of them. They must have had a good beating somewhere. Captive balloons up.

31 March Wednesday Fine day. Sausages up, at nine in the morning they were hauled down.

1 April Thursday Beautiful day. Went to Miss Mellin's; she took us to see how Miss Weir was and then we went downtown. Captive balloons up. Cannons going. Jim Kirkpatrick has died of wounds.

2 April Friday Beautiful day. Captive balloons and guns. After dinner Baby and I picked some anemones in the Bois.

3 April Saturday Varied weather but no rain. After dinner Baby and I went downtown. A great many Germans about. There was a crowd looking up into the sky saying there was an aeroplane, we could not see it. Lord Rothschild is dead.

4 April Sunday Easter Sunday. Had two beautiful big eggs full of bonbons. Rainy day. Went with Baby to Children's Service. Mr Gahan baptized four children.

5 April Monday Raining all day. Stayed at home.

6 April Tuesday Varied day. Had a big walk with Baby near to The Espinette. Mrs Rossen, Mrs Simms, Mr and Mrs Gahan came to tea. The Germans say they have crossed the Yser, Daddy says it is all bosh.

7 April Wednesday Fine day. No news.

8 April Thursday Several hailstorms. Saw an aeroplane, Allied, terribly high and a funny square signal in the morning. Baby, Joséphine and I went to the Palais de Glace in the afternoon.

9 April Friday Varied day. Took a letter to Mme B. Went to tea with Miss Doyle.

10 April Saturday Changeable day. No news. Mr Gahan has lost his bicycle.

11 April Sunday Lovely day. Captive balloons up. The Germans have had a great loss. Daddy took Baby and me up to the tennis to

1915

11. Ada Bodart, 1928, Amy's 'Mrs B.'

see the primroses. In the afternoon Arthur and I went to Children's Service.

12 April Monday Lovely day. Captive balloons up. Took a letter to Mrs B. After tea Mother took Baby and me to the dentist. All is going well with the Allies. Mr Campbell was seen by Mr Heidsig as an English soldier. A zeppelin passed over Brussels.

13 April Tuesday Lovely day. Captive balloons up. Went to the Vieux Marché. *The Times* not come into Brussels.

14 April Wednesday Rain and sunshine. Captive balloon up. Had a fight with a girl in the rue Americaine: she began calling me names and then thumped Baby in the back; I knocked her down. She began kicking and screaming. Thinking I had hurt her I went to pick her up; she got up and kicked me, so I went off. Auntie feeling very weak. Mrs Jarvis very ill.

15 April Thursday Beautiful day. Captives up. Miss Mellin took us to Trois-Couleurs; I picked a basket full of anemones, took tea at the restaurant, walked to Quatre-Bras, took the tram from there to Tervuren and then came back. Cannons very loud.

16 April Friday Fine day. Sausage up. Saw some Bavarians coming down the chaussée de Waterloo, singing though they were tired; they evidently came back from a battle.

17 April Saturday Fine day. Sausage up. Cannons going.

All that happened while we were at Middelkerke from *The Times*
>
> Coast Patrol in Action
> Germans Shelled
> Dash on Calais Foiled

Rear-Admiral Hood's dispatch, published today, describes the exploits of the Anglo-Flotilla off the Belgian coast in October and November. Most valuable work was done in checking the German advance on Calais, and 'the greatest harmony and enthusiasm existed between the Allied flotillas.' On October 30 Rear-Admiral Hood hoisted his flag in the *Intrepid*. Some splendid deeds of bravery are mentioned in the dispatch.

Admiralty, April 13

The following dispatch has been received from Rear-Admiral the Hon. Horace L.A. Hood, C.B., M.R.O., D.J.O., reporting the proceedings of the flotilla off the coast of Belgium between October 17 and November 9, 1914.

Office of Rear-Admiral,
Dover Patrol,
November 11, 1914.

Sir, – I have the honour to report the proceeding of the flotilla acting off the coast of Belgium, between October 17 and November 9.

The flotilla was organized to prevent the movement of large bodies of German troops along the coast roads from Ostend to Nieuport, to support the left flank of the Belgian Army, and to prevent any movement by sea of the enemy's troops.

Operations commenced during the night of October 17, when the *Attentive*, flying my flag, accompanied by the monitor *Severn*, *Humber*, and *Mersey*, the light cruiser *Foresight*, and several torpedo-boat destroyers, arrived and anchored off Nieuport Pier.

Early on the morning of October 18 information was received that German infantry were advancing on Westende village, and that a battery was in action at Westende Bains. The flotilla at once proceeded up past Westende and Middelkerke to draw the fire and endeavour to silence the guns.

A brisk shrapnel fire was opened from the shore, which was immediately replied to, and this commenced the naval operations on the coast which continued for more than three weeks without intermission.

During the first week the enemy's troops were endeavouring to push forward along the coast roads, and a large accumulation of transport existed within reach of the naval guns.

On October 18 machine-guns from the *Severn* were landed at Nieuport to assist in the defence, and Lieutenant E.S. Wise fell, gallantly leading his men.

The *Amazon*, flying my flag, was badly holed on the waterline and was sent to England for repairs, and during those early days most of the vessels suffered casualties, chiefly from shrapnel shell from the field guns of the enemy.

The presence of the ships on the coast soon caused alterations in the enemy's plans, less and less of their troops were seen, while more and more heavy guns were gradually mounted among the sand dunes that fringe the coast.

It soon became evident that more and heavier guns were required in the flotilla. The Scouts therefore returned to England, while HMS *Venerable* and several older cruisers, sloops and gunboats arrived to carry on the operations.

Five French torpedo-boat destroyers were placed under my orders by Admiral Favereau, and on October 30 I had the honour of hoisting my flag in the *Intrepid*, and leading the French flotilla into action off Lombartzyde. The greatest harmony and enthusiasm existed between the Allied flotillas.

As the heavier guns of the enemy came into play it was inevitable that the casualties of the flotilla increased, the most important being the disablement of the 6-inch turret and several shots on the waterline of the *Mersey*, the death of the Commanding Officer and eight men and the disablement of 16 others in the *Falcon*, which vessel came under a heavy fire when guarding the *Venerable* against submarine attack; the *Wildfire* and *Vestal* were badly holed, and a number of casualties caused in the *Brilliant* and *Rinaldo*.

Enemy submarines were seen and torpedoes were fired, and during the latter part of the operations the work of the torpedo craft was chiefly confined to the protection of the larger ships.

It gradually became apparent that the rush of the enemy along the coast had been checked, that the operations were developing into a trench warfare, and that the work of the flotilla had, for the moment, ceased.

The arrival of the Allied reinforcements and the inundation of the country surrounding Nieuport rendered the further presence of the ships unnecessary.

The work of the squadron was much facilitated by the efforts of Colonel Bridges, attached to the Belgian Headquarters, and to him I am greatly indebted for his constant and unfailing support.

> I have the honour to be, Sir,
> Your obedient servant,
> Horace Hood
> Rear-Admiral, Dover Patrol

List of Ships which took Part in Operation off Belgian Coast

Venerable, Attentive, Foresight, Brilliant, Sirens, Severn, Humber, Mersey, Vestal, Rinaldo, Wildfire, Bustard, Excellent, Crane, Falcon, Flirt, Mermaid, Myrmidon, Racehorse, Syren, Amazon, Cossack, Crusader, Maori, Mohawk, Hazard, Nubian, Viking, Submarine c. 32, Submarine c. 34, Dunois, Capitaine Mehl, Francis-Garnier, Intrepid, Aventurier.

18 April Sunday Beautiful day. In the morning went to the cemetery with Daddy and afterwards picked a bunch of primroses at the tennis. Baby and I went to Children's Afternoon Service at Christ Church. Captive balloon up.

19 April Monday Beautiful hot weather. Had tea with Mrs Jarvis who is very ill. Captive balloons up.

20 April Tuesday Unsettled weather. Had tea with Mrs Simms.

21 April Wednesday Changeable day. Met Mrs B.: she has changed her house because she is watched, she went to Vilvorde to get off some Englishmen, one of which has been staying in her house. Captive balloon up.

22 April Thursday Fine day, chilly now and then. Captive sausages. Saw the automobile with ladies in it. Germans put up a notice that bicycles are not allowed to run. Beastly shame. Miss Mellin took us to the Petite Espinette, we walked back through the Forest. Funny sort of signal very high up.

23 April Friday Cold day. Funny black kites have been sent up by the Germans: a rumour went that they were aeroplanes chasing each other, but since 9 o'clock they have been in the same place. A few days ago the Germans were repulsed from the Yser. A woman going to Termonde saw 150 German cannons coming back from the Yser.

24 April Saturday Rain now and then. No papers are allowed to come across the frontier.

25 April Sunday Fine day. Daddy took me to Etterbeek to see the captive balloon on the Plaine des Manoeuvres. It is enormous and the shape of a whale. Went to Children's Service and afterwards to tennis.

26 April Monday Lovely day. German came this morning to know about Charlie. The Italian priest of Father Lecourt's who had been taken by the Germans has been sent to Germany. Captive balloon up.

27 April Tuesday Beautiful hot day. A whole lot of provision German carts and stores passed through Brussels. After school went up to tennis and played two sets of tennis. A boy of Charlie's school came to tell us that two German officers had been to ask where Charlie is.

28 April Wednesday Lovely hot day. The Germans have sent up two signals: one white, one brown. A German bicyclist came in the afternoon saying he had a letter for Charlie: we told him he wasn't here. After school went to tennis.

29 April Thursday Lovely day. Captive balloons up. Went through the forest to the Petite Espinette with Miss Mellin.

30 April Friday Saw a zeppelin at 9 a.m.: on it was the letters LZ 38. Lovely day. Went to tennis after school. Captive balloons up.

1 May Saturday Beautiful day, rather hot. Mother and Daddy had to go and inscribe themselves for the GG's, rue du Méridien. Miss

1915

Mellin took us to Trois-Couleurs to pick bluebells: it is like a blue carpet of them. Captive balloon up. Shower in the afternoon.

2 May Sunday Very hot, rain now and then. Went to Children's Service and afterwards had tea up at tennis.

3 May Monday Varied weather. A lot of kitchens and carts passed through Brussels. Went to tennis afternoon. Daddy fell out of the tram; was brought back by several people. The doctor came and bandaged his knee.

4 May Tuesday Fine day. Daddy feels pretty stiff, but will go out. Went to tennis. In the evening a thunderstorm.

5 May Wednesday Very hot day. A storm in the afternoon. The LZ 38 zeppelin I saw: it is only half the size of a proper zeppelin. The Germs were all drilling and pretending they were at a battle in the Bois. Thunderstorm in the afternoon. Great victory for the French.

6 May Thursday Lovely day. Captive balloon up. Baby and I went downtown in the morning. We saw a poor young fellow (who evidently had been selling English papers) taken by two Germs. Miss Mellin took Arthur and me in the Bois. The Germs have put up a notice that no French and English can go in the country.

7 May Friday Very close day. Went to tennis after school.

8 May Saturday Hot day. Two queer signals in the air. Mother went to see Mrs B. There she saw twenty English soldiers playing down in the cellars. In the garden they have prepared two ladders in case any Germs came they need only scramble over. A German submarine has sunk the *Lusitania*, an English ship with 2000 passengers on board. We don't know yet if they were saved or not. Baby has got pains in his throat, legs and arms and has got fever.

9 May Sunday Beautiful day. I went to see the English soldiers at Mrs B.'s. One of them picked a big bunch of white lilac for Mother, and Hilda, Mrs B.'s girl, puts a forget-me-not in their button-holes every morning. There are eleven of them and they each signed their names on a handkerchief. It is said that 650 passengers are known to be rescued out of the *Lusitania*, the rest we don't know. The captive balloon hasn't been up for several days: a signal is up instead. Baby is beginning to have spots on his face. Arthur and I went to church and after to tennis.

10 May Monday Lovely day. The doctor came and said that B[aby] has the measles. Arthur is staying a few days at Miss Mellin's for fear of catching it. Two signals in the air.

11 May Tuesday Lovely day. The rash is all out on B.'s face. At 5.15 p.m., at least 50 Allied aeroplanes were flying over Berghem. Mrs B.'s house is again being spied on. The Belgians round about her house have given her away. Four more English soldiers came to her this morning. They are all in a terrible funk each time a bell rings. If a suspicious-looking person rings they scramble up two ladders that are at the end of the garden. Mrs Jarvis is very bad, people think there is no hope of her living. 1500 passengers of the *Lusitania* have been drowned, so only 500 have been saved. Captive balloon up.

12 May Wednesday Baby is worse: he coughs a great deal, and does not eat anything. He has received his first real watch. Mother gave it to him hoping it would cheer him up; he was delighted with having it and keeps it on a chair at his bedside. The doctor came after supper; he said B. had a great deal of fever. Mrs B. has been advised to escape again from her house and leave the soldiers behind, because on Friday the Germs will make a raid at her house and make her prisoner till the end of the war. I don't know if it's true nor does Mrs B., but she says she'll take her risk. Baby had a bad night.

13 May Thursday Rainy day. The doctor came in the afternoon: B. has his eyes hurting a good deal, feels very weak, and has still a lot of fever. He talks of going back to school tomorrow; the doctor has advised Mother not to leave him alone, in case he was to uncover himself and catch cold. Mother is sleeping with him.

Copy of *The Times* of April the 8th
Effect of Poison Gas
Sufferings of the Victims

The *Liverpool Daily Post* publishes today the following from a letter just received from an English officer of high rank:

But this latest phase of murder – asphyxiating gas – if I wrote from now till the end of the war I could not say anything about that. Of all the devilish crimes of which the Germans have been guilty since the war started this one is far away the most devilish, and to try to excuse it on the ground that it inflicts a quick and painless death far different from the tornado of shells we let loose at Neuve-Chapelle is blatant lying. We have a lot of the men who have been gassed in our hospitals. Their moans are awful, and they sit up swaying about fighting and gasping for breath. Their faces and bodies are a muddy purple black, their eyes are glazed, and foam comes from their mouths. Their lungs are turned to liquid, and the doctors say they have the appearance of men on the point of death from drowning. Nurses and doctors work night and day to give relief.

To Our Fallen (*Times* 28.12.14)
Ye sleepers, who will sing you?
We can give our tears –
Ye dead men, who shall bring you
Fame in the coming years?
Brave souls ... but who remembers
The flame that fired your embers?
Deep, deep the sleep that holds you
Who one time had no peers.

Yet maybe Fame's but seeming
And praise you'd set aside,
Content to go on dreaming.
Yea, happy to have died
If of all things you prayed for –
All things your valour paid for –
One prayer is not forgotten
One purchase not denied.

But God grants your dear England
A strength that shall not cease
Till she have won for all the Earth

From ruthless men release,
And made supreme upon her
Mercy and Truth and Honour –
Is this the thing you died for?
Oh, Brothers, sleep in peace.

R.E. Verniede

14 May Friday Rainy and windy day. B. had a better night and seems better today. Mrs Jarvis is very ill. 16 German carts and stores passed down the avenue Louise. At 10.30 a.m. Mrs Jarvis died. The doctor said that B. has a little bronchitis.

15 May Saturday Fine day. Captive balloons up. Baby is about the same; he seems to have a little more fever. Near avenue de la Cambre, saw mounted Uhlans and a great many ammunition, provision carts. The doctor came to see Baby and told Mother that he just escaped having a pneumonia. Rain about dinner-time. Mrs B. was told to go to the Kommandantur.

16 May Sunday Fine day. Captive balloons up. Went with Daddy to the cemetery at Uccle and to see Mr Kirkpatrick's nice garden; he gave me a bunch of lilac, iris and forget-me-nots out of it. B. is much better. The cannons are heard from Uccle.

17 May Monday Daddy went to Mrs Jarvis's funeral and then on to the cemetery. Rainy day. The other day Mrs B. was told to go to the Kommandantur: she went, and by clever tricks she managed to get round the Germans by pretending she was helping them, or else they would have kept her prisoner. She has now got rid of all the English but one and has gone back to her old house and she has made the Germans sign a paper that they must not be allowed to go into her house. B. is much better.

18 May Tuesday Rainy day. There is talking going about that all the English, male and female, will be sent out of Belgium, the men to Germany and the others put on the frontier. Arthur is still at Miss Mellin's. On the 13th of May the Consul of Rotterdam wrote in the paper that some Germans had made 40 English officers prisoners and burnt them alive in a stable, and some Canadians which they crucified. These are the diabolical things those brutes do. We heard today that Dr Depage's wife is drowned on the *Lusitania*. He has an ambulance [hospital] at La Panne. There seems to have been a great victory on the Allied side, many people are talking and saying: 'Have you heard the good news?' etc., etc., but we can't get to the end of the story.

19 May Wednesday Dullish day. Daddy's ankle is worse. The doctor came to see Baby and thinks he's getting on splendidly, and will perhaps be able to get up on Sunday and go out on Monday. He is now pealing a lot.

20 May Thursday Lovely day. Captive balloon up. Daddy's pupil told him that somewhere in the country outside Brussels some Germans had taken a priest and sawed both his legs, hung him up five times, brought him down each time that they thought he was dying, just to torture the poor man: he is still living. The Indians are now giving the Germans a rig-up. Baby's appetite is coming back.

21 May Friday Very hot day. Captive balloon up; it had three hearts and half-an-hour after only two. The sweet-shop woman near Arthur's school has offered it a franc if he will draw her a picture of King Albert. The Italians are going to join the Allies. We heard today that Connie has got a baby boy, and Archie also a boy.

22 May Saturday Captive balloon up, but came down very soon. Frightfully hot day. The doctor came to see B., says he is getting on, but has got a 'congestion pulmonaire' in the back. A zeppelin, the same LZ 38, passed near our house four times: people [said] it had been on the go ever since 5 a.m. In bed heard the Germs three times playing a big band, they seem on the qui vive. Near Daddy's pupil's house there were a parrot at the window and it was whistling [a musical bar with notes drawn in]: 'Nous sommes foutus.'

23 May Sunday Lovely hot day. Went up at tennis with Daddy in the morning. B. is out of bed and dressed but cannot go out of the room. A white kite has been sent up by the Germs instead of a captive balloon.

12. Charlie, Connie and her first son Desmond (b. 13 May), and Tommy, London, 1915

24 May Whit Monday Beautiful hot day. Daddy took me for a walk in the morning through the Bois and then on to tennis. Jean gave me a nice bunch of roses: the first roses of the tennis. The Germs have sent two white kites up in the air: one goes up then the other goes down, always in opposite directions. B. is rapidly getting better.

Mensonges des Allemands dans le *Wochenschau*

503. Scène dans une tranchée anglaise.
Un Anglais qui tend sa bourse à un Allemand qui vient l'assaillir. Qu'avait en tête ce défenseur de la patrie britannique qui, perdant contenance en voyant l'Allemand foudre sur lui, présente à l'ennemi son porte-monnaie rempli, après avoir jeté son fusil? Cet incident est notaire. Le mercenaire anglais s'enrôle en entendant sonner les écus à ses oreilles et fait la guerre comme il fait tout autre métier bien payé. Il suppose le même point de vue chez l'adversaire. Ce cas, dépeint ainsi, est le pendant de la conduite des prisonniers anglais qui voulaient serrer la main en camarades à leurs vainqueurs comme après un match de foot-ball.

E. Zimsner

This was copied out of the *Wochenschau* to show what lies the Germs say. They suppose that every cowardly thing they do the English do.

25 May Tuesday Italy declared war to Austria on Sunday night at 12 o'clock. The Germs are too furious for words. Daddy has given me two pots and I have planted some sweet-peas and some pinks. All night trains passed.

26 May Wednesday Frightfully hot day. Five captive balloons, they look black. Mrs Munzinger is very, very ill.

27 May Thursday Fine day. Two little signals. Mr Jarvis sent me a bundle of little odds and ends of poor Mrs Jarvis's. I weighed myself at the chemist's: 39 kilos 90 grammes. Mr Cuissart told Daddy that Mrs Munzinger is nearly dead. We read in *The Times* that we have had a great victory, many losses, continual fighting for 13 days. The Germs loathe the Italians; they used to hate the English, but the Italians!

28 May Friday Fine day, colder. An English man-o'-war has been sunk and an American cargo-ship too, the English was sunk in the Dardanelles. The captive balloon has got five hearts today, four black and one white and is very high. Joséphine is not well: she has cramps and shivering fits.

29 May Saturday Fine day. Captive balloons up. Mrs Munzinger died at 5 o'clock in the morning. In the morning I went up at tennis to get some roses and other flowers.

[There follows 'Petit Dictionnaire de Boche', in French, for seven pages, which I have not included. It is a satirical piece directed against the Germans, possibly from *La Libre Belgique*.]

30 May Sunday Coldish day. Daddy and I trammed to the Prince d'Orange and then we walked right through the forest to Boitsfort, and nearly lost ourselves. We heard the cannons well in the forest. Captive sausages.

31 May Monday As I was taking Daddy to the club a little boy came up to us holding a dead sparrow, and said: 'Sir, this is a new antiquity, it is a chicken which the Kaiser is going to have for his breakfast.' The doctor came, says that B. can go out tomorrow for an hour.

1 June Tuesday Poor Charlie's birthday. No news from him yet. Daddy and Mother go to sign at the rue du Méridien. Miss Drury is very ill. Eight little leaves are springing up in my pot of pinks. The Meyers are all gone away for fear of the Americans having a bad time with the Germs in Brussels. B. for the first time since his illness has gone out for a walk. Hot day. Captives up. Mrs Munzinger is buried.

2 June Wednesday Hot day. Captives up. Baby and I went to feed the rabbits up at tennis in the morning, and after tea we went to the Bois. Daddy said that the Germs have shut up Malines and nobody can go in or out, so the inhabitants will starve, and we shan't have any vegetables. A zeppelin or an aeroplane again went to England and threw bombs. The Allies now wear masks to protect them from that awful gas.

3 June Thursday Very close day. Captives up. New troops come in to Brussels. Auntie fainted before dinner. A little boy about 12 or 13 years came up to me and asked if he could buy my buttons from me: I naturally refused. He was a Belgian boy scout and he took messages to England, Calais and Dover for the soldiers, and had received a bullet in his right hand. He also was for the Red Cross. Baby's room has been disinfected. My plant of pinks is getting on beautifully; I have two little leaves on the sweet-pea plant.

4 June Friday Very hot day. Captives up. Baby and I after tea went to the lake and we went to fetch Arthur back from Miss Mellin.

5 June Saturday Very hot. Saw a zeppelin this morning. Captives up. Mr Nasmith was married to Miss Kirkpatrick at Christ Church at 2.30 this afternoon. Auntie feeling very sick. Mrs B. is being watched again so in a fortnight she is going to change her 'domicile'; she has now four English soldiers with her and she can only go out at 5 o'clock in the morning for fear of being seized upon. When she heard that we had not any news from Charlie, she said: 'What not yet any news, well I will dress as a soldier and go and fetch him back.' A zeppelin has thrown 90 bombs on Ramsgate and the neighbourhoods. It is supposed that a French vessel and a Dutch vessel have been torpedoed. Von Bissing has turned off the whole committee of the Red Cross and has taken the 200 thousand francs because he pretends that they were spending the money to get men off to the front. Malines has been shut up because the Germans wanted all the workmen of the Arsenal, 5000 of them, because they want them to work for them; the workmen have positively refused, saying they would rather starve than work for them. They have pulled up the tram-lines. Such an injustice they have not done yet in all their abominable things throughout the war. The zeppelin I saw this morning was Number 39, an old-fashioned one.

6 June Sunday Baking hot day. My plants are getting on beautifully. Captive balloon of Etterbeek went up late this morning. Arthur, Baby and I had tea up at tennis. A zeppelin passed quite near our house at 8.16 p.m. and came down at Etterbeek; we saw it again at 9 p.m. going in the direction of England: perhaps to deposit a few bombs there. No. 37.

7 June Monday Frightfully hot. Captive up. At 3 a.m. Mother came tearing up the stairs to wake me up, the cannons were making an awful noise. We both went up in the garret and from one of the windows we saw lights, smoke: they were bombs which the Allies were throwing from aeroplanes. They smashed the zeppelin and the shed was all burned up at Evere, 30 soldiers wounded. Bravo! three cheers for the Allies! George Weir died. Saw several small mitrailleuses on the avenue Louise. Another zeppelin came a cropper at Ghent at 4 a.m. B. and I went to tennis and we heard the cannons.

8 June Tuesday Baking hot day. A thunderstorm in the afternoon. Captives were up till the storm broke out. Daddy says that they were French aeroplanes that bombarded the zeppelin sheds: an English German spy told them where they were situated. Daddy went to George Weir's funeral service.

9 June Wednesday Very hot. Roumania bought half a million warboots from America: that shows they will march! The Germans have forbidden any Dutch papers to come into Belgium. We went up at tennis after 4 o'clock. Now it is said that they were two English aeroplanes that threw bombs over the zeppelin shed at Evere.

10 June Thursday Mother's birthday. Very hot day, several thunderstorms. We all went to Meg Butcher's birthday party. The Germans have taken back Przemyśl.

11 June Friday Much cooler, rain. Strawberries are already very cheap: 25 centimes for a pound. In yesterday's thunderstorm the big-cornered house of the avenue Longchamps, near Mrs Simms's, was struck by lightning: they had to fetch the firemen. The Misses Weir and the Misses Etherington are all going to England soon.

12 June Saturday Fine day. Black Maria or captive balloon up. One of the 'Hohenzollern' Dautzenbergh has been made prisoner by the Allies. The Turks want to make peace. Mother had a letter from Uncle Fred who is now staying with Aunt Polly: it looks as if he is in Switzerland for there is a Swiss stamp on the letter. People cannot have any more passports to go to Holland. There were some

13. 27 rue Africaine, St Gilles, Brussels, the Hodson home from 1904

mitrailleuses and ammunition carts passing down the avenue with those 'Pigs' singing 'God save the King'. Doctor Nicolet is gone to England. Baby has a cold so he did not go to school. New moon.

13 June Sunday The zeppelin which was attacked on the 7th was by one of our naval airmen, Flight Sub-Lieutenant R.A.J. Warneford, between Ghent and Brussels. He dropped six bombs upon the airship which exploded and fell to the ground in flames, etc. Another English ship, the *Ocean*, has been torpedoed and sunk in the Dardanelles, with the loss of 500 men. Cardinal Mercier came to preach at the St Gudule cathedral a few days ago; he had to walk eight miles for those horrid Germans would not give him a lift. Arthur and I went to Children's Service and then on to tennis. B. went out in the pony carriage to the château of Mme Errera at Boitsfort with Georgie. Auntie saw a great many scouts, and she said they did not look a bit like German scouts. Lovely day.

14 June Monday Black Maria is up and a small black signal. Lieutenant Warneford has received the VC, the Legion of Honour from France and a letter from the King for his noble deeds. Three cheers for him! Arthur saw a zeppelin. Baby suffered a great deal today: Doctor says he mustn't go to school tomorrow. Went up to tennis with Dad in the afternoon. Fine day.

15 June Tuesday Lovely day. At about 5.30 p.m. the Germs sent a round signal high up in the air and brought it down a few minutes after. Yesterday Arthur went and did a lot of jumping and today he has to stay in bed because his back hurts him so.

16 June Wednesday The Russians have had a great victory in Galicia. Fine day. Black Marias up.

17 June Thursday At four a.m. I woke up with a start: Bang, bang, bang. I jumped up at my window: couldn't see a thing excepting Black Maria, went up to the loft and there I saw bombs flying high up in the air and making an awful noise; another Allied aeroplane I suppose! Mary Panquin invited us all to tea and we enjoyed ourselves very much. She took us to a fête at the school where there was a very clever juggler.

18 June Friday Lovely day. Nobody yet knows what the aeroplane did the other day. Black Maria of Etterbeek isn't up, but the others are. B. and I went to tennis after school.

19 June Saturday Lovely day, rather cool. Black Marias up. In the French communiqué they say they threw bombs on the Rheims cathedral: the truth-telling Germs say it is a lie.

20 June Sunday Lieutenant Warneford the great English hero is dead. He was trying a new aeroplane with another American near Paris and fell 300 metres and was killed. Poor man! The Germs have now stopped every single communication between Holland and Belgium, they have not yet been so strict about it. Arthur is very sick today, suffers a great deal from the head and cannot eat anything without being sick. B. and I went up to tennis: there we could hear the cannons very well. Lovely day. Black Marias up. The train which was going to take the people off to the place to go to England has been put off by the Germs.

21 June Monday Doctor came, says A[rthur]. has an 'Embarras Gastrique'; he suffered a good deal today. Mrs Evans is dead. Lovely day. Black Marias up.

22 June Tuesday Lovely day. Mother and Daddy have gone to spend the day at Louvain. A. isn't suffering today. Sausages up.

23 June Wednesday Lovely day. Black Marias up. Doctor says A. is better and can go out now. He is very pale.

24 June Thursday We went to Oda's tea-party. Very warm day. A. not feeling very well. Sausages up.

25 June Friday Baby's ninth birthday: he had a tea-party up at tennis. Meg and Joan Butcher, Richard and Rore Corrock, Oda Karaper, Georgie Cuissart and his nurse came to the party. It rained nearly all day, but it got beautiful at about teatime. Black Marias up. B. lost his purse with 1 f. 50 in it.

26 June Saturday Beautiful day. In going to tennis this afternoon B. and I saw a sort of big balloon flying about with a piece of white stuff hanging from it. The cannons I heard up at the tennis. Before poor Lieutenant Warneford was killed, Auntie read that he had been feeling very gloomy and dull and that he turned to his friend the aeroplane and said: I feel that I am going to be killed, and that I shall never see my mother's face again. Black Marias up.

27 June Sunday We have at last got news of Charlie. Uncle Fred wrote to say that he has heard that Charlie is in England and in good health. A. is very pale and feels all time so weak. We went to tennis after lunch and there was a roundish black thing in the sky: some people said it was an aeroplane, some said it was a sort of signal of the Germans. Beautiful day.

28 June Monday Rain and sun. Arthur is in bed with a sore throat. As the 'Sausage' wasn't up, there were two sorts of kites in its stead.

29 June Tuesday Lovely morning, in the afternoon there were showers. The 'Sausage' did not go up till nearly 6 p.m., it was still up when I went to bed. The men who bring *The Times* at the club have been captured.

30 June Wednesday By one stroke of the pen the King has struck off 8 of the Knights of the Garter: Emperor of Austria; German Emperor; King of Wurtemberg; German Crown Prince; Grand Duke of Hesse; Prince Henry of Prussia; Duke of Saxe Coburg; Duke of Cumberland! That is a great honour for Germany! King Albert has been named the Knight of the Garter. There is a notice put up that any person wearing either relics of the Allied army or flags, etc., will have to pay 600 marks or several months' imprisonment. Very changeable day, the sausage was up in the morning but was brought down when it rained.

1 July Thursday I went this morning with Daddy and Mother to the rue du Méridien for them to sign, and then on to the dentist. Auntie had a sort of congestion attack on going to bed. Miss Mellin took Arthur and me for a lovely long walk to Watermael and back. We passed the shed of Etterbeek and there was nothing in it, nor was the Sausage up in the afternoon, though it was in the morning. Lovely day.

2 July Friday Fine day. Sausage up. We are all in great anxiety: Daddy is not yet in and it is eleven o'clock of night. I went round to somebody, one of Daddy's friends, and we've been sending word round and nobody knows what has happened. Raymond fetched Father Lecourt and he cheered us up a bit, and Raymond then wanted to go to the Kommandantur to hear if he's been taken, but he cannot go without a passport. Daddy came back at 11.30 p.m.: he had been locked in the club, nobody knew he was still there.

3 July Saturday A zeppelin has been brought down in Holland, and the officers in it had all sorts of views they had taken of the country and maps. Now as the Belgians are forbidden to wear their colours they now wear the ivy-leaf and the English wear the red rose. Arthur, Baby and I went to tennis. Frightfully hot day. Sausages up.

4 July Sunday Mrs Peiser's birthday. Lovely day, very hot. Daddy took us to Waterloo at 9.30 a.m. We saw the Monument Gordon, which had been repaired in 1863 by his brother Admiral the Hon. ble J. Gordon. Then the Belgian monument, upon which was written: Belges morts le XVIII Juin MDCCCXV en combattant pour la défense du drapeau et l'honneur des armes. We went away from the monument of Blüchet and it was too far to see the French one. Daddy then took us to the Panorama: it was magnificent! one could have sworn we were in the midst of the battle. Then Arthur, Baby and I went up to the lion but there were Germans all round it, so we soon came down again. The swallows have built a nest in the lion's mouth. There were 226 steps to it. We then went to Hougoumont and had lunch under an apple-tree, and while Daddy was resting we went to visit the farm of Hougoumont. The farmer told us that at the Waterloo battle there had been a tremendous fight in his farmyard, and his grandmother who was then 15 years of age was in the midst of it all. After that Daddy took us to refreshen ourselves at the only Brown Hotel left. While Daddy was resting we walked to Braine-l'Alleud, bought some sweets there, then came back to the Hotel after having passed the Ferme de la Haie-Sainte and the Belle Alliance. After having spent such a lovely day we took the steam-tram at 5 p.m. and came home. We heard the cannons well.

5 July Monday Very hot day. Mr Morgan was shot at by a German professor in America because they said he had given a sum of money for the war funds: he was wounded in two places, and he is the greatest American millionaire. *The Times* thinks that the war will still go on for three years. Baby and I went to tennis after tea. A little black thing was flying in the sky this afternoon. Auntie been feeling very poorly.

6 July Tuesday Lots of people say that Holland is going to go to war with us. Sausages were up this morning but Etterbeek was afterwards brought down. Very hot day. A thunderstorm in the night.

7 July Wednesday Lovely day, but very windy. The new notice up is that people can travel without passports excepting near the frontier. Doctor came to Auntie today.

8 July Thursday Ethel Mellin, the Weirs, the Etheringtons, etc., have all gone off to England at 5 a.m. Mother got a letter from Uncle Fred to say that Charlie is doing military work in England, and enjoys it very much. Very windy day. We went to tennis in the afternoon. Instead of the Sausage there are two black signals up.

9 July Friday Fine day. Sausages up in the morning, black signals in the afternoon. After school we went to tennis and Arthur and I played tennis against Miss Winiasha and Alma Moodie and we beat them. Mrs B. has again changed her house and she won't tell anybody but Father Lecourt.

10 July Saturday Beautiful day. Sausages up in the morning but after dinner there was a round black thing. Doctor came today and he finds her very weak. Mother and I went to town morning.

11 July Sunday All the Germans in South Africa have surrendered themselves to General Botha, and Captain De Wet has been made prisoner for being a traitor. Dullish day. Went to church in the morning and played tennis in the afternoon. Sausage up.

12 July Monday Rainy morning, sunny afternoon. Charlie has at last written to say that he is very well, and is staying with Aunt Polly,

1915

and has seen Uncle Fred, Connie and Jack. We went to tennis after school and in coming back Wilhelmina fell out of my pocket and broke. Auntie has been very ill today, in agonies of pain. Some Germs went into the Clinique of the rue de la Culture this afternoon [Edith Cavell's clinic].

13 July Tuesday Poor dear Uncle Algie is dead: as he was walking along the front at Hove, it was pitch dark, for fear of enemy aeroplanes they had to put all the lights out, so he fell down the area steps and was killed poor fellow! Lovely morning, at 5 p.m. it poured with rain. We went to tennis after school. A funny sort of balloon was up in the afternoon.

14 July Wednesday Lovely day, but after 6 p.m. it rained. French national fête today. Auntie had another bad attack of pain. Doctor was fetched.

14. Tommy, Jack and son Desmond, and Charlie, London, 1915

15 July Thursday Charlie has enlisted in the Royal Fusiliers. Jack was able to write through Mr Watts and has sent a photo of dear old Tommy in the Lovat Scouts' uniform and one of himself, Connie and the Baby. Fine morning, rainy afternoon. Went to tennis and heard the cannons.

16 July Friday Went to market to fetch a lot of fruit for jam. Lovely morning, but at about 6 p.m. it poured. Went to tennis and we saw I think like a parachute in the air. Auntie is very weak and poorly. B. had a toothache in the night.

17 July Saturday Rainy day. B. and I went to the dentist in the morning. A rumour is going about that the Kaiser is in Brussels and goes in the night to the convent in our street, in the newspaper *La Belgique* I saw that he is in Poland. Auntie seems a little better today. Mother and I have been making cherry and gooseberry jam. A white flower on my plant.

18 July Sunday Rainy morning, fine afternoon. Went to tennis. In the morning went to see Miss Mellin. The 'Sausage' does not go up any more.

19 July Monday Arthur's birthday. Lovely day. Eric Wansart and André Panne went to the cinema with Arthur, Mother and Baby, I stayed with little Auntie. Arthur had a cake of the shape of a cannon ball, it was full of cream.

20 July Tuesday I have written a long story about my experience during the bombardment of Middelkerke, and am going to write them in books and sell them. Lovely day, a shower at dinner-time. Baby and I went to tennis. Arthur got a nasty bump on the head at school.

21 July Wednesday Belgian national fête. All the shops shut, people wearing the edelweiss. Germans will not allow any processions nor festivals to be made. Every house and every shop and café is shut up. The town is as quiet as death. We put our shutters down. We went to tennis, no nets were put up. Beautiful day. Sold two of my books.

22 July Thursday Mrs B.'s girl [Hilda] came this evening with a French soldier in hiding who was wounded by a Uhlan. Mrs B. has got still as many soldiers as she had before and will not give her address to anybody. Lovely day. Went to tea at Miss Doyle's.

23 July Friday Stormy day, rain and sunshine. Sold another of my books. In the paper we read that 30 thousand and sixty-nine Iron Crosses were given till the end of March, and 68 Victoria Crosses were given up to the end of June. There is scarcely an officer without a medal.

24 July Saturday Showers every now and then. Two days ago two German soldiers were shot in the Royal Park by their officers because they refused to fight. Very far away I saw a small black signal of the Germans. Baby and I went after school to the dentist and downtown. The paper *La Belgique* has been punished for five days because it wrote something against the Germans in it.

25 July Sunday Changeable weather. Went to church in the morning and to tennis afternoon.

26 July Monday The German Governor-General of Brussels, Von Bissing, has his brother interned in England. Fine day, went to tennis after school.

27 July Tuesday Changeable weather. Two Englishmen have escaped from Ruhleben in Germany. Baby and I went to the Botanical Gardens and to the monument 'Liberté' place des Martyrs. On the 21st the Belgians covered the monument and the sort of cellars below, of flowers.

28 July Wednesday Rain and sunshine. Baby's holidays have begun: he was supposed to have four prizes but as it is wartime they did not give any. Went to tennis after dinner. Mother took me to the High-Life after supper.

29 July Thursday Lovely day. Miss Mellin took us to Boitsfort and we saw a great many Belgian scouts. The cannons were rather loud.

30 July Friday Lovely day, stormy feeling in the air. Great victory for the Italians, over a hundred German officers taken prisoner. Baby and I went to tennis.

31 July Saturday Arthur's holidays have begun. Lovely day. Went to tennis.

1 August Sunday Very hot day. Went to church in the morning. Arthur dined at Mr Jarvis's. Went to tennis. Terrible boat accident in Chicago [the SS *Eastland* rolled over while tied to a dock; 844 passengers and crew were killed].

2 August Monday Very hot day. Daddy and Mother gone to sign at the rue du Méridien. Arthur, Baby and Mother went to the Kommandantur to ask the Kommandant leave to see the English wounded, he could not.

3 August Tuesday Changeable weather. Mrs B.'s boy [Philippe], who is thirteen, has been taken up by the Germans because he will not allow the name of the person who prints the *Libre Belgique*. Goodness knows when he will be let out. The captive balloons are not sent up any more. Sir Arthur Hardinge, the British Ambassador at Madrid, had a bad fall in the lift well, but he is recovering.

[The first page of Amy's new diary, which starts below, lists about thirty-seven pupils at her school in 1916: 'Nous des élèves de l'Ecole Moyennade St Gilles, 1916', and the names of professors, not included here.]

4 August Wednesday Just a year since war was declared. The notice is: that nobody is to wear any sign of mourning for the occasion, all the shops must be opened, but at 7 p.m. they must shut, everybody must be indoors by 8 p.m., if not they will have a fine of 10,000 marks or five years in prison. As I was in the chaussée de Charleroi at 20 minutes to seven there were eight sentinels walking on each side of the pavement to prepare for seeing everything shut. Rain and sunshine. Very funny signal in the air. Went to tennis after dinner.

5 August Thursday Lovely day. The Belgians had a lovely time last night, they sang the national songs and stayed out in the streets. The Germans have taken Warsaw. Miss Mellin is getting up a play, we went to the rehearsal this afternoon. Miss Cavell is taken.

6 August Friday Showery day. Went to tea at Miss Ada's.

7 August Saturday

> Lieutenant J.G. Smyth, 15th Ludhiana Sikhs, won his VC on May 18th. Each of the brave men with Lieutenant Smyth was awarded by the Indian Distinguished Service Medal. The men in the regiment believe that Lieutenant Smyth bears a charmed life for he has had his cap blown off by shells five times, has had bullets through his clothes, and lately while he was lighting a cigarette the match was taken out of his fingers by a bullet.
>
> (*The Times* 30 July)

Two military Bulgarian airmen were killed at Sofia the 29th of July. Miss Mellin took us to Berghem. Rainy day. Heard a troop of Germans playing 'God save the King' on their flutes and drums.

8 August Sunday Drizzly morning, fine afternoon. Went to tennis. American tournament going on. The Germans have offered Mrs B.'s boy 1000 marks if he will say the name of the author of the *Libre Belgique*, but he will not open his lips.

9 August Monday Hot day. The cannons have been very loud. Went with Daddy downtown in the morning to choose the prizes for the tournament. Went to tennis this afternoon. The Germans say that all the shops must be shut on the 20th of this month on account of the fun they had on the 8th. All the German civilians are going away from Brussels.

10 August Tuesday Very hot day. Storm in the evening. Miss Cavell has been made prisoner in the Kommandantur, Mrs B. is in hiding and her little girl is at Mrs Aileen's. Mlle de Smet and Mr Cass have won the tournament prizes. Baby and I went to buy my first watch downtown with the money earned from my books. We went to tennis this afternoon.

11 August Wednesday Very hot day. Baby and I went to the dentist in the morning. Played nine sets of tennis.

12 August Thursday Mr Jarvis and a great many English are going to England today. Mme Cuissart and family are also gone. Lovely day. Took Baby to Boitsfort in the morning to Mr Bauer's castle. Arthur and I went to tennis. In Tuesday's storm 10 thunderbolts were seen to fall.

13 August Friday Hot day. Mr Meredith, the English wounded soldier at the Palace, has had a leg and an arm cut off, is dying and the Germans are still going to send him to Germany. We went to rehearse the play and the dance at Miss Mellin's this afternoon.

14 August Saturday Lovely day. Miss Mellin took us downtown in the afternoon to send off some parcels to the prisoners in Germany. We went then to see the rue de l'Escalier and the rue du Dam, two streets which, on the 4th of August when they had to shut up the shops, mocked the German sentinels and threw things on their heads, so the Germans say that from the 9th to the 22nd of August all the inhabitants of these two streets must shut up their houses and be indoors by 7 p.m. When we passed at 6.30 they were already beginning to close. New German troops came in.

15 August Sunday Changeable weather. Daddy took me to the cemetery at Uccle in the morning. Arthur and I went to tennis. Jean Nicolet was taken to the Kommandantur last night but was released this afternoon, nobody knows why. There is a report that Reverend Crawford is dead. The Germans are just a day's walk from St Petersburg. Mr Carl Ehrlich and his wife came back from France this morning.

16 August Monday Rain and sunshine. Arthur and I went downtown in the morning; in coming back we saw a German car with officers and a poor man tied up on the bench of the car going to the Prison St Gilles. These are the numbers of the tram-men who are German spies: 313 – 917 – 702 – 1223 – 971, etc. We went to tennis in the afternoon.

17 August Tuesday Stormy day. Mrs B. and Miss Cavell have been taken up and are in the Prison St Gilles. We went to tennis in the afternoon.

18 August Wednesday Fine day. Arthur has an abscess in his ear, but he goes out. No English papers come across the frontier so we don't know any news. There were two kites up in the air. We went to tennis in the afternoon.

19 August Thursday Changeable day. Went to tennis this afternoon.

20 August Friday Anniversary of the entrance into Brussels by the Germans. Lovely day. Daddy and I played tennis against Mr and Madame Back. Over two years since Daddy last played. It was false about the Germans being a day's walk from St Petersburg, but they have taken Kovno.

21 August Saturday Rainy day. Arthur's abscess has burst. Went to tennis this afternoon.

22 August Sunday Lovely day. We went to church this morning. Daddy and I played tennis against Mr and Mme Back and beat them: our revenge of their having beaten us the first time. Tournament going on.

23 August Monday Lovely day. Baby and I went to see Miss Drury this morning, and we went to the cinema this afternoon when in an interval the man played the 'Brabançonne' and 'Vers l'Avenir'.

[There follows: 'Communiqué du Niewe Rotterdamoche Courant et Vaderland', 19 August, about 'La France et la Guerre', in French, five pages – not transcribed here.]

24 August Tuesday Lovely day. Baby and I went to play hide-and-seek at the Plaine de Berkendael this morning, and to tennis this afternoon.

25 August Wednesday An American ship has been sunk by a German torpedo, and several people have been drowned and 36 very much wounded. Had a lovely excursion to Quatre-Bras with Mr Gahan's Sunday School and brought back a big bunch of heather. Lovely day.

26 August Thursday Very good news on the side of the Allies. The English have taken Gallipoli, and have sunk 8 ships (the Germans only allow 1), all the Turks are surrounded by the English and the Italians are coming too. A million English are embarquing in Holland etc. they will perhaps fight at Hasselt. This is what I heard today, but whether it is true I do not know. Lovely day. Baby and I went to tennis this afternoon.

27 August Friday Very hot day. After dinner an Allied aeroplane passed over Evere and Etterbeek: immediately the Germans began firing. We rushed up to the garret and saw all the shells which had burst high up in the air then we went into the street and all the sky was full of bullets, but we could not see the aeroplanable [sic]. We don't know yet if it damaged anything. Went to Miss Mellin for the rehearsal. Heard the cannons in the night.

28 August Saturday Very hot day. Daddy and I went to see the Resurrection Church. Played tennis and heard the guns.

29 August Sunday Fine morning. Played for the first time in a tennis tournament with Henry Neusister, but we had to stop soon for it rained. Went to church this morning. Last night there was a thunderbolt.

30 August Monday Yesterday we heard of the death of Doctor and Mrs Fay's son-in-law, who was a captain, and died a dreadful death from the explosion of a shell. Stormy day. Played in the tournament till 5 p.m. for it rained.

31 August Tuesday Lovely day. Finished the tournament this afternoon. Mrs B.'s boy has been at last let out of the Kommandantur and is now with his sister but Mrs B. is still in the prison of St Gilles.

1 September Wednesday Fine morning, rain at 1 p.m. Went to tennis. Mother and Daddy signed at the Méridien.

2 September Thursday Rainy day. Auntie feeling very weak. The Germans have taken nearly all the nickel pennies, so now they are making pieces of money in zinc.

3 September Friday Pégoud, the great French aviator, has been killed. He was attacked in his aeroplane by the Germans and fell on the French line, never to get up again. The saddest funeral I have ever seen passed down the rue de l'Aqueduc this morning: the death of a general who has been a prisoner in Germany and had been sent back to his home a fortnight ago on account of his health. The coffin was draped with the big Belgian flag and the streets were crowded to see the coffin pass. He was only 56 years and lived 11 rue Moris. The Germans woke us up this morning at 5.30 with their fifes and drums. Rehearsal at Miss Mellin's this afternoon. Showery day.

4 September Saturday Lovely day. Went to town in the morning. Baby and I lunched at the château de Mr Bauer, Boitsfort. Went for a beautiful drive in the pony-carriage and came back at 4.30 p.m. with a lot of grapes. A lot of trains passed.

5 September Sunday Fine day. Went to Christ Church and to St Jacques, where they played 'Vers l'Avenir' and the 'Brabançonne'. Tennis this afternoon. The name of the general who died a few days ago was General Maes, a member of the tennis club. Mr Simmons has been named a captain, Captain Larking a major; Tommy Reichardt, an officer, they are all in the war.

6 September Monday Lovely day. New troops have come in to Brussels. Went to tennis this afternoon. Arthur has at last had his wish: a box of oil-paints.

7 September Tuesday Miss Mellin had all our photos taking in our fancy-dresses of the play at the Compagnie belge this morning.

Outward Bound
By an Officer who has since fallen in Gallipoli

There's a waterfall I'm leaving
Running down the rocks in foam.
There's a pool for which I'm grieving
Near the water-ousel's home
And it's there that I'd be lying
With the heather close at hand
And the curlews faintly crying
'Mid the wastes of Cumberland.

While the midnight watch is winging
Thoughts of other days arise,
I can hear the river singing
Like the saints in Paradise;
I can see the water winking
Like the merry eyes of Pan,
And the slow half-pounder sinking
By the bridge's granite span.

Ah! to win them back and clamber
Braced anew with winds I love,
From the river's stainless amber
To the morning mist above,
See through cloud-rifts rent asunder
Like a painted scroll unfurled.
Bridge and hollow rolling under
To the fringes of the world.

Now the weary guards are sleeping,
Now the great propellers churn,
Now the harbour lights are creeping
Into emptiness astern,
While the sentry wakes and watches
Plunging triangles of light
Where the water leaps and catches
At our escort in the night.

1915

> Great their happiness who seeing
> Still with unbenighted eyes
> Him of theirs who gave them being,
> Sun and earth that made them wise.
> Die and feel their embers quicken
> Year by year in summer time,
> When the cotton grasses thicken
> On the hills they used to climb.
>
> Shall we also be as they be,
> Mingled with our mother clay,
> Or return no more it may be?
> Who has knowledge, who shall say?
> Yet we hope that from the bosom
> Of our shaggy father Pan,
> When the earth breaks into blossom
> Richer from the dust of man,
>
> Though the high gods smite and slay us,
> Though we come not whence we go,
> As the host of Menelaus
> Came these many years ago;
> Yet the self-same wind shall bear us
> From the same departing place
> Out across the gulfs of Saros
> And the peaks of Samothrace.
>
> We shall pass in summer weather,
> We shall come at eventide,
> Where the fells stand up together
> And all quiet things abide;
> Mixed with cloud and wind and river,
> Sun-distilled in dew and rain,
> One with Cumberland for ever,
> We shall go not forth again.

(copied out of *The Times* of Friday, August 27 1915)

Beautiful day. Went to tennis this afternoon. Cannons very loud.

8 September Wednesday Beautiful day. Daddy took us for the whole day to Quatre-Bras. Walked from Woluwe to Quatre-Bras. We passed the beautiful property of Mr Parmentier on the avenue de Tervueren, where there were some Belgian wounded soldiers sitting in the garden. Came back with a basket full of blackberries and a bunch of heather. Mrs B. was tried today.

9 September Thursday Yesterday morning a zeppelin was smashed in two at Zerrien, near Berghem: it was on its way to England and in the fog it knocked against a chimney and was smashed. One zeppelin less. Poor old Paddy Palmer has died of wounds. This afternoon Arthur, Baby and I went to spend the afternoon at the Château de Bauer at Boitsfort. Jack Jenkins is going back to New York tomorrow. Lovely day.

10 September Friday Lovely day. The porter of the Carlton has been taken to the Kommandantur. This afternoon went to Miss Mellin's for the rehearsal.

11 September Saturday Lovely day. Playing in an American tournament with Mr Bigwood. A zeppelin has been flying over London and has done a lot of damage around St Paul's Cathedral, one is not quite sure if the cathedral has been touched. Arthur saw a captive balloon in the direction of Uccle.

12 September Sunday Lovely day. A German officer came into church this morning. Went to tennis this afternoon with Baby.

13 September Monday Lovely day. A zeppelin passed last night. Great victory for the Russians. Saw some mitrailleuses this morning. Went to tennis. Vera Levy and Georges Delcoigne have won the tournament.

14 September Tuesday Fine day. Went to tennis this afternoon. Mrs B. was not tried the other day.

15 September Wednesday The zeppelin which went over London threw 150 bombs, but it was so high up that the cathedral was not touched, but 6 men and 11 women were killed. Mr Cruger managed to get over from England a letter from Jack enclosing two photos

1915

15. Charlie and Tommy, London, 1915

of Charlie and Tommy side by side, both are soldiers. Charlie will be coming to Belgium on the 20th to join the army on the Yser, Tommy will be going to Turkey. Paddy was only two days in the trenches when on the 8th of August he was shot in the head and died on the 28th. From beginning of war to August 31, 1915, on all battlefields of the British army and navy:

Dead:	4905 officers
	70992 men
Wounded:	9973 officers
	241066 men
Missing:	1501 officers
	63466 men

16 September Thursday Dull day. We all went to the cinema in the afternoon.

17 September Friday Fine day. Saw four battalions of Germans, three guns, etc., going to the front. There was a mounted German Colonial officer, he looked more of a brigand. The Germans are turning the Persians against us. The Persians have threatened to murder the Russian and the English Consul, they are going about in disguise. Went to the rehearsal at Miss Mellin's.

18 September Saturday Mrs B. is now at the Military Hospital because she has got ill. The play is given this afternoon at Miss Mellin's for the profit of the Belgian soldiers.

19 September Sunday Lovely day. At 1.30 p.m. an Allied aeroplane passed over Brussels. We saw it this time. Immediately the Germans fired at it. It was throwing down papers and everybody fought to get them who saw them fall. I wonder what was written on them.

20 September Monday Poor old Charlie is leaving England today to go to the Yser, and Tommy is leaving to go to the Dardanelles. God bless them! Two new German flags have been put on the Palais de Justice. There was a great banquet given in London a few days ago for the honour of the sinking of the 50th German submarine. The aeroplane which we saw yesterday was a Belgian one, and it threw down a lot of French papers. A lot of trains passed during the night and morning. This is what was copied out of a paper which was thrown out of the aeroplane:

> Front percé par les Russes en Galicie par les Français en Lorraine. Nous serons ici dans deux mois. Courage!

Went to tennis this afternoon.

21 September Tuesday Lovely day, rather cold. Went to tennis with Baby this afternoon, from there I heard the cannons.

22 September Wednesday Lovely day. Cannons very loud. Went with Baby and the Butchers to play in the sands at Uccle and then to tennis.

23 September Thursday Lovely day, rather warm. Went to tennis this afternoon.

24 September Friday Two Belgian spies were shot by the Germans yesterday morning. Changeable weather.

25 September Saturday Rainy day. The Spanish Minister of Brussels is very angry against Von Bissing because he asked for Bissing not to kill the two Belgian spies and Von Bissing gave his word that he would not have them killed and the next day they were shot on the Plaine de Manoeuvres of Etterbeek. Mother took Baby and me downtown this morning, and we went to tennis this afternoon.

26 September Sunday Fine day. Two Belgians had been plotting at Schaerbeek to blow up a certain bridge so as to prevent the German troops from coming in: they have been taken and are condemned to death. Went to church this morning: harvest festival, two men played the violin. Went to tennis this afternoon. Perrin was beaten by the young Gräffe boy in tennis in the Carl Ehrlich Cup.

27 September Monday Showery day. Holidays are over. Baby and Arthur been to the school at the place de Parme.

28 September Tuesday The English are advancing successfully towards Lille. At 4 p.m. an Allied aeroplane passed over Brussels. There was a great deal of cannonading by the Germans who were firing after it. Somebody said a man had been killed by a piece of shrapnel which was sent up to shoot the aeroplane, near the Bourse. Auntie is very weak and seedy today. Fine day, rather chilly.

29 September Wednesday Changeable day. There were several aeroplanes which passed yesterday, though I did not see one. They threw down papers on which there was written that there was very good news on the side of the Allies. A great many Germans been taken prisoner.

30 September Thursday Cold day, showers now and then. Went to town in the morning. Saw a little spot on the place du Sablon, where a shrapnel had made a stone sink more in the earth than the other stones, when the aeroplane passed on Tuesday.

1 October Friday Daddy and Mother gone to sign at the rue du Méridien. Fine morning, wet afternoon. Went to tennis in the afternoon.

2 October Saturday Lovely day. Gräffe, aged 15, has beaten Carl Ehrlich in the final, and has won the Ehrlich Cup. Went to tennis afternoon. German officers and soldiers are deserting the army and German police go in certain houses to find them.

3 October Sunday 20 Declarations of War from July 28th, 1914 to the 4th of August, 1915.

> July 28th 1914 Austria Hungary against Serbia
> August 1st 1914 Germany – Russia
> August 3rd 1914 Germany – France
> 3rd of August 1914 Germany against Belgium
> 4th of August 1914 England – Germany
> 5th of August 1914 Austria Hungary – Russia
> 6th of August 1914 Serbia – Germany
> 11th of August 1914 Montenegro – Austria Hungary
> 11th of August 1914 France – Austria Hungary

13th of August 1914 England – Austria Hungary
23rd of August 1914 Japan – Germany
25th of August 1914 Austria Hungary – Japan
28th of August 1914 Austria Hungary – Belgium
Nov. 2 Russia – Turkey
Nov. 5 France – Turkey
Nov. 5 England – Turkey
Nov. 7 Belgium – Turkey
Nov. 7 Serbia – Turkey
May 23 1915 Italy – Austria Hungary

Went to town with Mother in the morning and to tennis in the afternoon. Cannons very loud. Lovely day.

4 October Monday 37 German deserters were shot yesterday. A collision of German trains of wounded soldiers happened at Etterbeek. Auntie had a very bad night, and today is sick. Fine day.

5 October Tuesday Rainy day. The Germans are forbidding people to sell maps of the war, and from the 15th of this month they say that they will search the houses to see if there are any maps. Went to town this morning.

6 October Wednesday Great excitement: the newspaper sellers are shouting: bombardment of Metz by French aviators. The Germans would soon stop them if they heard them calling it out. Rehearsal of the same play, dances, songs, etc. at Mlle Schöller's and Miss Mellin's after school.

7 October Thursday Lovely day. Mrs B. [Bodart] and Miss C. [Cavell] have been tried today. Acted the same play, *A Hero*, for the same fund at Miss Mellin's. Cannons very loud.

8 October Friday Dull day. Mother rather seedy. No news yet of Charlie and Tommy.

9 October Saturday Auntie had a very bad attack of faintness this evening. New Governor of Brussels of the German Kultur. Foggy day.

'Miss Cavell Was Shot': The Diaries of Amy Hodson, 1914–1920

10 October Sunday Auntie very weak. At 5 p.m. great excitement. Several aeroplanes came, great cannonading from the Germans from Berghem, Evere, etc. I saw four aeroplanes. One disappeared far away, another went in the midst of the bombs, then two more came. Funny things like fireworks shot up at it, shrapnels, bombs, etc. Met Mrs B.'s children coming back from the Kommandantur, and they said that they spoke of Miss Cavell being shot, and as she has not had half so many Tommy Atkins as Mrs B. they are very much frightened of their mother being shot too. Went to church this morning and to tennis this afternoon. Lovely day. Cannons heard.

11 October Monday Another Allied aeroplane came at 7 a.m. I did not see it this time nor did I hear the Germans firing at it, though they did. Mr Butcher, as well as several other Englishmen, has had a notice to go tomorrow to rue du Méridien, nobody knows why. Fine day. Funny signals up. Cannons very loud.

12 October Tuesday Miss Cavell, Princesse de Croÿ, Mr Séverin etc. were shot this morning by those fiends! Outrageous thing! Several people who saw Miss Cavell yesterday said that she was perfectly calm and dignified. She has died like a martyr. Heaven punish those

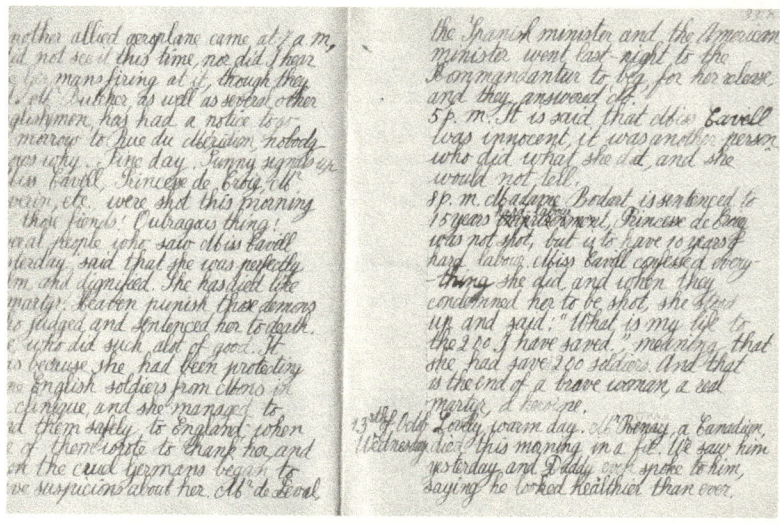

16. Two pages from Amy's diary, 11–13 October 1915, about the execution of Edith Cavell and sentencing of Ada Bodart

demons who judged and sentenced her to death. She, who did such a lot of good. It was because she had been protecting some English soldiers from Mons in her clinique, and she managed to send them safely to England, when one of them wrote to thank her and then the cruel Germans began to have suspicions about her. Mr de Leval, the Spanish Minister, and the American Minister went last night to the Kommandantur to beg for her release, and they answered 'No.'

5 p.m. It is said that Miss Cavell was innocent, it was another person who did what she did, and she would not tell.

8 p.m. Madame Bodart is sentenced to 15 years' hard labour, Princesse de Croÿ was not shot, but is to have 10 years of hard labour. Miss Cavell confessed everything she did, and when they condemned her to be shot, she stood up and said: 'What is my life to the 200 I have saved,' meaning that she had saved 200 soldiers. And that is the end of a brave woman, a real martyr, a heroine.

13 October Wednesday Lovely warm day. Mr Rönne, a Canadian, died this morning in a fit. We saw him yesterday and Daddy even spoke to him, saying he looked healthier than ever. Miss Cavell was shot at the Tir National of Evere.

14 October Thursday (Journal: *La Belgique*)

Condamnations

Par jugement du 9 octobre 1915, le tribunal de compagne a prononcé les condamnations suivantes pour trahison commise pendant l'état de guerre (pour avoir fait passer des recrues à l'ennemi):

A la peine de Mort
1. Philippe Baucq, architecte à Bruxelles
2. Louise Thuliez, professeur à Lille
3. Edith Cavell, directrice d'un institut médical à Bruxelles
4. Louis Séverin, pharmacien à Bruxelles
5. Comtesse Jeanne de Belleville à Montignies

A 15 ans de travaux forcés
1. Herman Capiau, ingenieur à Wasmes
2. Epouse Ada Bodart à Bruxelles

3. Albert Libiez, avocat à Wasmes
4. Georges Derveau, pharmacien à Pâturages

10. Princesse Marie de Croÿ à Bellignies à 10 ans de travaux forcés.

Dix-sept autres accusés ont été condamnés à des peines de travaux forcés ou d'emprisonnement allant de 2 à 8 ans.

Huit autres personnes accusées de trahison commise pendant l'état de guerre on été acquittées.

Le jugement rendu contre Baucq et Cavell à déjà été exécuté.

Bruxelles le 12 Octobre 1915
Gouvernement général Boche.

Lovely day. Captive balloon up at Forêt. Milly Selby has died of wounds. Went to tennis this afternoon.

15 October Friday Foggy day. They say that Von Bissing's son is a prisoner in France, and if the Germans shoot another civilian in Brussels the French will shoot him.

16 October Saturday Foggy morning, fine afternoon.

17 October Sunday Another beastly zeppelin has been over England and 15 soldiers have been killed. Went to church this morning. Private service for Miss Cavell. Miss Mellin took me home to lunch and then we went to the cemetery of Ixelles, where a new English soldier has been buried, Ernest Howard. Then we went to town. Dull day, a bit foggy.

18 October Monday Dull day. Daddy got a letter from Conn enclosing a very good photo of Charlie and Tommy in khaki. Doris has had brain-fever and has now a little girl [Kathleen, b. 29 May]. Conn is leaving for New York today.

19 October Tuesday Fine day. Several German buildings were burnt when the aeroplanes came over. It was Von Bissing who signed Miss Cavell's sentence.

20 October Wednesday Went to see Miss Drury this morning. This afternoon I went with Miss Mellin to the 'Caissette du soldat belge' for the name of a Belgian prisoner in Germany. Cold day.

21 October Thursday In the tram yesterday I sat in front of two German women spies, there are heaps of them in Brussels and they go in the trams for nothing, only showing a blue card. Play is going to be given at Madame Paquet's, *Rumpelstiltskin*; went to the rehearsal this afternoon. Mademoiselle Anita gave me a lesson of violin. The Germans say that it is all the inhabitants of Brussels faults that the aeroplanes came the other day, and if they come again they have threatened to punish us. Fine day. Everybody over the age of 15 years of age must be provided with a new 'Carte d'Identité'.

22 October Friday Daddy spent two hours at the House of Commons [Maison Communale] yesterday for his identity card, there were so many people.

[There follows a short extract in French from Reuters on 17 October, titled 'La France Déclare la Guerre à la Bulgarie', then a short article from Reuters of the same date entitled 'Les Victimes des zeppelins à Londres'.]

Lovely day. Went to Charlie's school today to fetch his things and his scout's uniform.

23 October Saturday Cold day. England has declared war to Bulgaria. Victory for the Russians. Everybody must give up their arms or else they will be severely punished. Saw a German motor with three women being taken to the Prison St Gilles, one was crying.

24 October Sunday The Russians made 12,000 prisoners, all Austrians. Went to church this morning, the hymns were accompanied by a violin. Went to tennis this afternoon and saw two big round things floating in the air. German signals I suppose. Cold day. Cannons very loud.

25 October Monday Rainy day. Went down to town this morning. The doctor cut Auntie's foot again.

26 October Tuesday A monument is going to be set up for Miss Cavell in England, everybody is giving a shilling. Next Friday a service will be given for her at St Paul's Cathedral, where the Prime Minister [Asquith] will be present. Lovely day, rather cold.

[Article in French follows titled 'Au Sénat Anglais – Londres, 20 Octobre'. I have replaced it with the Hansard transcription from the House of Lords:]

> THE MARQUESS OF LANSDOWNE ... We have been during the last few months continually shocked by occurrences each more terrible and moving than its predecessor; but I doubt whether any incident has moved public opinion in this country more than the manner in which this poor lady was, I suppose I must say, 'executed' in cold blood not many hours ago. It is no doubt the case ... that she may by her conduct have rendered herself liable to punishment – perhaps to severe punishment – for acts committed in violation of the kind of law which prevails when war is going on. But I have no hesitation in saying that she might at any rate have expected that measure of mercy which I believe in no civilised country would have been refused to one who was not only a woman, but a very brave and devoted woman, and one who had given all her efforts and energies to the mitigation of the sufferings of others.
>
> I am able to tell my noble friend that a full Report relating to the circumstances under which Miss Cavell was executed was forwarded to the Foreign Office yesterday by the United States Ambassador. We learn from this Report that the representatives of the United States and of Spain at Brussels up to the very last moment neglected no opportunity or effort in order to obtain a commutation of the death sentence passed on Miss Cavell, or even to obtain at least a period of suspense before that sentence was carried into effect. Those efforts failed. The material portions of the Report to which I refer will be published without delay.
>
> With regard to the second part of my noble friend's

Question, I am able to tell him that two French ladies have been condemned to death on a charge of sheltering British and French fugitive soldiers. These ladies were to have been executed on Monday last, but I am glad to be able to add that as the result of strong representations made by His Majesty the King of Spain and by the Pope the execution of these sentences has been postponed pending consideration by the German Emperor of the reports on both cases.

27 October Wednesday Lovely day, cold. Went to the undertaker's with Daddy to order a coffin for a lady.

28 October Thursday Went to town this morning. Rehearsal at Mlle Paquet's this afternoon. Rainy.

29 October Friday Dull day, might be warmer. Seemed to hear the cannons. Auntie had a very bad crisis of pain last night and is feeling rather bad today.

30 October Saturday Just a year ago since we came back from Middelkerke. Daddy and I went to the American Consulate this morning. Lovely day. Nobody is allowed to watch the trains.

31 October Sunday Went to church this morning. Service at the church rue Belliard for the Jubilee of the 50th year of the Orphelinat of Uccle. Nine more people were shot this morning. Fine day.

1 November Monday, All Saints' Day Mother and Daddy went to inscribe themselves at the rue du Méridien. King George has had a fall, and General Joffre is in London. Arthur and Baby have holiday today and tomorrow. Baby and I went to the Trocadero, where 37 musicians composed the orchestra, every instrument was used. Rainy day.

2 November Tuesday Rainy day. Arthur, Baby and I went to tea with Jules and Georgie May.

3 November Wednesday Mr Spong is now at Ruhleben with Mr Simms. He says it's a paradise in comparison to where he was imprisoned. The cold is dreadful there, and they have had a big fall of snow. Rainy morning, clearer a bit in the afternoon.

4 November Thursday Fine day. This afternoon we went to Mlle Paquet's for the rehearsal of *Rumpelstiltskin*. Everybody over 15 years of age must have their identity card to go out with.

5 November Friday Guy Fawkes Day. Fine day. Connie and the Baby [Desmond] have arrived in New York.

6 November Saturday Foggy morning, cold day. Went to town this afternoon. Joséphine gone at 2 p.m. this afternoon to fetch her identity card and came back at 6 p.m., so many people.

7 November Sunday Fine day, cold. Went to church this morning and to Children's Service this afternoon. Several more people been shot.

8 November Monday Brand Whitlock left Brussels last Saturday. The Germans have given Mr de Leval his *demission* on account of his taking the part of Miss Cavell and he is leaving Brussels tomorrow for the south of France with his wife and Roger till after the war. Cold day.

9 November Tuesday King Edward, the Peace-Maker's birthday [Edward VII]. For a few days German motors are constantly going down our street. Windy day, tempest in the night.

10 November Wednesday Soap is so frightfully expensive. There is a rumour that in all the big houses where people have gone away, German soldiers will inhabit these houses. Very windy day.

11 November Thursday Lovely day. Went at 5 p.m. for the rehearsal at Mlle Paquet's. Heard a great many trains last night.

12 November Friday Two new German flags were put up yesterday at the Palais de Justice. More people sentenced to death and to prison. Rainy day.

13 November Saturday The new notice is that more arms have been found and so German soldiers will lodge in all the big empty houses. There was a fight between two men in front of our house this morning. One of the men had stolen the purse of the other man, and he would not give it up. Finally he escaped and people were running after him, screaming: 'Thief! thief!' Went with Daddy this afternoon to see what the Germans have done in Mr Hooper's house. Rainy day. A year ago Mr Simms was taken.

14 November Sunday

New York Herald
Nice, October 22, 1915

To the Editor of the Herald: –
Dear Sir, Has anything more horrible, more revolting, been known than the execution of Miss Cavell? The Angel of Death must surely have veiled his face in sorrow at the mere possibility of such an outrage. The officer did his duty, did he? If he had had a spark of honor in his breast, the brute would have preferred to put a bullet through his own head in preference to assassinating a weak, defenceless woman under such circumstances. And those wretches call themselves 'honorable' men! In the name of posterity, I demand that the name of the officer be ascertained if possible and made known publicly, so that it may pass down to history in conjunction with those of Gessler, Torquemada, and other fiends, as an example of ferocious cruelty and brutality.

Yours sincerely,
H.W. Davenport

A boy of 14 years has been shot for looking at the trains. Cowards! Cannons going the whole day. Went with Arthur and Baby to the cinema of the rue du Bailly this afternoon. Fine day.

15 November Monday Daddy's birthday. Anniversary of King Léopold, holiday for schools. Got a bad cold. Cannons heard. Lovely day.

16 November Tuesday Lovely day, very cold. The nine provinces of Belgium must pay 40 millions monthly for the welfare of the German soldiers.

17 November Wednesday Madame Bodart has been sent to Germany, and the Germans have taken the new Clinique of the rue de Bruxelles so Miss Cavell's nurses are going to England in the special train soon and Miss Jemmett also. Trains passed all night. A little snow this morning.

18 November Thursday Sleety day. Went to tea to Mlle Paquet's to try on the costumes.

19 November Friday Very cold day. Seemed to hear the cannons. L'Abbé Petit, Charlie's friend, been taken up.

20 November Saturday Freezing day. The Germans are taking every single horse in Brussels for their transports. Cannons very loud.

21 November Sunday I heard a great many trains last night and early this morning. Went to church this morning. Very cold.

22 November Monday Icy cold day. Madame Jane Davy is very ill, she vomits blood.

23 November Tuesday Auntie's birthday. Very slippy, several people fell. For nearly a month no *Times* come into Belgium.

La Libre Belgique, **Novembre 1915**

Bulletin de Propagande Patriotique
Régulièrement Irrégulier
Adresse Télégraphique: Kommandantur Bruxelles

Aux Héros de l'Yser

Ils sont tombées, les preux, au soir de la bataille;
Ils avaient tout le jour combattu sans répit,

Et voici que soudain hideux et sans entrailles,
De son geste méchant, la mort les a saisis.

Ils sont là terrassés et gisant sous la neige,
Dans la bise d'hiver qui gémit autour d'eux,
Et sous le blanc linceul qui, clément les protège,
Leur bouche baise encore la terre des aïeux!

Ils sont là, jeunes gens, la face epanouie
Respirant l'énergie, et la force et l'honneur;
Ils ont été fauchés, au printemps de la vie,
Et leurs yeux, en mourant, n'ont pas versé de pleurs!

['Très Bien' is written in pencil below this verse.]

Car ils sont morts héros de la croisade sainte,
Défenseurs de la cause éternelle du Droit;
Ils sont morts glorieux, et leurs lèvres éteintes
Chantaient en expirant la Belgique et son Roi ...

Ne pleure pas, ô mère aimante et bien-aimée,
O père, dont l'exemple a formé ce héros!
Votre fils est au Ciel. Son âme immaculée
Va goûter près du Dieu la paix et le repos.

Novembre 1914

Vive le Roi

Mercredi, 5 août 1914. Au parc de Bruxelles. – L'orchestre vient de jouer les hymnes nationaux: Brabançonne, Marseillaise, God save the King, que l'assistance a écoutés debout, religieusement. – Trois heures et demie: Une sonnerie de clairons au garde du Palais Royal. Les gardes civiques qui occupent le Palais des Académies se précipitent, et, à la 1830 képis sur la crosse des fusils renversés acclament avec enthousiasme une automobile qui passe ... Vive le Roi! C'est ainsi qu'Albert Ier quitta sa capitale pour l'armée.

'Quand le Roi Albert et ses soldats reviendront bien des gens deviendront fous – fous de joie!'

24 November Wednesday Horrid day, wet and cold. The peasants will not sell their potatoes, so we have great difficulty in getting them.

25 November Thursday Rainy day. Went with Arthur and Baby to the cinema. Cannons very loud.

26 November Friday Big fall of snow. Cannons going the whole day. Scarcely any potatoes to be had, eggs are at 0f38.

27 November Saturday Snowy morning. Had a good slide and fall on the avenue Louise. Cannons very loud. Went to dentist.

28 November Sunday Bitterly cold day. Went to church this morning. Baby and I went to the Bois de la Cambre after dinner. The lake was full of ice, but it was forbidden to go on it. Arthur sat on a nail and I fell on my back.

29 November Monday Rainy day. Cannons not as loud as yesterday. General Joffre has been dismissed, so the Germans say.

30 November Tuesday Mr Back, musician, had been called out in the German army; on Sunday they took him and they only gave him three hours to stay in Brussels. It is not true about Joffre. Went to town this morning to buy Mother some fancy-work for Christmas. Rainy day, snow all melted away.

1 December Wednesday Mother and Daddy gone to inscribe themselves at the rue du Méridien, and an officer told them that they will have to go every week. Mr Back goes today or tomorrow. Rainy day.

2 December Thursday Mr Back has not yet gone. Rainy morning. Went to tea and for the rehearsal at Mme Paquet's.

3 December Friday Rainy day. Went to town this morning. Baby has had a bad cough. Doctor says he must not go out for two or three days.

4 December Saturday The English people must go every Tuesday to sign at the rue du Méridien. Rainy day. Mother and I went to town this morning.

5 December Sunday Lovely warm day. Went to church in the morning. Two funny German signals in the air. Raymond Collart, the poet, came to tea with us. He gives Arthur music lessons twice a week. Cannons very loud.

6 December Monday St Nicolas day. Lovely warm day, very windy. Went to the cinema with Baby, but they were shut.

7 December Tuesday The place Louis Morichar or place de Parme was full of Belgian horses at 9 a.m., which the Germans are taking. Sentinels at every corner of the streets so we could not pass there, excepting the children who have to go to school. Cannons rather loud.

8 December Wednesday Beautiful day. Poor Mr Back went to Germany yesterday: it was most touching when he bade farewell to his children.

9 December Thursday Some time ago Mother made Daddy a pair of pyjamas and she was very proud of them: last night, in bed, Daddy was fumbling about for the matches. Mother asked him what he was doing: 'Hang this pyjama', says Daddy. 'I'm looking everywhere for my pocket.' The pocket was sewn on the top of his shoulder. How we laughed! Went to town with Daddy and then to the American Consulate. Rainy day.

10 December Friday Auntie very giddy and weak. Went to town this morning. Rainy day.

11 December Saturday Rainy day. Went to the dentist this morning. Very high wind arose at 11.30 a.m., got nearly blown away.

12 December Sunday Went to church this morning and this afternoon. Rain at intervals. Cannons very loud.

13 December Monday Snow and sleet. Cannons louder than ever. Went in 11 shops for sugar: none to be had except in a small sweetshop at 1f10.

14 December Tuesday From the 20th all the English have to go and sign at the rue du Méridien every Tuesday, as well as all the French, the Russians, the Japanese, the Italians, etc., every week. Lovely day, rather cold. Cannons going every minute, 4 or 5 bangs together. Trains all night.

15 December Wednesday Big battle on the Yser. Several members of the Union Club saw an aeroplane yesterday morning. Baron Winspeare's wedding to a Russian lady. Arthur went to see *Julius Caesar* with the poet and Armand Parmentier. Cold day. Cannons are heard.

16 December Thursday Cold day. Mr Halet has married Mlle de Lavelaye. Miss Mellin fetched us for a small rehearsal of songs which we are to sing at her house on the 22nd or 23rd for the British Women, and then we went to tea at Mlle Paquet's to rehearse *Rumpelstiltskin*. Haven't any news of poor Charlie for a long time. Jean Nicolet and many other boys have managed to leave Brussels and they have reached England safely, from where they are going to the front. God bless them! Léopold Back has the measles.

17 December Friday Baby has a bad cough, so he has not been to school today. Rainy. Cannons rather loud.

18 December Saturday The same German who fetched Daddy once in the motor to go to the Kommandantur came this morning and said that they had seen Charlie and that if within 24 hours Daddy does not say where he is, Daddy will be taken up. It is now 12 a.m. Mother has just rushed off to get Daddy from the club. 1 p.m. Daddy has to go the Kommandantur on Monday, at 8.30 a.m. Rainy day. Cannons very loud this afternoon. Baby still coughs so he does not go out. Went to town this morning.

19 December Sunday Cannons going all day, louder than ever. Captive balloon flying about. Lovely day, rather cold. Baby and I went to church this morning. Went to town this afternoon.

20 December Monday Daddy took me to the Kommandantur with him, where we had to go in an awful room. The Germ said:

'Where's Charlie?' Daddy said he did not know. 'You do know,' said the Germ, 'for here is a letter which I have received to say that Charlie has been seen, and you will just stop here till he has been found.' I was shaking with fury. Then I spoke up: 'Do you think that Mother would cry so often if Charlie were here? Besides Daddy is not responsible for his son when he is in a school.' He got calmer at that. But all the time he was talking sneerely. At last he said: 'Well, it is a pity to keep you in when it is such weather (it rained two minutes after), and I suppose you would rather spend your Christmas at home than here. Scootum.' I could have shot him. Dull day.

21 December Tuesday Snow and rain. Daddy and Mother went to sign at the Méridien. Went to a rehearsal and to tea at Miss Mellin's.

22 December Wednesday Rainy day. Got a raging toothache. Big party at Miss Mellin's for the British Women. The programme was composed of: a Dutch clog dance, all of us together; Suzanne de Baeker and her sister recited; Mrs Morison recited; Joan Butcher and Pussy Poeleart danced a Grecian dance; Mme Poeleart sang 'Home sweet Home', 'The Little Girl Milking her Cow'. We all sang 'Soldiers in the Park', and 'God save the King', and then had a bully good tea.

23 December Thursday Went to town this morning. Last dress rehearsal at Mlle Paquet's. The Russians are doing well. Cannons rather loud this afternoon. Rainy day.

24 December Friday Big Christmas party at Mrs Butcher's and there was a lovely tree. We all had a nice present and crackers. I had a brooch. Mother and I went to town this morning. I wonder if Santa Claus is going to fill up my stocking. Rainy day. Arthur's and Baby's holidays begun.

25 December Saturday Christmas Day, war still going on. Lovely Christmas party at Mme Paquet's and we all acted *Rumpelstiltskin*, which was a success. Found my stocking full of things. Went to church this morning, and lost Mother's umbrella. Lovely turkey for dinner. Cannons very loud. Arthur bought a watch.

26 December Sunday Lovely day. Cannons going. Baby and I went to church this morning and I found Mother's umbrella. Met Mr Watts, and he's heard that our play was a great success, and he thinks that Villalobar, the Spanish Minister, wants to have it played for some Russian children. Baby and I went to the Trocadero this afternoon to see the life of Jesus Christ.

27 December Monday Varied weather. Cannons very loud. Arthur and I went to town this afternoon.

28 December Tuesday Mother and Daddy went to sign at the rue du Méridien this morning. Went to tea with Georgie May. Cannons going. Fine day.

29 December Wednesday Train leaving for England at 7.30 p.m. today. Mr and Mrs Morison, Mrs Green, etc., are going. I went at 6.30 a.m. to the Gare du Nord with Daddy to see them all off. They pulled a lunatic woman out of a cart to send her in a train, and she would not go. Cannons very loud. Baby and I went to see *Mark-Antony and Cleopatra* at the High-Life. There were a lot of male and female spies in the station. Fine day. The Germans have a signal up at 3 p.m.

30 December Thursday Lovely day. Cannons going. Auntie is very bad today: she tried to remain out of bed, but she nearly fell, her head was so giddy. I am also feeling rather sick.

31 December Friday A lot more people shot. The Germans were going to shoot a girl, but then they released her because they thought her too young so she is instead condemned to hard labour for life. Rosine, Raymond and Mme Tadini are leaving tonight for Italy. Many trains passed last night. We went to see *Les Trois Mousquetaires*. Windy day. New troops and mitrailleuses come in.

1916

1 January Saturday New Year's Day. I received a lovely big box of chocolates from Mrs Heineman. New German flag on the top of the Palais de Justice was put up yesterday, and today it is torn in three parts 'Made in Germany'. For three days a red notice has been put up every day of a lot of men and women condemned to death. This afternoon Miss Mellin took us to Schaerbeek, where we walked all along the 'Canal Maritime' to Laeken, it was very windy. Auntie is very bad today.

2 January Sunday We all had our photo taken in the costumes of *Rumpelstiltskin*. Went to church this morning and this afternoon. Doctor came to see Auntie and finds her very bad.

3 January Monday Arthur and Baby have gone back to school. Abbé Petit is condemned to two months in prison. Lovely day. Went to tea at Miss Doyle's. Baby is sleeping at Miss Mellin's.

4 January Tuesday A P&O sunk by a German torpedo. Daddy and Mother went to the rue Méridien this morning. Dull day. Went to have a dancing lesson at Miss Schöller's. Auntie is terribly weak.

5 January Wednesday At 2.15 p.m. Auntie rang her bell: she was in dreadful pain: her ears were ringing like a thousand bells, her head was splitting, and it lasted for nearly 2 hours. She is today frightfully weak. Doctor was sent for: he said Auntie had a fever of nerves. Lovely day. Mr Van Halteren is condemned to 8 months' imprisonment.

6 January Thursday Rainy day. Lunched at Miss Mellin's. Auntie is a little better. Mrs Scappa took us to the cinema, and after we went to tea at Miss Mellin's. New flag on the Palais de Justice.

7 January Friday Auntie is still a little better, but she had a bad night. There are a lot of Germans in the house next to the Union Club. Windy day. B. still at Miss Mellin's.

8 January Saturday In *The Times* of the 30th of December there have been a great number of casualties amongst the Lovat Scouts at the Dardanelles [half-brother Tommy's regiment], and also in the Royal Fusiliers [brother Charlie's regiment]. The German flag of the Palais de Justice is again all torn. Cannons are going. Doctor came and is pleased with Auntie. I am sleeping with her tonight. Showery day.

9 January Sunday Lovely day. Cannons very loud. Arthur went to Boitsfort with the poet, and I went to church. Daddy treated us to see the last series of *Les Trois Mousquetaires* at the High-Life: the place was crowded. The Germans have taken twenty horses out of the Lannoy brewery.

10 January Monday It is a good thing that Mr Burls left Brussels, for two days after a letter was sent to his house that he, a man who cannot walk, was to present himself to be sent to Germany. I went to the Alimentation this morning to get some rice, sugar and macaroni, and there were so many people that I had to wait 1 hour and 40 minutes, the people say they wish for peace so that then they won't have to 'faire la file' for cheap soap, sugar, flour, grease, etc. Rainy day.

11 January Tuesday Mother and Daddy went to the rue du Méridien at 8.30 a.m. The man who denounced Miss Cavell is the son of a Belgian Lieutenant-Colonel, and he was walking near the station when two men sprang on him: one shot him through the arm, and the other through the heart; he also denounced some people who wanted to go to Holland and so a good thing to get rid of a wicked man: he was paid a thousand marks by the Germans. The coal-carts are now dragged by men as there are scarcely any horses left. We went for our dancing lesson this afternoon at Mlle Schöller, which Miss Mellin is giving us for a little time. Auntie had a fidgety night, and is in great pain today. Rainy.

12 January Wednesday A group of Belgians are plotting to kill as many Belgian traitors as they can find, but it must be kept a dead secret from the Germans, for the other day in a tram a man was talking about Miss Cavell's traitor, when suddenly a German thumped on the shoulder, saying: 'Ho! ho! young man, you seem to know a lot about that affair; come along with me to the Kommandantur'; and he took him off. One of the English men-o'-war, *Edward the VII*, has been sunk by a Turkish mine, but all the crew is saved. All the English have left Gallipoli. Lovely day, cannons going. Auntie very poorly. Had tea at Mme Paquet's. Another spy has been killed. Sausage up at Uccle.

13 January Thursday Very windy day, cannons are loud. Auntie is a little better, and she treated us to the Trocadero. A little snow came down. Big explosion at Lille.

14 January Friday Rainy day. Doctor finds Auntie worse. Mother and Daddy dined out.

15 January Saturday The Germans say they have taken Cettignë, the capital of Montenegro. Germans have shot a lot more civilians. Auntie a little better. Rainy day.

16 January Sunday Lovely day. Went to church this morning. Went for a lovely walk to Viviers D'Oies with Mr and Miss Mellin. Cannons very loud. Sausage up at Linkebeek. Lord Lonsdale says that by August we shall have the Allies' flags flying in Brussels. Won Mr Mellin's [...].

17 January Monday Lovely day. Cannons going. The province of Brabant must pay 10,000 marks for the murder of Miss Cavell's traitor, and Schaerbeek must pay 5,000 marks as the population let the man escape: the Germans also want to know with what firearms the men shot the spy with. Went to town this morning. Dreamt that the Germans had killed their Kaiser, no such luck. Mr Bauer is dead. The Germans have a new flag up on the Palais de Justice and they have taken Mrs May's pony. Miss Mellin took me to town this afternoon to try on some dancing shoes. Arthur went to see the *Bossu* with the poet. Rainy evening. Doctor finds Auntie very bad.

18 January Tuesday Mother and Daddy gone to the Méridien. Rainy day. Auntie very poorly, she has given me a lovely gold brooch of hers. Went to our music lesson and on to tea at Miss Mellin's. B. still at Miss Mellin's.

19 January Wednesday Auntie seems a little better. Lovely day.

20 January Thursday Lovely day. Went to Joan's birthday party. The Minister of the Foreign Office in London says that English women without any occupation in Brussels had better leave.

21 January Friday Rainy day. Baby has come back from Miss Mellin's.

22 January Saturday Fine day. The king of Bavaria is in Brussels for a visit: what cheek! The German flag is again torn on the Palais de Justice. Doctor has given Auntie all different medicines as the others don't act any more, she is feeling rather bad today. Doctor cut Arthur's feet, because he has been suffering a great deal lately.

23 January Sunday Lovely day. The two men who murdered Miss Cavell's traitor have been caught by the Germans in trying to get across the frontier, and will probably be shot. Arthur in bed. Auntie suffering. Went to church this morning. Father Lecourt came to lunch. Baby and I went to the Bois this afternoon with Miss Mellin's dog. Cannons going.

24 January Monday Rainy day. Auntie still in bed. Scarcely any castor oil left. Auntie a little better.

25 January Tuesday Lovely day. Mother and Daddy went to the Méridien this morning. Baby and I went for our dancing lesson this afternoon. Doctor says Arthur must not dance any more on account of his foot.

26 January Wednesday Fine day. A lot of Germans have been in Miss Stanger's house to look for arms. Baby has small bronchitis, but he goes to school. Doctor finds Auntie improving. The floods are dreadful in Holland, from the Zuyder Zee. Auntie better.

1916

27 January Thursday Kaiser's birthday. New German flags everywhere. All the Germans have their pointed hats on today. Auntie feeling low-spirited and sick. Arthur's stomach is hurting. Baby and I went to see Miss Drury, who has turned Belgian, this afternoon. Rainy day. Bread getting nasty again.

28 January Friday Auntie stayed up a little this morning, but she was frightfully weak, nearly fainting. Rainy day.

29 January Saturday Fine day. There are about thirty refugees from Westend, Louvain, etc. in Wiltcher's Hotel, in Brussels.

30 January Sunday Fine day. Arthur stayed at home on account of his foot. Baby and I went to church this morning and in the afternoon we went to see *Captain Grant's Children* of Jules Vernes at the High-Life.

31 January Monday Daddy went to the American Legation and Mr Whitlock showed him a letter, dated from the 5th of December, from Uncle Fred, saying that Charlie crossed to England as a refugee, palmed himself off as being 19 years of age, and the brave boy enlisted, and then he crossed to France, is in the 22nd Royal Fusiliers and is working in the trenches. His commandant has written to Uncle Fred that Charlie does his work beautifully and that if anything happens to Charlie, he will let Uncle Fred know. God bless Charlie! Tommy was still in England when the letter was written. A train of English people was supposed to leave on the 10th of February, but the Germans have put it off for another fortnight. Auntie cried when she heard about poor Charlie, not yet seventeen, being in the trenches. Cold day.

1 February Tuesday Daddy and Mother gone to the rue du Méridien. Lovely day, very cold. Went to our dancing lesson at Miss Schöller's. Cannons faintly heard. Tin-kettles (German band) passed 7 a.m.

2 February Wednesday Fine day, freezing. Went to the Alimentation this morning. Doctor says Baby must stay at home for a few days on account of his throat, he finds Auntie very weak. Another zep. been to England, and a Taube has dropped several bombs in Paris and has done a great deal of damage. Fine day, very cold.

3 February Thursday Lovely day, cold. Went to the Alimentation for some rice and had to wait for 2 hours 35 minutes. Mrs Leivey invited me to the cinema and then we had tea in the chique tea room, next to the Trocadero. Cannons going. Charlie been away a year.

4 February Friday The English people in Brussels have had two scares in the last two weeks: they nearly all want to go to England because a rumour is going about that the Germans are going to intern us. No sugar to be had. Everything gone up tremendously: butter 3f50 a pound, cheese 3f10 per pound, black soap 2f25 per pound, etc. etc. Colonel Wynne went to get a passport to go to England and the Germans have locked him up because he is a colonel. Colonel Ford has also been locked up for 17 hours, but fortunately he is let out. Goodness knows what devilish tricks they are up to. Somebody says that Von Bissing has been murdered by some Germans. No such luck. Windy day.

5 February Saturday No more potatoes to be had, everybody is trying to make provisions, but we can only get a tiny quantity at a time: such as 1 pound of butter. It is not Von Bissing who has been murdered, but the governor-general of Ghent by his own soldiers. Baby can go out now. Miss Mellin took us in a cab and we went to town. Doctor cut Arthur's foot again. One can't open one's lips in town about the war, there are such heaps of spies, women spies more than men. Lovely day. Mme Haley has a small property somewhere in the country, and yesterday she got a letter at Boitsfort, where she is now staying, headed 'Par l'Autorité Allemande', writing that they have cut down her walnut-trees, three of them, each worth 500 francs, that she is to pay 42 francs, and lastly that they employed a man, who lives near her place and whom she sometimes sent for to see after a few odds and ends in her garden, has broken a bone in felling the trees, meaning that she, Mme Haley, is responsible for it. She has written back to say that she does not understand head or tail of the matter, and that she never asked them to cut down her trees. Those trees were the beauty of the place. The bread is quite brown.

6 February Sunday The zeppelin L 19 has fallen in the North Sea. It had gone over Holland (it had no right to do so) and was coming back from England, when it fell and a little fishing-boat was passing, the Germans were on the top of the zep. screaming to the fishermen to save them. They said: 'See you blowed first, we are going back to Grimsby to tell the Admiralty you are there; we don't want you to take us to Germany, we all know your tricks. Goodbye.' We have not yet heard what was the end of the zep. The Germans have published it in every paper, calling it 'English inhumanity' because they were not saved. Prince Léopold of Belgium is now at Eton with one of King George's sons. Cannons going. Went to church this morning. Arthur staying in bed. Fine day. No potatoes for dinner.

7 February Monday Lovely day. Went to tennis to get some parsley, and I picked some daisies and a crocus. Arthur in bed, B. gone back to school. Cannons going.

8 February Tuesday Rainy day. Mother and Daddy been to the Méridien. Cannons going. Went to dancing class. Arthur's foot paining, still in bed. No potatoes.

9 February Wednesday Lovely day, cold. Doctor says Arthur can go out, and he has gone to the High-Life with the poet. No potatoes and no sugar. There seems to be good news of the Allies.

10 February Thursday Big snowstorm in the night, but a lot of rain today. Heaps of trains of wounded passing night and day. Daddy managed to get us some potatoes today. The Germans take all the potatoes and then sell them to the people who work for them. Went to a small party at the Gahans. Cannons going.

11 February Friday Rainy day, very cold. Arthur gone back to school. Auntie is feeling very faint today. Sugar-candy is used instead of sugar.

12 February Saturday The flag is torn in rags at the Palais de Justice. Mother suffers from the ear. Rainy day, cold.

13 February Sunday Rainy day. The Australian man who plays the violin at church has been told to bring himself and his carpet-bag to the Kommandantur, that means he is to be interned. One of the men who shot Miss Cavell's traitor was the son of Mrs Jay's serrurier [locksmith], and he has been shot: the red notice is put up everywhere. The poet came to tea this afternoon and he plays the piano like an artist, which he is. Went to church this morning. Cold day. A French ship sunk and 600 lives lost.

14 February Monday Rainy day. Went to town this morning and this afternoon. Auntie has bought me Beethoven's music for my birthday at the Maison Beethoven. Managed to get a pound sugar.

15 February Tuesday Mother and Daddy gone to the rue du Méridien. Lot of snow fell in the night, rain had melted it all away. Terrific wind early in the morning. Auntie not well. Went to Miss Schöller's. No potatoes.

16 February Wednesday Very windy day. No potatoes. Butter is sold en cachette. Went to town this morning. Mrs Brand Whitlock, Mrs Peiser and Mr Ehrlich have all lost their pet dogs in the last few days. Arthur is going after tea to the High-Life with the poet.

17 February Thursday Sunny weather, hail at intervals. Mother's ear is cured. No potatoes. Went to Oda's party.

18 February Friday Rainy day. Auntie very weak. No potatoes, no brown sugar, nor any other sugar. An inferior kind of butter, called 'era', cost 10 pence a pound before the war, is now two shillings and is still going up dearer. No butter to be got under 7 shillings a kilo, and then there is very little of it.

19 February Saturday Mr Bigwood, who was taken a year ago, is still at the Kommandantur, so is Colonel Wynne. I got a card today from Holland from Hetty. A tiny new flag is on the Palais de l'Injustice. No potatoes. Rainy morning, fine afternoon.

20 February Sunday The Russians have taken a fortified town in Turkey. The Germans are furious. Lovely day, fairly cold. Went to church this morning. The poet has lent me a 'Symphonie de Haydn'. No potatoes.

21 February Monday Fine day, very cold. Auntie is very much in pain, the doctor says that she is worse than last time. Got half a pound of loaf-sugar, our delight. No potatoes for dinner. Colonel Wynne is in the same place as Mr Bigwood is.

22 February Tuesday Mother and Daddy gone to sign at the rue du Méridien. Very cold day, a little snow. Went to the dancing class. No potatoes. Cannons very loud.

23 February Wednesday My fifteenth birthday. Mother took me to town in the morning, snowing all the time. We went and had some hot chocolate and some cakes, had dinner out, came back to tea, and went to the cinema afterwards. Arthur and Baby were invited to the cinema with the poet. Snow all day long, bitterly cold. Cannons so loud I can hear them from my window.

24 February Thursday Mother is ill, and in bed. Fine day, freezing. Could hear the cannons in bed last night. The poet has sent me a piece of music which he composed for my birthday. Baby and I went to town this afternoon. No potatoes yet, how we miss them!

25 February Friday Colonel Wynne has been sent to Germany. Freezing day. Daddy and I went to the rue du Méridien this afternoon to get my card as I am fifteen. I shall have to sign every Tuesday. No potatoes. Mother is better, but Auntie is keeping in bed today. Saw two Belgian wounded at the Palais des Académies with their Belgian caps on.

26 February Saturday Black soap costs 5f40 the kilo, butter 8 francs. No potatoes. Cannons very loud. Snow in the night. Cold day. Germans have taken the fort near Verdun.

27 February Sunday Daddy heard today from Jack that Tommy has had a commission as officer and Charlie writes very cheerfully to Jack. Went to church this morning. Baby and I went to Boitsfort after dinner, and Arthur went in the forest with the poet. Cannons loud, very cold. No potatoes. Mother got a sore throat, is in bed.

28 February Monday Miss Mellin is rather bad. The Germans are advancing in France. Went to town this morning. Candles are so rare and dear that Auntie has had a gas light put up in her room. Cannons very loud. Mother out of bed, still suffers.

29 February Tuesday Went to sign at the rue du Méridien 10. The French have taken back the fort. Mother and I then left some magazines for the English wounded at the Palais des Académies. No potatoes. Lovely day. Went to the dancing lesson. Got a lot of chilblains.

1 March Wednesday An English passenger boat has been sunk by a mine near Dover. Got a pound of sugar and 12 potatoes. Miss Mellin is better; went to see some poor in the rue Haute with her. Lovely day. Misery is dreadful with the poor.

2 March Thursday Lovely day. I have to have a 'Carte d'Identité', went to town with Mother to get my photo taken for it. Several more people condemned to hard labour. Baby and I went to see *Siegfried* at the High-Life, avenue Louise.

3 March Friday Trains passed all night. Cannons very loud, especially tonight. Rainy day. No potatoes.

4 March Saturday Snow in the night, rainy day. Cannons going. I measure 1 metre 61 [5 ft 4 in.]. No potatoes. The Portuguese have taken 35 German merchant ships which had the cheek to go into their harbour.

5 March Sunday Lovely day. Cannons very loud. Went with Daddy and Arthur to see a studio of painting, and then to church. Auntie in bed. No potatoes.

6 March Monday Snowy day. Went to the Maison Communale to get my Carte d'Identité. Lost 1 mark. Spent 2 hours 30 minutes at the CRB for a pound of sugar. Cannons going. No potatoes.

7 March Tuesday Went to sign at the rue du Méridien. Cannons very loud last night and today. Snow all day long. Went to the dancing lesson at Mlle Schöller's. No potatoes.

8 March Wednesday At Braine-l'Alleud a German officer shot himself because he was told to burn the dead bodies of the wounded which were brought there. Had awful pains and was sick in the middle of the night, am staying at home today. Snow in the night. Auntie is very weak today. No potatoes.

9 March Thursday Auntie is staying in bed because she felt so faint. Very cold day. No potatoes. I am better.

10 March Friday The Portuguese have declared war with Germany. A new red paper has been posted on the walls that 7 people have been shot at Mons and 2 condemned. Great fall of snow in the night. Cannons going last night. No potatoes. Cold and snowy day.

11 March Saturday Rainy day. I brought back ten kilos of potatoes from Stockel at 0f20 a kilo. The Germans have been twice to Auntie Flo's house to inhabit it, but Hannah has got 1 or 2 CRBs men to lodge in the house, so that the Germans can't take it. Auntie is very poorly today. The Germans allow the French have taken back the fort of Verdun.

12 March Sunday Went to church this morning. Cannons rather loud. Baby and I went to see Miss Drury. Lovely day.

13 March Monday Lovely warm day. Auntie had a bad night. Cannons going.

14 March Tuesday Went to sign at the rue du Méridien and went to the dancing lesson in the afternoon. Beautiful warm day. Cannons rather loud. Butter has gone down to 7 francs the kilo.

15 March Wednesday Rainy morning, fine afternoon. The Allies are doing very well.

16 March Thursday Fine day. Miss Mellin took us to the Bois and we picked some anemones, and had tea in a pâtisserie. Cannons very loud. Doctor finds Auntie bad again.

17 March Friday Lovely warm day. Went to town this morning.

Miss Mellin asked us to go to her house after supper to do a dance and some songs for a meeting of the BW [British Women] next Wednesday. Auntie very poorly. Mme de Banterlé is dying.

18 March Saturday Hot day. Daddy thinks he heard an aeroplane at 4.30 a.m. and another one has been seen at 8 a.m. Funny signals out. Auntie a little better, but nearly fainted tonight, so weak.

19 March Sunday The Germans prevent people carrying potatoes in some country places. It is forbidden to make soap unless the oils are bought from the Germans. Beautiful hot day. Went to church this morning, and to tennis to pick some primroses this afternoon. Cannons have not been so loud as today for a long time, the tennis was shaking. Auntie is keeping in bed. Saw a black signal moving about.

20 March Monday At 10.15 p.m. last night Auntie had an awful attack of pain, which lasted a long time. The doctor came this morning and he says it is a kind of neuralgia. Lovely day. The potatoes are finished, so J. has gone to Stockel to try and get some at 2.30 and came back at 9 p.m. without any.

21 March Tuesday Went to sign at the rue du Méridien. Warm day. Auntie very poorly. No potatoes. Dancing lesson at Miss Schöller's.

22 March Wednesday Rainy day. No potatoes. Von Bissing has written a very impertinent letter to Cardinal Mercier. Did a dance at Miss Mellin's for the BW and then we sang and had tea. Went to town this morning. Auntie a little better. Mme de Banterlé died on the 18th.

23 March Thursday Snowy day. The Germans have posted up that nobody is allowed to send any more food to the Belgian prisoners, evidently they are frightened that there won't be enough for their German pigs (casques à pointe) in Belgium. They don't mention the English prisoners, because they know that if they starve our soldiers, the English will starve the German prisoners. No potatoes. We have had to get a new Carte de Ménage for rice, grease etc. J. went to get it and had to wait 3 hours and a half.

24 March Friday The influenza and the grip are very much about. Little Stephen Heineman, Simone and Jacques have got it. Snow has been falling all night and all day without stopping. No potatoes. Uncle Fred is giving up his house here, and he and Auntie Flo are always going to live in England. Miss Mellin invited us to tea and then we went out for a walk with her.

25 March Saturday Lovely day, rather cold. J. got 6 kilos of potatoes at 0f13 the kilo at the Alimentation for a week. Miss Mellin has made me a present of a sweet little watch of hers and a lovely book of Beethoven's Sonatas with his portrait in full on the cover; went to have my tooth filled up and then to town with Miss Mellin.

26 March Sunday Mother is very sick, is staying in bed. Rainy and snowy morning, fine afternoon.

27 March Monday Mother is up, but feels rather faint. Auntie had another bad attack of pain last night. Changeable day.

28 March Tuesday Went to sign at the rue du Méridien. Windy day. Dancing lesson at Miss Schöller's.

29 March Wednesday Rain and sunshine. Arthur goes out with the poet every Sunday and every Wednesday afternoon.

30 March Thursday Lovely spring day. This morning I went to take some tennis cards for the annual meeting to several houses, and this afternoon I helped Miss Mellin to put Mrs Stocks's toys, etc., safely away in the Church of the Resurrection.

31 March Friday The Royal Fusiliers are fighting splendidly near Ypres. Haven't had news of Charlie for ages. Lovely day. Got some beans, macaroni and vermicelli at the CRB in the rue de l'Amazone. No rice and no potatoes. Lovely day.

1 April Saturday Lovely day. A policeman came this morning to ask if we had any potatoes in our cellar. No potatoes. Auntie is a little better.

2 April Sunday Beautiful day. Arthur has gone out in the country for the whole day with the poet, and Baby is spending the day with Miss Mellin. Went to Christ Church. No potatoes and no sugar.

3 April Monday At 6.30 p.m. we saw a zeppelin passing over the Trinity church, a bomb hanging from it. The beast was evidently going to England; one of them has been brought down in the Thames. Lovely hot day. Went to town this morning. After lunch Auntie had an awful crisis of heat in the head and difficulty of breathing.

4 April Tuesday Dull day, stormy feeling in the air. Auntie is very poorly. Went to sign at the rue du Méridien this morning. Dancing lesson this afternoon. No potatoes. No sugar.

5 April Wednesday Another Belgian woman has been shot as well as several men for having sent people across the frontier. As we can't get sugar we have to use sugar-candy at 2f20 the kilo; carrots cost 0f80 the kilo, soda 0f25, gingerbread 2f50, coffee 6frs, tea 8frs and more, candles 0f50 and 0f75 each, meat is dreadfully expensive, rice 2f50 the kilo in shops; the cheapest biscuits are 3fr the kilo, petit-beurres 4f50, etc. etc. More zeppelins have been playing Old Harry in England. Arthur is in bed with a rash on his face. Doctor says it is not serious but he must keep in bed for a few days. Colder day. Went to town this morning.

6 April Thursday A. is better but must not yet go out. A Dutch boat has been torpedoed by a German mine. Went to town this morning, and this afternoon Baby and I went to the Bois and picked a lot of anemones, and then some primroses and some violet and white violets at the tennis. Auntie is still very, very weak.

7 April Friday Rainy day. A. is better and went out today. The Allies are doing very well. Stayed at home today. No potatoes.

8 April Saturday Baron de Lavelaye's son has been killed at the war. All dogs have to wear their muzzles. The doctor finds Auntie very bad. Dull day. King Albert's 41st fête day.

9 April Sunday Fine day. Went to church, and after lunch B. went to see Miss Drury and then to town. Arthur has gone to Waterloo for the whole day with the poet. No potatoes yet.

10 April Monday Lovely day. Mother and I did the spring-cleaning of poor dear Charlie's room. Auntie is very giddy tonight. No potatoes and no sugar or rice.

11 April Tuesday Went to sign at the rue du Méridien this morning. Dancing lesson this afternoon. There is a rumour that all the refugees are going to be sent out of Wiltcher's Hotel and 200 German women will lodge there and work in bureaux. Auntie is very weak. No potatoes.

12 April Wednesday Rainy day. At 12 p.m. Auntie had an awful crise, she rang her bell violently, and she was delirious for a long time, and all today she has not recovered. No potatoes. The Germs shoot all dogs without muzzles, yet they go about with dogs unmuzzled. Daddy won't let Arthur go to the poet any more. Emile de Lavelaye died on his mother's birthday.

13 April Thursday J. has got us 6 kilos of potatoes from the Alimentation. Showery day. Arthur, Baby and I spent the afternoon in the big mountains at Uccle, where we saw a lot of trains passing, and we heard the cannons. Auntie is still very weak, but a little better.

14 April Friday Showery day. Daddy got a pound loaf sugar.

15 April Saturday Opening of the tennis. Auntie had another attack last night. Showery day. Went to town this morning and to tennis this afternoon. Holidays have been for the boys. Cannons going.

16 April Sunday Lovely day. Went to church this morning and to tennis this afternoon. Cannons are heard.

17 April Monday Wet day. Had a bad night, and am feeling seedy today. Went to play bumple-puppy at tennis this afternoon. No potatoes.

18 April Tuesday Have got awful pains, and had to go to the rue du Méridien, but when I came back I went to bed and stayed there all day: have also got a little fever. Rainy day. Miss Mellin has given Arthur a sweet little saxon canary, and we call it Jack. No potatoes. Got a pound of white sugar.

19 April Wednesday Rainy day. I am still suffering; but I feel better than yesterday; am staying at home today. Jack sings. No potatoes.

20 April Thursday Fine day. J. got 6 kilos of potatoes from the Alimentation. Auntie had an attack of the ears this afternoon. Baby is suffering from headache and I from stomach-ache. Baby and I went to tennis this afternoon.

21 April Friday Good Friday. The Russians have had a great victory, the German papers are full of it. Baby is alright, but I am still suffering. More Belgians have been shot. Lovely day.

22 April Saturday Rainy day. Mrs Heineman has sent me a huge Easter egg, with three sweet handkerchieves, a pair of kid gloves, a purse and some chocolates in it. Doctor is uneasy about Auntie.

23 April Sunday Easter. Lovely day. J. has an attack of 'bouderie'. Mr Kite, one of the Americans of Auntie Flo's house, came to lunch today. Went to play tennis. Cannons are heard.

24 April Monday Beautiful day. Went to tennis this afternoon. Cannons are going. Lots of Americans come to tennis. No potatoes.

25 April Tuesday Went to sign at the rue du Méridien. Went to tennis this afternoon, and we saw three beastly zeppelins. Sausage up.

26 April Wednesday The General-Governor of Belgium, Von der Goltz, is dead! Thank goodness! Cannons were rather loud yesterday. The English have sunk a German submarine. Very hot day. Beppie Back has had the scarlet fever. Went to tennis after dinner. No potatoes.

27 April Thursday At 7.20 p.m. yesterday another zeppelin passed over the Trinity church, and we watched it a long time. Very hot day. Got a pound of white sugar and some potatoes.

28 April Friday Miss Mellin took us to tea at Châlet du Gymnase, and then we had a lovely walk round the lake. Heard lots of trains passing and the cannons going. Mr Cuissart's mother is dead. A zeppelin has been brought down in France. Mrs Carl Ehrlich saw a German train full of asphixiating gas. Auntie has got up but is feeling very ill. Lovely day.

29 April Saturday Lovely hot day. Miss Mellin took us to tea at Trois-Couleurs, and we picked two baskets full of bluebells. Cannons going all the afternoon, and lots of trains.

30 April Sunday We spent the day at Georgie's château at Boitsfort and we had a lovely time in their garden which has 1400 acres. The Allies have advanced their hour one hour, so the 1st of May all Belgium is going to do it for 6 months. Cannons going. Lovely day.

1 May Monday Lovely day. Went to tennis and then to tea at Miss Doyle's. Everybody is getting mixed up with the new time.

2 May Tuesday Went to sign at the rue du Méridien. Lovely morning, thunderstorm this afternoon which lasted over two hours. Went to tennis and then to the dancing.

3 May Wednesday Lovely day. Went to tennis this morning to fetch Mother a huge bunch of lilac. Auntie seems to suffer from the heart.

4 May Thursday Lovely day. Went to tennis this afternoon and there were two signals flying over it. Auntie has a good deal of pain.

5 May Friday Terrible hot day. I got a pound and a half of loaf sugar. Great wind in the night. No potatoes.

6 May Saturday Hot windy day. Eggs have gone up to threepence each. No potatoes. Went to town this morning, and to tennis this afternoon. No news of Charlie and Tommy for a long time. Auntie is not at all well and the doctor is uneasy about her.

7 May Sunday Fine morning, rainy afternoon. Went to church and after lunch to tennis. Eggs will perhaps be 0f75 next week. No potatoes.

8 May Monday Changeable weather. No potatoes. Arthur beat Mlle de Smet, the lady champion at tennis.

9 May Tuesday Had to sign at the Méridien. Rainy day. Went for our last dancing lesson. No potatoes.

10 May Wednesday Fine day. Went to town this afternoon. Auntie's head is hurting. Lilies of the valley are very cheap and there are heaps of them. No potatoes.

11 May Thursday Lovely day. Auntie had a very bad attack of pain at 2 a.m. Went to tennis this afternoon and in coming back we met the poet; Arthur talked to him but we have been forbidden to talk to him, why, I don't know; so Baby and I walked on. No potatoes. Cannons very loud.

12 May Friday Lovely day. No potatoes. Auntie feels always so weak now.

13 May Saturday Rainy day. Went to fetch a kilo of sugar at Mr Kirkpatrick's, which he was kind enough to give Mamma, et Mme Gräffe has sold us 2 kilos at only 1 franc the kilo. Went to tennis for half an hour after tea. No potatoes. Meat is an awful price.

14 May Sunday Foggy day. Baby and I went to St Jacques church to hear the 'Brabançonne'. Beef cost 10 francs the kilo. Went to tennis and had tea with Mrs Carl Ehrlich. No potatoes.

15 May Monday Rainy day, cleared up at 8 p.m. No potatoes.

16 May Tuesday Signed at the Méridien, and on our way we saw a great many ammunition carts going up the rue de la Loi, the band in front of them. A big red notice is posted up everywhere, that 3 men have been shot and seven condemned to penal servitude. Went to tennis this afternoon; the cannons were pretty loud. No potatoes. Lovely day.

17 May Wednesday Very hot day. Went to town this morning. No potatoes.

18 May Thursday Very hot day. Auntie's complaint is all coming back again. Went to tennis this afternoon. No potatoes.

19 May Friday Very hot. Doctor finds poor little Auntie very bad. He has been trying to ease her pains without using morphine, but he is very much afraid that he will have to give her morphine soon. Mr Delcoigne [Belgian architect] is very ill. Went to tennis this afternoon. No potatoes. Cannons very loud.

20 May Saturday Very hot. Auntie is suffering a good deal. Had a row with the gas-woman, so Arthur and J. took a long string with a paper-ball at the end, and we knocked and bumped it on her head. No potatoes.

21 May Sunday Mr Delcoigne died this morning of a double pneumonia, and all the members of the Lawn Tennis Club are going to subscribe for a wreath. Terribly hot day. Auntie had another bad night. Went to church this morning and to tennis at 3 p.m. No potatoes.

22 May Monday Suffocating heat. The members on the Committee of the Lawn Tennis Club have subscribed for a magnificent wreath for poor Mr Delcoigne. The neighbour's cat crept into our house last night, and at 3 a.m. we heard something running up the stairs. What a fright we had, and it was only a cat. Big hailstorm and thunderstorm this evening. Cannons very loud tonight. No potatoes.

23 May Tuesday Went to sign. The hail which came down in town yesterday was as big as pigeons' eggs, and over 1000 francs of damage has been down at Hirsch in the rue Neuve; all round the

Halles people are picking up bits of glass; all the best strawberry beds of Berghem St Agathe, etc. The funeral of poor Mr Delcoigne passed our house at 10 a.m. Lovely day. The boys have gone out with the whole school to the Bois des Capucins. Went to tennis this afternoon and then to Miss Schöller. No potatoes. Cannons very loud.

24 May Wednesday Lovely day, rain at 5 p.m. Went to dentist and all his windows were smashed the other day by the hail. Have got an awful headache. No potatoes.

25 May Thursday No potatoes. Showers now and then. Went to tennis, and my head and throat were hurting a great deal. Willy Gräffe has again won the Ehrlich Cup for this year.

26 May Friday Had an awful earache last night, and this morning my head is just splitting so I am stopping in bed. No potatoes. The doctor has given Auntie a certificate that she must have white bread because the brown is very bad for Auntie so we get it for her every two days.

27 May Saturday Rainy day. Auntie's head is going round the whole time. No potatoes. I went to tennis.

28 May Sunday Lovely day. Went to church, and to tennis this afternoon. No potatoes.

29 May Monday Lovely day. No potatoes. The woman of the Papeterie de l'Espérance, rue de l'Amazone, had her house searched by the 'Pigs' and a *Libre Belgique* was found so she's taken up. Colonel Wynne has been sent back from Germany to the Palais des Académies because he is ill.

30 May Tuesday Went to sign at the Pigs. Rainy day. No potatoes.

31 May Wednesday Lovely day. No potatoes. Went to tennis this afternoon and at 5 p.m. the cannons suddenly became very loud and in a quarter of an hour they stopped.

1 June Thursday Poor Charlie's seventeenth birthday. I wonder how he is spending it, poor boy! Lovely day. [...] Ascension Day. No potatoes. Went to tennis this afternoon.

2 June Friday There is not a piece of sugar in the house nor in the shops, excepting Pottin sells some brown sugar at 6f40 the kilo. Mother has bought 2.5 kilos of potatoes at 0f60 the kilo.

3 June Saturday Doctor says I have a very bad throat, my cold has been going on ever since I caught that wetting in going to order Mr Delcoigne's wreath. Thunderstorm this afternoon. The English and the German ships are fighting in the North Sea.

4 June Sunday Went to the Carmes this morning and the sermon was all about deserters who leave the army. Went to tennis and a German signal was flying all over the place.

5 June Monday Showery day. Charlie is now in England because the captain finds him too young a boy to be in the trenches.

6 June Tuesday Went to sign and this afternoon I went again to the Méridien and to the Pass-Zentrale, place Royale, to find out when is a train going to England for I think I am going to England.

7 June Wednesday Showers now and then. Lord Kitchener and all his staff have all been drowned by a mine which knocked against their ship [5 June, on HMS *Hampshire*; he was a cousin of Jack Jenkins]. Went to tennis this afternoon.

8 June Thursday Fine day, rain at 4.30 p.m. We went to Meg Butcher's birthday party this afternoon, and there was a lady there who played the violin beautifully; Meg is getting on very well with her violin.

9 June Friday Showery morning, fine afternoon. Went to the market to get Mother a lot of flowers for her birthday tomorrow, and this afternoon I went to tennis. We have to use honey for sugar.

10 June Saturday Mother's birthday. Cannons going all day. Went to the tennis this afternoon. The Russians have had a great victory.

11 June Sunday Rainy day. Went to church and there was a service for Lord Kitchener. Went to tennis, thunderstorm, and the cannons were very loud all day long.

12 June Monday Rainy day. Since the 1st of June we have not had a single day without rain. Baby and I went to the High-Life this afternoon.

13 June Tuesday Rainy day. The Russians are still taking a heap of cannons and things from the Austrians. Went to tea at Mrs Simms's.

14 June Wednesday Showery day. The papers have been stopped by the Germans for a few days for having put in about Russia's great victory. Went to the dentist this morning.

15 June Thursday Showery day, very cold. Went to tennis this afternoon.

16 June Friday First fine day. Went to town this afternoon.

17 June Saturday Lovely day. This afternoon the Americans had a match of baseball at the Léopold Club and then they all came up to tennis. Tournament of the Ehrlich Cup.

18 June Sunday Anniversary of the battle of Waterloo. Kitty's birthday and also the poet's. Baby and I went to tennis this afternoon and had tea with Mr Mellin and Jean Bruyère. Fine day.

19 June Monday Dry morning, wet afternoon. J. went to the rue de Constantinople for sugar at 1 p.m. and she came back at 5.20 p.m. without any, such crowds there were.

20 June Tuesday Butter is very scarce again, 8 francs the kilo; eggs, threepence; potatoes, 90 etc.; meat 8 and 10 francs; black soap, 7 frs; biscuits, 8f60; oil, 16frs the litre, etc. All the CRB cars are stopped because the owners have noticed that their Belgian chauffeurs all steal the essence [petrol] and then sell it, so they have given them the chuck and are going to get some foreign chauffeurs. Went to sign this morning. Captain Kendall Browning, our cousin, Chaplain on board the *Indefatigable*, has perished with 1200 others. [An error. The naval chaplain who died was Kendall Browning's brother, Rev. Guy Arrott Browning, on 31 May during the Battle of Jutland. He was the nephew of her father's first wife.] I got some sugar after waiting from 8.15 to 11 a.m. Rain at 5 p.m. Auntie is suffering a lot. Cannons very loud.

21 June Wednesday First summer's day. Lovely day. Cannons very loud this evening.

22 June Thursday Very hot day. Went to tennis after breakfast for some flowers, and went to play there this afternoon, cannons going all day. Mr Dun, an American in the CRB, has won the Ehrlich Cup. At Ruhleben the prisoners would be absolutely starved if people did not send them parcels.

23 June Friday Suffocating day. At 8.30 a.m. there were two signals just like aeroplanes on both sides of the moon. Went to town this morning.

24 June Saturday Showery day, very warm. Went to town this morning, and to tennis after lunch, where I played in the American Tournament with Mr Henri Neusister.

25 June Sunday Baby's 10th birthday. He invited Meg and Joan Butcher, Eric Wansart and Georgie and Miss Hazeldine to tea, and after tea we all went to tennis. Lovely hot day.

26 June Monday Lovely morning, stormy afternoon. Went to Miss Mellin's this morning, and her father cut me an orange rose from a tree which he'd bought at the Brussels Exhibition, in 1910. Went to tennis after lunch.

27 June Tuesday Rainy day. Went to sign. Auntie is suffering again. Baby has a canary now.

28 June Wednesday Showery day. Mr Dupuiche has had 6 months' imprisonment and 1000 marks to pay for having called the Germans 'bandits'; he is now let out and they have given him back 500 marks. Young Bigwood is let out. Went to tennis. Auntie is very weak again and she suffers a lot. Cannons going.

29 June Thursday Rainy morning, fine afternoon. Went to spend the afternoon at Mrs May's château at Boitsfort. The English have taken a place near Ypres and are doing splendidly. Cannons pretty loud.

30 June Friday Rainy morning, beautiful afternoon. The Germans have forbidden any peas or carrots to be sold, for they pretend that they are going to make preserves for the winter. Now, when Baby is angry with anybody he hides their things which they want the most.

1 July Saturday Beautiful day. I have received an invitation from some foreign people in the rue de la Vallée, and I am to begin on Monday. Am full of excitement packing up. Went to tennis this afternoon.

2 July Sunday Lovely day. Mother and I went to town this morning to buy my necessaries.

3 July Monday Lovely day. At 9 a.m. I went to Mrs Sainderichin's place for the children. Just before I left Auntie had a very bad crisis. [...]

4 July Tuesday Went to sign at the Méridien. Rainy day.

5 July Wednesday Changeable day. When we went to bed I played the clown for Elsie and Costia.

6 July Thursday Mme Sainderichin allowed me to spend the afternoon with Mother and Auntie: I found Auntie very ill, and I came back at 7 p.m. Mr Fugenne came to supper. I saw Mr Heineman and Mr Meert in the CRB. My room is next door to Elsie's and Costia's. Very unsettled day. Heaps of Germans are committing suicide like that they won't have to go to war. The Arabians have turned the

Turks out of Arabia. There is an 'on dit' that King Albert has lost a finger from his left hand.

7 July Friday Showery day. Nothing new. Mrs Heineman sent me a lot of chocolates 'remedy for home-sickness'.

8 July Saturday Showery day. Went home this morning to invite Arthur and Baby to come to tea tomorrow. [...]

9 July Sunday Fine day. [...] Arthur and Baby came to spend the afternoon, as well as Hilda De Witte and Marcel Prist. We played hide-and-seek in the grenier, etc., and Baby saw this morning a Belgian cuffing a German sailor because they were requisitioning his hotel; after having well cuffed the Pig, the Belgian was taken up.

10 July Monday Lovely day. [...] Anna has got awful stomach-ache, so I went to get Doctor Vaucleroy, and at the same time he told me that Auntie is very weak. Elsa had a cold so she has not been to school. The Backs have to go to Berlin.

11 July Tuesday Went to sign at the rue du Méridien, and I met Daddy, so I trammed to the club with him and we talked. Mr Fugenne came to lunch. Fine day. [...] Anna is alright again, except now and then she suffers.

12 July Wednesday Fine day. [...] Went to Boitsfort this morning to take Miss Gifford a present from Mme Sainderichin.

13 July Thursday Rainy day. [...] Went to market for Mme Sainderichin. This afternoon I spent the time with Auntie and Mother. I have never seen Auntie look so terribly weak, she has not eaten anything today.

14 July Friday Rainy day, fine afternoon. Went to the Alimentation after having taken Costia to school with Anna. Mother came to tea this afternoon and after tea I went to the High-Life with Costia and Elsie. [...] Mother told me that Auntie is in awful suffering for two days.

15 July Saturday Lovely day. I practised my piano for 2 hours.

16 July Sunday Rainy day. Went home at 2.30 p.m. and found Auntie terribly bad; she has a 'congestion' pneumonia and has 107 degrees of fever. Doctor Vaucleroy has found a nurse for Auntie, who put a lot of silver on her back to draw out the flesh, but the things dropped off, for she has no flesh. While I was with her this afternoon, she was very delirious. She does not eat anything and has great difficulty in breathing and coughing at times, poor little Auntie. Miss Mellin is keeping Baby to spend a few days with her while Auntie is so terribly bad.

17 July Monday 4000 English prisoners in Germany are being starved to death. Rainy morning, lovely afternoon. I am leaving Mrs S. tomorrow, but she wants me to come every afternoon. Auntie is worse, her cough is dreadful and she is terribly delirious, she has a 'pneumonie pulmonaire'.

18 July Tuesday Went to sign at the Méridien, and then I came home. Auntie has not said a word until 7.30 p.m., but the whole day she has got the death rattle, is unconscious of everybody around her. When she speaks one can't understand what she says. I have left Mme S., like that I shall be able to help Mother with poor Auntie. Tonight the death rattle is worse and she groans horribly. Doctor says no hope. Rita is keeping Arthur with her as well as Baby so as not to worry Mother. I went to fetch the Doctor again at 9.15 p.m.; what he said was: she will not live the night.

19 July Wednesday At about 2.30 Auntie's death rattle was much worse, her bed shook with it. Suddenly she stopped, opened her eyes, gave three huge sighs and she was dead. Poor darling! her sufferings are all at an end. (I saw her spirit over my bed.) She never said a word. Daddy took me to the Uccle cemetery to choose a piece of ground for the darling. The undertaker came to take her measures. Arthur is 12 years old today. Lovely day.

20 July Thursday Miss Watt came up to dear Auntie's room yesterday, and today Mrs Simms and Hannah came. At 7 p.m. the men came and put poor darling Auntie into the coffin. Daddy saw that she was

1916

put in gently: she had her hands on her mother's portrait. Daddy and I went to the Maison Communale this morning to order her carriages. Lovely day. Mrs Simms, Miss Doyle, Miss Stanger, Hannah, Joséphine and Daddy have brought some beautiful flowers.

21 July Friday Awful day for the national fête! Poor dear darling's burial. Mother, Arthur, Miss Mellin, Miss Watt and I bought some flowers. The nurse cut a lock of Auntie's hair for Mother and me just before she was put into the coffin. Mother, Daddy, Arthur and I went to the cemetery, and we each threw a shovel full of earth over her coffin when it was put in the fosse. The dear darling is now at peace, and may she evermore be happy for she deserved it. Lovely day. Captive balloon up. Gordon Simmons has been killed. A. and B. have come back from Mr Mellin's house.

22 July Saturday Dull day. Baby and I went to town this morning, and to tennis this afternoon.

23 July Sunday Fine day. Mother took Baby and me to church this morning, and this afternoon I went to the cemetery with Mother and Daddy, and then I went to tennis. Young and old Bigwood are free now.

24 July Monday Fine day. Brussels has to pay 1000000 frs to the Germs. Went to town with Mother this morning, and at the place St Catherine we saw a little girl run over by a milk cart.

25 July Tuesday Dull day. Went to the Méridien with Daddy this morning, and this afternoon I went to tennis.

26 July Wednesday Lovely day. Went to town this morning and to tennis afternoon.

27 July Thursday Very hot day. Went to town this morning and to tennis at three o'clock with Meg and Joan [Butcher], who invited us to tea. Meg played the violin and I accompanied her on the piano.

28 July Friday Very hot. Went to town this morning, and to tennis this afternoon. Cannons loud. Explosion in a house in our street.

29 July Saturday Suffocating day. Boys' holidays have begun. Went to tennis this afternoon. Mr Marcel Bormans has had a bad accident.

30 July Sunday Lovely day. Went to church this morning, to tennis this afternoon.

31 July Monday Very hot. Stayed at home all day. Cannons heard.

1 August Tuesday Very hot. Daddy and I went to the Méridien. At 3 p.m. Mother and I took Auntie some flowers at the cemetery and then I went to tennis.

2 August Wednesday Baking hot day. At 1.30 p.m. we heard gunshots: out into the street I flew. After looking for several minutes we saw 2 aeroplanes and some time after another one appeared. The Germans fired from the Palais de Justice for about half an hour. There were altogether 6 or 7 aeroplanes, French and English. Went to tennis this afternoon. Cannons very loud.

3 August Thursday Terribly hot. Feeling rather seedy. Went to tea at Miss Doyle's.

4 August Friday Much cooler. Daddy got a letter from Uncle Fred, saying that Charlie is doing very well in England and all the family is very. It is just 2 years today since the war broke out. Miss Mellin took us to the Prince d'Orange.

5 August Saturday Fine day. They say that a bomb fell on the avenue Longchamps on Wednesday and that a man was killed, but it is not quite certain. Went to town this morning. Mrs Nicolet came to tea with Mother. Went to tennis this afternoon. It feels rather cold today. No sugar for a long time.

6 August Sunday Lovely day. Went to church this morning and to tennis this afternoon. Cannons going. No sugar.

7 August Monday Dull day. The aeroplanes of last Wednesday dropped a bomb on the shed of Etterbeek. Baby and I went to town this afternoon. We all have to use small packets of sugar which come to 4f50 the kilo and next month it will cost 4 francs.

8 August Tuesday Went with Daddy to sign at the rue du Méridien. Beautiful day. Mr Sperry has presented a silver cup to the club for ladies' singles, which has to be won in 3 consecutive sets or 15 times in all. Mlle M. van Goethem has won it today against Mlle de Smet. The Germs have shot the captain of the Brussels ship because he captured one of their submarines. England is more outraged about it than about Miss Cavell's case.

9 August Wednesday At 6.30 a.m. I was awakened by loud bangs. I screamed out: they are firing at aeroplanes. We all rushed to the loft and the sky was full of bullets. We saw 2 or 3 aeroplanes and it went on for over half an hour, and the Uccle sausage was up: when the firing was finished they brought the sausage down. Beautiful day. Went to tennis. Kind of sound balloon up at Uccle.

17. Garden party at the Brussels Lawn Tennis Club, 18 June 1890. Connie, aged nine, is in the white dress to the right of the table. She gave a speech and presented a bouquet of flowers to Mrs Lyon, wife of Hon. E.B. Lyon of the British Legation, who were leaving Brussels for Washington. Standing behind Connie is possibly Hussey Vivian, 3rd Baron Vivian, diplomatist, who also gave a speech

10 August Thursday We went out picnicking for the holiday at Rouge-Cloître with Miss Mellin and Mlle Henriette Delmont, the artist painter. It rained a little bit, but on the whole it remained fine. Dad got a letter from Con.

11 August Friday Lovely day. B's canary flew away, but Arthur caught it again in Victoria's garden. Went to tennis this afternoon.

12 August Saturday Very hot day. Went to town this morning and would have been run over by a tram if a German had not given me a violent push on to the pavement. At 6.30 p.m. a small balloon was sent up very high and then brought down immediately after.

13 August Sunday Dull morning, lovely hot afternoon. Went to the church of St Josse Ten Noode and to tennis this afternoon where the men's singles for the C.E. Cup began this afternoon. Mr Léon came to tea.

14 August Monday Showers, wind, very close. Miss Watt came to tea. Henry Matthysen is the winner.

15 August Tuesday Went to sign with Mother and Baby, and then I went to the dentist. We all went to tennis this afternoon. Showers every now and then.

16 August Wednesday Warm day. Went all alone to Vilvorde in the tram and from there I walked near Eppeghem. Left the house at 2.15 p.m. and came back at 8 p.m.

17 August Thursday Fine day, big shower and rainbow at 7 p.m. Mother lunched and had tea at Boitsfort with Miss Gifford. Went to tennis this afternoon. Perrin won the C.E. Cup.

18 August Friday Went to town this morning and to tennis this afternoon.

19 August Saturday We can't get any more butter in shops. Went to tennis this afternoon. Stormy kind of weather.

20 August Sunday Fine morning, stormy afternoon. Mother took us to Rouge-Cloître for lunch and Arthur and I had tea at Mrs Westwood's, at Boitsfort. A large Italian boat has sunk.

21 August Monday Showers. The Germans are taking a certain quantity of flour from every baker, so we have less bread.

22 August Tuesday There have never been so many English at the Méridien as there were today. After that Mother took we three to town. Went to tennis this afternoon. Cold day.

23 August Wednesday Lovely day. Baby and I went to the Vieux Marché, and after luncheon we went to tennis where we saw a zeppelin very high up at 6.30 and at 7.30 p.m. we saw it again.

24 August Thursday Lovely day. Captive balloon at Uccle Observatoire at 8.30 a.m. and signal at 6 p.m. Went to tennis this afternoon. Matthysen beat Gräeffe again.

25 August Friday Hot day. Went to market with Mother. At 8 a.m. the Germans fired at an aeroplane but for very short. Went to tennis this afternoon.

26 August Saturday Lovely day, small storm at dinner time. We all spent the afternoon at Mr de Bauer's château at Boitsfort. Lots of trains passed at the bottom of their garden while we were there. Cannons rather loud.

27 August Sunday Went to Christ Church this morning and to the cinema this afternoon. Shower day, storm at 7 p.m. The Germs are building super zeppelins which can go up at 5000 yards.

28 August Monday A few showers. Nothing interesting.

29 August Tuesday Germany has declared war to Roumania yesterday, and Italy has declared war to Germany. Went to sign at the rue du Méridien, and to tennis this afternoon, where at 6.45 p.m. there was a huge double storm which lasted till 8.30.

30 August Wednesday Terrible windy night and today also. Went to tennis this afternoon. From the 20th of this month all the bicyclists must give up their tyres to the Germs, whether old or new. Now the chief occupation for men, women and children is bicycling. Everybody is furious.

31 August Thursday Lovely day. J. gone to Halles. Went to tennis.

1 September Friday Went to town this morning and to tennis this afternoon. Mother has a tea party this afternoon.

2 September Saturday Lovely day. Greece has joined the Allies. Went to town this morning and to tennis this afternoon. Saw a zeppelin very high up at 7.45 p.m.

3 September Sunday Lovely day, rain at 6 p.m. Mother and I went to Christ Church and this afternoon to tennis. I had tea with Mrs Peiser at tennis.

4 September Monday Rainy day. The cheapest ham costs 12 frs the kilo. Everything is very expensive, especially the fruit and vegetables, and it is getting worse every day.

5 September Tuesday The zeppelin which we saw last Saturday has been brought down in England. Went to sign at the Méridien this morning and then to the dentist. After lunch went to tennis. Showery day.

6 September Wednesday Lovely day. At Lille the famine is dreadful: butter, 20frs the kilo, one egg 1f75, dog meat 8frs.

7 September Thursday At 10 p.m. last night my room was lit up and huge bangs were heard. Naturally I jumped out of bed. My first idea was fireworks. The whole house woke up and it proved to be Allied aeroplanes which were dropping quantities of bombs on the German buildings. At 10.45 it began again, but it lasted much longer. All the sky was lit up with bombs, awful row. We saw several aeroplanes: they looked like large moving stars. Naturally the Germs fired at them and one of the shells fell through a house near the Hôtel des Monnaies, killed a girl, smashed the line of the tram. The Germs have taken 625 millions of francs from the Banque nationale to pay their loan. Comtesse d'Oultremont is sentenced to be shot for having let some men pass the frontier. Fine day. Went to tennis. Mr Hocks is dead.

8 September Friday Lovely day. Went to tennis this afternoon. The winner of the Sperry Cup is Mlle van Goethem.

9 September Saturday Lovely day. Went to tea with Miss Gifford at Boitsfort.

10 September Sunday Lovely day. Went to Christ Church this morning and to tennis this afternoon.

11 September Monday Fine day. Went to tennis.

12 September Tuesday Went to sign at the Méridien. Had tea at tennis with Frida Meert and her mother. All the inhabitants of St Josse and Bruxelles have to be indoors by 8 p.m. on; all the cafés and cinemas must be shut at that time, because the Germs say they sent up signals at the aeroplane the other day. Lovely day.

13 September Wednesday Showery day. Daddy heard the trains at 2 a.m., and some say they must have contained German troops.

14 September Thursday Showery day. Went to tennis this afternoon, and had a long talk with […].

15 September Friday Cold day. Mother took us all to town this morning. […] Went to tennis. Perrin has won the Ehrlich Cup.

16 September Saturday Cold day. The Germs have shot 2 Belgians for having sent some recruits across the frontier. No butter.

17 September Sunday Fine day. Went to tennis this afternoon and had tea with Suzanne Romedenne.

18 September Monday Pouring wet day. No news.

19 September Tuesday

Proclamation de l'Aviateur qui a survolé Bruxelles le 6 Septembre au soir

Belges!
La fin approche:
Devant Verdun l'admirable et héroïque résistance de l'armée française a brisé la formidable offensive allemande. Sur la Somme les armées françaises et anglaises avancent victorieusement.

En Volhynie, et en Galicie l'armée autrichienne est mise en déroute par les armées russes et les débris soutenus par des corps allemands et turcs ne parviennent pas à enrayer la pousée continue de nos alliés.

Les Italiens ont rejeté l'envahisseur du Trentin et ont enlevé après des efforts magnifiques des positions inexpugnables de la Goritza.

Enfin la Roumanie s'est rangée du côté du droit.

Belges, vous ne serez plus longtemps sous le joug de l'envahisseur. Votre Courage, Votre Dignité, Votre Fiéreté indomptable font l'Admiration du Monde.

Notre Vaillante Armée Vous Rejoindra Bientôt Avec L'Aide De Nos Puissants Alliés.

Elle Chassera L'Ennemi Du Sol Natal. Le moment de la Déliverance approche. <u>Courage</u>.

Vive les Alliées!!
Vive la Belgique!!
Vive le Roi!!!

Paris le 5 Septembre, 1915

Showery. Went to sign at the Méridien. Today is the last day that bicycles are allowed to roll.

20 September Wednesday Showery. Went to town this morning, and to tennis this afternoon. [...]

21 September Thursday Fine day. Went to tennis. Cannons pretty loud this afternoon.

22 September Friday Lovely day. Went to town this afternoon.

23 September Saturday Beautiful day. Am playing in the Ladies' Singles for the Sperry Cup against Yvonne Jensens. Sausage up.

24 September Sunday Lovely day. In coming back from tennis yesterday we saw a huge zep at 7 p.m. Sausage up at Uccle, and brought down at 8.30 a.m. Went to tennis.

25 September Monday Lovely day. Three zeppelins passed at 9.15 p.m.

26 September Tuesday Went to sign without my 'Identité' because I lost it. The man told me that I have to pay 5 marks and get a new one for next Tuesday, but Mother found it when I came back. Very hot day. Went to tennis this afternoon.

27 September Wednesday Big cannonading of aeroplanes at 8.15 a.m. from all directions. I saw 2 aeroplanes and they dropped some bombs. It lasted very long and then they sent up two black signals. Lots of people have been killed and wounded in the avenue Brugmann, rue de la Vallée, etc. We went to see the damage in the avenue Brugmann; 7 houses had all the windows smashed and blood was in front of one of the houses where 2 people had been wounded. In the Chausée de Waterloo there was a group of houses also the windows smashed, and a policeman had been telling the people to keep indoors when a shell blew his arm off and he was taken into an apothecary's. In the rue Vanderkindere 2 children and a woman have been hurt; rue de la Vallée, a lady was having her bath when a shell fell through and blew her arm off, etc. They say that the Germans fire the wrong way on purpose to hurt the people. Fine morning, rain at 2.30 p.m. and fine at 4 p.m. Mlle Van Goethem has the Sperry Cup for ever now.

28 September Thursday The policeman who was wounded yesterday is dead from loss of blood. Fine day. Went to tennis this afternoon. Cannons very loud.

29 September Friday Daddy is going to send me to school in the rue de Parme, and I went this morning to pass an exam: to know which class I am to go into. Fine day. Baby and I went to tennis.

30 September Saturday Went to school this morning and I can pass from the 5th preparatory into the 1ère Moyenne on Monday. Went to the Léopold Club [founded in 1893, in Parc Brugmann] to see a match of baseball played by the Americans. Pastry cooks are forbidden to sell cakes by Germ law.

1 October Sunday We did not go yesterday to the Léopold because Miss Mellin took us to Koekelberg the highest point of Brussels. Lovely day, rather cold. Went to tennis and Meg and Joan [Butcher] took me to their house to tea.

2 October Monday Holidays are over and we all go back to school. At 7.30 p.m. last night there was a noise just like an aeroplane; it came back 6 or 7 times and we could see nothing, but searchlights I could see from my window. At 6 a.m. we saw an aeroplane. Firing from every quarter for half an hour. Sausage up.

3 October Tuesday I have a certificate to only go once a month to sign, being a scholar. I go every Tuesday and Saturday afternoon to Mme Seeldrayers to speak English with Manette and play and have tea with her. Rainy day. Another aeroplane 4 a.m.

4 October Wednesday Rainy day. Went to school.

5 October Thursday Showery. Had tea at the Racing Club ['Le Racing', a private club for tennis, athletics and football, founded by the British in 1881 in Uccle] with Manette and Germaine Seeldrayers.

6 October Friday Arthur's canary died this morning. Showery day. Went to town after school to buy a new hat with Mother.

7 October Saturday Had dinner at the Racing with the Seeldrayers and spent the afternoon there. Fine day, rain at 5 p.m. Baby's canary was found dead in his cage.

8 October Sunday Showery day. Went to tennis this afternoon.

9 October Monday Fine day. Went to tennis this afternoon. No butter, no sugar.

10 October Tuesday Went to the Seeldrayers this afternoon. Fine day.

11 October Wednesday Fine day.

12 October Thursday Fine day, windy. Had tea at the Racing with Manette and Germaine Seeldrayers.

13 October Friday Rainy day.

14 October Saturday Showery. Spent the afternoon with Manette Seeldrayers, her mother is feverish, and keeps in bed.

15 October Sunday Fine day. Went to C. Church and to tennis, where when it got dark everybody played hide-and-seek.

16 October Monday Showery. Cannons terribly loud all the day long.

17 October Tuesday At 11 a.m. a few shots were fired at a Taube, which the Germs took for an enemy. Spent the afternoon with Manette. Cannons very loud.

18 October Wednesday Went to the dentist after school. Cannons rather loud.

19 October Thursday Spent the afternoon with Manette and her cousins. When I came back at 6 p.m. the cannons were going tremendously. Eggs are at 44 centimes, black soap 9f75, cakes 40 and 50 centimes, potatoes 75 centimes, etc.

20 October Friday Freezing day, very fine. Cannons very loud from 3 p.m.

21 October Saturday Icy cold day, very fine. At 9.15 p.m. last night I heard a zeppelin. Had tea at the Racing with Manette Seeldrayers.

22 October Sunday Lovely day, very cold. Mother paid 11f75 the kilo of butter. An English submarine has sunk a German cruiser.

23 October Monday Mme Back and children have come back from Hungary and they come to my school. Lovely day. J.'s sister has come from Liège with her kids.

24 October Tuesday Black soap has gone up to 18frs the kilo. Spent the afternoon with Manette.

25 October Wednesday Nothing interesting.

26 October Thursday Wet day. Spent the afternoon with Manette. She wasn't well today.

27 October Friday We can't get any more coal in shops.

28 October Saturday Spent the afternoon with Manette only till 4 p.m. There were 3 rainbows. No more potatoes to be had.

29 October Sunday Rainy day. Went to church this morning. Cannons very loud.

30 October Monday Windy day, at 4.30 p.m. the sky was beautiful: huge black clouds between a bronze-tinged sky.

31 October Tuesday Fine day. Spent the afternoon with Manette. Sir James Freeling is dead.

1 November Wednesday, All Saints' Day Lovely day. A. and I went to the cemetery this morning and we all went to the country this afternoon. The Roumanians have had several big victories. The cannons pretty loud.

2 November Thursday Lunched with the Seeldrayers. We had holiday yesterday and today. Rainy day.

3 November Friday Lovely day. As we can't get any more potatoes people eat large turnips called choux-raves. Carl Ehrlich has been fined 100 marks or 10 days' imprisonment for having called the Germs thieves when he had to take his tyres. No potatoes.

4 November Saturday Rainy day. Mme Seeldrayers took us to the Palais des Sports at Schaerbeek [opened in 1913] which has been converted into an immense dolls' palace and she bought each of us a ticket for a doll which will be drawn out on the 1st of December and the money goes for the Christmas of the poor.

5 November Sunday Lovely day, very windy. At 6.30 p.m. I saw a star fall. Guy Fawkes's Day. No potatoes.

6 November Monday Showery day. No potatoes and no coal. Eggs are at 0f50 a piece.

7 November Tuesday Went to sign at the Méridien. Mrs Westwood is dead. B. and I went to the cinema after school. Rainy day. No potatoes.

8 November Wednesday The Germs are going to send all the Belgian men from 17 to 65 to Germany to work for them. Went with the school to the Palais des Sports for the dolls' show. Rainy. No potatoes.

9 November Thursday No potatoes.

10 November Friday J. has got some potatoes from the Alimentation. Cannons very loud. At the Germ. school a girl was sent away, having been seen to meet an officer in coming out of school. Next day the officer turns up and threatens to shut the whole school if they punish the girl, and now nearly all the girls meet some officers at the break-up. Lovely moonlight night.

11 November Saturday In a week or two the Germs are going to cut off all the gas and electricity. Spent the afternoon with Manette. Had a good report at school.

12 November Sunday Went to the Racing with the Seeldrayers and some of their friends. Cannons loud.

13 November Monday Very foggy morning. In coming back from the Racing yesterday I had a rare old tumble down a hill.

14 November Tuesday The English have had a great victory. Spent the afternoon with Manette. At 6 p.m. the cannons were very loud. A convict of the St Gilles Prison was found hung in his cell. Drizzly day. Mme Desquin, our concierge at school, is unwell.

15 November Wednesday Daddy's birthday and St Léopold, so we have holiday all day. Went with Daddy to the church library this morning and he treated us all to see *Ivanhoe* at the High-Life. Cannons very loud. We bought 2 kilos of potatoes at sixpence the kilo, and that's cheap.

16 November Thursday Lovely day, freezing. Rita Mellin took us to town this afternoon and she bought me a dear little cupid. Cannons really loud.

17 November Friday Lovely day, freezing. Great excitement all over the town because the burgomasters will not give up the names of the chômeurs [the unemployed], so all the Hôtels de Ville are surrounded and the burgomasters will be imprisoned till they give up the list. No potatoes. Lovely moonlight night.

18 November Saturday Mr Watts has made up his mind he is going to quit work and he is going back to America: he is not well enough. It snowed last night, but it rained this afternoon, so there is no more snow. Spent the afternoon with the Seeldrayers. The Taverne Royal has been fined 85,000 marks for having served some meat the other day. No potatoes.

19 November Sunday Dull day. Went to church this morning and to Mirelle's house to tea. The boys went to the Cinéma Trianon where there was a fight between a German officer and a Belgian civilian because the G. wanted the B. to give him his place. The B. cuffed the G. till he was black in the face, but was taken up by 5 Gs who came in just then. No potatoes. Cannons pretty loud.

20 November Monday A notice is put up that from tomorrow all the belligerents must be indoors at 7.30 p.m.; all cafés and cinemas also because some national manifestations have been taking place. Mme Burveniche, our singing teacher, gave me 4 points out of 8 for my singing with Eugénie.

21 November Tuesday It is so funny tonight: at 7.30 p.m. not a soul in the street, all the shops are shut and the trams are empty. Lovely day, foggy night. Spent the afternoon with Manette. Cannons very loud. Big lights in the sky.

22 November Wednesday Emma Gaeslinck, a girl of 1ère B., has got into an awful row because she has imitated her aunt's signature and has never shown her report because her aunt beats her. The Roumanians are doing bad. At 8.30 p.m. a zeppelin passed, but it was so foggy nobody could see it; it came back twice at 10 p.m. and it stayed a huge time. Cannons terribly loud all night and all day. Francis-Joseph of Austria is dead [Emperor Franz Joseph]. Mlle Bens brought one of her tortoises with her to school to show it to us.

23 November Thursday Poor dear Auntie's birthday: we took some flowers to her grave and then we stayed and played amid the fields. We were watching huge lights signalling of the Germans from every direction, on the top of a hill where there was barbed wire, when suddenly the wire gave way and A. and B. rolled down the hill and I stuck at the top. The Gs sent freely in the air several gas balloons from the Uccle Observatoire. Cannons very loud. We still have to be back at 7.30 p.m. Zeppelin at 8.30 and 10 p.m.

24 November Friday Rainy day. J. and I went for a little walk at 6 p.m. till 7.30 p.m. At the Porte de Namur at 7 all the restaurants and cinemas shut. Shops are lovely for St Nicolas. Zeppelin passed again at 8.30 p.m.

25 November Saturday In the chemical lesson we all underwent an electric shock. Two people have been caught at the Gare du Midi because they were later than 7.30. The Germ took their Carte d'Identité and the next day they sent to sell the furniture till the 10,000 marks are paid up. No potatoes again.

26 November Sunday Spent the afternoon at the Racing Club with the Seeldrayers. J. had to come back at 7.30 instead of 10 p.m., it being her day out. Cannons very loud. No potatoes.

27 November Monday Foggy. No potatoes. Mme Vereest, the Professor of 2ème Moyenne, has lost her father. Cannons pretty loud.

28 November Tuesday Manette is having her portrait painted by Pirot, and her Mother, Mr Hasen, and I went with her to the painter's studio, at the top of a huge house in the rue Royale. Afterwards we went home and rehearsed the play *La Jalouse*, which we are going to act for St Nicolas. No potatoes. Foggy.

29 November Wednesday Two zeppelins have been brought down. We have some potatoes, but no sugar.

30 November Thursday American Thanksgiving day.

1 December Friday Freezing day. Miss Vander Est has married Jean de Pauw.

2 December Saturday Spent the afternoon with Germaine and Manette Seeldrayers and Claire, a friend. Mlle Bens is ill.

3 December Sunday This morning I went to town and this afternoon I went to the Racing, but we came home early for it was so cold. Cannons loud.

4 December Monday Cannons very loud, but this night they were terribly loud. Snow fell in the night, but rain came after.

5 December Tuesday Mother took me to the Palais des Sports for the tombola and Arthur won two beautiful guns made by the wounded soldiers at Liège. Signed at the Méridien and spent the afternoon with Manette. Cannons very loud. No potatoes.

6 December Wednesday, St Nicolas A zeppelin passed last night at 7.15. Denise Bernard and Suzanne Courrouble put me some nice things to eat in my desk. No potatoes, no oranges, no spéculaus [Christmas biscuits]; everything terribly expensive. As it was St Nicolas, Mlle Mercks let us do the 'tour du monde' at gymnastics: we have to go all round the salle on all the instruments, and each time that we touch the ground with our feet we have to begin all over again: it's great fun. Denise Bernard is my greatest schoolfriend, she is just three days older than I am. I am the tallest of my class, which contains forty-one girls. A zeppelin passed at 7 p.m.

7 December Thursday Cannons pretty loud. The Germans have taken Bucharest, the capital of Roumania.

8 December Friday There is a talk that Greece is going to war against us. Léopold Back is going to have an operation in the throat.

9 December Saturday Spent the afternoon with Manette and her cousins.

10 December Sunday Went to church this morning, and to the Racing after lunch, where there was a big football match. Signal in the sky, and cannons terribly loud. Lovely day.

11 December Monday Mlle Bens came back to school today, for she is better. Signal up at 8 a.m. and cannons very loud, especially at night.

12 December Tuesday Rain, snow and sleet. Mr Léon is very ill.

13 December Wednesday The Kaiser is asking for peace, not without a reason. Eggs are at 55 centimes, butter 12 frs, oil 25 frs the bottle, black soap 15 frs; the cheapest military biscuits 6 frs the kilo, potatoes 75 and 1 fr. Lovely day. Cannons louder than ever.

14 December Thursday Rainy day. We went to the Kursaal of the chaussée d'Ixelles this afternoon.

15 December Friday Rainy day. Went to Manette after school; she was in bed with fever and a bad cold. Cannons very loud.

16 December Saturday Cannons very loud. The French have had great success. I don't like Mlle Bens any more because she is very unjust to the girls who are not in her sleeve. Manette's fever is higher today. Cold.

17 December Sunday Went to church with Arthur and we all had tea at Mrs May's. J. came back at 8 p.m. with her sister and the 5 kids; they were stopped by the Germs, and all began to howl, so they are all spending the night in our house. Cannons very loud.

18 December Monday Now people may come in at what hour they like, but public houses and shops which don't sell food must shut at 7 p.m. I went with the school to the Picture Exhibition done by the Belgian prisoners in Germany, rue Royale. Am feeling seedy.

19 December Tuesday All the Preparatory Section have holidays because croup, scarlet fever, measles, etc. are raging. Two zeppelins passed at 5 p.m. Spent the afternoon with Germaine and Manette Seeldrayers. Snow fell at 6.15 p.m.

21 December Thursday Lovely day. I went to the High-Life and saw: *Mais mon amour ne meurt pas*. I have never seen anything so lovely. Edouard, a violinist of the Olympia, played a piece during an interval. Very windy, lightnings in the sky.

22 December Friday No butter.

23 December Saturday Holidays begin today at 12 p.m. We were all invited to the Xmas party at the Butchers. Among the friends there were two very nice Canadian girls: Mary and Ruth Peters. Tempestuous day.

24 December Sunday Heavenly weather. A German biplane came at 1.45 p.m. I went to church this morning, and to the Seeldrayers this afternoon. Manette is still unwell.

25 December Monday Santa Claus filled my stocking up. The first thing we did was to go into poor little Auntie's room, and there stood a big Christmas tree. I received a big packet of chocolate and a box of lovely ancient notepaper with my initials from Mrs Heineman; a box of sweets, some odds and ends and three francs from Mother; an envelope containing five francs from Carl Ehrlich, etc. We all went to church this morning, and to the High-Life to see *Le Fils de Lagardère* this afternoon. As it was a short programme we went to the Eden-Théâtre in the rue Neuve. Rainy day. Mme Remy is dead, it is very sad for her husband and her two little children.

26 December Tuesday Miss Drury has sent us 5 francs to buy chocolates. Spent the afternoon with the Seeldrayers. Manette is worse, they think it is measles. This morning I went to town and bought a bracelet and a ring. Lovely day.

27 December Wednesday Lovely day. We all went to the Majestic Cinema in the rue Neuve. No potatoes.

28 December Thursday Lovely day. I could not see Manette because she has got the measles.

29 December Friday Wet day. Coffee has gone up to 30 francs the kilo; eggs, 65 centimes; petits-fours, 20 francs the kilo; caviar, 180 francs; turkeys, cheapest 75 frs; geese, 65 frs, etc.

30 December Saturday Wet day. Went to the dentist and to the Parc Marie-Louise.

31 December Sunday Wet. The Germs are going to requisition all the copper they see which is not used as ornaments.

1917

1 January Monday Wet day. The Senne has overflooded with the quantity of rain we are having. A big part of Fôret and several parts of the town have also been overflooded. Mr Noblet has died quite suddenly at The Hague. Baby and I went to the Scala to see *Veronique*, acted by Angèle Van Loo. Mother received a huge basket of fruit from Lady Phipps. Cannons very loud. Daddy has a bad cold.

2 January Tuesday Went to sign at the rue du Méridien. Took some flowers to Auntie's grave and a German aeroplane passed over my head. Ixelles, Uccle and Forest are all under darkness, because of the floods produced by the Senne. Cannons very loud. Mr Watts left Brussels by the 1.50 train.

3 January Wednesday We all go back to school. Mr Graham is going to be sent to Germany on Saturday because he denied to the Germs having ever been in the army. He has immediately flown off to the American Legation. The floods are worse. Whole cellars are under water, as well as fields. Denise, Suzanne and I amused ourselves by putting handfuls of confettis in all the shut umbrellas so that when the girls open them they'll receive showers of paper in their faces. Mrs Simms came to tea. Rainy day.

4 January Thursday Drizzly weather. A thief stole at a chemist's shop in the rue du Bailly. Baby and J. went to see the floods at Fôret; he came back feeling very unwell. Spent the afternoon with Manette; she is alright again, but her mother suffers from the heart, and the doctor has advised her to go to Switzerland so they are all going to try and get off. Denise did not come to school today.

5 January Friday Lovely day. J. had an awful fight with her brother-in-law, who nearly smashed her head with a hammer. He was going to give her a bang on the head when her sister called out: 'Don't forget she is a woman.' Over 500 people came crowding outside their house. Poor J. came back to us, having received that threat from her brother: 'Mind, don't go and do any mischief, and never show your face in this house again.' B. is better, but as he has a little fever he is keeping in bed today.

6 January Saturday Wet day. Spent the afternoon with Manette. [...] B. went to school.

7 January Sunday Lovely day. Spent the afternoon with Manette. After tea her parents, Mr Hazen and Mr Konig did some music. Mr Hazen sang: 'Ave Maria', 'Les Yeux' and several other songs.

8 January Monday It snowed all night and rained all day. A theft was committed at no. 84, in front of our house.

9 January Tuesday Sleety. Guns have been going all day near Brussels, people say it is to celebrate the Kaiser's birthday. Spent the afternoon with Manette.

10 January Wednesday Cannons pretty loud. Rainy day. Suzanne Courrouble's mother suffers from awful crises, just like poor little Auntie used to have. It was not the Kaiser's birthday yesterday.

11 January Thursday The Germs have taken 90 horses from Wielemans Ceuppens, the big brewery. The Crown-Prince has got a new kid [Wilhelm, the German Crown Prince, and his new daughter Princess Cecilie Viktoria Anastasia Zita Thyra Adelheid of Prussia]. Snowy day. Spent the afternoon with Manette.

12 January Friday Snow and sleet. Pepper costs 50 francs the kilo. Léopold Back has been operated in the throat.

13 January Saturday Cannons very loud at 2 p.m. Doctor says Manette must rest for a while because she is so weak, so won't go so often. Mr Simms and Dicky Biggs are going to be set free.

14 January Sunday Went to Christ Church. We all want to the Cigale – the programme was very interesting. Harry, a comic clown, sang some very clever songs, and then there was a couple of duetists, The Harry Mans, which was wonderful. Snow fell this morning. Cannons very loud in the night.

15 January Monday Everything covered with lovely woolly snow. Germaine Nacher's dog was run over.

16 January Tuesday Snow with frost. Firing very hard. The verdurier [grocer] and his wife of the rue de l'Aqueduc are in prison.

17 January Wednesday Snow fell all night. Cannons very loud. Denise, Suzanne and I are in an awful row with Mme Scheppers, because we were caught snowballing.

18 January Thursday The row is still going on. The Grand Bazar and Franchomme are shut up because they did something which the Germs do not like. Cannons going.

19 January Friday Tomorrow there will be great excitement because quantities of chômeurs have to present themselves at the Gare du Midi with a blanket, etc. They are going to be sent to Germany. Freezing. Cannons still going. Roumania and Russia are making an offensive [...].

20 January Saturday Everybody must be in by 10 p.m. till new order. Freezing all day. Robert Noblet has been caught trying to cross the frontier.

21 January Sunday Lovely freezing day. We all went sledging at the Bois de la Cambre with some friends. Jean has made us a sledge.

22 January Monday I have lost my report of school in the street, now I am in for a row! Lovely freezing day. Denise and I are separated during recreation because the prof. imagine we plot scrapes.

23 January Tuesday Went to see the Conservatoire Royal de Bruxelles in the rue de la Régence. I went into several of the music-rooms.

All the taps are frozen, we couldn't have any water. Freezing. Trains passed all night.

24 January Wednesday At Anderlecht 2000 chômeurs have been sent to Germany. Freezing hard.

25 January Thursday B. and I went for the first time to skate at the inundated farm of Forest. We had a ripping time; met a lot of friends, and then I went sledging with Denise on the avenue Besme.

26 January Friday Freezing. Daddy says that he never remembers such cold in Belgium. All our taps are frozen, so we have no water. Cold wind.

27 January Saturday Kaiser Wilhelm's birthday. Freezing hard. After tea I went with Mother to the Butchers. North wind blowing.

28 January Sunday We all went skating at Forest, and we met a lot of friends. They are also skating at the Etangs d'Ixelles, Cap Nord, etc. All the taps are still frozen, excepting the kitchen one, which runs drop by drop. The Allies have made two advances, one in Roumania and one on the Somme.

29 January Monday There is a report that the Germans have asked for peace. Freezing. Mlle Eymal, our drawing-mistress, is very ill.

30 January Tuesday Snow has been falling all day. An English cruiser has sunk a German submarine.

31 January Wednesday I now go to the music class of Mme Delinge from 6 to 7.30 p.m., and I am put in the 4th class. Baron Roest's uncle has been condemned to hard labour for life. The consul of Antwerp is looking after some chômeurs, who are too ill to go on working in Germany, and says that they have lost twenty pounds of flesh, having been so ill-treated. Streets full of snow. Stephen Heineman has the measles.

1 February Thursday Germany has written a mad letter to America that the coast of the Atlantic and W. Mediterranean is going to be blockaded by their submarines; and any ship they see will be sunk. An exception is to be made for two ships going from America to Falmouth and vice versa, specially painted. That means that America will be driven to war. The ship is only allowed to go once a week. Freezing day. We all went to the cinema.

2 February Friday Freezing hard. Sixty German soldiers have been brought into different hospitals with their legs frozen to death. Denise is not coming to school any more.

3 February Saturday The Germans requisitioned all the horses on the place Louis Morichar at 9 a.m. The order has been to give up all the copper. Went to the music class. Coldest day we've had yet.

4 February Sunday Freezing hard. The gasmen are shutting all the gazometers, and we have not a drop of water. Accidents are happening everywhere, all the pipes are frozen. Went to see *Néron et Agrippine* at the Select. Carl Ehrlich's birthday.

5 February Monday The Americans have broken off all diplomatic relations with Germany. All the American ministers and consuls must leave Germany. Denise Bernard has come back to school. A public tap has been put in the rue de l'Aqueduc, so we have some water, thank goodness. The American Senate has passed a loan of 500000000 dollars for the Army and Navy without interest. Freezing hard.

6 February Tuesday Went to sign at the Méridien with Daddy. The Americans have seized some German cruisers. The German and Austrian ministers have been sent away from Washington and have retired to Mexico. Coldest day we've had −10 degrees on Fahrenheit at 7.30 a.m. Exams began today.

7 February Wednesday Still freezing hard, mi is broken. Went to the music class. Mme Scheppers is now headmistress of our school.

8 February Thursday Olga Movaux has been sent away from school because she stole a purse which contained two gold rings. Baby and I went to the Cigale. There was a rather good tenor, and a funny clown.

9 February Friday Mrs Ehrlich is staying in bed today, because the house is so cold, there being no coal anywhere. The Escaut is frozen. Lots of seagulls have come to Brussels, because the seaside is so cold. Public tap is stopped, no water.

10 February Saturday The weather is getting less cold. Went to the singing class tonight.

11 February Sunday Lovely day. We all went skating this afternoon, and Arthur and I get along very well; I had eleven falls though.

12 February Monday It snowed a little today.

13 February Tuesday Fine day. All schools are shutting for want of coal.

14 February Wednesday A little colder. Went to the music class. Cannons pretty loud.

15 February Thursday Lovely day. Went to town and to skate. An American CRB ship has struck a mine and has sunk.

16 February Friday Lovely day. Tonight it has begun to rain.

17 February Saturday Von Bissing is shutting up all schools, private, free, etc. Today we all assembled in the préau [indoor playground] and Mme Scheppers read to us the letter for shutting the schools. Lots of girls cried, you bet I didn't. Went to the last music lesson. Rain and fog.

18 February Sunday I have got a new watch. Went to C. Church this morning. Cannons pretty loud. The Americans are going to stay in Belgium till further order.

19 February Monday Cannons very loud.

20 February Tuesday In bed I heard the cannons going.

21 February Wednesday A German officer and boy have taken a flat in front of our house.

23 February Friday My 16th birthday. We all had tea in town and to the cinema we went afterwards.

24 February Saturday Dull day. They say that the Kaiser and von Hindenburg are in Brussels tonight. Nobody is allowed to go into Austria with jewellery, not even a gold watch.

25 February Sunday Lovely day. Went to church this morning, and Baby and I went to the High-Life to see *Les Baderlans*, a historic piece in 10 parts. The place was cram full.

26 February Monday The Germans have sunk eight Dutch boats. Lovely day. Baby and I went to the Bois de la Cambre this afternoon.

27 February Tuesday Went to school this morning from 10 to 11. Manette invited me to her house, after tea Mr Konig took us to the cinema. Showers every now and then.

28 February Wednesday Foggy day.

1 March Thursday Fine day. We went to see a magic lantern at Miss Doyle's.

2 March Friday Went to see *Roman d'un Mousse*. Two German civilians came to our school this morning, so we were all obliged to go out from the concierge's parlour. How he swore! Snow and sleet.

3 March Saturday Today everybody has to declare their copper, linen, mattresses to the Germans. A fine scene this morning with her [Mother]: she said she hated, loathed the sight of me. Dined in my room.

4 March Sunday Went to C. Church. Lovely day, windy. She [Mother] beat me so that I ran away in the streets at 7 p.m.

5 March Monday Snow been falling all day. Came back last night at 10 p.m. She has kept me in all day, has taken my watch from me: breakfasted on a slice and a half of dry bread. Got an awful headache.

6 March Tuesday Went to sign at the Méridien. Daddy has told Father Lecourt all about Mother and I saw him today. He encouraged me and told me that if it becomes unbearable for me to stay at home he will try and get me to a boarding school. It was very nice of him. He also gave me 5 francs, because he says every girl must have a little pocket money to buy cakes or sweets, etc. And as Mother does not give me a cent and Daddy can't afford it, he is going to give 5 bobs every month, more if I want it. Very windy. A. and B. are supping with Mrs Gahan.

7 March Wednesday She won't let me go out of the house.

8 March Thursday Snow all day, rather cold. Stayed at home all day. The two boys have gone to the cinema. Wonder how long I shall have to be stuck indoors!

9 March Friday Bitterly cold! Snowstorm now and then. She let me go out today for commissions but I mustn't go to school till Monday. Mr Michaux sent a lettre recommandée saying that if Daddy does not pay him by the 15th what we owed him at Middelkerke he will put it into the hands of the 'Acquis de droit' [the 'holiday' in 1914 when war broke out?]. B. went to the cinema. A. to a friend.

10 March Saturday Rain and fog. B. went to the cinema. A. also at his friend's.

11 March Sunday Lovely warm day. She won't give me my watch back for a month, and only if I <u>behave</u> myself. It will be just like my four soldier buttons which she took months ago and pretends she has lost. Went to C. Church this morning. A. and B. gone to see a play acted at a boy's house. Spent the afternoon at home.

12 March Monday Showery. Went back to school this morning. We only go for one hour a day in the morning. I had to go and get lectured by the headmistress to whom she [Mother] had written that I was always going to cinemas, with bad girls, which isn't a bit true. Still, I let her say on; of course I couldn't tell her the true side. A. and B. went to town.

13 March Tuesday Wet day. As the weather is warmer we have class from 9 to 11.

14 March Wednesday Wet day. Count Zeppelin is dead.

15 March Thursday Lovely day. Baby and Mother went to town with Germaine Vandenlinden. Arthur went to his friend. Stayed at home and practised the piano.

16 March Friday Beautiful day. Mr Bormans is taken prisoner because he lied to cross the frontier. B. went to the cinema and A. to his friend. Sugar costs 10 frs the kilo.

17 March Saturday Lovely day. The Tsar of Russia has abdicated because of the numerous revolutions, and also because the soldiers will not obey him. An aeroplane passed at 9 p.m.

18 March Sunday Lovely day. The aeroplane which I heard last night threw some bombs at Margate. Baby and I went to church, and this afternoon we went to the High-Life to see a famous piece called *Glory and Riches* by Henri Bataille, and acted by Lyda Borelli. Franz Doehard played a piece of violin during an 'entracte'. No coal, no sugar, no potatoes, scarcely any bread, no oil, meat 10 francs the kilo, no butter, etc.

19 March Monday Rainy day.

20 March Tuesday The English and French are doing beautifully. Daddy beat Carl Ehrlich at billiards this afternoon. I am learning shorthand with Daddy. B. and I went to town this afternoon.

21 March Wednesday Snow. First spring day. Bitterly cold. The Germans fired off guns this afternoon.

22 March Thursday Hailstorms. Went with Daddy and M. [Mother] to the Savings Bank. Arthur went to his friend and B. to the cinema.

23 March Friday Very cold. Went to town with M.

24 March Saturday Freezing hard. Cannons very loud.

25 March Sunday Baby wishes Mother was a fairy. She's begun her beastly bullying again; kept me in my room when I came back from church and won't let me go out. Lovely day. Cannons very loud all day and especially at night.

26 March Monday Wet day. Cannons going all day.

27 March Tuesday Snow and hail. Went to Uccle. Some shots were fired at 2 p.m.

28 March Wednesday Fine day, very cold. After school I went to the General Post Office with Daddy.

29 March Thursday An Allied hospital ship has been sunk by a German submarine, and several CRBs coming with food have also been sunk. Lots of CRB men are quitting Brussels. Mother took Baby and me to the Eden. Wet day. Went to town this morning with Daddy.

30 March Friday Showers of hail and storm.

31 March Saturday At 2 p.m. there was a lightning and a clap of thunder. Showers. J. had to take our brass kettle and huge saucepan to the Germans. Holidays begun.

1 April Sunday, Palm Sunday I dined on eight beans. Another scene: she kept me in the whole afternoon because I did not come home in time to lay the table, which J. always lays on Sundays.

2 April Monday Our gas has been turned off because it can't be paid, and we will be in pitch darkness tonight. B. and I went to the Modern Cinema.

3 April Tuesday Snow whole morning and beastly wind. I have got a post to speak English to two girls of 10 and 14 every day, excepting Thursdays and Sundays, from 2 to 4 p.m. They live on the avenue Molière. Went to sign at the Méridien. They asked tenpence for a bunch of radishes.

4 April Wednesday Wet day. Went to Georgette and Suzanne Baes; their father is a big painter [Firmin Baes; they lived at 166 avenue Molière, Ixelles, in a Beaux-Arts house].

5 April Thursday America is on the point of joining the Allies. Went to the Cigale with J.

6 April Friday, Good Friday She called me a thief this morning and has washed her hands completely of me. I can go to the devil for all that she cares. Went to town with Georgette and Suzanne Baes.

7 April Saturday Snow. Cannons going. Went for a walk with S. and G. Then I went into their garden and saw the father's huge studio. B. went to cinema.

8 April Sunday, Easter Mrs Heineman sent me a chocolate egg. She [Mother] gave me nothing, didn't speak to me, excepting to ask me if I had stolen a letter with money in the letterbox. Went to Boitsfort this afternoon. She told me to be back at 5. Was a few minutes late, everybody was out, so I had to ask next door to let me get over the wall, which I did. Lovely day. Cannons going. B. went to the cinema.

9 April Monday Rain, hail and snow. Went to Uccle this afternoon. Baby went to the Eden theatre with her. My supper always is a wafer slice of bread and grease.

10 April Tuesday Same weather as yesterday. Went to S. and G. Baes. I had an invitation card for the High-Life, so I went and saw Sarah Bernhardt act in her play, *Adrienne Lecouvreur* [1913 film], and Hesperia. Franz Doehard played a beautiful violin solo.

11 April Wednesday At breakfast another scene began. She says she is paying four spies to spy on everything I do. Suzanne showed me some of her father's beautiful paintings. The best one is: *Belgium* [maybe *The Death of Ypres*]. One sees a tall woman who represents Belgium, holding her head with grief, all around her are ashes, cinders and some parts still smoking. It was painted in 1915. She and Baby have gone out again together, I suppose to the cinema. Cold and windy. All my time is spent in my room.

12 April Thursday Last night she locked me in my room without my supper. Thanks to Daddy I was released this morning. I went to Miss Watt; she was a dear and she gave me a cold leg of chicken and a delicious cup of tea. Then she paid me a lunch in town and gave me two marks. Went with S. and G. to Uccle to see about some hens, and after I went to the cinema. Baby and J. also went to the cinema. Cold day.

13 April Friday Took a letter to Von Bissing this morning [he died five days later]. Went to S. and G.

14 April Saturday Lovely day. Mme Halet has left for England. Went to the woods with S. and G. Georgette was not feeling very well, she had a pain in her side.

15 April Sunday Lovely morning, wet afternoon. Went to church this morning and to Boitsfort this afternoon. B's gone to the cinema. She gave me no tea and no supper.

16 April Monday School has begun again. Denise Bernard has come back. Suzanne Bourgeois, Suzanne Courrouble and I locked a whole class in, the $2^{\text{ème}}$ Moyenne A. Lovely day. Had tea with S. and G.: 3 slices of lovely homemade bread and apple jelly and butter; two pieces of paille feuilletée tart.

17 April Tuesday Snow and hail showers. Cannons very loud. At the place St Croix I saw a collision between the trams 82 and 30. All the glasses were smashed, and one or two of the tram-men were taken away badly wounded. Butter costs 20 francs the kilo. She has gone out to supper tonight.

18 April Wednesday At lunch she beat me and kicked me. She damned me; Daddy kept her away, but she made his hand bleed. She and Baby have gone to the cinema and are supping in town. I had half a piece of bread for breakfast, a tiny portion of rice and Daddy gave me his soup for lunch, no tea and no supper.

19 April Thursday A piece of dry bread for breakfast, and a dessertspoonful of rice for lunch. Went with S. and G. to their grandfather, who is also a painter. J. and B. have gone to the cinema.

20 April Friday Von Bissing is dead and all the cinemas must shut. I got a card from the Pass-Centrale in answer to my letter. After waiting over half an hour I went into a private room where a very nice officer received me. I have to fill in a paper and to go back tomorrow. [Amy seems to be trying to leave Belgium.] Went to S. and G.

21 April Saturday After school, at 10.30 a.m., went to the Pass-Zentrale. The man whom I saw yesterday says they will write to Berlin and see if my wish will be granted, and in a few days I shall get an answer. I met Mrs Nieslet and David there: they are going to Switzerland next week. B. and she have gone to town and A. went to the cinema with them. Went to S. and G. then had a delicious tea with [...]. Cold day.

22 April Sunday Beautiful day, cold. At 10.30 a.m. an enemy aeroplane flew over Brussels: it was a beautiful brand new one, I could not sleep till 2 a.m. last night, listening to the trains and wishing I was in one of them. Brought a bunch of flowers which I picked this afternoon in the beautiful park of Woluwe. B. went to the cinema. Had no tea.

23 April Monday Lovely day. At 9 a.m. an aeroplane passed, I think it was the same as yesterday. Went to G. and S., whom I've got very fond of. Went to see a beautiful piece of *Salâmbo* [film], at the Select.

24 April Tuesday After supper yesterday, Daddy called me down, while I was talking to him she suddenly sprang at me and gripped me at the back of my skull: it hurt. Daddy luckily released me; she slept in Auntie's room with the door locked. At 8.30 a.m. five new German aeroplanes flew over Brussels. Went to G. and S. She gave me no tea and no supper, so I had tea with Miss C. Beautiful day.

25 April Wednesday Colder day. Went to pick some anemones with G. and S. Another scene at lunchtime. She is telling everybody

1917

that I go out with bad girls, that I am a thief, a liar and a crapule [villain], etc. Had no tea. She supped out.

26 April Thursday Fine day. Went to see Henri Ollibaere's studio with G. and S. She gives me no more tea, so I had a very nice tea with Miss C. She took A. and B. to the cinema this afternoon.

27 April Friday At 10 p.m. there was a huge noise like an explosion. Went to G. and S.; had tea with Mrs Simms and went to town with Miss Mellin, who has made me a present of a brand-new coat. Cannons pretty loud. Daddy told me to get a packet ready, because at a moment's notice I may leave the house for good. Eggs cost 0f50 a piece.

28 April Saturday Today the eggs are at 0f75. Tennis has opened today. Went to G. and S., and then played tennis with Pierre Paquet. Cannons very loud. The new governor who has taken Von Bissing's place is now in Mr Brugmann's house. Fine day. She took up a chair to throw at me yesterday.

29 April Sunday Beautiful day. After her supper yesterday she said that if I was to come down she would scratch my eyes out, and as Daddy kept on calling me to come down, she came running up the stairs; pushed with all my strength against the door, as she could not come in to my room. A. spending the whole day out with his friend; she and B. have gone to the cinema and I went to tennis. Two Taubes flew over at 6 p.m. A Taube passed later at 8 p.m.

30 April Monday Beautiful day. 5 Taubes flew over at 4.30 p.m. Went to pick some flowers at the Bois with G. and S. She kept me in after 4 to keep the house, for everybody has gone out: didn't have a bite of food. Daddy lost 5 francs which had been put with some other money in an envelope: she immediately accused me. I hope they will find it for Daddy seems to think I have taken it. B. smashed a window: she said it was my fault for leaving it open.

1 May Tuesday Went to the Méridien with Daddy: we got there a few minutes before 11: the door was shut in our faces. Lots more people got there with us, so we will evidently have a fine. Went for the last time to G. and S. because Father Lecourt is sending me to a convent. Played tennis. A Taube passed at 6 p.m. Very hot day.

2 May Wednesday Said goodbye to my schoolfriends. Miss Mellin came to fetch me for lunch. We then went to buy my trousseau, a pair of dancing shoes, slippers and Mollière shoes. At 5 p.m. Daddy took me to the convent, rue Théodore Verhaegen [in St Gilles, about twenty minutes' walk from home]. The dormitory is very nice. We each have a little room without a door, only a white curtain, which leads into all the other alcoves. We have a plate of beans, rice and sugar and bread for supper. I have already made some friends. Anaïs, Marie Conception is a Spanish girl, and several others. We all go to bed at 8.30, a nun sleeps at each end.

3 May Thursday We get up at 5.30. Last night I could not sleep because a girl was snoring so loudly. We are allowed half an hour to dress, then we go to chapel. Breakfast at 7.30, religious reading at 8 a.m. then play till the class begins. There are over 100 boarders and 150 day girls. A lot of praying is done here. As I have no schoolbooks yet I am writing this during class-time. I have just received a note, slipped in a book; an unknown friend wrote it to ask me my name and if I will be friends with her. Her name is Yvonne Schoenmaekers; she is very pretty, but she is not a boarder. We lunch at 12 p.m., which is composed of rice soup, sometimes meat, vegetables. Lovely day. I am in the big class with the grown-up girls. We met Daddy in the Bois.

4 May Friday Very hot day. Daddy came to fetch me to go to the Méridien. My portefeuille, which contains my identification cards, letters, etc. have been stolen, as well as my nice piece of soap, out of my cupboard. I had to explain at the Méridien. The nuns are going to search every cupboard and desk. Every girl has to take the key of her cupboard wherever she goes. For several days the nuns say cupboards have been forced open. There was lovely music this morning in the chapel and Sister Christina sang. The thief threw my soap in the dirty basket.

5 May Saturday Suffocating day. Went to the swimming-bath with Angèle, Anaïs, Eva and Adèle and the 'concierge'. We left her there and we all went to buy some sweets. We got back long after tea, so we had tea, us five, together, which was very nice.

6 May Sunday Lovely day. Went to St Jacques church with some boarders this morning. This afternoon went to hear a speech of Mr Terlinden. We had potatoes for lunch.

7 May Monday Lovely day. A Taube passed at 8 a.m. Father Lecourt came to see me this afternoon.

8 May Tuesday Rainy day. I have always a headache in the afternoon now.

9 May Wednesday Lovely day. A G. aeroplane flew over Brussels.

10 May Thursday Lovely day. Miss Mellin fetched me this afternoon, and we went to the Quatre-Bras, had tea in a restaurant, and picked some bluebells. A Taube flew above. Miss Mellin bought me some lovely double-narcissus, which I gave to Sister St Charles. An old restaurant has been smashed in the rue Marché aux Herbes. 11 people were wounded and several killed. As it was so old it smashed of itself.

11 May Friday Very hot day. Yesterday Miss Mellin told me she had seen Mother the day after I left home. She came to ask where I was. Miss Mellin told her nothing, excepting that I was in a safe place. Mother is going to Miss Gifford's château at Boitsfort for change of air. I had my très-bien tonight.

12 May Saturday I had my two reports of both weeks today and I had all my points. Suffocating day.

13 May Sunday Terribly hot day. Went to St Gudule this morning and in coming back Sister Clarice let me see Daddy at the Union Club. He told me Mother is very ill, is so thin. Poor Mother. I suppose it was not her fault that she was not good to me. Went with some of the girls in the death-room of one of the lady lodgers of the convent, Mlle Monnom. She died this morning. I am very fond of Sister St Charles and Sister Christina. They are so good. Sister Andrew is very ill, but she is not in bed.

14 May Monday Thunderstorm at 5 a.m. and a huge one at 6 p.m. I lost my temper at teatime and I hurt Georgette Bormans. I wish I could keep in my temper. Terribly stuffy weather.

15 May Tuesday Lovely hot day. Diabolo is being played again. A lot of lilac is out in the garden.

16 May Wednesday Rainy day. A window-pane was smashed by diabolo.

17 May Thursday, Ascension Day Dull morning. Lovely afternoon. Went with Soeur St Charles and Soeur Clarice and the boarders to St Jacques's. In coming back we went to see the accident of the old house, rue Marché aux Herbes. Miss Mellin fetched me for lunch and then we went with her father to tea at Rouge-Cloître.

18 May Friday Huge thunderstorm, and enormous showers of rain from 1.30 p.m. to 3.30 p.m. A girl has lost a gold ring. A signal was flying about this morning.

19 May Saturday Showers every now and then. Have a horrid headache today.

20 May Sunday Very hot day. I stayed at home today, for I had a bad foot.

21 May Monday Went to bed early because I was ill.

23 May Wednesday Am feeling beastly sick.

24 May Thursday Still sick but am up.

25 May Friday Am better. Miss Mellin took me to tea at the Horloge and we bought lots of things. I brought back some flowers for Soeur St Charles. This morning we went with Soeur Christina to the St Gilles church to celebrate the 100th anniversary of the foundation of the Marist Fathers. Very hot.

26 May Saturday Lovely day. Very hot. Holidays till Tuesday for Whitsuntide.

27 May Sunday Terribly hot. Went with the girls who have not gone home to their parents to St Gudule. Miss Mellin fetched me for dinner and then we went to Trois Couleurs.

28 May Monday Boiling hot day. At 9 p.m. all the girls who did not go home and I accompanied by Soeurs St Charles, Christina, Maria-Cécile, Marie-Paula, Marie-Clarice and St Alphonse went for a pilgrimage to the Laeken Grotto. Crowds of people. A woman and a child fainted. We lunched and had tea at the Parc Rouge; we came back at 7.15 p.m.

29 May Tuesday Cooler. Daddy came to see me this morning and he brought me a ripping little silver watch, present from Mr Ehrlich. This afternoon Father Lecourt came. Soeur St Charles scolded me; it is the first time she has ever been so angry with me. I love her so much yet I am such a beast that I cannot even obey her.

30 May Wednesday Fine day. A Taube flew over this afternoon.

31 May Thursday I am no more friends with Yvonne [Schoenmaekers], she has too many.

1 June Friday There is a new boarder, a young kid. Very heavy weather. Had a delicious talk with Sister St Charles. Charlie's 18th birthday.

3 June Sunday Lovely day. Some German Taubes flew over Brussels this morning. Went to St Jacques church with the boarders. At 2 p.m. Daddy fetched me to go to tennis and there I saw Arthur and all my friends. Mother is at Boitsfort and Baby spent the afternoon with her.

4 June Monday A signal and an aeroplane we saw this morning. The new boarder is homesick. I was rude to Soeur St Charles.

5 June Tuesday Daddy fetched me to sign at the Méridien. When I got there I noticed I had forgotten my Carte d'Identité so I had to go back with Mlle Marthe. Stifling hot day. Soeur St Charles does not talk to me as she used to. She sees that it is no good, as I don't listen to her. She little knows how that I listen more to her than I have ever listened to anybody. But I forget. Have a terrible rival, Louise de Melina.

6 June Wednesday Last night I went to Soeur St Charles's dormitory to excuse myself for having behaved so badly. I remained with her for nearly half an hour. Oh! she was beautiful when I went in. She gave me a little religious book and has promised me <u>her</u> prayer book when I am more obedient.

7 June Thursday Suffocating hot day. Fête-Dieu [the Feast of Corpus Christi]. Went with the whole school, boarders, day girls and nuns, to the service at St Gilles, then this afternoon Miss Mellin and I had tea at Jette [north-west of the centre of Brussels].

8 June Friday Very hot and stuffy. Soeur St Charles has given me her black prayer book. Huge thunderstorm when we got to bed. Soeur Christina lit something up in the dormitory so as to stop the lightning from being quite so light.

9 June Saturday I am the 4th out of 32 girls for the Belgian exam.

10 June Sunday Mother's birthday. Went to St Gudule with the boarders. Very hot. Thunderstorm at 7 p.m. I got 20 sentences on obedience for punishment from Soeur St Charles and ten from Soeur Marie-Clarice for having jumped out of the window into the garden. Père Chanoine made a sermon in the chapel this afternoon.

11 June Monday I like Yvonne, the new girl, very much. Two inspectors, sent by the Germans, came to the Ecole-Gratuite to see if the children learn Flemish. The lady inspector who visits the school was sent to Germany this morning.

12 June Tuesday A few claps of thunder at 3 p.m. Last night a lady sang Mme Butterfly in a house on the avenue du Parc and from the dormitory we could hear her beautifully. She has a very cultivated voice. Francine, Rosa, Marie-Lucie, Eugénie and I rehearsed *Red Riding Hood* which we are acting for the Mother Superior's birthday. Very warm.

13 June Wednesday A few thunder shots this afternoon. Very close.

14 June Thursday Lovely day. Went for a walk with Sister Christina and the girls this afternoon. Gave a music lesson to one of the small girls. Soeur St Louis has given me a very nice piece of music, a slow waltz: it is very pretty. I should love to become a Roman Catholic. I have discovered that that religion is the real true one. How much better the girls feel when they have confessed to the Reverend Father. I saw Daddy at the window of the Union Club.

15 June Friday No lessons today because it is the fête of the Sacré-Coeur. Yvonne is not well so she is going to be only half-boarder till she is cured. Every morning I am going to try and polish Soeur St Charles's shoes, when I can find them. I have discovered the place where she puts them. Terribly hot. Got a note from Daddy last night to say he is coming to fetch me on Sunday afternoon.

16 June Saturday Soeur Christina has given me the permission to carry Soeur St Charles's books every night to her dormitory and have a small talk with her when I have been good. I have come out second for the French exams: 18 points ½ out of 20. Maxence presented me with a bunch of peonies last night. Miss Mellin came to see me this evening.

17 June Sunday Beastly warm. Went to St Jacques church this morning with the boarders, and this afternoon Daddy came and sat in the garden with me.

18 June Monday Very close and stuffy. Between 12 p.m. and 1 a.m. there was a big thunderstorm. The chapel did look lovely this afternoon. It had got quite dark suddenly at 5 p.m. so the candelabras were lit. Lovely flowers were on the altar, it looked just beautiful. I am playing a duet with Rosa for Soeur Supérieure's birthday.

19 June Tuesday Two big thunderstorms today. Big rehearsal of everything today. A gentleman sang last night.

20 June Wednesday Eve of the Big Saint, Saint Louis. We all fêted Soeur Supérieure this afternoon. Quarrelled with Eugénie Van

Loo, who called me a hypocrite, so am not going to play in *Red Riding Hood*. Felt pretty seedy this morning. The tea-tables were decked with lovely flowers.

21 June Thursday Lovely day. The girls acted, danced and played the music this afternoon to celebrate St Louis. An aeroplane flew over the convent this morning.

22 June Friday Showery. We thought we wouldn't be able to go for the excursion. It rained cats and dogs at 8 a.m. till 9.30 a.m. so every class began praying to stop the rain. At 9.30 we all went off, day girls as well, to Koekelberg. Made myself ill with gooseberries as green as leaves in spring, strawberries and cherries. Heard a very nice sermon at the Basilica de St Pierre. A kid fainted. Sat near Soeur St Charles in the tram in going, in coming back Anaïs sat near her, so was in bad temper. Soeur Louis is ill, so S. St Alphonse give me music lessons.

23 June Saturday Showery. S. St Charles has given me the Evening Prayer to copy as punishment, cause I laughed during prayers. My craze for the violin has begun again.

24 June Sunday I could not go to S. St Charles's dormitory last night as punishment. Presented my excuses to her this morning; she wouldn't accept them. A great change seems to have come over her towards me: she seems quite indifferent with me, when with Laure she laughs and talks by the hour. My character must be getting terribly jealous. Went to St Jacques this morning with the boarders. At 2 p.m. Soeur St Charles, Soeur Christiana and another nun took some of the big girls to a speech at the Salle Mercelis. A young Brother spoke beautifully and there was a little music. I have got S. St Charles's photo and I put it in her prayer book; come back from the speech, look and photo disappeared. Have smashed my watch. After congregation Frère Chanoine spoke to me about Catholic religion. He showed me so beautifully how that religion alone is the real, true one. Fine day. A lady fainted in church.

25 June Monday Baby's eleventh birthday. S. St Charles has taken the book because she says I don't pray. She won't let me go to her dormitory any more. No luck. Weather is much fresher.

26 June Tuesday Laurence pleaded for me and after some little time S. St Charles said: 'Very well, if she can find any books she can come tonight.' So thanks to Laurence I had a talk with her last night. Big thunderstorm during the night.

27 June Wednesday Showers every now and then. Lovely music last night in a neighbouring house. I am now going to learn the violin. Miss Mellin came this afternoon: she says Mother is worse.

28 June Thursday Dreamt Arthur came to see me. He looked very pale. I took him in the garden and introduced him to S. St Charles. When he saw her he got still paler than he was before, and went away. When I asked him the reason he said: 'Because she looked so like Mother when she was well.' And true enough she did look like her, same size and stoutness. Went to town with S. St Charles and the girls. A new boarder has come.

29 June Friday Big storm during the night. Lots of lightning. For some reason S. St Charles wants me to mortify myself in not going to her for nine evenings. Now it isn't fair: I can't speak to her all day because Laure is with her; but I console myself with the thought of the few happy minutes spent with her at night; but even that is stopped. She has so many that like her, there is no lack of rivals. There is a dear goat in the garden.

30 June Saturday Rainy day. S. St Charles keeps a death's head, a skeleton, on her writing-table. I wonder why.

1 July Sunday Went with the girls, S. St Charles and S. M. Clarice to the Carmes. Daddy fetched me to go to tennis at 2.30 p.m. Arthur and Baby were there. Came back early because I hate going to tennis. Mother is worse, Arthur told me. She always sleeps in Auntie's room. I asked him if I could write to her. He immediately said No. Mother said anything which comes from me will be torn up unread. When I got back I disobeyed; instead of going to the schoolroom I went elsewhere so I had to do a punishment and, worse still, I couldn't go to S. St Charles tonight. Cannons going.

2 July Monday As Soeur Christina had to see about the big girls' exams, S. St Charles said the meditation this morning, the best I've ever heard. Free time because it is the Visitation of the Virgin Mary. Soeur St Alphonse won't let me learn the violin till the holidays. Soeur St Charles has forbidden me to go to her tonight because I talked during study.

3 July Tuesday Daddy fetched me to sign at the Germans. They are now sending to Germany a lot of the Belgian aristocracy, for instance Comte d'Oultremont, Duc d'Ursel, and many more of Daddy's friends. Father Lecourt came this afternoon. German aeroplane was seen at 6 p.m.

4 July Wednesday Everything going on the same. I was very nearly not going to her dormitory.

5 July Thursday Lovely day. Went to town with S. St Charles and the girls. Talked with her nearly the whole way.

6 July Friday Lovely day. The moonlight last night was beautiful, I thought it was already daylight. S. St Charles only will let me carry her books to the dormitory and come away because some girls jabber instead of going to bed.

8 July Sunday Thunderstorm at 9 a.m. the sky was pink. S. St C. has again forbidden me to go tonight because I answered her rudely this morning. I give it up, it is impossible to be perfect. Daddy came to see me at 2.30 p.m.: he brought me my watch mended. Wet day.

9 July Monday I went all the same to her dormitory, without her knowing it, to arrange her table near the window. Jamina, the goat, is dead. After supper Soeur Christina got out the gramophone and we spent a jolly evening.

10 July Tuesday Nasty damp day. Felt pretty seedy this morning but it's passed.

[There follow two pages of most of the poem 'L'Expiation', in French, by Victor Hugo.]

11 July Wednesday Last night S. St Charles said to me: 'If you find me so severe, Amy, why don't you like another sister instead of me?' Fancy saying such a thing. Why, the severer she is, the more I love her. Nothing would make me change. Oh she did talk so beautifully. Bethmann, the German chancellor, has given his demission [he was forced to resign in July 1917]. Good news on all sides, all Bavaria has refused to go on fighting. The Germans are evacuating many places in the Flanders. At Düsseldorf a lot of rows are going on: the Hohenzollern and officers told the soldiers to fire on the civilians; instead of firing on the civilians the soldiers fired on the officers. Hope peace will soon be signed.

12 July Thursday This morning in going into chapel I suppose I was taking my time. S. St Charles took me roughly, by the arm. Lost my temper and refused to go to the service, but I went all the same. Now as if it is not enough that Laure pores over her desk in her class, but now when it is not her it's her sister. No room for me, two's company, three's none, that's how the world goes round. No roses without thorns. Love her more and more.

[A new notebook starts below. The first sixteen pages are in French written in 1917, not diary entries, followed by a few lines of shorthand. Then Amy starts with the same date.]

12 July Thursday Lovely day. Miss Mellin took me to Wemmel [north of Brussels city centre]. It was beautiful there.

13 July Friday Warm day. S. St Charles would not accept my excuses. We all went to the Parc Duden and picked some flowers. It's a ripping place with a castle in it. Several German aeroplanes passed today. The girls who went for their exams the other day all got their diploma, so two of them, the nicest, Adrienne Bolie and Hélène Romainville, left for their holidays tonight.

14 July Saturday Lovely day. Am really mad with joy. Soeur Christina called me this morning to a small room where a professor of violin was, and I am to begin with him on Wednesday. I can't believe it's true. While going to bed S. St Charles gave me back her prayer book but in it I found a photo of her with Laure.

15 July Sunday Lovely day. Went to St Jacques with the girls. Another rival turned up, another Laure. It increases every day. Am getting desperate. S. St Charles tells me that it isn't she who put that photo in the book, and now it's disappeared and think I am hounded. S. St Charles does not look well today. Little Georgette Govens fell down and bit her tongue which has produced a horrid cut, and another girl fell and hurt her wrist.

16 July Monday Am not going any more to her at night because I have discovered that she does not care for me, so am not going any more.

17 July Tuesday Soeur Bernardine is suffering. I went to S. St Charles tonight and she says it's all an idea. It's all very well to say that, but why does she not like me to give her flowers, to arrange her table at night, to carry her books for her, etc?

18. Arthur in Coquitlam, BC, Canada, 1972. From left to right: Doris's son Kendall Walker, Doris's grandson Conrad and wife Rose, Arthur, Arthur's son Chad Hodson and daughter-in-law Sharon

18 July Wednesday Just a year ago at 9.30 p.m. that poor Auntie quitted this earth. Miss Mellin came this afternoon. Can't help noticing how ill S. St Charles looks. The violinist didn't turn up, had an engagement. Thunderstorm at 6.30 p.m.

19 July Thursday Arthur's thirteenth birthday. Not a word have I said to S. St Charles the whole day; it's awful. Miss Mellin took me to town this afternoon, had hot chocolate at Marchal's. A young violinist, the brother of a day girl, is dying, it is very sad, because he thinks he's getting better, and it's just the contrary.

20 July Friday Second awful day, not a word have I been able to say to her. Exams are all finished, thank goodness. S. St Charles combed me. Fine day. Blanche Bataille being the friend of the violinist's sister feels his death, which is almost certain, very much. Miss Mellin and Mme Deltan came for a few minutes this afternoon.

21 July Saturday There was a most beautiful concert given in a house on the avenue last night. By turns a man played the violin divinely, a lady and a gentleman sang 'l'Angelus de la Mer', Madame Butterfly, and all kinds of lovely things. It lasted till near midnight. Holiday today for it's the national fête. We all went to the service at St Gilles; the choir-boy was very fidgety and impatient to get the service over. Georgette Bormans and several other girls left for their holidays today. This afternoon we acted and played before the girls and some of the nuns as a kind of last rehearsal before Soeur Marie-Christina's birthday. Recited 'The Death of Sir John Moore'. Saw my star last night from my bed.

22 July Sunday Lovely day. Soeur St Charles went with us to St Gudule. Daddy took me to tennis this afternoon. He says Mother looks still thinner than before, she said very little, has no taste for anything. Last night the girls who are acting and I played hide-and-seek in a long kind of underground hole; we shut ourselves in, and as it was pitch dark we sat on nails, ladders, splinters of wood, etc. Bumped my head well in getting out. Went to her last night.

23 July Monday When I went to her tonight she let me know that she doesn't want me to go any more, and this time I have made up my mind never to go again. What I think is this, that somebody else goes and takes her books instead of me. I asked her the reason why: 'Because you are not "convenable"' was the expression. We all got kissed by Soeur Marie-Christina as it's the eve of her fête.

24 July Tuesday Had my violin lesson with Mr Veydt and he's lent me his violin. Mr Wauters, the inspector, came this morning and gave us pictures. At 2 p.m. we all went to the 'Gratuites' and acted before the girls what we are going to do tonight for Soeur Christina. Everything went off very well. Four times we had to do the 'Voyage à Paris'. At 9.15 p.m. we went to bed, cannons terribly loud in the night. Lovely day. Laure and her sister sat near S. St Charles.

25 July Wednesday Thunderstorm this morning. Forgot to write down the other day that some Allied aeroplanes came over Brussels at 7 a.m. The Germans fired after them, don't know the result. We all acted and sang and recited again this afternoon for Soeur Christina and the girls.

26 July Thursday Girls are packing up, classes being washed out. Played 53 pages out of the violin music.

27 July Friday Beautiful weather. Last lesson day, Monsieur le Chanoine came at 2.30 p.m. and gave us all the quarterly reports. Lots of girls have gone back for their holidays.

28 July Saturday More girls left today. Very warm. Cannons going fast tonight. Helped to clean out Soeur Marie-Paula's class with Soeur St Charles and Soeur Christina, etc. As S. St Charles wouldn't let me help her in her class I was determined to work with her, and so I did, but Laure turned up worse luck. Things are not going as well as before; so goes the world.

29 July Sunday It's fun when there are such few girls. Warm day. Think there was a mad woman in the street last night, when we all were in bed; there was a woman's loud scream then lots of shouts after, as if somebody wanted help. Don't know the result. At lunchtime it suddenly got so dark that we could not see ourselves.

<u>Emploi du temps</u>

7h ¼ <u>Déjeuner</u>
7h ½ <u>Charges</u>.
8h à 9h. <u>Récréation</u>.
    9h. <u>Visite au St Sacrement</u>.
9h ½ <u>Etude</u> - <u>Ecriture</u> - ouvr. man.
10h ¾ <u>Récréation</u>.
11h. <u>Etude</u> - <u>Ecriture</u> - ouvr. man.
12h. <u>Dîner</u>.
12h ½ <u>Récréation</u>   Répétition de
2h. { <u>Lecture et</u>   Salle de   violon
    { ouvr. man   piano
4h. <u>Goûter</u>
5h. <u>Chapelet</u>
5h ½ h. <u>Etude</u>. <u>Ecriture</u> ouvr. man:
6h ¼ h. <u>Lecture Spirituelle</u>.
6h ¾ h. <u>Prière du soir</u>:
7h. <u>Souper</u>
7h ½ h. <u>Récréation</u>
8h ¼ <u>Coucher</u>

    Le 30 juillet 1917 - Bruxe. St Gilles.

19. Amy's boarding-school timetable, 30 July 1917

Rain came pouring down, thunder and lightning. Thought the end of the world was coming, but it wasn't. We are still all living. Getting on with my violin. I wonder how I could have remained so long without having learned it.

30 July Monday Another deception; today we're all changing from the big dormitory to the first floor, when I was longing to go to the second. There are only fifteen girls left.

31 July Tuesday Had a rotten night. Went to the baths this afternoon.

1 August Wednesday Am to keep silence for the whole day cause I spoke after breakfast and was caught by S. St Charles. Cold day.

2 August Thursday Went for a small walk to the Parc Duden with Soeur Christina and the girls; we had to come back soon because it began to rain. Said 500 Ave Maria this afternoon to obtain lots of 'indulgences'. Don't know that word in English. Jesus granted one of the biggest. Soeur St Charles let me go to her tonight and I had such a delicious talk with her. But the time always goes so quick when I am with her. Am feeling rather seedy.

3 August Friday Wet day. Nothing new. When I went to practise my violin found a string broken.

4 August Saturday Several girls are feeling ill today. Just three years since the war began. Dreamt last night that Miss Mellin came to tell me that Lady Phipps was adopting. An auto was waiting for me outside. Was searching everywhere for Soeur St Charles and at last I found her in a big room. It was so awful to have to say goodbye to her. She gave me two kisses, instead of three. At last I went off in the car and came to Lady Phipps's lovely château in the country. Nothing could take away my thoughts from Soeur St Charles, and when I woke up how pleased I was to see that it was only a bad dream. Soeur Marie-Clarice is not well today.

5 August Sunday Lovely day. S. St Charles came with us to the church in the rue Neuve. Had tea with Daddy at tennis. Cannons going.

6 August Monday Went to the St Gilles park with the girls. Stormy feeling in the air.

7 August Tuesday Went to sign with Daddy at the rue du Méridien. We need not go any more nor the French either.

8 August Wednesday Went to the park with the girls. Went to her last night; for the 1st time she asked me to fetch her book.

9 August Thursday Thunderstorm last night. Spoke to M. le Chanoine. He's told me to write to him a letter expressing my wish which he will send to the Cardinal. Laurence has put her hair up, she's nineteen.

10 August Friday We went to town with Soeur St Charles. Mr Veydt is very pleased with my violin.

11 August Saturday Had a beastly night. Felt sick and pains. Citine was delicately carrying a plate with American bifsteak, when Germaine Wauters went up to her and said: 'Let's see what's in it.' She gives it a punch and down goes the plate, smashed to atoms.

12 August Sunday Lovely day. Assisted a very nice service in town. Soeur St Charles etc. accompanied us. The yearly retreat for the nuns began at 8 p.m. last night and we are not allowed to them till Friday. German aeroplane passed.

13 August Monday Scarcely a sound is heard throughout the house. A reverend father preaches four times a day for the nuns. Am looking forward to the retreat for girls which is beginning on the 26th. As we had kept quiet for the whole day, Soeur Christina told us to play and have a good time after supper and by gaudy! we did. We played hide-and-seek and blindman's buff. Lovely day. Few showers. Soeur St Charles appeared at lunchtime.

14 August Tuesday Not to disturb the retreat I carry my violin up to the loft of the Patronage and there I practise the whole morning in peace. Have not been allowed to say one word to Soeur St Charles, scarcely saw her, only at chapel time. She looks quite pale and ill. Lovely day.

15 August Wednesday Lovely service of chapel this morning in honour of the Virgin Mary's fête. Soeur St Charles came for a few minutes in the dormitory this morning and half an hour in the schoolroom after lunch but couldn't speak to her. Aeroplane passed yesterday at 5.30 p.m.

16 August Thursday Mlle Catherine lost the keys which open her door; nobody knows exactly who hid them as a joke. She had to go in by the window. They disappeared at 12 a.m. and now it's 6.15 p.m.

17 August Friday Georgette Bormans has been run over by the tram and will be operated tomorrow in the foot. As nobody has accused herself about the keys which were found in a desk, the culprit is me. Soeur Christina said the other day that nobody can have a good place in heaven without having passed by a little suffering, so I expect all the girls will look upon me as a thief and a sneak. But as long as my conscience is quiet, what matters it? I have no idea who on earth has done it, but if she had been found out she would maybe have been sent away. I don't know if I'm doing right, but I pity the poor girl who is keeping it quiet. I have lost all trust, and in Soeur Christina's eyes she told me. She can't understand how I could have slept last night with such a sin on my conscience, but I only thought of it this morning.

18 August Saturday Soeur St Charles sent me to Sister Superior's parlour to get scolded because I practised my violin in the loft instead of going to chapel. She didn't keep me for more than three minutes. As luck would have it Anaïs was also waiting to get a scolding. A whole lot of young girls have come to pass their exams. Among them is an English girl, Marg Pitts.

19 August Sunday I could not go to bed without telling Soeur St Charles the whole truth about the keys. She is the only person who knows. The other people still think me guilty. The culprit has not yet been found out, and never will be I expect. We went to St Catherine this morning with S. St C., etc. Daddy took me to the Léopold Club to see the greatest lady tennis champion play, Mlle Van Staeten, then we went on to tennis and had tea out there. Lovely day.

20 August Monday Laurence, Mimi, Laure de Molinari and Germaine with all the young ladies went off at 6.30 a.m. to the place in town where they are to pass their exams. Soeur St Charles said a beautiful meditation. Lovely day.

21 August Tuesday Henri Seret and Marcel Bormans are both prisoners in Germany for having tried to cross the frontier. Two new nuns have come with the girls who are passing their exams, Soeur Apauline and Soeur Camille. Flore Deujck is leaving for Pêches at break of day tomorrow to learn how to become a nun. Soeur Louis and Soeur St André left for Pêches this morning to regain their health. We spent the whole day at the Bois de la Cambre with Soeur St Charles, Soeur Maria-Cécile, Soeur Marie-Paula and Soeur Marie-Clarice. Lovely day. Laure Lessine has come over for two days and she came to the Bois with Soeur St Charles. Cannons loud.

22 August Wednesday Beautiful weather. We spent the morning at the Parc Duden. Cannons very loud.

23 August Thursday Spent the whole day near the 'Ferme Rose'. Picked some blackberries and heather. A big storm broke out at 5 p.m. We had to take shelter in a farm, but trees were smashed in two and a big chestnut tree was uprooted. Rosa Secleppe has come back to school.

24 August Friday Began my second position for the violin this morning.

25 August Saturday Because I hid Germaine's hat Soeur St Charles was furious. Of course it was a stupid thing to do, but I thought it would be such fun to see her searching for it.

26 August Sunday Lovely day. Several signals flying about. Am kept in silence till lunchtime because I wouldn't go out. So first I hid in the chapel but Soeur St Charles made me go down. As I wouldn't move Soeur Supérieure was fetched, but I was already in a cellar. When the girls were all gone, Soeur Supérieure saw me and I have to write out choice sentences on a solitary bench. Anyhow I didn't go out, that was what I wanted. I know why I'm getting so horrid, it's because I don't pray so well the last few days. The retreat begins today at 5 p.m. Hope I shall be better for all the sermons.

27 August Monday I sleep now in Emily's bed because a lady is sleeping in mine. A Reverend Father says four sermons a day. The one I liked the best today was the fourth about Death. A whole lot of girls and ladies have come to do the retreat. The boarders have to go in a small room of the Patronage. Soeur Philomène and S. St Charles do the 'surveillance'.

28 August Tuesday The Reverend Father preaches very well.

29 August Wednesday Soeur St Charles scolded me terribly today. Twice I knocked my glass of water over the table. She says I'm following the devil, that I must be mad. It was terrible the way she talked, but I guess I deserved it.

30 August Thursday Last day of the retreat. Rd Père Cyrille blessed our medals and all the religious things. Asked him several things I wanted to know and he counselled me to pray a lot to the Virgin Mary. S.S.C. wouldn't let me speak to her last night. She was just going downstairs and told me to go to bed, but I remained on the stairs till she came back again. It would have been better if I hadn't because all she said was: I told you to go downstairs. Down I went, not greatly relieved. Daddy came for a few minutes this afternoon. Emily was operated in the foot this morning.

31 August Friday A new girl has come. Didn't see a sign of S.S.C. till after 5.30 p.m. She scarcely comes with us now. I'm quite blue about her.

1 September Saturday Pretty cold. Germaine Georlette has left school for good. Spoke a long time with Germaine Wauters about S.S.C. Germaine was blue about her at the beginning. As it was the fête of St Gilles we went to church and then had a walk to town.

2 September Sunday Very windy. Daddy took me as well as Arthur and Baby to Waterloo. We visited the Ferme d'Hougoumont, where there is a small chapel belonging to a ruined castle; then we saw the Death well, the Ferme de la Belle Alliance, all the monuments and said good-day to the lion. We discovered a ripping plum tree and walnut trees. Robert Danly has crossed the frontier with Mr Bivoire. We met the Delcoignes at Waterloo.

3 September Monday Am following the advice of the Reverend Father. Already a change is coming over me: I try hard not to think of S.S.C. and, with some difficulty, I manage to do it. Rénée Roberhoid has come back; she sleeps next to me.

4 September Tuesday Lovely day. We all went to the Parc Duden with S.S.C. I haven't really spoken to her for a week. I'd gone off with three girls to pick some blackberries in the shrubs of the park when two guardians rushed out on us. The girls ran five hundred miles an hour and left me along with them. I explained to them that we weren't doing any harm.

5 September Wednesday Lovely day. Two aeroplanes passed at 6 p.m.

6 September Thursday Have got a violin of my own now. Soeur St Charles said the meditation this morning and will tomorrow also.

7 September Friday Last night it was pitch dark when I went alone to the chapel; only a dim light was burning.

8 September Saturday Went for a walk with S.S.C. and the girls. Soeur Madeleine left today, Madeleine is terribly sad.

9 September Sunday Lovely day. Went to Wemmel with Daddy, Arthur and Baby. When I came back, dead tired, Soeur St Charles gave me a lecture because I came down two minutes later than the others. Had to remain alone in the office whilst the others supped. I don't like her any more.

10 September Monday Mimi has sprained her ankle; stayed in the garden with her this afternoon. Laure de Molinari has gone for good. Got in an awful row because I mixed up all the girls' services for a joke; but we did laugh to see the boarders rushing about looking for their spoons, forks, etc.

12 September Wednesday My love for S.S.C. has come back, it never really went away.

13 September Thursday My fête. Tonight we're all going back to the big dormitory so we went to arrange our cupboards. Soeur St Charles did part of mine.

14 September Friday We're arranging all the classes for school begins on Monday.

15 September Saturday Miss Mellin took me out for an hour to get some things. In the morning there is no nun to wake us up as we are so few so we stayed in bed till 6 a.m. It was too late to go to Mass, Soeur St Charles came at 6.10 to make us get up.

16 September Sunday The girls and I went for a walk at Forêt this morning. At 4 p.m. we assisted a most touching service in Father Lecourt's church because it is the fête of Notre-Dame des Sept Douleurs. There was a procession round the church; it lasted an hour and a half. Cannons very loud. Lovely day. Aline Goble came back today.

17 September Monday Holidays are over. The girls came back the whole day. It was jolly at supper: the lights were lit and in the dormitory also. There are lots of new girls. I've gone up into Soeur St André's class.

18 September Tuesday More girls have come back.

19 September Wednesday It's too dark to play in the yard after supper so we all go in the big playroom. Soeur St Charles and some other mistresses played with us. It was fun, especially at musical chairs.

20 September Thursday Lovely day. Have begun again my piano. I have now one lesson of violin and one of piano a week. Miss Mellin took me to town; had a delicious ice at the Dutch shop, then we bought odds and ends.

21 September Friday Germaine Wauters is going to a boarding school at Louvain on Monday. Had a good fall at recreation time this afternoon.

22 September Saturday Mr Veydt is teaching me the third position [violin].

23 September Sunday Went to S. St Charles last night, haven't been for ages. Walked with the girls to the Bois there and back. Daddy came, but I was practising where I ought not to, and when I appeared Daddy had gone. S.S.C. keeps on trying to make me leave off learning the violin because she says it's against Daddy's will. It's curious how everything always goes against my learning it.

27 September Thursday The Germans were firing after people carrying potatoes at the Barrière de St Gilles. At Laeken 2 millions of francs worth of provisions have been burnt by the workmen at the Entrepôt. A lot of cheating had been going on and they heard that a list was going to be made and, frightened of being found out, they set fire to the building. Went to town with Miss Mellin; had tea and ice at the Italian shop, then we went to the Grand Bazar; she bought me two little cupid-dolls and a Japanese doll. Lovely day.

28 September Friday A new girl has come; she learns the violin.

29 September Saturday Blanche Bataille's cousin, Germaine Descamps, is a boarder. She goes to the Conservatoire for the piano, which she plays beautifully. Miss Mellin fetched me to choose a fur at Franchomme's. Lovely day. St Michael's fête.

30 September Sunday Went for a walk to Forest with the girls. Played tennis this afternoon and had tea with Daddy. Three aeroplanes, German I think, passed after lunch. The Germans are now taking every single thing which is in copper or brass: candlesticks off the piano, candelabras, artistic things.

2 October Tuesday Lovely day. Am learning Mozart's sonatas. Fête of the Adoration of St Gilles; all our class as well as Soeur St Charles's went to the church. Sarah Maes has gone back to her home.

3 October Wednesday Thunderstorm at 3 a.m. A fire engine was rushing up the avenue du Parc last night.

4 October Thursday Angèle Cheveral is now my friend. We went out for a nice walk to Forêt; there was a high wind, so we took off our hats. It was great fun; then we went to the Parc Duden and played there a while. Weather getting colder.

5 October Friday Soeur St Charles has forbidden me to do any music today as a punishment.

6 October Saturday Wet and cold. Am learning the double notes on the violin.

7 October Sunday Germaine Descamps has a piano of her own at the Patronage, and she let Angel, Germaine and I hear her play. Blanche sang. It was quite a lovely concert; the only drawback was that Soeur St Charles fetched me too soon and so I had to go out with the girls. Soeur Christina gave me permission to go to S. St Charles last night. Pretty cold.

9 October Tuesday Nearly had a fit this afternoon. The girls all began talking about Soeur St Charles going away. At teatime she suddenly left the refectory; I was told it was to arrange her luggage. Nearly blue with emotion, I got up and – what do I see but Hélène coming in with an enormous bundle. The girls all roared with laughter and said: it's Soeur St Charles's luggage. After having a runabout and asked all sorts of questions it turned out to be all a joke: they'd done it just to bother me. Germaine Wauters has come back to have particular lessons with S.S.C.

11 October Thursday Went with the whole school to the St Gilles Mass to celebrate the Holy Ghost's fête. Wet day. Never will Soeur St Charles allow me to carry her books for her; all the others may. It's rather hard. Again my good resolutions are spoiled.

14 October Sunday Was transported into heaven last night because I remained a while in S.S.C.'s dormitory. We went for a walk near the Midi this morning. Georgette Bormans came to see the mistresses. She told us how the accident happened. The doctors had to give her artificial blood, because she had none left. A priest came to administer her; they thought she was done for. Soeur St Charles was exceptionally nice with me this afternoon. It's difficult to say if I like Angel very much; it's of course S.S.C. who comes first. Today is the fête of St Thérèse, a saint very much liked in this school. Anaïs sang last night after supper and Blanche Bataille recited a lovely piece of poetry about a violinist. Wet day. Two G. aeroplanes at 4.30 p.m.

15 October Monday Lovely day, pretty cold. Two stars fell this evening.

16 October Tuesday Another G. aeroplane. Had such a ridiculous fall; I'd just finished accompanying Adrienne at the piano, when, in getting out of the little room, I tumbled head over heals into a coal back, knocked several things over. Instead of helping me up the girls all burst with laughter; what could I do but laugh with them? I felt the fall when I got up.

17 October Wednesday Now as Laure de Molinari has gone, her sister, Marie-Lucie, takes her place. She's nearly always with S.S.C. Smashed a string of my violin this afternoon. Lovely day.

18 October Thursday Lovely afternoon. Another rival: Rosa Appelmans; and the lucky girl is in Soeur St Charles's class. We walked to the Bois de la Cambre; in coming back I saw Arthur. G. aeroplane flew quite low at 3.30 p.m. Couldn't practise the violin.

19 October Friday Wet and cold.

20 October Saturday Zeppelin flew over Brussels several times today. Soeur St Charles was going to give me a yellow card today but she isn't now. Oh she was so nice this afternoon!

21 October Sunday Cold. Went to St Jacques with the boarders. Laure de Molinari is going to be a kind of mistress in the school. Cannons rather loud this afternoon.

22 October Monday For the first time the chapel was lit this afternoon. Soeur Seraphina gave me a good mark. Every night after supper, as it's pitch dark, I go up to the choir and say my prayers there. Only a dim light burns in the end part of the building; everything is as quiet as death.

23 October Tuesday The leaves of the tree in the school-yard are all on the ground. Soeur St Charles has told me not to speak to her any more because I disobeyed. Miss Mellin came this afternoon. Wet day.

25 October Thursday After lunch we went out for a walk to Forest. Very windy.

26 October Friday Went to the baths with Angel. All the dogs higher than forty cm must be given in to the Germans. No boot shop can have more than five pairs of boots in the window. After tea I went to Soeur St Charles to ask her if I could speak to her again; she would not listen to me.

27 October Saturday Rita came to see me this morning, and this afternoon I went to town with her; we had tea at a tart shop in front of the Gare du Nord; then she bought me a brooch and some chrysanthemums for Soeur St Charles. She had a small talk with S.S.C. Moon is veiled. After supper, Soeur Marie-Christina told Angel and I that we are not to go together any more, we are separated for good, because we write to each other.

28 October Sunday Soeur St Charles is so nice again with me. Went to St Gudule with the boarders. After lunch Soeur Christina let us dance in the playroom. Mimi played the piano. Now Soeur St Charles has separated me from Germaine Honoré. Cold day. We had the gramophone out this evening. Another new boarder.

29 October Monday It was so dark this morning to dress that the gas had to be lit. Soeur St Alphonse is teaching me 'Minuit, Chrétiens' to accompany with the violin for Soeur St Charles's fête.

30 October Tuesday Our class fêted Soeur St Charles this morning;

she gave us free time so we had no lessons. Two G. aeroplanes passed. Fine day.

31 October Wednesday Holidays begin today at 4 p.m. till Monday because of All Saints. Lots of girls are going home; Angel has left also. Soeur St Charles allowed me to go in her class with her pupils. We played several games and she told us our future.

1 November Thursday, All Saints' Day I almost hate Soeur St Charles now. She has taken my violin, has stopped me from going to the piano. Then she said that it was through me that Mother was ill, that I was fit to be in the streets, and all sorts of things. She made me copy out of a book till seven o'clock.

2 November Friday We had three consecutive Masses at chapel this morning: lovely singing. Soeur St Charles said a whole lot more horrid things this morning. Altogether everything is not going very well for the second day of All Saints' holidays. After lunch Soeur Christina took us to the Forest cemetery. Wet day. A whole day passed without having touched either my violin or the piano. The stove was lit in the schoolroom.

3 November Saturday At 6.30 a.m. we went to a funeral service at St Alène instead of going to Mass here. Soeur St Charles gave me ever so many punishments this morning; after lunch I got back my violin. Saw Mother this afternoon. Miss Mellin said it was better for me to see her. She would not let me go near her at first, but after Miss Mellin had spoken to her, Mother gave me a very cold kiss. She says she has not a spark of affection for me left in her. When I left she kissed me, but it was a much better kiss. I think she has got much thinner. Then I went to town, met Daddy, and I bought a basket with ferns in it for Soeur St Charles. The Italians are not doing very well.

4 November Sunday Soeur St Charles's fête. Cannons were pretty loud this afternoon. We went to bed at 7.30 last night.

5 November Monday All the girls have come back. Got a letter from Daddy. Am learning a rather pretty duet, 'Arlequine', with Mimi;

we have to play it when the girls practise their gymnastics for Soeur Supérieure's fête. At 4 a.m. the cannon was going. Am feeling rather seedy, throat is hurting.

6 November Tuesday Several girls have brought to school a whole lot of little pink things which one puts in toy revolvers, and every now and then a girl accidentally or purposely puts her foot on it and it makes a frightful noise. Lots of pupils have their yellow cards because of that. Laure de Molinari has given me my yellow card because I laughed when she came to the 'surveillance'.

7 November Wednesday Now Germaine Bassyns says she likes Soeur St Charles. I don't believe it. Angel has given me back my photo, because she pretends I'm Alix Menton's friend.

8 November Thursday We went to the cemetery of Calevoet; in coming back we had to tram because it was too late. Soeur St Charles has already sent my flowers out of her class, as she said she would do the first time I disobeyed.

9 November Friday Soeur St Charles has again taken my violin away: it happened after tea in the 'salle de piano'. Nearly every evening the girls rehearse the 'Massues' hymn, and Mimi and I play a duet. Laurence is learning the duet too, so I'm only playing it for the moment. Drizzly weather. Anaïs came this afternoon for a little while.

10 November Saturday Soeur St Charles has given me back my violin and the little doll. Angel has made it up again. Germaine Bassyns says it is not true that she likes Soeur St Charles. I knew it.

11 November Sunday Daddy took Arthur and me to Hal [south of Brussels]. We visited the church, and there was a lovely service. The German band was playing outside the House of Commons [town hall, Maison Communale]. Jack Jenkins is a lieutenant. Daddy told me that Mother fainted dead away at the Trocadero the other day. Arthur has passed his exams. A retreat is beginning tonight at 7.30 for the boarders by the Reverend Père Someville. Georgette Bormans has come back as a boarder.

12 November Monday I forgot to put yesterday that all the way to Hal there were big trees cut down; the Germans force men to cut them so that they can make guns with them.

13 November Tuesday Soeur St Ch. has got all my 'billets'. I had to tell her where I put them and she went to fetch them.

14 November Wednesday Renée Ledrut suffers from a sore on her side. Today is the 'confession générale'; the girls all feel so happy when they come back from the confessionnal.

15 November Thursday King Albert's fête. The closing of the retreat was at 10 a.m. A touching Mass was held this morning with a sermon; every single girl went to Communion. Had a private talk with the Reverend Père Someville. Renée Ledrut read a compliment out to the Father before he left and he gave us a benediction. Went out for a walk with the girls after dinner. Some day girls brought me a sparrow which they had caught and couldn't fly. It escaped out of my hands, tried to fly, but banged itself against a window. The poor

20. Lieut. Jack Jenkins (far left), Royal Army Service Corps, probably Boulogne, c. 1918

little thing has broken its legs. A girl put it back in the garden for the parents to come and fetch it. The central heating was lit today.

16 November Friday Soeur St Charles read all the 'billets'. Lessons have begun again. A new girl has come.

17 November Saturday Mr Veydt is very pleased with the progress of my violin. Georgette Bormans suffers with her foot.

18 November Sunday Am punished for the whole afternoon. Soeur Christina has given me a lot to copy out; I mustn't practise the violin nor the piano today. Soeur St Charles has made Alix give up all her 'billets' which I have written her. Angel, Alix and I had a scolding from Soeur Supérieure about these wretched bits of paper. I wrote on a slate from 1 p.m. till 7 p.m. After tea the girls rehearsed the gymnastics. Angel felt ill at supper. We passed in front of our house this morning, with the boarders, saw Daddy but I couldn't speak to him.

19 November Monday I am separated from Angel, from Germaine, Alix and Juliette. Just as I was speaking alone to Angel in the yard Soeur St Charles fell upon us. She took Angel to Soeur Supérieure; I stayed behind. After chapel Soeur St Charles spoke a long time. She says I'm absolutely corrupted, that I was possessed with a devil, and lots more. Soeur St Charles coughs a good deal. Soeur Christina put us in silence at lunchtime, but as it was Queen Elisabeth's fête we were allowed to talk after five minutes of silence. Another new boarder, a big one.

20 November Tuesday Soeur St Ch. has given me thirty sentences to write out. Remained in solitary confinement from 2.30 till 4.15 in Soeur Supérieure's little room because I was rude to Soeur Seraphina and also because I disturbed the class. Couldn't do any music.

21 November Wednesday We had holiday today because it was the fête of the Virgin Mary's Presentation to the Temple; all the boarders remained in the study-room. Received the first big smack from her hand this morning. Marie-Lucie de Molinari is going to play the duet instead of me because I've not been good. Again a new boarder.

Laurette Mignon has been sent away from school. As tomorrow is St Cécile we're all going to fête Soeur Christina tonight, as she is a musician, as well as Sr Alphonse, Sr Maria-Cécile. Great excitement this morning; a mouse was running in the yard. The girls all began to scream. Martha Mauroy killed it with a spade.

22 November Thursday Sr St Charles has taken my violin away again, but for two weeks this time. Soeur Christina has forgiven me and I can play the duet with Marie-Lucie. Miss Mellin took me to town this afternoon; we had ice and hot chocolate in a tea room in the rue Neuve; there was lovely music, two violins, a cello, and a grand piano. The piece they played is called 'Paillasse'. I haven't been able to speak to S.S.C. for goodness knows how long. At 3 a.m. the cannons were very loud. The Reverend Père Someville called me in the 'parloir' this afternoon; he has been kind enough to inquire about my becoming a Roman Catholic; he says I must wait till I come of age because everything would go well so long as I was at school, but if I were to leave I wouldn't be able to go to Communion, etc. Marthe Soupart is not well.

23 November Friday Marie Conception came this afternoon; she's thinking of becoming again a boarder.

24 November Saturday I couldn't have my (music) violin lesson because Sr St Charles has not yet given me back my violin, so Mr Veydt played me something on his. Soeur Séraphine washed my hair and in a quarter of an hour it was dry near the 'calorifère'.

25 November Sunday For the first time since I'm at boarding school Soeur St Charles has congratulated me, because I put on my black coat. Went out for a walk with the girls; it was very windy and the girls' hats kept flying off. S.S.C. has promised me my violin for half an hour before teatime. We rehearsed the things which are to be played in December. It is now Eva Demeuze who carries Sr St Charles's book for her at night. It snowed for the first time this evening.

26 November Monday Angel is not at all well; she spits blood and barely eats. Did not practise my violin; Sr St Charles has locked it up in the cupboard of her class.

27 November Tuesday Jeanne Hensmans is expelled. Sr St Charles gives me now my violin every day for a little while, but then she takes it back after. Angel is no better.

29 November Thursday Jeanne Hensmans came today in a pitiable state to fetch her things. Her father, so furious at her being expelled, knocked her head against a red-hot fire; the poor girl is almost blind and all her head is bandaged. She must suffer! Went out for a walk with Sr St Charles and the girls. I did not have my violin today because Sr St Charles caught me with Angel last night.

30 November Friday The girls were speaking last night about a German mad soldier who has been running about the St Gilles streets in his shirt with a knife in his hand. Luckily an officer soon caught him. S.S.C. made (made) me go to the office for tea because I came down late.

1 December Saturday Angel is sulking because I prefer S.S.C. to her; Brigitte wants her to be her friend. Emma Schoetens's sister Irma is now a boarder.

2 December Sunday S.S.C. is punishing me the whole day because I answered her rudely. It all began about my violin; she said I shouldn't have it till I was put on the pavement, then only she would give it back; so I went to Soeur Supérieure, who said I could have it back but that I was to be punished in another way. I had forty sentences and all kinds of chapters to write out. After tea we all went to see some acting at the Patronage; it lasted till 7 p.m. It was great fun. Angel wants to make it up, but it is useless if she wants me to prefer her to S.S.C.

3 December Monday At 6 a.m. when we were going to the service at chapel, in the yard there was a lot of ice with snow over it; some of us slid and played snowballing. It was quite dark, and the stars and moon were still out. Last night a new little boarder came in who has just lost her mother. S.S.C. was awfully nice to me.

4 December Tuesday A lot of snow fell during the night; we had great fun with it in the yard and in the garden. S.S.C. has given me back my violin for good. Mr Maurice accompanied me with his violin, and we got out a very pretty waltz. I want to break with Angel, but she won't. There is another new boarder. We can only burn a small quantity of gas by German order. The cannon was going all night. In looking for my pencil the schoolroom's blackboard tumbled down, knocking over with it a table, a flower-pot, only a plate was smashed. After supper St Nicolas is going to pass and tell each girl her faults.

5 December Wednesday St Nicolas and Père Fouettard ['Father Whipper'] were awfully well got up; they passed in the small classes this afternoon. Jeanne Colpart and I are going to play a waltz on the violin on Saturday. It is freezing hard tonight. Angel gave me a sweet little baby-doll tonight.

6 December Thursday We all found some nice surprises on our plates at breakfast. We have holiday today. Angel gave me a 'bonbonnière' with fondants in it; two pictures; from Alix I got a box of ripping notepaper; from Léonie a medal and a bag of turnips; from Juliétte a purse like in olden times and some apples. The girls rehearsed nearly all day. Soeur Christina told us tonight that there will be very [little] light dating from tomorrow, because the Germans have given order that, after 6 p.m., not a light can be seen from the streets; who disobeys has a fine of 10000 marks. Pretty cold.

7 December Friday S.S.C. has hurt her finger. A zeppelin passed this morning. We fêted Soeur Supérieure this evening; each boarder got three kisses from her. We had holiday this afternoon. The chapel is lovely this afternoon to prepare the big fête of tomorrow, la fête de l'Immaculée Conception. S.S.C. and several other mistresses are busy putting up big curtains and sticking paper on the windows so that the Germans can't see the lights.

8 December Saturday We had to go to bed in pitch dark last night. The keys of the dormitory could not be found, so we were obliged to go by the balcony; we kept falling against each other; also we have to dress without a light. There was a beautiful High Mass this morning. I saw S.S.C. wipe her eyes.

9 December Sunday Wet day. The party went off pretty well last night, only all the girls who had to sing got sore throats. After the congregation we played everything all over again for some ladies; we had supper at 8 p.m. S.S.C. cried again this afternoon. She scolded Angel severely because she came to the table where I eat.

10 December Monday I was told today that S.S.C.'s brother has been killed recently at the war: that is the reason why she is so often sad lately. The exams begin today. All the stars are out tonight.

11 December Tuesday It is Laurence Deckers's birthday. Soeur Christina sent me to Soeur Supérieure because I gave a letter to a girl to take to Miss Mellin. Emilie Favresse has come back almost cured. My violin string smashed this afternoon. S.S.C. had put up some big curtains in the schoolroom and in the playroom to prevent the light being seen from the outside.

13 December Thursday Went out for a walk with S.S.C. and the girls this afternoon.

14 December Friday Some keys have disappeared from off Soeur Marie-Paula's desk since Wednesday, and this morning Soeur Supérieure called me; she insists that I have hidden them, and that if they are not found soon all the blame will fall on me. Went to the baths this afternoon. At this moment Soeur Christina has just caught the three Flemish girls disobeying, and they have to remain on their knees on the ground as punishment.

15 December Saturday At breakfast, because I was talking to Eva behind the backs of Laure and Ferdinande, S.S.C. sent us both to Soeur Supérieure. I didn't go, so S.S.C. says I am to write the whole day tomorrow. She has separated Eva from me, because we laugh too much. There is a new, tall nun, Soeur Virginie. As soon as it gets dark the Germans send lights as signals in the air. The English have taken Jerusalem.

16 December Sunday At St Jacques church this morning a boy suddenly got a fit and he began screaming, his eyes were starting out of his head, and his face was ghastly white. Daddy came this afternoon and we went to tea at Mrs Simms's. Sir Francis Villier's youngest son has been killed at the war. It is now Eva who carries S.S.C.'s book and shawl to her at night.

17 December Monday Livine Peeters had a lovely 'bonbonnière' full of sweets in her desk and it has been stolen, as well as two buns. A little snow came down.

18 December Tuesday It was Angèle Vanderbiss who stole the sweets, and other things. She was expelled this afternoon. Emma Genevois, Aline Dend and several other girls left for their holidays today.

19 December Wednesday Last day of work. Holidays begin this afternoon. [Five lines in pencil in French follow, including 'C'est vous que je hais le plus ici! ... Amy et Angel'.] Soeur Supérieure gave the reports. Renée Vandenbergh has smashed another doll of mine.

20 December Thursday Angel left this afternoon. There are only about 25 or 30 girls left. There was a lot of ice in my basin this morning. It is freezing hard.

21 December Friday Freezing hard; the trees are covered with a fine snow which has all kinds of designs. The ice was so hard in our basins this morning that we had to bang jolly hard before getting out a little water. We change dormitory tonight. I am sleeping on the first floor.

22 December Saturday Blanche Bataille coughed all night. An aeroplane passed this afternoon. It is not as cold as yesterday.

23 December Sunday We had quite a musical morning. Germaine Descamps and Rosa Secleppe played the piano, I played the violin and we sang. There are two new little girls. S.S.C. would not let me go to her last night.

24 December Monday Snowy weather. Went to the Christmas party at Mrs Butcher's; Arthur and Baby were there.

25 December Tuesday, Christmas Day There was lovely music this morning at chapel. Spent the day at Miss Mellin's. Daddy came after lunch. I came back at 8 p.m. The girls were already all in bed. It snowed all day. S.S.C. was very nice.

27 December Thursday Everything is full of snow. Cannons rather loud. Emilie Favresse speaks and sings every night in her sleep.

28 December Friday Soeur Marie-Clarice is ill. Sunny day.

29 December Saturday Spent the day with Miss Mellin; we went to Miss Watt. The Russians have made peace with Germany; it is outrageous.

30 December Sunday Spent the day with Lisa, we made some toffee, played the piano and I had a very nice time.

31 December Monday Rita fetched me this evening to spend a few days with her. S.S.C. kissed me before I went. I took my violin with me; Rita accompanied me after supper. At 12.15 p.m. I went to bed; we saw the New Year in and the Old Year out. Snowy day. Rita's big doll, Vera, kept me company in bed. S.S.C.'s first kiss.

1918

1 January Tuesday Jean Bruyère and the general came to wish us a happy New Year. After tea Rita brought me to school for a few minutes to see S.S.C. Played the violin after supper.

2 January Wednesday Spent the morning at the BCF [the British Charitable Fund] and wrote down the names of the people. Valentine and Mlle Tillmann lunched with us. Rita took me to see the poor of the 'impasses' of the rue Haute with Soeur Antoinette; they are terribly in misery [alleyways in the ancient quarter of Marolles]. Saw S.S.C. a few seconds.

3 January Thursday Went again to the BCF. At 12.30 a.m. some Allied aeroplanes came over. The Germans fired after them. Had tea and played the violin at Miss Tillmann's house. Afterwards I came back to school with Rita. S.S.C. coughs.

4 January Friday A lot of girls have colds. Rita fetched me to get some boots this afternoon. Freezing hard.

5 January Saturday S.S.C. was ill at chapel this morning, she had to get out before it was over. I was a long time with her last night in the dormitory, and this morning. She allowed me to go in her class with her. I have given her my promise to work better after the holidays. Went to see Father Lecourt with Germaine Pierre. There is a new boarder: Esther; she is a pianist of the Conservatoire. We have gone back to the big dormitory.

6 January Sunday Soeur Christina took a few of us to a lovely Oratorio at the Salle Patria. S.S.C. says I may sleep on the second floor if I ask Soeur Supérieure, so I went and I shall have the answer tomorrow. My throat is hurting.

7 January Monday Holidays are over; the boarders are coming back. Woke up with a bad headache and a sore throat. At 4 p.m. Dymphna took me up to bed. S.S.C. came seven times, and the sixth time she told me something which nearly made me wild with joy; it was this: tomorrow I am to change dormitory and can sleep on the second floor. Angel came to me for a few minutes.

8 January Tuesday Head is better but throat pretty sore still. It is snowing. Elisa helped me to carry my things into Germaine Deboeck's cupboards because it is in her cubicle I am to sleep in; I still think it is but a dream. There are several new boarders.

9 January Wednesday Am quite better now. My bed is next to the window, quite near S.S.C.'s. I can see the stars at night. A lot of snow has fallen during the night; in the yard I was up to half my leg with snow. There are the whole time flashlights in the sky. Cannons are going very loudly.

10 January Thursday Emilie Favresse's leg is very painful. Olga Debuisson is suffering very much with glands in her throat. Now it is the other side of my throat which is hurting. Such a mess everywhere; the snow it's all melting. Have begun my fourth position on the violin this afternoon.

11 January Friday I have given up being Angel's friend; I can't love two people here.

12 January Saturday S.S.C. not at her usual place at Mass this morning. Angel has lent me S.S.C.'s photo for one day; it is there in front of me as I am writing this. Rita came after tea.

13 January Sunday Lovely day. S.S.C. is not nice with me today; I don't know why. Livine Peeters received the sad news today of the death of her aunt. Anaïs has come back.

14 January Monday Snow. There are some ripping slides in the yard. S.S.C. has not spoken to me once today, excepting when I spoke to her, and then it was in such a funny way. Angel tells me she can't like another girl, she wants to go on with me; I told her she can, but not to be my friend, because S.S.C. does not seem to like it.

15 January Tuesday Another awful day passed without speaking to S.S.C. I've noticed that she likes Rosa Appelmans. One of the Flemish girls got ill at teatime; thought she was going to have a fit. Mr le Chanoine made us a little speech. Weather much warmer; rain and wind. Am learning the fourth position on the v.

17 January Thursday Wet day. S.S.C. is still as cold. Had tea at Miss Watt's; Rita fetched me.

19 January Saturday Eva Demeuze has come back; her sister is dying. Cannons pretty loud. Spoke to Mr le Chanoine.

20 January Sunday This morning after breakfast. S.S.C. told me to fetch my black coat. I wouldn't and told her I didn't know where it was; so she said I could take all my things out of my cupboard and go elsewhere. Then she dared to mention that the coat I had hidden in the place where I have hid Soeur M.P.'s keys; so S.S.C. did not believe me and she the whole time made me think she had. We went to sing in the choir of the Barnabites church for the 'salut'. Cannons very loud.

21 January Monday A little girl of S.S.C.'s class fainted away; I saw her in the playroom. Renée Groanendael ran away from school by the door of the day-scholars; they are looking for her. S.S.C. would not let me get into bed before I'd told her where I have hidden my black coat. It must have been about 10.30 p.m. before I got into bed. I nearly fell asleep all dressed on the mattress when I felt somebody touching me on the shoulder. It was Soeur St Charles. She spoke to me a while and then I had to make my bed; pleased I was to get into it. The cannons are so loud that the windows of the study-room are shaking at times. As the weather is getting warmer we now play in the yard instead of in the playroom.

22 January Tuesday Eva has lost nearly all her affection for S.S.C. so she says. She prefers several other people to S.S.C. Renée came back last night with her father. As I am writing the cannon is going incessantly.

23 January Wednesday Laure is beginning again to go a lot in S.S.C.'s class. Angel is suffering again. Got letter from Daddy.

24 January Thursday Henriette Maes threw her ball on the roof, so, with the aid of two girls, I got up on it. S.S.C. caught me and because some girls opened a little window to let me in she punished them and she won't let me practise my violin. We met the poet on the avenue Louise. S.S.C. came late in the dormitory last night.

25 January Friday Eva told me false, she does like S.S.C. Angel has an 'hémorragie'. Remained a long time with S.S.C. in the dormitory last night. Am feeling rather seedy. Lovely day. The sky is quite blue, dotted here and there with little pink or white clouds. At 2.15 p.m. an aeroplane was flying in the airs; we don't know if it was an ally or an enemy.

26 January Saturday Went to bed immediately after supper. S.S.C. let me sleep with her shawl near to my bed. Am fonder of her than ever.

27 January Sunday Jeanne Deruisseau fainted away in the dormitory this morning and Renée Groanendael fell off her chair in a faint at chapel. Kaiser's birthday. The Germans sent off guns from the Palais de Justice. Daddy took me to see Miss Drury. Angel has gone home for a few days because she's not well. Sydney Wiltcher is dead.

29 January Tuesday Eva was with S.S.C. in her class before classes began this morning. All the wool has to be taken out of the mattresses and given to the Germans, so the girls sleep on mattresses stuffed with straw, dead leaves and horse hair.

30 January Wednesday At 1.30 p.m. the Germans fired after some Allied aeroplanes; we could see the shots in the sky from the yards. Marie-Henriette Gosens has a beastly white finger: she suffers a lot from it. Emilie Favresse has left for the hospital.

31 January Thursday Went to town with Rita, had hot chocolate and cakes at Werthy's. Fine day. Saw a G. aeroplane going over the station.

1 February Friday S.S.C. was not well during the morning service, she had to sit down after Communion. Alix suffers painfully with her foot.

2 February Saturday Purification of the Virgin Mary; the whole school went to the service at St Gilles. A G. aeroplane flew very low at 2.15 p.m. S.S.C. threw my weekly pink card into the fire and has taken my musics because I went to the piano instead of doing some extra problems. Yes, since Eva and Cie [and co.] have come back it is not the same.

3 February Sunday It is now 6.45 p.m. Eva is laughing and talking with S.S.C. while I have to do a punishment. S.S.C. has separated me for the whole day from the girls and have got to write the whole time. Last night, as I had not done my punishment, I had to do it in the dormitory. Heard another aeroplane. Wasn't allowed to do any music. Lovely day.

6 February Wednesday S.S.C. took my diary on Sunday, but she has given it back to me now. Alix can scarcely walk, she knocked her foot the other day, and has to keep it up on a chair. S.S.C. is very nice to her; what a difference to me! Since Sunday S.S.C. had not said a single nice thing to me.

7 February Thursday Angel and Eva are converting themselves. There was a high wind all night. In opening my desk I found a paper with a whole lot of rubbish written on it; I passed it on to Anaïs and we both began laughing. S.S.C. saw it and made me give it up to her, and now this holiday afternoon I have to write out a punishment instead of practising my violin. Wet day. Emilie Favresse is being operated today.

8 February Friday Wet day. Angel is thinking of being a Carmelite; I have got much fonder of her since she has changed so. After tea there was a meeting for the 'congréganistes' and the 'aspirantes'.

[Two prayers in French follow, including one by St Stanislas.]

10 February Sunday I have given Eva S.S.C.'s photo because I'm not going to like her any more; I shall not be jealous any more when I see her with E.D., with L.M., A.B., etc. Today is the Consécration de la St Vièrge; eight of the older girls wore white veils because they are 'congréganistes', which is a big honour. The mistresses kissed the c. and the 'aspirantes'. I saw S.S.C. kiss the girls who like her. And I was not jealous.

11 February Monday It is now Eva who speaks with S.S.C. at night. I see now that it is a farce to attach oneself to somebody on earth. Am trying to make the girls believe I don't like S.S.C. any more; it is terribly hard but it's the best thing. S.S.C. speaks to Eva just as she used to with me.

12 February Tuesday Soeur Christina brought out the gramophone last night; when it played the 'Brabançonne', instead of standing up like the other girls, I remained perched on the windowsill; of course Soeur Christina was very angry and said out loud what she had to say. After that S.S.C. almost knocked me down the stairs because I did not salute her in passing in front of her. Altogether I seem to get badder and badder everyday. If S.S.C. was nice all would go better. Lovely day. Citine had a fight with Laurence, and she is now crying bitterly; tears of repentance. We had no lessons to do today.

13 February, Ash Wednesday Georgette Bormans was ill during the night, so I went to see what was the matter with her. She was suffering a lot. After a time S.S.C. went to her. The priest put a black cross on all our foreheads to remind us that we are dust and that we shall return to dust. Wet day. [There follow four lines in French, in pencil, seemingly by someone else, not transcribed here, and what seems to be Amy's response in French, in ink:] *Parce que celà ne regarde ni vous ni personne.*

14 February Thursday Lizzie fetched me to have tea with Rita. Miss Watt and Mr Gahan came; I played a few pieces of violin. Esther has lent me two pretty berceuses which I am going to learn. The weather is colder. There is another new boarder.

15 February Friday Angel has given me back my photo; our friendship is broken. Mme Mignotte, one of the old ladies, died this morning at 9 o'clock.

17 February Sunday It is absolutely impossible to go on pretending I don't like S.S.C. any more. It has all come back again, even more than before. Cannons going.

18 February Monday Mme Mignotte was buried this morning. Soeur Christina told us this morning at the Méditation that the Germans are going to take the big bells of all the churches in Belgium to make ammunitions; it is a perfect sacrilege.

19 February Tuesday I went to bed before the girls last night and I remained in it later this morning. Had two dreams: the first was a horrible one. I dreamt that S.S.C. was going to leave us till Easter. It was awful, especially at the last lesson which we had with her. Then the second dream was about Mother. We were reunited again, and she was kissing me. Then Daddy seemed angry that I loved Mother so much; I told her it was with her I wanted to live and not with

21. Newspaper photo of 'Representatives of the British Colony in Brussels' presented to King Albert, c. 1919. Rev. Gahan is far right, Ernest Rust Hodson third from right

Daddy. She was sweet! If it would only come true! Rita came for a few minutes this evening, with the news that Mother says I can see her on Thursday afternoon for a little while; so part of my dream has come true.

20 February Wednesday Georgette Bormans has gone back to the hospital to have an operation in the eye, because she can't see any more with her left one. Mrs Peiser is dead.

21 February Thursday I went to see Mother and (we are) she kissed me as if we had never quarrelled. I remained with her about an hour, then she accompanied me with Baby to Rita's where I played a small piece on the violin. So my dream has come true! She says I can go back to her if I like but that I am happier where I am. Then after tea Daddy came.

23 February Saturday Am seventeen today. S.S.C. was the first person I saw this morning. Lunched at Rita's then Arthur came to town with us. Dymphna Deckers likes S.S.C. as well as Irma Schoetens. Mme Niekop has fallen down the stairs.

24 February Sunday Went to the service at St Jacques with the boarders. After tea we went to see the girls of Soeur Celestina's class act and dance; there was violin and piano. It was very pretty; but I got ill in the middle of it, so I went to bed. S.S.C. brought me a glass of water long after supper. Hélène Romainville has the measles; she has been carried into another room. There is a new French girl, Henriette.

25 February Monday I have promised S.S.C. to try and be good every day in class and to do all my lessons but I broke my promise this morning when Mlle de Molinari gave us our lesson; she sent me out of the schoolroom. Still I am going to try hard now to be good.

26 February Tuesday S.S.C. was awfully severe tonight because I disobeyed, and going again with Angel. Oh: why is it I can't keep a promise properly?

27 February Wednesday Soeur St Charles refused to let me carry her books for her, and when after supper I asked the reason, why she said it was because I was so disobedient. But she let me keep her shawl, because I was obedient all day about not going with Angel.

~

[Diary 3 ends with a poem Amy has composed in French, in pencil, about Soeur St Charles, which includes the words 'aimer c'est souffrir'. Alas, I have no diary from 28 February to 27 November 1918. I presume that it was lost rather than that Amy, so prolific, stopped writing for nine months, so unfortunately there is no account of the end of the war.

There is an odd passage in her brother Henry's memoirs, 'This Is My Life', written about sixty years later:

> During the later part of 1917, my Mother and I along with my brother and sister, had the opportunity of travelling to England as 'exchange prisoners of War', although my Father had to remain in Brussels. It was a wonderful experience for us all, and we all arrived safely in London after a weird experience. Luckily for us we had relatives living in London, and soon found a home right in the heart of London. Needless to say, we had a wonderful time exploring the City ... I will always remember how we were all fascinated by the Underground Railways in the City, and we three travelled many many miles on the price of one ticket. One Xmas Day we only arrived 3 hours late for our Xmas Dinner, and were none too popular, believe me ... Soon after the Armistice, we all returned home to our home in Brussels, and resumed our schooling activities there. My sister entered a Convent, as she was rather keen on eventually becoming a Nun.

Amy was certainly not in England for Christmas in 1917 or 1918, and was in Brussels for the whole of 1917. Perhaps Henry was wrong about the year, and she went with her brothers and mother to London in 1918, and that is why there is a gap in her diaries. When the diaries resume she is a day girl and no longer a boarder, but that doesn't seem to be the only change. She has converted to Roman Catholicism and often writing in French. Maybe she did go to England and there were more awful scenes with her Mother. But there is no mention of having been to London in her later entries. For example, on 9 December 1918 she writes in French: 'If Daddy asked me now to go to England, I would go.' She uses the verb *partir*. If she had been to England she would perhaps have used a different verb.

In late 1918 Arthur and Henry were at a boarding school in England. Mother Annie and Henry did not return to Brussels until sometime between 20 February and 14 March 1919 (see Amy's diary entry), some three months after the Armistice. It is possible the relative in London was my grandmother Constance Jenkins, Amy's half-sister.

Amy sometimes now writes her diary entries in French. I have translated these, shown by the asterisks.]

~

28 November Thursday Daddy got a letter today from Conn saying that Mother is very well and Arthur and Baby are at a very good boarding school. I wonder how Baby will enjoy the discipline! Tommy is a lieutenant in the Lovat Scouts and Jack an officer in the GEA. Charlie may turn up at any moment as well as the others. Spent the afternoon with Rita; we had tea at home and then we went to town; we saw some more poor English prisoners coming from the North Station: they had walked from Waelhem. About 2000 Tommies left this morning to go back to their homes in England, Scotland and Ireland. Soeur St Charles is looking so very pale and is very black under the eyes. The girls say she coughed a lot last night, and of course she doesn't look after herself; it is she who dressed my finger now.

29 November Friday *I went to confession at St Joseph; as the Reverend Father didn't come I went to Parlai. Finally I left, because the porter told me after a wait that the Reverend Father had just left the confessional; since Daddy is returning earlier this evening I had only time to take the tram and come home.*

30 November Saturday *From this evening I am going to put my new doll and my bear in my old room where I never go, so that I will not be tempted to play and talk with them. I will keep them there until the Monday after the 8th, the day after the fête of the Immaculate Conception, as that will be a little sacrifice to offer to the Blessed Virgin. Ave Maria!*

1 December Sunday *I tried to persuade Joséphine to go to confession; she agreed to read my 'Preparation and Manner of Confessing'. Also, after more persuasion, I think that she will go. Daddy coughed a lot yesterday evening. Recently I've thought that I would like to enter a convent and become a nun. It seems to me it would be good there, the only way to save myself, because later when I am thrown into the world, no one there will prevent me from falling. Ah! if only Mother loved me. All my dolls are going tomorrow to the poor children of St Nicolas. I've kept two: Boutchala and the new baby. For two days it seems that the Blessed Virgin is displeased with me: yesterday evening when I went to bed, when I said goodnight to her, it seemed that she didn't reply as usual.*

2 December Monday *Oh! Mary, I've again been really naughty today! Madame was even forced to send me out of the classroom. And that's how I prepare myself for your beautiful fête of 8 December! No, Mary, I cannot continue in that way, or else where will

22. Charlie, Jack and Tommy, London, 1915

I fall? Alas! low: Oh tender Mother, hurry and place me under your mantle, sheltered from all danger. But I don't deserve such grace after all I did today. Pardon me, Mary, and tomorrow I will be well behaved; but without you I cannot keep my good resolutions. Give me your help, Mary, in that way I will not succumb so easily. Ave Maria!*

3 December Tuesday *Today was even worse than yesterday: Sister St Charles doesn't want me near her any more; she told me: Go away. No, I can no longer endure it. After 'salut' I again tried to ask Sister St Charles; all that I got was that I gave you my response this afternoon. Eh! well, that's good; so that no one can say again that I always laugh during study, I left the pensionnat even though S.S.C. sent Esther to tell me to come back. I openly resisted again. Arrived at the Barrière the idea came to me to go to confession; the brother porter told me that Reverend Father Someville won't return until next Thursday. And I came home, where I threw myself on Auntie's sofa; when I got up I was much calmer and from the utter dejection I felt a quarter of an hour previously, now I plan to start well again in class tomorrow. Oh! I wanted to be dead and interred this afternoon; I completely detest myself.

Sister Ernestina has dressed me as St Nicolas for the little children of the Comité. They really believed I was St Nicolas. On coming back from the school this morning I saw lots of Alpine soldiers with their cookstoves and their war ammunition; they were going to Germany. I don't know whether to see Pauline again; I would like to. Oh! I don't know what I want to do, only she bores me. Here is a day given to the demon.*

It is so funny that we have not yet received a letter from Mother, I wonder why that is. Oh, it has been just awful today: really, if it goes on like that I shall ask Daddy not to let me go to school any more. It gets worse and worse every day. Just before I was leaving tonight S.S.C. told me that I was not to go to Communion tomorrow morning if I do not go and confess my sins. She just hates me now, and no wonder for I am a perfect beast. Well I shall confess to a priest at St Gilles tomorrow at Mass. Santa Claus is coming for the boarders this evening, as I am a day girl he won't come to me. I wonder what he will say to them. What fun we did have last year! Soeur Christina told me yesterday and today that instead of improving I was just doing the contrary. But why is it? I saw Georges Delcoigne in his Belgian uniform yesterday. Soeur Ernestina came in our class this morning with two little girls from the Comité; Blanche Trappe had the basket in which the girls who liked could put in the toys for the poor's Santa Claus. Poor teddy and the dollies were placed in the basket, so that is the last I shall ever see of them.

5 December Thursday *The pupils wished Sister St Charles a good fête for St Nicolas. I went to confession this morning at St Gilles to a Reverend Father whom I didn't know; he told me that I must have a great devotion to the Sacred Heart and that I must receive Communion often, fine.

I went to town with Rita this afternoon; she is very worried about her father who isn't well at all; he has awful headaches. An English nurse, Nurse Stokes, has returned from Calais by car; she drove it herself and she spent the night at Rita's, and this morning she returned to Calais. She was the director of the Institut du Docteur Depage at La Panne and her devotion to the wounded and dead was admirable. She will try to send a nurse from London to look after Mr Mellin. Tommy was named Captain, and Captain Tanner is Colonel. The two brothers of Juliette Couder have come back from the army. Sister St Charles blessed me this evening.*

6 December Friday *On the occasion of the fête of St Nicolas we all received a large spéculaus at school. Sister St Charles coughs a lot again and this evening she wasn't well at all. Sister Christina allowed us to watch the boarders' dress rehearsal for Sister Superior's fête. My finger isn't healing; this afternoon it made me quite ill. This evening I began to think that I would like to go for good into a convent; all worldly pleasures fill me with horror now. How could I delight in seeing all these dramas and stupidities? Ah! where would I be then, Mary, if I hadn't known you and loved you? Renée Ledrut has returned to Brussels; she is married to the brother of Sister Marie-Clarisse. I had a huge fright this evening after supper. As Daddy was out I went to the living room to play the piano; while I played it seemed to me that twice I heard the door handle turning; after the second time I quickly opened it, but I saw nothing, so I played again. Suddenly I thought I saw something like a white scarf near the staircase. I was so frightened that I stayed as if nailed to the spot for several minutes. It was possibly nothing at all! But even so I was really scared.*

7 December Saturday *I left the pensionnat at 10 o'clock this morning because Daddy wanted me to replace him at the library, because he had to go to the Netherlands Legation. We had a letter from Constance this morning; she writes that Tommy is in Namur; he is a captain and a motorcyclist. He is coming to see us soon now. But there is no news about Charlie. Sister St Charles suffers a lot on the left side and her cough is getting worse and worse; she left the chapel at the end of the 'salut'; that means that S.S.C. suffers. All the higher classes went out this afternoon to go to a demonstration of thanks to Mr Hoover, the head of the CRB. But when we arrived near the Grand-Place a policeman told us that it had been moved somewhere else. S.S.C. didn't come with us; I am sure that it's because she wasn't feeling well. Now, this evening, S.S.C. is again really angry because I didn't wish 'bonne fête' to Sister Superior with the boarders. But what is worse is that S.S.C. told me: 'Is it because you see my suffering that you think that I will forgive more easily? And now, don't try to come near me.' No, it's useless, I don't know how to be as wise as S.S.C. wants me to be. I try, and always, always it's the same, or worse. What can I do so as not to totally despair? I have almost nothing to offer to the Blessed Virgin tomorrow and it's her fête.*

8 December Sunday *Fête of the Immaculate Conception. Everything is against me today; I wanted to go to at least two Masses this morning and I couldn't go to one. Then I went to the pensionnat and after having looked for an interminable time for S.S.C. I found her at last with a cold worse than yesterday. S.S.C. made me understand that it's absolutely useless to go near her, that she will not take an interest any more in me because since I have given my hand to the devil I can go to him. And all that because I again resisted yesterday evening in going alone to the yard instead of joining the boarders for the fête of Sister Superior. Eh! well, it will be better like this, because I can never be as well behaved as S.S.C. wants. I wish I were dead!

Daddy promised Joséphine and me 2f50 the day when we

bring him a letter from Mother. Poor Daddy! He is starting to worry about not getting any news. Miss Gifford invited me this afternoon, but I didn't go because I wanted to go to the 'salut' at the Eglise des Carmes.*

9 December Monday *Yesterday evening after supper I went to watch the fête that the boarders had prepared for Sister Superior. S.S.C. has really red eyes and she coughs a lot. I think that I won't stay for study in the evening because I always do something wrong. Today Sister Marie-Clarisse made me leave the refectory because I [...] just when Sister Marie-Clarisse lit the gas. Also I shall see S.S.C. less and perhaps I will begin to forget her. Oh! I don't know how to go on like this. If Daddy asked me now to go to England, I would go. How could I stay here on my own, having no one that I like that I can talk to? No, S.S.C. told me that I must no longer go near her, that it was useless.*

10 December Tuesday *S.S.C. hasn't said a good word to me today, also I was happy not to go to classes this afternoon. Sir Francis Villiers invited Daddy to a solemn service celebrated at the grave of Miss Edith Cavell at the Tir National. Daddy wanted me to go with him. The Minister of Spain, Villalobar, and Brand Whitlock were there. Also Francis Villiers placed a wreath on the grave of this martyr on behalf of their Majesties the King and Queen of England. Afterwards, after taking Daddy to his club, I went to see the Rev. P. Someville and I stayed for the 'salut'. When I got home I was overjoyed to see a letter from Mother for Daddy and an English newspaper. She says that Arthur and Baby are both at boarding school, and they are all right about it. Mother writes that she cried a lot when her beloved Baby left. Poor Mother! How she must suffer to see herself separated from all those who are dear to her. Tommy was seriously wounded on the hip and he was blinded by asphixiating gas. Now he is out of hospital and is going to Germany. Arthur and Baby have what they have always wanted: a scout's uniform and a watch. The Blessed Virgin has answered my prayer because I asked her so much over the last few days to let us have news of Mother.

Yesterday there was a really beautiful 'salut' at the chapel in honour of the fête of the Immaculate Conception; Sister Christina played the violin.*

11 December Wednesday *S.S.C. kept me in at 11 o'clock because I hadn't done my exam well on Hygiene. Oh! she's talking so rudely to me now! She is not coughing so much. Daddy received an invitation for the Théâtre de la Gaîté; it was a company of English soldiers called 'The Chequers'. They sang and played well. It was a sort of potpourri. I went there with Joséphine and then Daddy came. Again I've got to go to bed knowing that S.S.C. is angry. Oh! it's terrible, how long will it last? Is that why I became a Catholic? No, what can I say? It's a punishment that Jesus has sent me because I have been so wicked. We still have no news of Charlie.*

12 December Thursday *Mother and Arthur have written to Daddy this morning; they still don't know anything about Charlie, no one knows where he is. I spent the afternoon with Rita; her father is very ill. Nurse Tilleman is looking after him for the moment while waiting for a nurse from England. While I was at Rita's, Mabel Stokes and Dr Pirrat arrived from Calais in a car. The doctor promised me that he would search for news about Charlie. Someone did a dirty joke on me this morning at the pensionnat; I was really late, and leaving at noon I discovered that my pockets had been totally emptied: 2 pairs of gloves, my rosary, six centimes, a letter and trifles had all disappeared. Despite the resolution that I made, I went back to the pensionnat this evening. It's all that S.S.C. said. OK. And I had to return home like this! I wasn't naughty yesterday or today. Even the pupils think that I am ill because I don't laugh like before. Ah! yes, it's important to laugh and show a happy face to Daddy, otherwise he'll ask what's the matter. But I want to cry, cry all the time. Oh! if I were a boarder, what a day I would have – I must ask tomorrow.*

13 December Friday Daddy forgot to tell me yesterday that Mother has had a very bad fall from a bus. She was left half-unconscious and has hurt her elbow very much. Again today S.S.C. kept me in at 11.30 to learn my 'Commerce'. It is getting more horrid every day; her cough is much better. I have bought Daddy a new pair of woollen gloves for a Christmas present to make up for the one I lost of his. But I shall not give it to him till Christmas morning.

*Constance wrote to us again; she says that Jack is at Tourcoing and that he will do his utmost to come and see us. Tommy was seriously wounded twice: for the moment he is stationed in Namur;

23. Ernest and his daughter Connie, Broadstairs, Kent, 1932

but we still know nothing about Charlie. Soeur St Charles isn't angry any more this evening; I have received her blessing.*

14 December Saturday *Oh! I am happy this evening, S.S.C. was adorable today; I was able to go to her in her classroom after tea.*

15 December Sunday *Miss Gifford invited me this afternoon; there were several people there: a general and three ladies. After that I went to 'salut' at Eglise de La Sainte Trinité, then I went to S.S.C.'s; she was still nicer than yesterday evening; her severe air was completely gone this evening. Oh! Mary, give me the strength to continue to be well behaved, in that way Sister St Charles will never again be angry. I had the misfortune to break one of the beautiful little Japanese plates at Miss Gifford's.*

16 December Monday *Oh I don't know what I'm doing. On going home at midday, Daddy told me that Tommy is in Brussels and that he's coming to see us at 12.30. We are waiting for him now so impatiently. Daddy is walking up and down in the room; oh! thank you, Mary, you are good to have answered my prayer again. But where is Charlie? It's now 9.30 in the evening; Tommy came at 12.30; he lunched with us and then I went to tell the happy news to S.S.C. I stayed near her in class for almost an hour. Oh, the Blessed Virgin has been good to me today. Tommy has gone out with Daddy this afternoon, and tomorrow Tommy will take me out with him. This evening after supper Tommy and I went out, he wanted to take me to the cinema, but as soon as he saw I didn't want to he took me to a pâtisserie and bought me chocolate and cakes. Then we went to town and after buying some things we returned home. It's twelve years since I last saw him! He came from Yvoire this morning.*

17 December Tuesday *This morning, before lunch, I went to Holy Communion, then I said to Sister St Charles that Daddy wanted me not to go to school today, nor possibly tomorrow, because Tommy had returned. Mrs Heineman invited us three to dinner at 7 o'clock. I told Daddy that I didn't want to go for various reasons. I don't know why, or, at least, yes, I know why Daddy would like me to like this woman but I will never do it. Tommy absolutely wants me to go there; Mary, I will do this mortification and I offer it to you. I went out with Tommy all afternoon; he had fun putting my hair up and pulling it. We went to see M. Jean Davy, then Sister St Charles and Sister Christina. Then Tommy took me to town and we drank chocolate and ate cakes in a pâtisserie. At 6 o'clock he had to meet Daddy to go to the club and I returned for a little while to the pensionnat. Terrible news arrived when I was there; I saw S.S.C. coming back from the parlour crying: her father is dead! Oh! Mary, console Sister St Charles, she loves you so much; it's also because you love her that you have sent her this big cross. Poor Sister St Charles! I went to Mrs Heineman's to ask her to excuse me this evening. No, I can't have fun knowing that Sister St Charles has sorrow and suffering.*

18 December Wednesday *Yesterday evening I went to bed at 11 o'clock and Tommy came up later than midnight; he goes this afternoon to Namur and from there, after a little while, to Cologne.

I went out with him until 8 o'clock; we went to Rita's, but we couldn't see her. Her servant told us that Mr Gahan had come to give Communion to Mr Mellin; he didn't recognize anyone, not even Ethel who had returned from England. The doctor thinks that he won't last the night. I had an awful dream last night about Mr Mellin; he was dead, and poor Rita was desolate. Then Tommy bought me meringues and squares of mint; then he took me to the rue Hôtel des Monnaies; there I said goodbye to him and I went to the pensionnat while Tommy went to rejoin Daddy at the club. I only saw S.S.C. for a moment and then I went to 'salut' at the Eglise des Carmes; then I returned to the pensionnat to be by Sister St Charles. Oh! if I ever have to leave Sister St Charles I won't support it. Why does this thought haunt me all the time today? No, is it that, Mary, S.S.C. might leave?

Mother and Baby have written a long letter to Daddy. Arthur and Baby are now with Mother because the holidays have started. I don't know what's the matter with me today. It's silly but I can only cry. Oh if I could only become a boarder again! Only there was I happy. But I don't deserve to be happy because again today I resisted S.S.C. When will I really be humble and submissive? It's miserable to be like this.*

19 December Thursday *Mr Mellin died this morning at 6 o'clock. I went to St Joseph's this afternoon, and was happily surprised to see Sister St Charles and Sister Marie-Paula also there. I went back with them to the pensionnat and S.S.C. let me go into her class. Constance has sent a Christmas present to Daddy, of money, and she writes to Daddy to give me ten francs of it to buy myself a present.*

20 December Friday *Oh! today was a terrible day; firstly I woke late; I didn't say my three Ave Marias on my knees as I was late and my whole day was given to the devil. I didn't pray well at Mass at 7 o'clock because all the time I was abstracted. In class I laughed and distracted the pupils by stupidities. Then, worst of all, when Elisette was upset because S.S.C. had taken her notebook of poems, I took it from her desk and gave it to Elisette. I showed a bad example to the pupils who were there. Sister St Charles, having learnt about that, was really angry, and now I've caused her sorrow. I detest myself. There, at your feet, Mary, by the chapel I asked all the time to die. Happily you haven't granted my prayer, Mary, because where should I be hurled. Oh! Mary, why have I been like this on the last day of classes. Tomorrow the holidays start. I had to go home this evening without S.S.C.'s blessing. Oh! I am ungrateful, without heart. I had a letter this morning from Auntie Flo. In England, Mother, Constance and others are doing all possible research to have news of Charlie, with no result.*

21 December Saturday *Mr Mellin was buried this morning. I stayed with Rita in the dining room while others went to the interment. M. A. Max came to present his condolences; Rita showed truly admirable courage. The coffin was in the living room; Daddy went in the car with Sir Francis Villiers; the others followed the funeral procession in cars; the service was at the Protestant church in rue de Stassart [the Anglican Church of the Resurrection]. Mme Deltan, Mlle Volger and I were with Rita. She said that her father barely suffered, only at 3 in the morning, the day he died, the chambermaid called Rita: her father had a terrible headache. The doctor hadn't wanted until then to give him a morphine injection, but he gave him opium to help him sleep. He gave him two injections which eased his pain. Poor Rita, how she must painfully feel the loss of her father. This afternoon I went into town to buy things for Daddy and one or two presents to give at Christmas. Then I went to the 'salut' at the Carmes; during the third decade of the rosary my head started spinning and I suddenly felt peculiar; I opened my cardigan and I thought it would pass; but no, it got worse, I no longer held on to my chair. Finally I left the church and after a few minutes I was better. I went to say goodnight to Sister St Charles and before I went she blessed me.*

22 December Sunday *Oh! I regret now having told all my past life to S.S.C. I knew that when she knew it she wouldn't want to see me any more. I went to the pensionnat at 2.30 this afternoon; I stayed until 6.30, and I only spoke to S.S.C. for ten minutes. The way that she asked me what I was doing was enough to assure me that my presence was insupportable. When I arrived, as the pupils were in the chapel, I went on the swing with a few young girls in Sister Séraphina's class. I went after S.S.C. spoke to me at the chapel and I stayed there an hour and a quarter; to stretch my legs I went a bit

1918

24. Church of the Resurrection, rue de Stassart, Ixelles, Brussels. Built by Rev. C.E. Jenkins and his brother Rev. J.C. Jenkins, consecrated by the Bishop of London 23 October 1874

to the yard and the cat kept me company. He was the nicest to me this afternoon. After assembly I asked S.S.C. to bless me; it would have been much better not to have said it, because previously not a word, when I was well behaved, left her lips; on the contrary. Why do I not keep out of the way? Oh! it's the last time that I will go there. But I don't know how to be better behaved than I was today and yesterday. Oh! Mary, I know that you send me this to punish me for what I did the other day. But tomorrow maybe you will lift the punishment. Tell Sister St Charles not to speak to me like that. She made me believe, before this, that I was pardoned.*

23 December Monday *This afternoon I took a letter to Rita's, then I went to a magnificent 'salut' at the old convent where I went when I was six or seven years old. Someone sang 'Ave Maria' in the rood-loft; she had a superb voice. Then someone played some music on the cello. Finally I went to say goodnight to S.S.C. Again I returned in a state worse than yesterday, only I went back to her and now I am fine. S.S.C. says that I must come tomorrow evening to sleep in the pensionnat so that I can go to Midnight Mass. Oh! Jesus, I want so much to receive you on your birthday. Last year, I was so sad to see all the pupils go to the Holy Table, and I couldn't. Alas, I was a Protestant. Jesus, maybe Daddy will give me permission to sleep at the pensionnat. I will be near S.S.C. This evening Daddy said that it was ridiculous to go to Midnight Mass. He said: You see it's ridiculous; you aren't a Catholic. If only he knew! ...... Oh, Mary, can I not go?*

24 December Tuesday *After Mass I took my night things to the pensionnat. I chatted with S.S.C. then I went to get holly at Jean's. At 3.30 I was at St Joseph, then I had tea at Georgie May's. There were two children there: Vera and Alexis. We played and as soon as I'd gone they were going to start decorating the Christmas tree. When I got to the convent the pupils were in the dormitory; I was able to sleep in my old alcove. Oh! again I was truly happy, there, so near S.S.C. This evening, at last, I didn't say to you, Mary, to remind S.S.C. that I think of her. At 11.30 we got up to go to Midnight Mass in the chapel. Oh, it was beautiful. Baby Jesus opened for us his little arms so that we could go to him, and I received him. As I had been to confession this afternoon, that big sin I'd committed against S.S.C. didn't weigh any more on my conscience. It was the first time in my life that I'd gone to Midnight Mass. The choir, accompanied sometimes by a violin, was very beautiful. Also, what showed so well the beautiful fête of the nativity of Our Lord was that fine snow covered the roofs and the grass in the garden. After Mass we ate in the refectory, then immediately afterwards we went back to bed. Oh poor Daddy, how can he pass a day so beautiful without going to glorify the Baby Jesus.*

25 December Wednesday, Christmas Day *We got up at 6.30 this morning; at 7 o'clock we had two consecutive sung Masses in the chapel. Immediately afterwards I greeted Daddy with a Happy Christmas. He was very happy with the gloves I gave him. All morning it seemed I was going to get bad news, and this evening when I was with S.S.C. she told me that she was leaving on Friday at 4 in the morning but that she will come back probably on Monday. Four days of awful torture. Oh! Mary, protect S.S.C. during this long journey; bring her back as soon as possible. Before going home I went to a beautiful 'salut' at the Eglise de la Sainte Trinité.*

26 December Thursday *It was magnificent this morning to see everybody go to Holy Communion; everyone, grown-ups and children, young and old going to receive Jesus in their hearts. My foot is really well; this morning, when I got up, I almost couldn't put my foot on the ground and I limped. S.S.C. pierced the part that hurt and when I returned home it no longer hurt. I had tea with Rita and Ethel. They had invited an English soldier. I left early as I had to take a letter to Mme de Somsée and I got lost in the middle of the wood. I thought I'd never get out. Finally after a good hour I found myself on avenue Louise and I went quickly to the pensionnat. My foot started to hurt this evening again. I said goodbye to S.S.C. this evening; she leaves at 4 in the morning, but I will be very brave, because Mary will help me to pass those days that I won't see S.S.C.*

27 December Friday *Sister St Charles has gone! Daddy has gone to change German money into Belgian; after the 31st of this month German money will no longer be accepted. This afternoon I was photographed for a new identity card. We met Angel and she walked all along chaussée de Charleroi with Joséphine and I. After that I went to 'salut' at the Eglise des Carmes and I asked the Blessed Virgin to bless me for S.S.C. Then I took a letter to Rachel; then I went home, soaked by the rain. A whole day has passed without seeing S.S.C. Still two to go, and on the third she will return.*

28 December Saturday *Ave Maria. After Mass I went to Alimentation. I saw the Reverend Mother of the old convent where I went when I was six or seven. She was very pleased to see me again because she had learned that I was Catholic. She kissed me; it's more than ten years since I last saw her, but I immediately recognized her. While I chatted with her, Mother Oedecie came in and the three of us chatted for over half an hour. Mother Oedecie was really nice, she said that when I went into Sister Rose's class I was attracted to the Catholic religion. But my parents took me out as soon as they discovered it. After that I went to 'salut' at St Joseph. Since I got there a bit before the 'salut' I went near the Virgin by a little altar. And today, exactly, the priest brought the Holy Sacrament and displayed it on this altar. I was thus the nearest to all the faithful of Jesus and Mary. During the sermon, which was about the Blessed Virgin, the priest and his two assistants sat in front of me. I felt a bit peculiar, there, behind the priest. Coming out of the 'salut' a man who was walking behind me called me. I pretended not to hear. He continued, then he came nearer and asked if I would like a chocolate tart. I continued walking; if he came even nearer I was prepared to tell him in English that I didn't understand French. Happily he took a different road to mine. My foot really hurts this morning; pus is coming out and it is really enflamed around the part that hurts.*

29 December Sunday *After Mass I went to make music at the pensionnat; I accompanied Germaine with some songs, then I went home. This afternoon Daddy took me to the Léopold Club where there was a great football match. English against Belgians. It was very interesting. During an interval Highlanders played the bagpipes, marching around the ground. The drum major all the time made elegant gestures all the while he was beating time. The English won (3 to 2). I got a Christmas card from Mother this morning and Daddy got a long letter, and also one from Constance.

Mother thinks to return with Uncle Fred as soon as they can. She writes that Arthur is as bad a child [*enfant terrible*] as before. He broke a beautiful vase and the owner demanded 25 shillings from Mother; he lost a ring belonging to the granddaughter of the house, another 25 shillings; then he totally broke a chair in Mother's room, destroyed a superb cushion belonging to Constance and finished a whole pot of jam that a boarder had put on the table near Arthur: Arthur thinking it was a present for him had emptied it. And finally, as he ran in the park he overturned Desmond's cart; the latter fell out and banged his head. Arthur hates being at boarding school; he doesn't get on with the teachers. He is now on holiday, like Baby. Arthur delivered a speech to 300 boy scouts and he was presented to the Duke of Connaught. On Christmas Eve Arthur and Baby hung their stockings at the foot of their beds and they found them full the next day. On Christmas Day they spent most of the day with Constance, who had prepared a beautiful Christmas tree for them. Charlie is in a hospital in Germany; he has poisoned feet. We haven't had news from him for a long time because the Germans moved him from one camp to another so that we couldn't write to him. I asked the Blessed Virgin this evening to give me a blessing from S.S.C. Oh! tomorrow it will be S.S.C. who will give it to me herself with her own hands. Oh, Mary, will S.S.C. return tomorrow?*

30 December Monday *When I went to the photographers this morning I'd lost the ticket that they'd given me the other day; so I had to pose again. That's stupid. This afternoon I went to see Miss Drury, then I wanted to go to 'salut' but after I'd stayed twenty-five minutes at the church, since the 'salut' wasn't about to happen, I hurried to the pensionnat. Sister St Charles still hasn't returned. I waited a quarter of an hour at the place where tram 14 stops, but Sister St Charles didn't get off. But I am not going to cry, it's the Blessed Virgin who will bring me happiness tomorrow. Mother has bracelets for me that were made in 'An Aeroplane and tank manufactory'. Jack is in Boulogne and he will do all he can to spend a few days in Brussels with Daddy.*

31 December Tuesday *S.S.C. still hadn't returned when I went to the pensionnat this morning; if she still hasn't come back this afternoon I will go to the Gare du Luxembourg to wait for all the trains until 6 o'clock. Daddy dines at the English Legation at 1 o'clock, so I will eat on my own. Today was the worst day since Sister St Charles left. I waited two hours at the Gare du Luxembourg, then the train arrived. Everybody left the station, but no Sister St Charles. Suddenly I saw a nun, then two. They were foreign sisters. Oh, everything has been against me today. Finally I went to 'salut' at the Eglise des Carmes, again I asked the Blessed Virgin for the blessing of S.S.C., then for the third time today I went to the pensionnat, hoping that S.S.C. had come via another station. Oh! Citine can well wish me a good and happy new year. I think that it will start well. When I think of last year's New Year's Eve, when Rita came to fetch me and I was able to give my best wishes to Sister St Charles first of all, and now .... I have been brave until today, but if S.S.C. doesn't return tomorrow. It is now 9 in the evening. Joséphine is in bed and Daddy has gone to a ball given this evening at the Hôtel de Ville in honour of the Prince of Wales [the future Edward VIII]. I wonder where S.S.C. is at this moment; is she also all on her own?

11.30. I have just finished my translation. Daddy still hasn't returned; I am going to bed. Have a good and happy new year Sister St Charles; if I can't wish it to you close to, I am doing it from afar. Alas, from a long way away.*

1919

1 January Wednesday *At 1.30 this morning Daddy returned from the ball. He came to my bedside and wished me a happy new year. He sat at the foot of my bed and told me all he had seen at the ball. He spoke a bit to the Prince of Wales, but as I was half asleep I don't remember what. At midnight, when I was in bed, I saw beautiful fireworks set off in a garden quite near us. Sister St Charles has still not returned. And she had promised me that she would return on Monday. I saw a football match at the Léopold Club this afternoon, English against Belgians. We were beaten this time, but also our side had one soldier less since he was injured while playing. After taking Daddy to his club I went to 'salut' at St Joseph's, then I spoke to the Reverend Father about what I must do on Saturday, because Mrs Heineman has invited me to go to the Théâtre de la Monnaie to see *La Tosca* with her and Nelly and I don't want to go, especially on Saturday. He told me there was nothing to prevent me going, I must go in the spirit of mortification, but I must ask the Blessed Virgin during Communion to find a pretext for me not to go.*

2 January Thursday *I spent the afternoon at Rita's, then I went to the pensionnat, hoping to see S.S.C. But no, the Virgin Mary without doubt wants me to detach a bit from S.S.C. A day will come when either S.S.C. or I must leave. Oh Mary! this sacrifice will cost me still more, much more than that of my violin. My foot hurt a lot this evening. Mother has sent me illustrated newspapers from England.*

3 January Friday *I went to look for my photos, then Daddy took me to the Review of the English troops at the entrance of the Bois de la Cambre. Amongst the crowd I couldn't see anything, but when Daddy recognized Sir Francis Villiers standing in his motorcar we got through the crowd and, despite a policeman making a sign for us to stop, we got beside Sir Francis Villiers in the middle of the road. King Albert, on his white horse, watched the Review; for one hour and three-quarters we were close to King Albert. He talked to the General of the English brigade; behind him was the English military staff, the King's head groom, and the Earl of Athlone. Oh how I would love to be a soldier when I see them marching past like this; it was magnificent, and the crowd was enormous. The name of the General who was all the time at the side of the King is Sir H.S. Jeudwine. I was at the 'salut' at St Gudule because it was Cardinal Mercier who presided and who consecrated Belgium to the Sacred Heart of Jesus. At last, Mary, I have seen Sister St Charles, and I thank you with all my heart, if I still have a little. Mother has written to Daddy and she says that poor Charlie has completely 'broken down'. Uncle Fred has handed over a packet of letters to Mother that Charlie wrote to him and in which he says how he was punished in front of the others attached to a gun for two hours for several days because his soldiers did not want to obey him; he was angry. Poor Charlie!*

25. Review of the 55th (West Lancashire) Division, Brussels. On horseback: King Albert I and (left) General Hugh Sandham Jeudwine. Far right in the motor car is Sir Francis Villiers, British Minister to Belgium, possibly his daughter Marjory, and Lady Villiers, 3 January 1919 © IWM

5 January Sunday *Yesterday evening I went to see the opera of *La Tosca* at the Théâtre de la Monnaie with Mrs Heineman, Mrs Jensen, Nelly and another woman. I told S.S.C. before I went and now she is cross, and this evening, when I went to say goodnight, she replied really coldly; I asked for my diary and she gave it to me without saying anything. It's really good on her part but, Mary, I don't want to cry any more because S.S.C. is cruel; I see now that she delights in torturing me. Isn't it terrible enough to have spent eight days without seeing her but now that she has returned it's even worse than when she was away? Oh! but I will remain silent, otherwise I will say things that I will regret afterwards. But tomorrow, Mary, I will not walk to the pensionnat; help me to courageously offer this sacrifice tomorrow when going to receive Jesus. Oh! Mary! when I think that since I have known Sister St Charles I have taken her as a mother but now it's finished. She doesn't want me any more. Oh this cursed theatre, never again will I go, or if I am forced I will shut my eyes. The whole time. Besides, the music wasn't beautiful and the actress was frightful, but she sang well. Oh! Mary, I guess the reason that you send me this is that you don't want me to attach myself to one creature. You want me to only love God and you. Ah, if I could, how happy I would be! From today I am going to do it, Mary, but I beg you to help me. Tomorrow I will not go to see Sister St Charles, nor Tuesday, no more perhaps. Mother has written to Daddy, telling him that she will have enormous difficulty in getting a passport because she was born in Hamburg.*

6 January Monday *Constance writes that Charlie is in a hospital in London and that she went to see him the day she wrote to Daddy; how happy Mother will be to see him again. Constance sent me a gold brooch and a button from Charlie's uniform. Arthur wrote also a very nice letter to Daddy. I met Elisette this morning and she came with me to the Maison Communale to find a document that all foreigners must have to show that they didn't have relations with the Germans. I spent a moment at Rita's and in the afternoon I went to 'salut' at the Eglise des Carmes. I have kept my promise, I haven't seen Sister St Charles. Daddy brought me a bag of pralines from Mrs Heineman.*

7 January Tuesday *Mother saw Charlie at King George's Hospital in London; he came back from Germany via Denmark. His thumb is poisoned as well as his legs. Mother didn't see a doctor because for four days she has been suffering, and when she is in bed she almost doesn't know how to breathe. After Mass I went with Daddy to the Plaine des Manoeuvres at Etterbeek to see hundreds of machine guns, field guns and caissons that the Germans abandoned in Belgium; it was interesting. This afternoon I went to the Grand Bazar then to confession and 'salut' at the Eglise St Joseph. I asked the Blessed Virgin to give me the blessing that Sister St Charles gave me before; alas, all has changed now. I should return to school today since the holidays are finished, but I will go tomorrow.*

8 January Wednesday *Oh Mary, it is impossible, I don't know how to keep this resolution to no longer be near Sister St Charles; for that, I must leave Brussels for good and it must be impossible for me to return to her. Oh I love her! Will you not be angry with me, Mary, because you see that I can't do anything good when S.S.C. doesn't speak to me. Also, S.S.C. was really severe today, but I really deserved it because I was unbearable, but, oh! this evening when I was with S.S.C. I was in Paradise. I received her blessing and now I am much happier than yesterday. Captain Bueley has died of influenza [*la grippe*]. From today I've promised S.S.C. to do a novena in honour of the Blessed Virgin, to study hard all my lessons, and to properly do all my devoirs.*

9 January Thursday *This afternoon I went to play at Manette's, then I said goodnight to Sister St Charles.*

10 January Friday *I went to Mass at 7 o'clock at St Gilles and I was next to Sister St Charles the whole time at Mass. Paule Flandre has come back to the pensionnat.*

11 January Saturday *Ave Maria. Charlie has written a long letter to Daddy telling him all his adventures. He never received a single packet nor letter that we had sent to him in Germany. He is getting much better now; he has received a letter from King George V and he will have two medals. Carl [Ehrlich] has returned from London and he brought the brooch and the button from Charlie's uniform.*

1919

12 January Sunday *I saw a motorcar run over a motorcycle. I screamed and didn't dare look. Since Daddy didn't see it he asked me what the matter was. Then we saw the two men stand up, laughing; they weren't at all hurt. After 'salut' I said goodnight to S.S.C.*

13 January Monday *Baby returns tomorrow to boarding school at Broadstairs. I had an awful nightmare last night.* [This is the nightmare that she has written in her 'conscience diary' for 13 January, in English:]

> I dreamt last night something which I am wondering if it means that I am not to go back as a boarder. It was night and Daddy woke me, saying that Mother and the boys had come back. I flew down and only caught a glimpse of Mother because she wanted to speak to Daddy, so I asked Arthur how it was that he was not at school. He said that masters had sent him away because he was always up to mischief. I kept thinking about going back to the convent, and when I saw Mother afterwards I asked her if I could, and she said: No, not yet. She then said she wanted to go to the post office. I asked her if I could go with her, and she let me. Then we passed through a cemetery. Mother and I knelt down on a tomb. All round us were small statues of the Blessed Virgin; as I was looking at one it suddenly began to move and it said: Yes. I screamed and pointed it out to Mother, and she could see nothing. What could <u>yes</u> have meant, I wonder?
>
> After that we traversed a wood and suddenly I discovered Mother was no more by my side. Half maddened with fright I rushed about everywhere, trying to find her, but I couldn't. Then Rita appeared on the scene. I beseeched her to try and find Mother; as I was saying that I saw a black figure lying on the ground at a little distance from us. I ran and ... it was Mother. She was groaning and when I was by her she said: My legs are broken. I fell upon her and cried, beseeching her to try and tell me what had happened. She said some mysterious person had suddenly rushed out upon her and given her a tremendous blow; she also had two books which the person had left her. Mother told me to read one, but as I saw that it was

[And that is where Amy's account ends.]

15 January Wednesday *During the lessons with Sister Marie-Paula and Sister Ernest I was better behaved than on all other days this morning, and S.S.C. still found a way to talk to me as if I had committed numerous faults. But what am I supposed to do? Every time that S.S.C. sees me laugh or be amused it's a catastrophe. Yet it wasn't in class that I threw my muff after Alix, and for that, when I was with S.S.C. after the 'salut', she replied to me: I do not reply to a rude pupil. Then she called that Pauline and I left. But I will bore her no longer now; P. can go to her as much as she wants. It's always like this; yet P. has her mother here .... but I will keep silent.*

16 January Thursday S.S.C. has not said <u>one single</u> word to me today. Spent the afternoon with Rita; we went to see a house in the rue de Belle-Vue which Rita is thinking of getting because this house where she is living is too big for her alone. Polly bit my finger, the unlucky one which is beginning to hurt again. I am not going to ask for S.S.C.'s blessing any more because it is too awful when she refuses it to me. Mary will now give it to me every night; I know she would not refuse it to me.

17 January Friday Tommy has come home for a day; he came to lunch then he took me to school, not without having taken me into a pastry cook's, and he bought me some cakes and chocolates. He is staying at Delock's hôtel and will come round here again tomorrow morning. S.S.C. is still worse today; well, I am just sick of going to school. I went to the 7 a.m. service at St Gilles but today I was not next to S.S.C. as I was last Friday.

19 January Sunday *I was with the pensionnat at the Eglise des S.S. Barnabites; it's the day when all children can dedicate themselves to the infant Jesus. We sang the 'salut' and I returned home still more disheartened than before I went. Why? Without doubt because I laughed coming down from the rood-loft. Then I went to the 'salut' at the Eglise de la St Trinité; I asked the Blessed Virgin to bless me; then I went to the pensionnat to say goodnight to S.S.C.*

20 January Monday *Another day of past martyrdom! It's really encouraging to learn her lesson well and then not to have to recite it! I cut my finger and, in going to Holy Communion, I didn't know what to do to stop the blood flowing; the finger that the doctor had cut begins again to make me feel ill. God has sent it to me because I want so much to start playing the violin again. I never can again because this finger prevents me.*

24 January Friday Poor Daddy is awfully worried about Mother. Connie has written to say that Baby won't go back to school. He was to have gone back Tuesday the 14th and on Sunday only Uncle Fred discovered he had not gone back at all. Mother said she could not possibly let him go for he cried so at the station. Uncle Fred is very angry because the school was paid for a whole year in advance. Daddy thinks Mother will do something desperate. Connie also asks Daddy if I would care to go out to South Africa to Doris in a little while; Daddy thinks it would be the best thing for me. As the Reverend P.S. was absent I went to confess to the R.P. Chaîneux. I met Mr Gahan; he made me a long speech about my not going to his church. It was on the tip of my tongue to say: I don't belong to your church any more. Luckily I remained mum.

25 January Saturday Soeur Marie-Paula could scarcely speak today for her throat is rather sore. There are Tommies everywhere now, they are lodging in all houses which they can get for tomorrow is the big Review. General Butler has sent Daddy an invitation for the reserved places near the Palace.

26 January Sunday Everything is covered with snow and the sky looks as if a lot more is to come down. At 11 a.m. I went with Daddy to the reserved places at the gate where the guests go in for the Court Ball. It was a fine show. King Albert reviewed the British troops with the Prince of Wales, Prince Albert and the Earl of Athlone. The Marquis de Villalobar and Lord Vivian spoke to some people near to us. Vicomte de Spoelberch was there also; he is awfully like Cherry. He told Daddy that at their château at Rixensart the bagpipes go three times around the castle every day after lunch. As the tram-men are still on strike we had to walk home through the snow. This afternoon I went to a lovely evening service at the Carmes; a tenor sang most beautifully, and they played the cello. After that I went to school. I knocked a few snowballs after the girls and then went up to the evening service. Monsieur le Chanoine read out the names of the girls who are accepted as 'aspirantes'. I was one of them. So in a fortnight I shall belong still more than ever to the Blessed Virgin.

27 January Monday *Justine came to school this afternoon wearing mourning because her father has died of influenza. Sister Marie-Paula is in bed; she also has influenza. Sister St Charles held her head several times as if she was suffering this evening. Oh! Mary, don't let S.S.C. get ill. I got first-class snowballs on my neck and back today, and again because I laughed and I amused myself the whole day, in the evening I wanted to cry. Oh can I continue for long to keep this resolution of no longer going so often to S.S.C.? It's terrible. Every time I see her I want so much to talk to her, to chat to her.*

28 January Tuesday *Jack has come back from Boulogne this morning and he can stay until Saturday. I wasn't in class this afternoon

26. Review of the 3rd British army corps outside the Palace, Brussels, 26 January 1919 © IWM

because I went out with Jack. First of all we went to see Bounote, the painter; then Fernandez, and then we had tea with Miss Drury. After that Jack and I went to eat at Buol's. As it was too early for supper we went to High-Life, from where we went to look for Daddy at his club in order to dine in town. The day was the most *mondaine* and worst since the happy day when I started at the pensionnat. Ah! beautiful days, will you never return?*

29 January Wednesday *I am not dining out this evening, no, I don't know. Jack and Daddy are not coming back. Today I've been told that I am two-faced, ungrateful, etc. Oh! it's cruel to say that! Ah! but it is true, nothing more can touch me.*

30 January Thursday *Sister Marie-Paula is really ill. Poor Esther does not know if she can see her. Sister St Charles let me go to the Porte de Halles with her. This afternoon I went out with Jack. We went to see Rita, then had tea in town and finally looked for Daddy at the club. Jack and Daddy are dining at Mr Heineman's this evening. Jack told me that Edward John [Palmer], who is only seven, is a true genius at music. He composes whole pages; he sightreads as well as a person reads a book and he plays Grieg, etc.*

27. Lieut. Jack Jenkins with his men, Royal Army Service Corps, probably Boulogne, c. 1918

31 January Friday *No, it's impossible, I cannot continue any more like this without speaking to S.S.C. Every evening she will now give me her blessing when I have deserved it. Daddy and Jack didn't return at midday. Jack goes to Boulogne tomorrow morning at 5 o'clock and this evening he is sleeping near the station; we dine at home, then I helped him organize his suitcase. It is now 8.30 and he is about to go. He will meet Daddy in town and they will eat together for the last time. In wanting to tidy his hair back I broke his glasses.*

5 February Wednesday *I was too happy yesterday; today everything has started again. It is impossible for me to stay well behaved for two consecutive days. It is me who made Pauline's mother cry? Eh! well, that is not true, that's all. I would like to be dead and buried if by that I don't cause sorrow any more to anyone. After all ... . Oh! I will stop. Sister Marie-Paula is better. The days of the martyrdom are starting again. S.S.C. has no more confidence in me because she has told me for some time that I lie. Ok, if I am a liar it isn't surprising that Sister St Charles treats me like a stranger. I spent the afternoon at Rita's; her leg hurts because the doctor gave her an injection. Baron de Lavelaye came to have a cup of tea with Rita; she said that I had made a lot of progress. Happily a person can say at least a little good about me. Afterwards I went to say goodnight to S.S.C. God bless her! I have made a portrait of a spiked helmet in our courtyard and Joséphine was in a bad mood because I dirtied her kitchen with snow but she found afterwards that it was to admire the *chef-d'oeuvre* on the marble top that she now she laughs.*

9 February Sunday *I am now an 'aspirante'; this afternoon Monsieur le Chanoine put a ribbon with the medallion of the Holy Virgin around the necks of the new 'congréganistes' and the 'aspirantes'. Oh! Mary, today I am still more your child than yesterday. Do not let me ever forget my promise that I made you this evening. Always be my mother and let me always be your child. Good Mother, I love you! Sister St Charles gave me a frame containing a picture of Our Lady of Lourdes. Daddy had a headache all day.*

13 February Thursday *Mother has at last written to Daddy; she has influenza and has been suffering badly. She is doing all she can to get a passport to return to Brussels with Henry, who doesn't want to be at the college. Mother says that she can no longer put up with this independent life. Rita told me that I could return as a boarder as soon as Mother returns. I was so happy an hour ago and now Daddy finds the idea ridiculous. The Blessed Virgin will arrange all well if I pray well. I saw an old Scottish lady with Rita, then I went to say goodnight to Sister St Charles who at the moment has an awful cold. I knew that sooner or later it would happen. Oh! Mary, cure Sister St Charles and Mother!*

14 February Friday *Colonel Wynne is dead. The Blessed Virgin has answered my prayer: Sister St Charles doesn't cough as much as yesterday.*

15 February Saturday *I went to confession this afternoon and on returning I saw Sister St Charles and several boarders removing the snow from the courtyard. I helped and when all was almost done I did something stupid: I was going up with a bucket of water for S.S.C.'s class and a stupid desire came to me to throw the water from the bottom to the top of the balcony. I did it and Marie-Henriette got it. S.S.C. is now very angry. Oh! what a calamity! When will I be serious? Daddy got a letter from Tommy this evening; he is now in Germany.*

16 February Sunday *I met S.S.C. and the boarders this morning. At 3 o'clock I watched a beautiful 'salut' at the Eglise des Carmes. A beautiful Blessed Virgin was carried in procession, followed by barefoot Carmelites and men carrying flaming torches and finally the Holy Sacrament. When I went to say goodnight to S.S.C. she told me that she had news for me which would give me huge joy, that now I would perhaps be free to do what I wanted, because S.S.C. believes that she is leaving. No, is it, Mary, that Sister St Charles is going? [...] If they take S.S.C. away from me I will have no one in the world. Oh! Mary, I beg you not to let S.S.C. leave. I promise you that I will behave better.*

17 February Monday *This morning all the 'classes du balcon' went to Mass at 9 o'clock at St Gilles in order that the war doesn't start again, because today, it is said, the conditions of peace will be decided. I had a letter from Auntie Flo. Oh! Mary, I do not know what's the matter this evening, but I no longer want to live like this. No one loves me; what does it matter if I am ill or if I suffer, no one will notice. I know that I deserve that the whole world abandons me, because I have committed so many sins in my life. But now that I am behaving well, why is there no one who loves me a little? The only creature to whom I am really attached, you are going to take her away from me? No, surely, Mary, you won't do that! Punish me in whichever way you want; send me all sicknesses, even death, but I beg you, please, don't let Sister St Charles leave. If you take S.S.C. from me I would have nothing. Mary, I promise that I will behave well: today I was and tomorrow I want that too.*

18 February Tuesday *I don't dare write my diary this evening because the promise that I made to the Blessed Virgin was totally broken. I was so naughty that S.S.C. suffered this evening. Oh, I am so cruel! Therefore, when I laughed so much in class, I upset Jesus, the Blessed Virgin and S.S.C. I was with S.S.C. in class from 5.30 until almost 7 o'clock. Before leaving she gave me her blessing. Oh! she is good and I am so ungrateful. My foot really hurt this evening, I can't put it on the ground without it really hurting. Thank you, Jesus, because now I must suffer in order to atone for all my faults today. The armistice has been lengthened.*

19 February Wednesday *I didn't go to classes this morning because I can hardly walk; I could only go to Mass and receive Jesus at the Eglise de la Sainte Trinité. Sister St Charles put some ointment on my foot: it's better this afternoon.*

14 March Friday *It's been a long time since I last wrote my diary and a lot has happened since then. Mother and Henry returned from England and the hope that I have of returning as a boarder has vanished little by little. Oh! Mary, can I never return? I <u>detest</u> being a day pupil; even when I was a boarder I could barely know all the day pupils; now still less. I think that S.S.C. has a fever this evening; she doesn't look well at all. Sister Marie-Paula called me a madwoman this morning; I thank her immensely for that. Oh! I don't <u>know</u> how to behave well. Almost every day I have good resolutions in the morning and after scarcely one hour in class they have vanished. What a martyr! The holidays will start soon and I will see Sister St Charles even less then now.*

16 March Sunday *Mother is not well this morning; she has gone to the Anglican church with Henry. After dinner I went to Rita's; she is much better. Finally I went to the pensionnat and I only saw Sister St Charles for a tiny moment. My foot is beginning to hurt again and this evening, returning, it really hurts. From tomorrow I must absolutely begin my Lenten fast.*

17 March Monday *At the moment I am in the study-room; the sky is completely black and strong rain falls, I think it's hail. Laure de Molinari and Laurence Deckers have gone to Pêches this morning; it is the last time that we will see them dressed in non-religious clothes because they are taking the veil. I saw Sister St Charles in church this morning.*

18 March Tuesday *I am so happy today because I have been well behaved the whole day. Sister St Charles gave me a notebook about the Blessed Virgin, which I can copy for her.*

19 March Wednesday *On the occasion of the feast of St Joseph we went to a lovely Mass at St Gilles; this afternoon Germaine Honoré gave a little lecture on the Belgian Congo. I was at the side of Sister St Charles during the Mass. At 5.15 there was a very beautiful 'salut' in the chapel.*

21 March Friday It really is encouraging when I've tried and tried hard to be good this week to have S.S.C. telling me that she is going to send my report home to Daddy. Now I've not had a single bad mark the whole week and just today of course everything must go wrong.

22 March Saturday I've been a perfect beast this afternoon; because S.S.C. would not allow me to go to confess I answered her and made myself detestable all during study time. But what made me so bad is that she said I was a thief, a liar, a hypocrite, etc. I know I'm a horrid creature, but I'm not those three things she calls me, anyhow. S.S.C. has taken away the book she said the other day

I could copy for her. It really is encouraging when I've tried hard to be good all the week to finish it like that.

23 March Sunday Went to confess and the R.F. said I <u>must not</u> answer and show the bad example to the girls, for if I go on I shall have an abominable character later on. It's bad enough already, if it gets worse, well .... Spent the afternoon with Rita. Madame Wilmars came to tea, so while they were talking I went and played in the garden with Alice. I did not go to S.S.C. today, for if I am a liar, etc., etc., she must hate the very sight of me.

25 March Tuesday Today is the fête of the Annunciation of the Blessed Virgin; we had temps libre. How I do hate that kind of temps libre. Always something must happen to make the day be given to Satan instead of to Mary. What is becoming to me? I'm simply detestable now, more than ever. The girls went to church this morning, I didn't go 'cause I hadn't any money with me, and so I went to B.'s room and practised there. S.S.C. came to find me there and she told me a bit of her mind.

26 March Wednesday Eva likes S.S.C. again, and I'm sure she is the girl S.S.C. is so often speaking about who, after having received two observations in one week, is now completely changed to her advantage. Wish I were like her. I feel as if I shall never be good. What do those girls do to keep to their good resolutions? There, yesterday I promised to be good, and I've just been laughing like a fool.

27 March Thursday I went to the British canteen with Daddy; went to see Rita for a moment and then went to evening service at the Carmes. After that I went to say goodnight to S.S.C. Mother has gone to see the *Raid on Zeppelins* at the High-Life with Henry. My foot is hurting horribly. Tommy has just come out of the hospital; he had to have a piece of shrapnel, which had remained in his leg, taken out. He hopes to come over and see us soon.

28 March Friday S.S.C.'s cough is beginning again. Somebody has written on the blackboard in the study that the Easter holidays are from April the 12th until May the 1st: eighteen days I shall wish I'd never been born.

30 March Sunday *Mass at St Gilles; 'salut' at 2 o'clock at the pensionnat. I looked for my violin at S.S.C.'s and I took it to Rita's. S.S.C. found the book that Daddy told me to read and I cannot go to Holy Communion before going to confession. Sister St Charles, will you give me this book?*

1 April Tuesday *Henry has a fever, he is staying in bed today. Since I didn't go to confession yesterday I haven't been to Holy Communion. I am also not going to Mass. S.S.C. has not wanted to let me go to confession this afternoon; when she was talking to Sister Marie-Clarisse I walked on the benches and I ran from the study-room. When I got to the Rev. Father's parlour, Dymphna was there and I came back with her. The Rev. Father told me that I must ask S.S.C. to humble myself as much as I can, that I must not answer back after receiving a comment. Eh! well, thank you, if he thinks that S.S.C. isn't severe enough, then what does he mean by severe? Finally, now, my conscience is at peace. What a frightful day has gone by!*

28. Henry and his father Ernest, and Jack's three children: Desmond (on the bench), Jackie (John) and Doris/Dorice on the grass, Broadstairs, Kent, 1932

2 April Wednesday *Auntie Flo has written to me; she says that she is sad that I have left their church, but since I love so much Our Lord Jesus Christ we can be united. I received Jesus this morning. I had to stay in class until 12.50 to do my arithmetic exam, which I had torn up. Henry is still in bed.*

3 April Thursday *Henry complains of a sore throat; his headache is better; he is still in bed. I spent the afternoon with him and we played together. Daddy thinks that Charlie is going to change his regiment; he wants to join the cavalry regiment of the Scots Greys. Tommy is in a hospital in Leicester.*

4 April Friday *I can do what I wish, S.S.C. told me. From today I will go every day to Mass at 7 o'clock at St Gilles. Since it's the first Friday of the month there will be a 'salut' in the chapel. S.S.C. still hasn't returned my book.*

5 April Saturday *I was next to Sister St Charles at Mass. Henry is getting better; he went to classes this morning.*

8 April Tuesday *We have a holiday today because of the birthday of King Albert. Henry and I went to the review and we saw the King and Prince Léopold twice. We met S.S.C. and the boarders.*

9 April Wednesday *For several days the whole school has been going at 4.30 to the church of St Gilles because a priest was preaching for the children; today the subject was the seriousness of mortal sin. S.S.C. let me work a bit in her class with her this evening. Tommy is really suffering; he was taken from Cologne to Leicester on a stretcher; they took the bullet out of his body, but he is in a bad temper and the wound isn't going well. Jack is now with Constance; he is demobbed.*

10 April Thursday *We polished our benches this morning in class. At 4 o'clock Mother took Henry and me with her to the fair at Laeken; I went on the big wooden horses instead of going to listen to the sermon at the church of St Gilles. Daddy told me that he hopes to go to London on Sunday. Tomorrow at 4 o'clock the holidays start! Oh! when I think about the happy holidays of

Easters past when I was a boarder! Never, never more will they happen again. Mary, can I no longer be a boarder again?*

11 April Friday *The holidays have started. S.S.C. gave me her blessing this evening. Sister St Charles, I don't want you to say that someone else has taken their place in my heart, it's not true.*

12 April Saturday *I went to bed at 1 o'clock this morning. At 10 o'clock I went to the library of the Anglican church.*

17 April Holy Thursday *There was no Mass at 7 o'clock at St Gilles; priests gave Holy Communion for almost one hour, so I went to the church of the St Trinité and I saw the procession and then the Holy Sacrament placed on a beautiful altar. Oh! it was so beautiful to see all these gentlemen kneeling before the King of Kings. After dinner Henry came with me to the British soldiers' canteen. Jesus has again answered my prayer: I was able to go to the Office of darkness; I went to seven churches this afternoon: les Carmes, the church of St Joseph, St Boniface, in chaussée de Wavre, St Croix, in rue Washington, and finally the church of St Trinité. I am happy; I didn't think that I would be so well granted my prayer; but ...... last year! Sister St Charles has forbidden me from coming near here from today. Oh! she is cruel. What have I done to her that she detests me so? S.S.C. also thinks that tonight when I go to bed my conscience will not be tranquil. Eh! well yes, she is still more tranquil now during class because I am not resisting any more and I don't disobey any more so much. Oh! how this mistress knows how to torture hearts!*

18 April Good Friday *There was no Mass at 7 o'clock, so, after having made a short 'adoration', I did the Way of the Cross. For two days S.S.C. hasn't come to church; I haven't seen her except scarcely two minutes at the pensionnat, and this short time, instead of being happy, was the opposite, because S.S.C. has again forbidden me from coming to her before I have changed my conduct. But what conduct? What have I done so criminal to make her like this? Oh! now, when Daddy comes home and says to me that I must soon leave to go to Doris, I do not want to be sad, because I no longer know how to be happy where someone finds me too much and deceitful, a liar, a hypocrite, etc. Sister St Charles is going away next week for several days! She is ill. I received her blessing this evening. This afternoon I went to pick flowers in the Bois for Mother and for Sister St Charles. Mother has invited an English soldier, a friend of Henry, and he's not leaving until 8.30.*

19 April Saturday *I stayed an hour and a half in church this morning, waiting for Mass to start. The priests chanted the litany etc. without music. Finally I left as soon as the bells and the music started, and naturally S.S.C. and the boarders entered the church. I still couldn't receive Jesus today. As I was leaving the pensionnat S.S.C. came in with the pupils, so I saw her this morning, but not this evening.*

20 April Sunday, Easter Day *I received Jesus this morning at the Eglise des Carmes. There was a magnificent Mass. Oh! the music was beautiful! Mrs Heineman sent me a box of chocolates, and I was in a really atrocious mood from the time I got home. After lunch I went to Rita's in her new house; Ethel and I took plants to the cemetery to put on the grave of Mr Mellin. Joe Heineman is dead.*

21 April Monday *She is cruel. Oh! I wish that I'd never known her. Why does she torture me like this? Tomorrow she is going and today she behaves like this to me. As if I knew how this ghastly cardigan fell from the balcony! But it's always my fault. Everything that happens is because of me.*

22 April Tuesday *When I went to the pensionnat this morning the pupils told me that I was too late, because S.S.C. left at 4 o'clock in the morning, and I didn't even say goodbye to her! If I continue to have a foul temper like this I don't know where I will end up: at the moment I am in an atrocious mood and I was like this all morning. I am beginning to think that the Blessed Virgin has abandoned me because I don't any longer feel her near me as I did before. I am really discouraged today.*

23 April Wednesday *My head really aches today; yesterday as well; it's spinning at the moment. Sister Marie-Clarisse returned several books that S.S.C. had said I could have before she went. Still two more days!! Mother and Henry have bad colds.*

24 April Thursday *Henry is in bed. At 11 o'clock I went to the wedding of Miss Bivort, a pupil of Daddy's. It was really beautiful; I believe that she really loves the Blessed Virgin because during the marriage blessing a man sang 'Ave Maria' very well, then he was accompanied by a violin and a cello. But it's disgraceful how people strike up conversation in church! When I got home from the ceremony M. [Mother] didn't want to believe that I had stayed so long at the church, she maintained that I had gone to see S.S.C. Oh! if only that were true! It's terrible to not be able to speak to S.S.C. in person; I am impatiently waiting for the evening because I will see her in my dreams. Still one more day! Last night I dreamt that on going to town I met S.S.C. and Sister Hélène-Maria. S.S.C. took my hand and we walked across fields together. Suddenly I saw lights in the sky, then loud shots were heard. I was very frightened, but S.S.C. squeezed my hand harder, and the scene changed and we were at the pensionnat. But it was only a dream!*

25 April Friday *Last night I dreamt that Sister St Charles didn't want me to carry her books because I had disobeyed. At 4 o'clock this afternoon I went to the pensionnat but Sister St Charles had still not returned, I won't see her until tomorrow. Henry is better but he's got to stay in bed one or two days more.*

26 April Saturday *I got up at 5.45 in order to do my Way of the Cross before Mass in order to see S.S.C. as soon as possible. Yes, I know well that I haven't seen her. I stayed in the pensionnat more than half an hour going from place to place and I didn't find her. It's now five days, five long days of torture that I've been waiting for her to arrive and .... oh! I don't want to love her any more, because to love is to suffer cruelly. At 10.30 I went to the library; after lunch at the Maison Communale and on returning I saw Sister St Charles near the sisters' study-room. When she saw me she asked me <u>what I was doing here</u>. As if she didn't know! S.S.C. is still cross with regard to the black cardigan, that horror! It's not surprising that I detest it so much. If I had known! .... Oh! carry on like this Sister St Charles and lead me soon to the grave.*

27 April Sunday I'll never, never, never be good! It's no good, my character is too bad. There, I've been crying and being a perfect fool just because I could not go to school this morning, then I wouldn't eat my lunch and went off to get M.'s sugar, but of course had to look in a moment at the school. I saw S.S.C., yes, half a minute, she only answered coldly to my good-day. Went to Rita's and at 5.30 tried my luck again. This time S.S.C. was sweet. I remained with her almost an hour. When I came back I found Daddy at home; he has brought me back a pink sweater from Conn. Charlie is again at the hospital because as he was coming out of a cinema some bad ones jumped on him and hurt him on the head. He has had to have it sewn up.

28 April Monday I sat next to S.S.C. at Mass. She was a darling when I went to her this morning, only she took a book away from me and had forbidden me to read it. Henry and I went to tennis and afterwards to the fair. We went into a circus and we saw a wonderful man who curled his body up like a snake. It snowed a bit this morning.

29 April Tuesday I was too happy yesterday morning; today a cloud has come. I could see the way S.S.C. answered to my good morning. I had not the chance to speak to her, for she was cleaning in the back yard, so she could not possibly have guessed that I went to tennis yesterday. Henry went back to school this morning. Having taken Daddy's letter to the Legation I went to school and found S.S.C. occupied with somebody. I asked to speak to her and she said, 'In a few minutes.' It ended by my only seeing her for two minutes for the Angelus was rung. Well, I'm not going to bother her any more. Tomorrow I shan't go to school. I shall try to content myself with seeing her at church. It is all beginning again with M. [Mother] I think. It is all jealousy because she imagines Daddy spoils me or something. Oh! Mary, you see nobody loves me, <u>do</u> not abandon me. Be my Mother always for my earthly mother does not love me. But I love you, Blessed Virgin! This afternoon I went to the C.N. d'Alimentation with Joséphine.

30 April Wednesday S.S.C. said again this morning that I was a storyteller, a hypocrite, etc., all about a book again. I must say she is not very consoling. Why is it that I can't let a day pass without going to see her? She doesn't want me, I only bore her. Well, tomorrow I shall try and do that great mortification. Mary, please do help me! When Daddy was on his journey back to Belgium he saw the tops of the masts of an English ship which had sunk with a crew of twenty men. She was carrying food over to England and struck a floating mine. After tea Henry and I went to the fair. Saw two Indian chiefs in a motorcar. A Belgian military went into a lamp-post at the Porte Louise.

1 May Thursday After 7 o'clock Mass I went to confess. I believe somebody reads this diary, so I am not going to write everything I think. I know M. at least has seen my conscience book for she told Daddy, and this morning that kind, good brother of mine threatened to tear up all my religious pictures on the wall if I tell Daddy Henry was touching and prowling into his books and papers. From today, being the 1st of May, month of Mary's, I have promised not to read any storybooks and not to buy any sweetmeats. Henry and I went to the circus at the fair; it was a very good show. Mother is suffering from a pain in the back.

2 May Friday It is just two years today that I came to school as a boarder, and never, never did I think I should become a day girl. No, I can't stand it any longer! I hate it, I hate it! Went back to school this morning, and, as usual, after I've been longing for this day to come, S.S.C. has been simply horrid. Oh! I'm not going to bother her any more; she has enough girls. When I get to South Africa it will be less hard for me to quit her. May that day come soon now for if she goes on like that I don't know what I'll do.

3 May Saturday I'm not going to like her any more. I remember those days when I was sometimes ill at school, S.S.C. would come many times to my bed. Her very sight made me better. I remember that day, in the summer holidays, when we went to the Pink Farm: I had gone far away from the sisters and the girls to pick some heather for S.S.C.

4 May Sunday I saw a fine religious procession; it came out of the St Boniface Institute. Went to town with Rita this afternoon.

6 May Tuesday We all went with the school to a cinema to see films of the terrible War 1914–1918. It was very interesting, but of course also very sad. S.S.C. simply hates me, she is just as cruel as can be, stopping me from going to the piano, etc. How I wish I could cease loving her! Why do I love her? She rarely says any nice things to me, always words which wound .... oh! I'm a fool, why can't I be good and reasonable!

7 May Wednesday Yesterday we heard lots of explosions; Daddy told us they were ammunition explosives at Groenendael; several people were wounded and the station and other things are very much damaged. Conn, Desmond and Jack have left London and are staying at a lovely place out in the country.

8 May Thursday Went to tennis with Daddy and played tennis with Mlle Jacquemin, went to see the rabbits and played with the two Heineman kids and Sylvane.

9 May Friday S.S.C. kept me in at 11.30 because I made noises with some grass. A row at lunch because Henry wouldn't eat some curry; he flew into an awful rage.

10 May Saturday Went to the Trinity church this morning instead of St Gilles; I find I can pray better there. I had two unlucky adventures this afternoon; first, Sister Superior asked me to replace Germaine a few minutes, then I had a catastrophe with the chair and all the girls set off laughing till Soeur Hélène-Maria appeared on the scene. Then after tea I wanted to get a ball on the roof and if my feet don't go through the pane. I thought I would land myself in the cloakroom, but I managed to scramble out, my knee is a bit cut and my feet hurt; but that was not all, if S.S.C. doesn't make it worse by saying all sorts of horrid things. I went to get the glazier and while I'm writing I see he is putting in the pane. I dreamt last night S.S.C. was going away to another convent as a Carmelite, and when I woke up I found myself blubbing like a baby. Mother and Daddy went to tea at the Legation.

13 May Tuesday Daddy had some invitations to go the North Station to assist the funeral service of Edith Cavell. Henry and I went with him. The station was decked in mourning and it was a very imposing sight. The coffin was carried by British soldiers accompanied by a military funeral band. Mr Gahan read the service in a pulpit draped in black. The martyr's two sisters and brother-in-law followed, then the coffin was put into the train, where it will be taken to England. I'm not good today. I was sent out of the schoolroom. When shall I be really serious? Monsieur Jean brought Mother a lovely big bunch of lilac this morning. *From today I will be serious.*

14 May Wednesday *Russia has declared war on Poland.*

15 May Thursday *I went to tennis with Daddy this afternoon and I played with Liliane and Henry. Esther told me today that Mlle Gabrielle is dead. Again I cannot go to Holy Communion because I do not want to promise to give my apology to Sister Marie-Clarisse in front of pupils. Arthur has written; he is at the seaside at Margate College. Mrs Jeffes and her two little boys came to tea this afternoon.*

16 May Friday *Going to class this morning I saw a child under a motorcar; he was yelling; policemen ran up and having lifted

29. Nurse Cavell's coffin was taken on a British gun-carriage from the Tir National, where she had been shot and buried, to the Gare du Nord, and thence to England, 13 May 1919 © IWM

the motorcar they freed the child and put him in a pharmacy in chaussée de Charleroi. Tomorrow I can't receive Holy Communion because I resisted too much after the 'salut'. But that sister! I know well that Sister St Charles wants me to become a teacher. Never, no never. Anything, but not that; there is nothing I detest more in the world. I left the pensionnat in a terrible rage at 6 o'clock; but it's she who forces me to act like this.*

17 May Saturday *I went to Mass at 7 o'clock at the St Trinité, but I left before the end because I felt so peculiar; my soul asked for its nourishment. Alas! it didn't receive it at all. Monseigneur de Sainte Alène gave me a picture of the Sacred Heart in class this morning. Mother and Henry went to a reception given by Mrs Gahan to see Bishop Bury, who came from England yesterday. Since the Rev. Father wasn't there I went to confession at the Eglise des Carmes.*

18 May Sunday *Uncle Fred is in Brussels. Henry saw him in church. I spent the afternoon at Rita's and I amused myself on a ladder cutting lilac; I carried a bouquet to Mme Benoit from Rita. Then I went to the pensionnat. Eva was with S.S.C.; the latter only gave me the keys to her classroom so that I could put the flowers there, that's all. Since I didn't want to return home in that fashion I ventured again to go to her; it was better. But it's no longer like previously. Finally, since Pauline knows how to put up with all that S.S.C. tells her and does to her, I will also try to become like her. There were again explosions this morning.*

19 May Monday *I woke up at 7 o'clock, so I couldn't go to that Mass, but I received N.S. at the St Trinité. For once S.S.C. was really kind to me today; I stayed with her for almost an hour. Oh Mary, I don't think about you as much as I did before; now it is always S.S.C. who fills my ideas. Ah! don't be cross, because I love you very much, yes, very much, good Mother.*

20 May Tuesday *I dreamt that S.S.C. had come to cover me up as before when I wasn't well in the pensionnat.*

22 May Thursday *I went into town with Rita this afternoon and after supper I went to the Laiterie du Bois with Daddy. He has received a letter from Doris, saying that she and Morty would be very happy for me to go to their home in Umtali and Daddy has decided to send me there, I think that I will return with Uncle Fred to England before I go to Africa. So I must therefore leave Sister St Charles!*

25 May Sunday *This afternoon I went to Reverend Father Lecourt's with Rita; I stayed there for the 'salut'. The Rev. Father promised he would research to find out if there are Catholic churches in Umtali. They all want to send me there, faraway from everybody. Well, may the holy will of God fulfil it.*

26 May Monday *Rita came to see Sister St Charles and they talked a long time; this evening I wrote to Daddy to tell him that I don't want to leave for Africa. Uncle Fred spent the evening with Daddy and Mother, and Henry and I went up to bed early; I stayed on the terrace until it was dark. There are a lot of green shoots starting to show in my reseda plant.*

27 May Tuesday *I clambered up the wall and went into the garden opposite to find our ball because the people were out. I went to confession with Adrienne and the Reverend Father told me I must do the impossible so as not to leave for Africa. That's what I am going to do; it's absolutely vital that I go back in May.*

28 May Wednesday *Not having had a favourable reply from Daddy I went to see Uncle Fred and he will come to the pensionnat this afternoon. Rita came to talk to Sister St Charles. At 2 o'clock I went to Rita's and, since Uncle Fred was there, I took him to the pensionnat. Now he is going to see Daddy and .... oh! happiness! may tomorrow I again be a boarder!*

30 May Friday *I was so happy yesterday and the day before, while today I am discouraged. Twice today I tried to make Daddy understand that I don't want to leave for Africa; he told me he absolutely didn't want me to return as a boarder. Oh! has the Holy Virgin abandoned me? Will she let me go there alone, among strangers, like a prisoner led to a strange land, far from those that she loves? No, is it not, good Mother, that you will let me return here?

Oh! I beg you to let me return near you. Henry is in bed, he has an abscess in his mouth. Sister St Charles must be ill because she was sitting at Mass, before the Elevation and after Holy Communion.*

1 June Sunday *Charlie is twenty years old today. After Mass at 9 o'clock at St Gilles I went to pick flowers at the tennis with Daddy. This afternoon I went to Rita's; Uncle Fred was there; then to 'salut' in the rue Washington. A young girl sang the 'Ave Maria' accompanied by a violin. It was magnificent; then an English soldier sang, then I went back to Rita's and, with Mlle Verbeckhoven, we drank tea in the garden. They now have a new project in mind; to send me to a cousin of Daddy's, Cardinal Bourne, who will put me in a convent in England. I have stopped fighting now: may they do to me what they want. I ended the day by going to Sister St Charles's class. There were two terrible explosions at Vilvorde yesterday evening; I heard them and Daddy even saw the lights. It's now been three weeks since it has rained; the crops are all dry.*

3 June Tuesday *I didn't receive Jesus this morning, because yesterday I was very naughty, and since Sister St Charles wasn't at the Mass at 7 o'clock I didn't know if I could receive Communion. Oh! if all this carries on I no longer know what I will do. My character becomes more and more abominable. Everybody detests me. The church was full of little girls dressed in white who made their solemn Communion; it was very beautiful. Oh! Life! Life! why am I still on this earth!*

4 June Wednesday *Henry is still not going to classes because he suffers again. Sister St Charles has a sore leg. Why must she always suffer like this? Yvonne Bodet has returned; she is a half-boarder. Oh! it's become terrible! It's no longer friendship, but the passion returns again in my heart (if I have one). And yet there are so many who love her; Elisa Demol loves her now. How I would like to detach myself from her! Is it because I am going to leave her, is it a horrible presentiment? No, it can't be. Please, Jesus, let me die near her.*

5 June Thursday *I went with Daddy to a reception at Mr Jarvis's; Mother and Henry came later. Since there were only important people, Henry and I were in the garden before and after tea. After that I took Henry to tennis, then I went to confession. The Reverend Father told me again that I must absolutely not go to Africa, but he found the other project with regards to Cardinal Bourne much better. He also said that I cannot live like this, carefree, and that I must think about my future. He also asked me why people wanted me to go and I had to give him the reason. Finally, I was at Sister St Charles's; I only saw her a moment because the Angelus sounded.*

6 June Friday *The first Friday of the month consecrated to the Sacred Heart of Jesus. After lunch I went to Uncle Fred's to ask him what was being proposed; the plan of London has vanished, and again the nightmare returns of sending me to Africa. This evening I tried again with Daddy.*

10 June Tuesday *Mother's birthday. I spent the night at Rita's because after the letter that Mother wrote to Daddy she no longer wants me to stay at home. I took flowers with Rita to Mother, who refused to see me; but before I left she let me kiss her once; afterwards Rita and I took my things to the pensionnat and this afternoon I returned as a boarder. I sleep in my old alcove. I can thank Sister St Charles and Rita for all this, because it's mainly because of them. Oh! thank you, thank you, Mary, now I am almost the happiest of boarders.*

11 June Wednesday *Father Lecourt came this afternoon; he showed me two medals that he had received from His Holiness the Pope. He saw Daddy yesterday at tennis and told him that I had returned as a boarder. Poor Daddy!*

12 June Thursday *It is very hot. During the night people played music at the Barrière de St Gilles. Rita came for a moment this morning to buy me a black hat and a ribbon, because now I must tie up my hair with a ribbon. A day girl told me that S.S.C. was again sitting during Mass at 7 o'clock at St Gilles, from which I must conclude that she is ill again.*

13 June Friday *Sister Marie let me play with the new little cat that I'm going to call Carlo; he is adorable. I wasn't at all well behaved today, nor yesterday either; I really believe that I am mad at moments.*

15 June Sunday An aeroplane threw down quantities of papers this morning; unluckily they fell on the roofs and trees; just as I nearly had one, Clémentine took it, but afterwards I managed to get one from a roof. Charlie came to see me and he brought me some chocolate, then Rita fetched me to dine with her; Uncle Fred and Mlle Verbeckhoven were there also. Charlie is going to Antwerp next Tuesday for a fortnight. Yesterday I saw the poet on the avenue.

16 June Monday S.S.C. is furious with me today, and no wonder for I am a beast. The big girls went to the funeral of Ida Dessy's mother, who died suddenly a few days ago.

17 June Tuesday S.S.C. wants me to decide what I want to do next term, whether I will go up into Sister Christina's class or remain in hers, but if I choose the last I must promise to work hard. Of course I shall choose the last.

18 June Wednesday Now S.S.C. simply hates me, I know. She says I tell bad things which are untruths, behind her back. All I said to Mimi was that S.S.C. was going to put a girl to watch me so that I should not speak to Mimi; and now S.S.C. thinks I said the other thing, which I didn't. Oh! is all this cruel torture going to begin again! If only I could stop loving her, but no, it is no more love, but passion which I have for her. I ought to be a hermit, always remaining alone, like that I should not sin so much, I hope. Instead of dressing this morning I went back to bed and when the bell rang S.S.C. told me I was to get up and go to confess at St Alène with Sister M.C., which I did; if I hadn't I would not have received Jesus today, because S.S.C. had forbidden me to approach the Holy Table after I'd been so naughty yesterday.

19 June Thursday We had free time today because it is Fête-Dieu and we all went to a big Mass at St Gilles. Antoinette fetched me at 12 o'clock, and, after lunch, Rita, Mlle Verbeckhoven and I went to the rue de la Loi to see President Wilson, the King, the Queen and Mrs Wilson on their way to Louvain and Malines; at 6.30 we saw them all again coming back from their visit. S.S.C. is not a bit nice with me today; yesterday night she was ill. That beastly Pauline is speaking to

30. Charlie, probably in London, c. 1919

her now; oh! how I dislike that girl. It is her who is making me like this; I'll go mad if she goes on bothering me like this.

21 June Saturday *Fête of Sister Superior; this afternoon we went to the adoration of St Alène. Berthe Deglune has won the first prize in the rudiments of music at the Conservatoire, and Esther has won the second; they both had 19 points and ¾ out of 20.*

22 June Sunday *We had a beautiful procession at St Gilles this morning; Justine and I were Guardian Angels. The mistresses of the pensionnat dined with the boarders; I was placed at Sister St Charles's table. The dinner lasted two hours; during this time the piano was played, people sang and declaimed. Esther and I played 'Le Ballet de Faust'. After supper we went to see the plays that the boarders performed for the fête of Sister Superior.*

23 June Monday *We went to Linkebeek for the whole day; unfortunately as I disobeyed in going with Pauline, Sister St Charles was very displeased in the evening.*

24 June Tuesday *I have a cut on my foot which hurts; Sister St Charles bandaged it. Renée and Paule Printemps have gone to the parlour crying; a taxi is waiting for them and they are leaving the pensionnat; it's said that they are returning to England. They don't have either a father or a mother! Many of the pupils from the first year went up today to Sister St Charles's, among others, Justine, Clara, Suzanne, Alix, Blanche, etc.*

26 June Thursday *Rita came to fetch me at noon; after lunch Henry and Uncle Fred came; the latter is going to England tomorrow and he gave me a whole packet of music that used to belong to Ethel. Then I went to town with Rita. S.S.C. doesn't want me to go with P., she has again strictly forbidden it. Not a single day passes now without something happening to distance S.S.C. from me.*

27 June Friday *Great fête of the Sacred Heart. The chapel is very beautiful today; the Holy Sacrament is displayed the whole day. I don't know any longer what to believe; some tell me one thing, others something else. What must I then do? It seems that P.'s résumé is totally different from mine. Who out of us two is lying? Ah! naturally it's me. That's what S.S.C. thinks. Oh well, she can believe me a liar, thief, hypocrite, whatever she wants. Why have I come onto this earth? To always be in the way everywhere I go. If I had not come back here as a boarder, this very day I would be on my way to London and from there to Africa. At times, oh, I would like to go far, really far from her and all the people who amuse themselves by making me suffer.*

28 June Saturday *I finally believe that it is finished with Sister St Charles, she detests me and can no longer bear me. Because of my resistance this morning I could not go to the Communion Table. That's the second time that's happened to me this week. Oh, where am I now going? But despite that she continues to detest me like this, it's not because of that that I will stop loving her. Oh! no, the opposite. Yet, it's stupid, it's ridiculous to attach oneself to someone who holds you in repugnance. <u>At 3 o'clock this afternoon, Germany signed the Peace Treaty at Versailles.</u> I went to confession with Reverend Father La Haye because Reverend Father Someville wasn't there.*

29 June Sunday *This morning we all went to the plateau of Koekelberg where a splendid altar has been erected in honour of the Sacred Heart. The King and the Queen were present, and his Eminence the Cardinal Mercier preached. At the Elevation, instead of ringing a bell they fired guns. The crowd was immense and lots of children fainted. We returned on foot at 1.30. Rita came at 9 o'clock and I went to the fair with her.*

30 June Monday *We had a holiday today because the pupils made their solemn Communion in the chapel. This morning we got up at 6.20 and after breakfast we played in the Parc Royal. Sister St Charles came with us but it's said that she is again displeased with me.*

1 July Tuesday *There were two Masses in the chapel this morning.*

2 July Wednesday *Fête of the Visitation of the Blessed Virgin to her cousin Elisabeth. I started my day badly and it continues to be bad. Oh! I despair about ever being correct. Every day it's the same.

There is not a single day that passes without Sister St Charles being angry; also, this morning, she said to me to go far away from her. Oh! yes, I go far away from her bodily perhaps, but in my heart .... never. I know well that I always bore her when I talk to her, eh! well, fate, it's just that I suffer now having committed so many sins. The whole class, separately, were photographed this morning, without the mistresses.*

3 July Thursday *Why do I repeat so much always that I am mad? I know well that I am. This afternoon we were caught in a thunderstorm: the boarders lost their way in the park while trying to find shelter. I found myself all alone, but afterwards I met three boarders and we got back to the pensionnat, soaked to the bone. Yesterday evening there was also a thunderstorm; I was afraid and S.S.C. came twice, but today again being a martyr starts. One can endure all for friendship.*

4 July Friday *That Sister M.-P.! I almost detest her; after Sister C. treated me like a madwoman yesterday evening she recalled it again in class in the presence of all pupils; Germaine H. said it at breakfast and when she met me. Now I cannot any longer go to bed with the

31. Amy's school photo, 2 July 1919, Institut des Filles de Marie, 6 rue Th. Verhaegen, St Gilles, Brussels. Amy is standing in the centre

pupils because I threw water over the boarders and Sister Christina told me that I've got to go up by the balcony.*

5 July Saturday *There was a thunderstorm this afternoon. Germaine Descamps has come back for one or two days.*

6 July Sunday *We went to see a really beautiful procession with Sister Louis; all the schools in St Gilles took part; our pensionnat represented Serbia; I would have loved to have been part of it but I don't have a Serbian costume; it was the procession of Peace and all countries were represented; at the back a large number of soldiers marched. A day full of disappointments for me. S.S.C. didn't say one word of encouragement today.*

7 July Monday *We had a holiday today by an order of the Commune. S.S.C. told me it's finished and that I must no longer speak to her for my permission; it's because I talked with P. We were on the swing this afternoon.*

8 July Tuesday *Rita fetched me for lunch; afterwards I went to look for music at Marian Carr's. Henry then came with a letter from Mother for Rita. After having been at the seamstress Rita and I went to tennis to see Daddy; he wasn't there; at his club, he had just left. Chance wasn't on my side. Sister St Charles has started coughing again.*

11 July Friday *I do not find that at all just; it is nearly all the newest pupils who are always performing in the plays for the fêtes. Sister M.C. does not want me to perform in the fête for Sister Christina; all the pupils who [...] for her and for Sister M.P. can perform. Why is it always the same? It's not fair, that's all; and if they think that I will play the piano, they are dreadfully mistaken. Every day this torture starts again: in the evening I think that Sister St Charles is no longer displeased; in the morning, early, my illusions have gone. It's time I got used to it, but no ...... it is cruel of her. Daddy has written to me and I can't have the letter <u>until I am well behaved</u>, S.S.C. said to me. Eh! well, I will not wait later than Sunday. I will never be acceptable enough to please this mistress.*

13 July Sunday *We went to the Eglise des Capucins with Sister St Charles; Rita came to fetch me for lunch.*

14 July Monday Big French fête. Didn't go to bed last night; sat on my bed. When I give a scream or do some foolish thing S.S.C. either says I'm mad or: do as you like; when P., who just loves being scolded, does as she can to make S.S.C. notice her well, S.S.C. just does. I suppose she'll not go and say, again, it's I who helps her to do all that for I simply detest her now. Beastly old hypocrite! The girls tell me, S.S.C. likes me; if she did she wouldn't have let me sit up all night. Oh! when shall I find some faithful friend? I've no one here. I went to town with a new sister from the Louvières and I saw Daddy in a tram. Soeur Christina left for Liège yesterday with the girls who are passing their exams at the Jury Central; our exams have begun too.

15 July Tuesday Last night it was made up, today it's something else again. She says it's stealing what I did in getting that bread. So I'm a thief now, what else? She's now used up all the names she could find. Whatever I do is wrong and sinful; that other girl said I could get that bread for she asked a nun before so I've not stolen. Oh! every day there's something. I'm just tired of it. I can simply not count upon anybody; they're all a set of tell-tales and hypocrites. Oh! if only Mother loved me I should not have searched affection anywhere but in her heart! I should not have this passionate love for a person who looks down upon me as a thief, a liar, etc., etc. Lucky are those who have a mother, a real one! May they never love anybody more than her.

16 July Wednesday Fête de Notre-Dame du Mont Carmel. The girls are all going to see the war films this afternoon and I can't go with them.

17 July Thursday Went for a walk to the Plaine de Berkendael with S.S.C. and the girls; we saw the Belgian wounded in wooden buildings near Doctor Depage's Institute. Oh! that passion is growing more and more every day; even when I'm preparing to go to Holy Communion her dear face is always present in my mind.

18 July Friday I believe S.S.C. must be ill for she has never been so strict as now. I wish Soeur Christina would come back; like that,

Soeur St Charles would not have so much work. Adeline Motte left this afternoon.

20 July Sunday Dined with Rita and then we went to the War Exhibition; we went inside a tank which weighs 48000 kilos; we saw some torpedoes too. When I got back to school I just saw the end of the girls' rehearsal. S.S.C. made me go into the office while the girls supped.

21 July Monday We went to see the King and Queen and all the royal family leaving the palace to go to the Te Deum; we saw Brand Whitlock, all the ministers in their grand uniforms; the judges and the advocates; after lunch S.S.C. took us to town to see the review of the schools at the Grand-Place; the Prince, the Princess and Mr Max [the Mayor] were at the large balcony of the Town Hall. Then we went to the rue Royale for President Poincaré. Marshal Foch arrived at the North Station at 6 p.m. We saw them with the royal family three times. We came back at 8 p.m. minus five girls. S.S.C. has not been at all nice with me today. Holiday today.

22 July Tuesday *This morning we went to see the grand review of the Allied troops; His Majesty the King, Marshal Foch were there at the front. Sister M. Christina gave me permission to go into the club because I saw Daddy at the window. It rained. In the afternoon the boarders went out again, but I didn't go because S.S.C. stayed in the pensionnat.*

23 July Wednesday *Going to Holy Communion, it seemed that a black veil had been placed in front of my eyes, my legs bent under me; I thought that I would fall. Then, coming back from the Holy Table I left the chapel and sat on the stairs because I couldn't walk any more; Sister Hélène-Maria found me and led me to the kitchen; afterwards I went out for some air in the courtyard and felt better. All day I feel unwell when I breathe, when I cough, when I laugh or when I speak. We went to the Comité to see the plays and at 6 o'clock we did the fête for Sister M. Christina; after supper we listened to the gramophone. Sister St Charles isn't well this evening; she has a headache.*

24 July Thursday *We had free time this morning on the occasion of the fête of Sister M. Christina. M. Poincaré left this morning; the gun was fired. At 2 o'clock Sister M. Christina and Sister Superior and all of us went to see the plays. After tea Rita came to fetch me to buy shoes. Sister St Charles is better today.*

25 July Friday *At 3 o'clock Rita will say the words which will make her a Roman Catholic; it's been a long time that she has wanted to change her religion.*

26 July Saturday *I went to the Léopold Club with Daddy and Henry to see a tennis match between M. de Borman and M. Lemmens (Belgians) against M. Lorrentz and M. Decrugis (French); the latter won the third match. After that we went to tennis and I played with Jimmy Heineman. Arthur returns from England with a friend this evening; Mother and Henry went to meet him at the station.*

27 July Sunday *Martyrs' day! This morning we went to Mass at St Antoine. S.S.C. says that I am only a beggar, etc.; I stayed at the piano from noon till almost 4.30, in that way my beggarly presence doesn't annoy anyone; and this morning I couldn't go to the study-room, even though pupils, among others P., were there. Alas that people are surprised that I am jealous ...... there is something in it.*

29 July Tuesday *Sister St Charles is really pale today. Henriette asked her if she was ill, but she replied no, that she was simply tired. My God, Sister St Alphonse told me that after the holidays Sister St Charles will perhaps have a transfer. No, that's not possible – naturally she will return.*

30 July Wednesday *Sister M.C. has again said to me that I am more to be pitied than blamed; Sister E. said it another way this morning in class. Nicely encouraging, I agree. Oh! bah! there are mad people in Paradise I think; perhaps they have a much nicer place than all these clever people.*

31 July Thursday *The cleaning of the classrooms starts; I cleaned Sister St Charles's classroom. At 6 o'clock Rita came and we went to town.*

1 August Friday *The announcement of positions took place this morning; I am 17th out of 22 pupils. Many boarders have gone home for the holidays.*

3 August Sunday *Pauline left this morning; S.S.C. didn't kiss her. Rita and Cécile, a cousin of Father Lecourt, came to take me to lunch; after that we went to the 'salut' in rue Washington and, at the club of young English Catholic girls, I danced with Cécile. She is very cheerful and kind; it's only 18 months since she joined the Catholic Church. Daddy went to England this morning.*

4 August Monday *Sister St Charles was again adorable yesterday evening, and today, from the little that I saw, she responded to me again so coldly. We are only eight pupils.*

5 August Tuesday It's simply unbearable this cruel way she answers me when I ask her something. As if it's not enough that I'm going away from her for a few days on Thursday. No, she wants to get rid of me, and she's quite right too, for I am detestable; but, oh, if she only knew how I love her, as much as she dislikes me. Rita fetched me for lunch, and, contrary to her habit, Sister St Charles did not say goodbye to me, and then I've got to go and enjoy myself through it all. Had tea in town; Rita bought me a chaplet and a silver chain; then I came back to find Soeur St Charles more severe than before. Well, I shall have to bear, it's my fault, I deserve it.

6 August Wednesday All the boarders and day girls have gone out to Eppeghem as a treat; Soeur St Charles is not going, so I'm not either. She thinks I love P.: and that it's because I can't go with her that I'm not going to Eppeghem. Well, if she wants to stick to that idea for ever, she may. I wish I were dead. It's been a perfectly beastly day for I'm the only boarder left today, and I'm just boring myself to death; scarcely seen anything of Soeur St Charles.

7 August Thursday We were allowed to stay in bed till 7 a.m.; at 8 we went to Mass at St Gilles with Soeur M. Christina. Blanche Bataille has got her diploma of the biggest distinction: she had the nine tenths of the points. Soeur St Charles did my hair this morning. *Arthur and Rita came to fetch me at the pensionnat; Sister St Charles took us all round the convent that one can visit; then we lunched in town, then I returned to the pensionnat to get my things. I saw S.S.C., she was really, really kind. I am going to spend a few days with Rita, then on Monday we go to Knocke until Friday, because on Saturday I'm going to the retreat 'de Pêches'. I saw Mother; she said virtually nothing to me, except that she is pale and is thinner and also a few words against my change of religion. Rita gave me a beautiful statue of the Blessed Virgin. Cécile and Arthur are dining here this evening and laughed a lot because Father Lecourt came and we played tricks. I went to bed at 11 o'clock.*

8 August Friday *Rita and I went to Mass at the Reverend Father Servites; at 11 o'clock we went to lunch in town. Afterwards I saw Sister St Charles a bit; she looked really pale and tired; it's not surprising because she went to bed at midnight. Poor Sister St Charles. Then we saw Mother; Joséphine is going to become a Protestant. Connie has a new child, a little girl; she is called Doris Margaret. Mme Deltan slept here tonight. Rita has bought me a beautiful little stuffed dog, his name is César.*

32. Ernest with his granddaughter Doris/Dorice Margaret (b. 31 July 1919), Connie and Jack's daughter, and grandson Desmond, Siasconset, Nantucket island, 1920

9 August Saturday *Henry spent the day with us; we lunched in town; then we went to Sister St Charles's. It was really hot today. I again went to bed yesterday evening at 11.30.*

10 August Sunday *After breakfast Rita and I went to look for tickets at the Gare du Nord and ordered tickets, a car for tomorrow at 7 o'clock. At 3 o'clock we went to the 'réunion' and Cécile and I left early. I went to Sister St Charles's, and stayed near her for two hours. Oh! she was so nice. What will I do without her? I returned with Pauline because the trams had stopped. Cécile came to supper and I packed before going to bed. I won't see Sister St Charles before Friday.*

11 August Monday *We got out of the train at Bruges instead of Blankenberge; it was again my fault; we stayed there one and a half hours; then we took the vicinal railway to Knocke village; from there the electric tram to the Grand Hôtel. Oh! the sea! It's so beautiful! After lunch Rita and I walked a long way, almost as far as Holland, on the beach and in the dunes; I went into the sea. The dunes are full of barbed wire, of trenches, etc., left by the Germans. From here we could see the ship that the Germans sank at Zeebrugge. The setting sun was magnificent; when it is dark I think that we are going on the seawall to see the phosphorescent sea. I have written a postcard to Sister St Charles. The Romdennes and the Allissons are here.*

12 August Tuesday *I had to sleep in Rita's bedroom because mine is too large and, since there are communication doors, I was afraid that in the night there might be an intrusion. I went to Mass and to Holy Communion at the church in Knocke village. I bathed in the sea. In the afternoon we went to Ziska in the dunes; everywhere there was barbed wire and destruction caused by explosions during the war. I climbed really high above the Hôtel, where previously were the gun turrets that the Germans built, and Marguerite Verbeckhoven showed me her studio and a mortar and all sorts of arrangements that the Huns placed up there.* Oh! I'm beastly homesick this evening; even this lovely sea does not stop me from longing to be near S.S.C. As I was in the sea .... oh! well, I mustn't be ungrateful. Still, it is hard to see all the happy children with their parents and me without mine. I'm sure Marguerite V. doesn't like me being here for she is beastly disagreeable when I say something wrong, etc. Well, I didn't ask to come; I'm much happier alone by the sea, for when I'm with them I've got to laugh and tonight I want to cry. Only three more days and I shall be near S.S.C., but I shall have to leave her again the day after for the retreat at Pêches. I wonder what she is doing now! *At 9.30 I went to see dancing on the seawall; before leaving I danced with Miss Marcks. Louise de Molinari is here. The sea is so beautiful and phosphorescent this evening; this morning I fell into the water with all my clothes on.*

13 August Wednesday *I went to confession this morning and the Reverend Father told me that I must adopt as my main aim the sign of the cross and that I must do it well. It's market day at Knocke, and Rita bought me a chain with a cross in mosaic; Rita isn't well today, I bathed in the sea and I think that a jellyfish touched me because my arms tickle a lot. This afternoon we went to have tea with a gentleman at the Châlet du Zoute; it was beautiful there in the middle of the dunes and by a wood of fir trees! Oda and Henri are at Knocke. An aeroplane flew above the sea and another above the dunes. One hears lots of explosions here; a gentleman told us that they are the boats that are blown up at Ostend. I picked flowers in the dunes and I gave them to the Blessed Virgin. The sea is so calm at the moment and the sun shoots its luminous rays on this page of stupidities that I write. There are lots of English and Americans here. I danced a bit on the seawall this evening, then I went to the seashore because it was superb at times; it was phosphorescent.*

14 August Thursday *I came back from church through the dunes and I saw the big battery called Wilhelm II and many houses in ruins. There was an armoured gun near the battery. I walked on the beach as far as Duinbergen, then I had a swim. The weather is magnificent. This afternoon we went to Ostend, via the ruins of Heist, Blankenberge, Zeebrugge, Le Coq and Ostend. It's really sad; we also saw English ships that had been sunk, among others *Vindictive* and *Brussels*. The weather changed this evening; there is a strong wind and the sea is almost angry.*

23 August Saturday Yesterday, I thought I should become a nun, but today .... no, never. Besides, how could I become one when I'm so jealous? I stay here for her, and the little I see of her is nearly always when A. is with her.

25 August Monday It is because she knows I love her that she treats me like that, and then she tells me that it is not true about her not standing me. What am I to believe? It's no good trying to be good to a saint, for laugh I must, even though I could cry my eyes out.

27 August Wednesday *I do not know what is the matter with S.S.C. today; everybody gives their opinion. We had silence during three meals and some of the fourth; silence during study. So as no longer to endure that I will go to the piano or the chapel when she supervises. In that way I will no longer see this scolding and these punishments which rain down.*

29 August Friday *Sister St Charles says to me that from today she has resolved to no longer talk to me when I am at fault, if I do not say to her, before this evening, what I think. Eh, well, no, I will not say it to her. Why must I say all this? It's now more than six hours and since the moment when Sister St Charles finished cleaning this morning she has all the time written alone in the classroom. It's not surprising that she is always so tired; that's not a holiday like this.*

31 August Sunday *Daddy comes back from England today. Rita and Cécile came for me at noon; poor Cécile, she is distraught because she has lost her prayerbook which has all her souvenirs of her admission into the Catholic Church. She will give 25 francs to the person who brings it back. We went to 'salut', then to Father Lecourt's club; he spoke for the last time because he is going for ever on Tuesday. This morning we went to the park with Sister St Charles and I was very naughty because, although she was so tired, I influenced the pupils to do all kinds of disobedient things. Mr Morrisson is dead.*

1 September Monday *The sisters return today from the first retreat at Pêches. S.S.C. is really pale.*

2 September Tuesday *I had to give my apologies to Sister Marie-Christina, to Blanche and to the pupils because I responded to a remark. Sister St Charles is really kind to me today; she made me a rosary.*

3 September Wednesday *Germaine Wauters came this afternoon.*

4 September Thursday *I was too happy yesterday morning; in the evening, or at least in the afternoon, the opposite of the morning carried the victory. But this Blanche ...... because of her I couldn't go to Holy Communion because I almost detest her. And to cap it all, Sister St Charles says it's me who makes her ill. Eh! well, that I don't believe, because I cannot think that that does anything to her. Why? Oh, I want to die for the hundredth time. Yesterday evening she coughed; no doubt it's my fault. Daddy came this morning, and I went to lunch at home with him; Arthur showed me how to ride a bicycle; afterwards I went to Mr Jarvis's and to tennis. Pauline is in the classroom with Sister St Charles at the moment. I hope that she will be kinder saying goodbye to her than she was to me this morning. Is it my fault that she is pale? It's not true, that's all.*

5 September Friday *Sister St Charles is getting ready to leave tomorrow; she gave me some bits of work and a book to copy before she returns. Rita and Cécile came this morning, but I couldn't go out because it's the last day that Sister St Charles is here.*

6 September Saturday *She left before 7 o'clock, as well as fourteen other mistresses. She said goodbye to me at 5 o'clock this morning, before she went to Mass. And now she won't return for ten long days. Oh! good Mother, help me to follow the rule of life that Sister St Charles showed me. I promised her to be well behaved. Can't I do it? Oh! I can't believe that she has gone. Now I must go back and forth outside her classroom without seeing her; it will no longer be with her that I carry the water for washing clothes, finally all is a void. And that for ten days! All morning I sewed in the classroom; I have made a rug and three small pieces of work. Near noon Rita and Cécile came and I went back with them for the rest of the day; we went to Dr Morhaue's and every day I must exercise and I must take 5 horrible pills at noon, because I am not strong enough. When I returned this evening, she wasn't there. I sent her a letter and I could only just write that I still haven't received any comment, that Sister Christina severely reprimanded me because I went out without a ticket.*

7 September Sunday *I was in the procession as a child of Mary, and I followed my heavenly Mother; I had a white dress and a veil and a blue sash. Oh! times past, Sister St Charles was with us, but today! Finally, I will be brave. Rita and Cécile came to take me for several days; in the afternoon we went to the club. Cécile and I went to sleep on the terrace this evening; it was good fun as it was so hot. Still nine more days!*

8 September Monday *Rita has an adorable little black cat and Cécile and I love it a lot. Today is the nativity of the Blessed Virgin; I gave her a bouquet of flowers at her feet in my room. C. and I laughed a lot yesterday evening before sleeping; this morning we went together to Mass. After breakfast we saw a Jewish marriage in the synagogue. I am in a foul temper. Mme Deltan lunched with us. Arthur and Henry went with us to the Bois de la Cambre, on Robinson island, and after lunch we all went out. Cécile and I slept again on the terrace this evening. We went to the fair this evening and I went to bed later than 11 o'clock.*

9 September Tuesday *Around 3 o'clock in the morning C. and I were so frightened on the terrace that our limbs were shaking. We were both woken almost at the same time and we heard a noise as if someone was in our room; it was terrible. I prayed to the Blessed Virgin to not let me die before seeing Sister St Charles again. An hour later we risked going in and went to Rita's room. Never again will we sleep outside. Rita came to Mass with me. We lunched in town. Cécile's arm really hurts; the doctor cut it. The little cat is blind. This evening I slept in the little room next to C.*

10 September Wednesday *I see now more than ever that Mother doesn't love me and that she will never love me. I went to the pensionnat this morning to change my dress and there Elisa told me that there is doubt whether Sister St Charles will come back. Oh! Mary, won't she return? Oh! that would be terrible if I don't see her again. Would I work like this on these pieces? We lunched in the Bois; this afternoon several people came for tea. Mme Deltan supped with us.*

11 September Thursday *Rita and I went to the Eglise St Croix this morning. Daddy came. We had lunch in the Bois.*

12 September Friday *Arthur and Henry came with us to the Bois this afternoon; they return to college in Margate next Thursday. It's awfully hot today.* It's simply beastly of R. to say I'm not straightforward. Why doesn't she call me a liar straight out? When I thought all that was finished .... Oh! I know she is tired of me, of course she is. But I want to go away, I never asked to stay. Nobody does love me, I know that. I wish I were dead. Oh! Sister St Charles, won't you ever come back?

13 September Saturday *We had lunch and then tea in town. Going to Mass I was almost knocked over by a bicycle; but I've only got a little bruise on my arm. This afternoon we went to the Wiertz Museum and I went to confession. When I visited St Gudule cathedral I saw a window on which was painted the portrait of St Charles Borromeo. Daddy dined with us this evening.*

14 September Sunday *I went to a second Mass in the cathedral of St Gudule. Arthur and Henry came to say goodbye. Mme Deltan dined with us. I dreamt that Sister St Charles had returned. This afternoon we went to the Girls' Club.*

18 September Thursday I'm sure Soeur St Charles is ill, for she sat down during Mass. And for the last three days she has been giving class at the Comité. I might as well have stayed with Rita for I scarcely see anything of her today. I've not seen her at all. I'm getting a bit sick of being here; that nun just bores me to death with her scoldings and her fine words. I nearly hate her. It's true I'm not paying here, so that's why they are so beastly to me. Antoinette fetched me to see the boys off; they are both going to Margate College. Rita is taking Cecily as far as Ostend and will then go on to Knocke for a few days. Cecily is going to her mother for she has to see a specialist about her arm. Daddy and Mother were at the station. They four have promised to write to me; I bet they won't. We went to bed at 7.45 p.m. because we made so much row in the yard. Last night, Lord! I was just whistling in the yard when in turning round I saw Sister C.'s eyes just glaring at me; but I am boring myself so today that I'd do just anything to while away the time. The cat came in the chapel during Mass; I did laugh.

19 September Friday Stayed in bed till 8 a.m. What is the good of going to Mass every morning if I can't improve? Row tonight because I put the light out after supper; then after chaplet because I got a fit of laughing.

20 September Saturday Oh! I do nearly hate that sister; she can't bear me and I can't stand her. The Reverend Mother is awfully sweet to me; she called me and said I was not to get always into mischief and that if I felt it coming I was to go to her and tell her. Well, if Sister C. spoke to me like that I should improve I'm sure.

21 September Sunday Feast of our Lady of Sorrows. First autumn day. My eye hurts rather. Doris has got malaria fever. Soeur St C. very cold and looks angry. Well, I've not done anything of which my conscience reproaches me very much. If she doesn't like to see me laugh a bit, well, I'm not going to care. Others have also gone through it all. If I could but leave here quite alone, never bother her any more! Well, I shall try again. After tea we went to Benediction at the Servites church; there was a procession of Mater Dolorosa round the church. Lovely singing. Very wet.

1 October Wednesday All the girls have come, heaps of new ones; it is like being in a new school! Oh! I'm just getting to long to go away now. Why did I ever come back? Sr St A. just blurted out this morning, when I asked what time I was to go to the typewriter, that I wasn't going to live off my hands but that I was to give lessons. I know that very well, she need not make it nastier for me; it's beastly enough living here on charity. Still, I never asked to come back in that way. I don't feel like a boarder any more. I wish people had more taste and not enjoy showing one's poverty. Of course I am poor for I've not a cent in the world which belongs to me; people who have all they want are always better looked upon than people who haven't it. Well, I'm going to try and not mind it. Patience for a while. Oh! Mary, do help me to bear it; really, at times I feel as if I should just pack my things, go back home, bear Mother's antipathy, anything better than living on this charity. I just loathe it! loathe it, hate it. I feel today as if I could never laugh again. I don't want to love her any more.

4 October Saturday Oh! never, never shall I forget how sweet she was to me last night! A mother could not have been sweeter; and after I'd been so naughty all day!

5 October Sunday I detest that girl to such an extent that if it goes on I shan't be able to go to Holy Communion any more. She's the biggest hypocrite of the school. Why does she come and tell me what S.S.C. says and does to her? We went to Mass at St Gudule. Rita fetched me to dine with her; after we went to the Girls' Club; came back to find the hypocrite had been manoeuvring again. Oh! I wish I were far, far away from here. That girl makes the cross of my school life. Will they never stop persecuting me?

6 October Monday C. tells me P. has a bruise which S.S.C. made yesterday. I wonder if it's true. What am I to believe? If it all begins again like before I think I shall go out of my mind. It was a liar she told me, for the girls say S.S.C. pulled her hair and bruised her face.

8 October Wednesday Got into a row because I took up M.'s part; poor kid, she's always crying and being punished. Soeur E. told Sister C. I'd criticized her, which wasn't true, so I had the honour of being called a demon amongst the girls. Then, as if that wasn't enough, S.S.C. scolded me too.

9 October Thursday I've done with the horrid creature now, she's the biggest hypocrite on the face of the earth. Last night as I was going to get some water P. came a little behind me, then went back to the yard where she knew S.S.C. was waiting for her. She would not say where she went, and of course S.S.C. thinks we plotted to meet there. That girl! I hated her so last night that I was not in a state to approach the Holy Table this morning, so I didn't go to Mass either. Rita came for a few minutes, she's going to England tomorrow.

10 October Friday Oh! Mother, I do wish you loved me. How much happier I should be! I should then never have got that passionate love for that sister. Why do I love her so? For over two years not a day, scarce an hour has passed that she's not present in my mind, and she .... ah! yes, to love is to suffer. But do I not deserve to suffer all this? Yes, Jesus, I thank Thee, for I am awfully naughty, but, oh! give me a mother and I shall be good. You know, Jesus, how cruel it is to feel I'm being kept here for nothing? I'm no more a boarder. I can only practise and type when there is room, says Sister A. And before, the hours and everything were settled. Well, dear Lady, you love me, don't you? for I love you. Alas! if I only could think less of her I should come and speak to you oftener. But I have tried so many ways. I shall try and bear it all for love of Jesus and you.

11 October Saturday Got a letter from Dad yesterday and today he is coming to fetch me tomorrow morning. I suppose that girl will do something else like last Sunday. Oh! why are people so false? She whom I thought I could have perfect faith in. No, why did she say that she did things to me which she would not do to others, because as I had no mother she would replace her to correct me? And now these girls tell me that she did drag P. by the hair, smacked her, pushed her etc.; and Bertha too, she smacks. Ah! but it's true, I'm no more a boarder. How can I feel comfortable in class, in the playroom, anywhere when I'm here out of pure charity? Ah! if I could but not love her so!

12 October Sunday Spent the day with Dad; called upon Miss Drury and Mr Jarvis; dined at home and had tea at tennis. Mr Spong brought me halfway home. Tram strike in Brussels; everyone has to walk or go about in a car.

14 October Tuesday My character's getting absolutely worse and worse; I simply can't teach these stupid kids. The majority don't even know their notes and they've no notion of music. No, I feel as if I simply can't go on like this; they must hate me for I've no patience with them. S.S.C. was coughing so yesterday study-time that she went out of the classroom. Today her cold seems better; God has answered my prayer, I think.

16 October Thursday Am giving English lessons in Sister Celestina's class twice a week. Got a note from Dad saying Edward's [Jenkins] come over for a fortnight to open the church two Sundays. He is coming to fetch me Sunday perhaps. We all went to the Scientific Museum after lunch. Sister St Charles did not come with us. My character's getting worse and worse.

17 October Friday S.S.C. seems discontented of me tonight. I suppose I've not been good again. Went to the baths.

18 October Saturday She's beginning again; she dares to tell me twice this afternoon that I'm waiting about for P.; first when I was coming back from the typing and secondly in the bathroom. She's doing it on purpose I know; she just loves rows; well I'm getting darned sick of them. I'm so mad with wrath that I almost hate her for saying such an insane thing. As if I'd wait to speak to P. in those places if I wanted an interview with her. Soon I shall dislike her as much as I've loved her; she'd better stop soon all this, if not I shall go with the creature all day long. It is she who's got such a vile imagination or it is out of horridness on her part. Well I'm not going on, I'm just madly furious.

19 October Sunday We all went to the woods this morning and we came back long past dinner time because the girls who led forgot the way home. Last night I got in a row because I walked out of the room without permission; it was to go after a girl whom S.C. had punished. The latter gave it to me hot and fetched me from the dormitory to write out lines, which I didn't do. So after a while as she saw there was nothing to be done she told me to go to bed but I went and sat on a bench in the yard. S.S.C. came and found me there. I apologised to S.C. because I saw it made S.S.C. sorry about my horrid conduct. She was very nice and gave me the hand. S.S.C. had a stitch which came on suddenly while she was dusting the stairs.

Edward J. fetched me after Benediction; he is a dear. We had tea in town and he told me I was quite right to have turned a R.C. as I believed in it. He spoke to me about Almighty God. He says Edward John [Palmer] is simply wonderful in music; he's only eight years old and he already plays Beethoven, Mozart, Grieg, etc.

1919

33. Rev. C.E. (Edward) Jenkins, Jack's older brother, 1914. In her 16 October diary entry Amy is referring to the Church of the Resurrection, built by his uncle (also Rev. C.E. Jenkins) and his father, Rev. J.C. Jenkins, who was chaplain there from 1874 until his death in 1894

He composed a wonderful music for Mass. We had to walk as the tramway-men are still on strike; then we fetched Dad from the club and they both brought me back to school. Had a letter from Rita; she is being confirmed today in Westminster Cathedral. Lovely day.

20 October Monday The Spanish flu seems to begin again, for several of the girls have it.

21 October Tuesday Soeur M.P. put me out of the class after I'd been 10 minutes in it. The girls are all going to see the war pictures tomorrow afternoon and I don't think she's going to let me go. Heard the first tram this morning; the strike is over.

22 October Wednesday Well, they've all gone and I've stayed behind; how could I go when she told me I might if I wanted to in such a funny way.

23 October Thursday I wish I had gone out to South Africa now; I'm getting tired of this life. I just loathe giving lessons. It was for her I came back; from today I'm going to try and love her less so that if I go away it won't be so hard. We went to the Botanical Gardens this afternoon. Lovely day.

24 October Friday I want to go away from here. I can't stand all this hypocrisy; I wrote to Daddy to ask him if I might go to Doris and the letter's disappeared out of my desk. Soeur St Charles took it and says she's going to send it to Rita. Now, since I whistle in my hands all the girls are trying to do it; a few have succeeded. It will be a row when they all get to know the trick. Went to confess here this morning because R. Father Someville is away for some time.

25 October Saturday Poor Carlo is dead; he was accidentally I suppose locked up in the loft, and was starved to death. Poor little beast, and he was my little friend. Conn and her two children and Nanny are off to join Jack in New York today. S.S.C. is nice with me, but I feel it is only to make me change my idea about going to S.A. [South Africa]. She coughed again in that awful way this morning; please, Jesus, don't send her that cough; let me have it instead of her.

26 October Sunday We went to High Mass at St Gudule Cathedral; I sat next to Soeur St Charles; she got a fit of coughing in the chapel, so she went out at the beginning of the fourth decade. Wet day.

27 October Monday There's a new boarder, an Alsacian kid. S.S.C. smacked P. tonight; I thought she wouldn't be nice very long to her.

28 October Tuesday Stayed in bed this morning because I couldn't receive Jesus for I was awful yesterday. Dear Lady, I want to be good; I am not going to laugh in church any more. The girls tell me that Sister C. gave out in the meditation this morning that she was grieved to say a girl, who was absent (I was in the dormitory), had laughed and made the others do the same in chapel yesterday; she also added that they were to say a decade every day this week to make up for the irreverence which was done by that girl to Our Saviour.

30 October Thursday Because S.S.C. was not going out for a walk with us, she told me to stay in; I refused, guessing what her motive was; so she fetched P. and asked her to stop. Isn't it maddening to have her always persecuting me about that girl. Keep on, I shall soon have had my share. Charlie was waiting for me when I came back; he took me to a picture-hall. It was a ripping American play. Charlie's here on a month's leave; after that he's going to London. Lots of girls have gone home for a few days for All Saints' holidays.

31 October Friday She's mad on me because Soeur Ernest asked Pauline, another girl and I to help carry a stove; as if I can help it. Oh! she's just maddening; I see now more and more that her one pleasure is to drive me into my grave!

1 November Saturday, All Saints' Day We went to a fine Mass at the Carmelite church. Lucie Streiff is going to her sister at Carcassonne. There are only a few girls left; I wish I were away from this place, they're only rotten the girls who are left and S.S.C. is as horrid as she possibly can be. I don't care, I'm boring myself to death here.

2 November Sunday First snowy day. We went to Mass at the Carmelite church. Got sniff from S.C. this morning because I spoke in the cloak-hall. I suppose she thought I was criticizing her again.

3 November Monday In the middle of the night I heard a man humming loudly in the street; twice he woke me up with the same sound. I'm sure he was a madman. We went to three Masses at St Alène at 6.30 a.m.; the snow covered the ground. There those girls are bringing S.S.C. ripping presents for her fête tomorrow, and I've got nothing but a stupid old franc to get her something. Several boarders have come back, tomorrow they'll all be here, what a bore!

4 November Tuesday I'm simply desperate today. And it's her fête! Last night cold, today cold. The girls have greeted her in class this morning and they have no tasks this morning. I've not been in class because I didn't give anything towards the present; besides I shan't be missed. I know why it is; P. came back yesterday and I did all I could not to find myself in her passage, when after supper she called me to tell me I was not to swallow the chewing-gum; that was all she said. S.S.C. just came in then, and of course saw us again together. Is this torture going to pursue me to my tomb? Will I never know what happiness is? What is the good of trying to be good? Oh! well I shall just keep away from all those creatures, the less I see of them, the better. We wanted to go to the baths but they were closed. The girls are back. The Rev. Mother has given me a pupil for shorthand. Got a card from Rita.

5 November Wednesday Mariette Williquet is dying; they say her tongue is already paralysed. Poor little kid! She didn't seem to be ill before she went home; we recited the chaplet to her intention. Another day gone by, another one less to live!

6 November Thursday Nothing revolts me so much as to hear how brutal she can be to some girls. Last night again B. got two smacks because she walked on a girl's foot. And that is what they call charity! What a boring day. Can't play, because if I do she'll say it's to be with P.; so I've got to stick on a beastly bench staring at those girls. I'm longing for Daddy to come and I shall tell him that I want to go to Africa; it's no good, I can't go on like this. I detest <u>all</u> the girls, the mistresses, everybody; it's all very well for her to say that it's my imagination; I just say it isn't; the facts are there to prove it.

7 November Friday Benediction today as it is the first Friday of the month. Daddy has written to say he is fetching me on Sunday; I've had to write and tell him I can't go out. And I wanted to see him so badly! Soeur St Charles, you must believe it is not for you I want to go away, no it's because I can't give lessons. I haven't the patience, I hate it. Ah! if you weren't here, it would not be I who should stay here. I know you think me ungrateful.

8 November Saturday Soeur Seraphina washed my hair this afternoon. That creature. She's beginning again; why is it that before, when I liked S.S.C. to scold me, why is it that she used to say I did it all on purpose to make myself 'remarquée'? And why is it she never tells that girl the same thing? Beastly injustice on her part. She's so absurdly blind.

9 November Sunday Daddy never came and I did not even have to play the piano. After supper I went to the yard after my visit to Mary, and I heard the swing was up, so I went. P. and some others were there. I suddenly heard S.S.C.'s voice so I shouted after P. to scoot. She made me believe she had gone; S.S.C. caught me and said what she had to say. I came back the other way, and saw P. still waiting near the stairs. She would have had ample time to go back to the girls without being seen, but no, she was waiting ……… and of course S.S.C. caught her, too. That's what comes of my trying to get the kid out of a row. Sister Christina's brother, a priest, is here for a few days, he said Mass this morning and we got up an hour later. Lucie Streiffe has come back.

11 November Tuesday R.P. [Reverend Father] Chaîneux is preaching our retreat, it begins after Benediction. Just a year today since the armistice was signed; snow fell during the night. Revolutions in Paris on account of the election.

12 November Wednesday The 4th sermon was on Hell; what an awful place it must be! Eternal sufferings, tortures, everything, and the worst of all, never to see God. The R.M. [Reverend Mother] says it is better for us not to go to Holy Communion till after the retreat is finished. Oh! Jesus, today, tomorrow and the day after, must I be deprived of that great treat?

13 November Thursday No Jesus again today; well, tomorrow I shan't go to Mass; oh! Jesus, I want you, I love you, and I can't come to your Holy Table before Saturday!

15 November Saturday Big fall of snow. End of the retreat. Te Deum sung at Benediction, and after the R.P. Chaîneux spoke and said goodbye to us in the playroom. Poor little Mariette died at 6 a.m.; the last thing she did was to gaze upon a crucifix. Lucky little mite! I'm sure she's near Jesus now. Holiday today for the King's fête. Dad's birthday. Receiving Jesus today at last!

16 November Sunday Charlie fetched me home for dinner; Mother was out; she wrote me a nasty note.

17 November Monday Some girls went to Mariette's funeral with Sister Christina this morning. Rita has come back but I was out so I did not see her. Sister S.C. coughed a lot last night. Got in a big row because I spoke in the ranks; we were all kept in silence during teatime. Freezing today.

18 November Tuesday Arthur has come out third of his class. Esther is ill in bed and in a room; I went to see her. Another stupid incident after supper: S.S.C. would say I'd gone to the yard to meet P.; always the same old song; it put me in a fever for the rest of the evening.

19 November Wednesday Father Brown came to see me this morning; he paid a long visit. Rita had sent him thinking I was in trouble about Mother's letter.

20 November Thursday Went out with Rita; Mr Jarvis's brother is dead.

21 November Friday Esther is better and up.

22 November Saturday Have got one of those awful mad fits on again; that girl! Her face is enough to put anybody in a mad temper.

23 November Sunday Beastly awful day; terrible temper and S.S.C. mad on me. Had dinner with Rita and Ethel, went to Benediction and Rev. Father Moore preached; after we went on to the club. Charlie was there; I had a walk with him and then he danced with the girls. S.S.C. has an awful headache tonight.

24 November Monday After supper I spied the prison door open; a mad thought rushed through my mind. I saw Rizia coming down the stairs, told her what I thought and in a jiffy we were out into the street; we went as far as the rue de la Perche [a three-minute walk!]; when we came back several girls and S.S.C. were looking for me to play the duet with E. I was lucky to get into the room without cross-questioning. I was such a beast today that S.S.C. cried over my conduct. How can I be so heartless!

29 November Saturday We rehearsed in front of Sister Zélie, who is here for a few days; I was dressed up as a Spanish policeman.

30 November Sunday Oh! I know now she hates me. Ah! yes, you call me a vile hypocrite, a liar. It's not true! You may do anything to me, beat me, kill me if you like, call me a thief, a beggar, but a hypocrite .... no, you've gone too far. And how many did you not repeat it? Oh! Mary, I do want to cease again loving her. She can't bear me, or else she would not have asked to stay at home instead of coming back so early. Oh! life, life is a misery when you can't depend upon anybody. She says it is to show off in front of the girls that I took Mathilde's part. As if there is a single one of those girls whom I should think it a great favour to be admired by her. What absolute nonsense! Rita fetched me to dinner; Herbert Silcox and Miss Stuerman were there. Afterwards we went to the C.C. Ethel is going back to England tomorrow. Eva Demeuze was with Sister St Charles when I came back. After supper I received a good blowing up and was again called a hypocrite. Saw Charlie at the C.C.

1 December Monday Have scarcely seen anything of her; excepting when I watered her plants and when she came and told Pauline to go away, and practise somewhere else because I was typing there. So she's still bothering about P. not speaking to me .... really one would think her one delight is to see people sad. I am glad to see her so nice with P., I wonder too how long it will last! For my part she may go on with me just as she likes. I shall try and show myself indifferent through it all. May God remove me soon from this earth so that I be no more a plague to them all.

3 December Wednesday Have a new pupil for English and shorthand twice a week in the morning. P. was helping Soeur St Charles to make flowers for the hoops this afternoon; my place is taken now, for I am no more a pupil but a beastly teacher; may it last long for her, longer than it did with me, for to laugh with her now, after all that has passed ……… no, I cannot. She says she is ill, what is she suffering from I wonder? Began a novena last night to Our Lady for Soeur St Charles to get better.

4 December Thursday Went to the Bank and to the Palais d'Été with Charlie and Rita; Charlie skated. Tommy has written to Dad to ask him if I would like to go out to Canada to him as a companion to his wife in the spring. This time I think I shall accept; I can't stay on here for ever, with all these people bothering me, spying upon me, etc. She may be as nice as she likes to me now, but I shall go. Santa Claus came tonight and told us our faults. Père Fouettard whistled when my turn came, then he said I was becoming an acrobat, getting out of windows; then that I nearly sent the typewriter out of window because the ribbon wouldn't work. A big thunderstorm broke out during Santa Claus's visit.

6 December Saturday Santa Claus's day; at breakfast we found little surprises at each one of our plates. At 2 p.m. we acted for the day girls. Soeur Celestina's girls gave me a box of notepaper.

7 December Sunday Beastly day; am in a vile temper. This evening we played for the girls of the Patronage.

8 December Monday Feast of Our Lady; heard High Mass at 6.30 then I went to St Gilles and heard another one. Oh! I want to go away from here; I nearly had a fight with Soeur Ernestina; I answer everybody. Soeur St Charles asked me to go in her class at 1.30; luckily I didn't for when I passed at 3 p.m. P. was there. Germaine Georlette has come back. Tonight we acted for the Reverend Mother, her relations and the people of the establishment. Flora and I stuck moustaches on.

1919

34. Tommy and Connie in 1956, in Edgware, Middlesex. Left to right (standing) Connie's daughter Dorice (she changed it from Doris), Tommy, and Connie's daughter-in-law Doreen; (sitting) Connie, with me on her lap, Tommy's second wife Eliza, with Doreen's daughter Diana on her lap. The wife Amy refers to on 4 December was his first wife

9 December Tuesday I could not receive Jesus this morning because I had called that nun a hypocrite. Oh! why am I getting like that?

10 December Wednesday Saw Rita this afternoon; she and Soeur St Charles agree that I stay on here another year. So another whole year of this life; how can I keep good? And then that girl goes up in her class, she'll take my vacant place. Oh! dear Lady, do, do help me to be brave. I am no more a pupil but that what I <u>hate</u>, a teach … Rita is going to England tomorrow, perhaps by aeroplane. A priest was murdered by a madman last Monday at 6 a.m. in the rue du Poinçon; he was coming back from his Mass. Marie Guigot saw him in a litter. Soeur St Charles is not looking well at all.

11 December Thursday Soeur St Charles has the grip, I think; she has pains all over and she did not go out for a walk with us. I knew something was the matter with her. It is freezing today. Rita is thinking of going over to England in an aeroplane.

12 December Friday Goodbye schooldays, your time is finished now. Very rare will be the days when I shall sit again on my bench in her class.

14 December Sunday We rehearsed the play this morning because we have to act again tonight. Charlie fetched me, and we went for a walk, then home with Dad. Mother was out. Charlie's not looking well. Daddy says he comes back nearly every day at 1 or 2 a.m. He's going to England on the 20th next, and Henry's and Arthur's holidays begin on the 17th. Henry is coming over, but A. is going to Leicester. Poor Dad suffers with his headaches. P. stuck like the other times all the time near S.S.C. during the play.

15 December Monday She's very cold towards me today, well I prefer that than those things which are false, false, false. What a fool I am to bother about what she says and does. P. is there for that. Patience for a while and then …….. goodbye.

16 December Tuesday S.S.C. took P. up to bed after tea because the latter said she's ill. I believe it's more jealousy than anything else for she's always asking: is Amy with S.S.C.? And this morning there wasn't anything the matter with her. They say tomorrow there is going to be an earthquake in some part of the world because three planets are going to meet; I think P. is in a funk.

18 December Thursday Rita and Mrs Morrisson came to fetch me and then we went to the Palais de Glace where Charlie was to meet us; we tried skating together; I had two falls. I said goodbye to him for he is leaving for England tomorrow.

21 December Sunday We went to 10 o'clock Mass at St Joseph's. Rita fetched me to dine with her, then we went on to Benediction and to St George's and St Patrick's Club. On our way back to school Rita and I went into a music shop to get some violin things for I'm taking up the violin again and she saw a lovely instrument there. The man played on it and it sounded fine. Rita is going to get it for me for Christmas. What a brick she is! and I'm going to have lessons too! I've got my old one back till I get the new one. This evening, after supper, Sister Christina, Mlle Alice and I played 'Minuit, Chrétiens', and something else on the violin for perhaps we will play for midnight service for Xmas. I asked the R.F. if I might take up the violin again after I'd promised Our Lady I shouldn't play any more; he said yes, on one condition, that I practise it with the idea of teaching later on, and not like before, out of passionate love.

24 December Wednesday Holidays have begun; while the reports were being given I stayed at the typewriter. What's the good of sticking with those girls when I'm no more a scholar? The girls went to bed at 6.30 because we are going to midnight service. I went at 10.30 and got up at 10.15 for I rehearsed some pieces of violin with Sister Christina, and we're playing for Midnight Mass and the 7 o'clock Masses. Soeur St Charles was in bed when I went up and she prepared all my night-things. What a dear! At 12.30 a.m. I received Jesus; after Mass we went to eat something in the refectory. The crib was awfully nice.

25 December Thursday, Christmas Day Henry fetched me home for dinner;

[Diary 4 ends here, with a semicolon. One can only wonder, presuming Mother was at home, what happened.]

35. Henry in Broadstairs, Kent, 1932, with Connie's children Jackie and Doris/Dorice, and their father Jack smoking his pipe

1920

[Diary 5 is the last notebook I was given, from 17 August to 20 September 1920. Diary entries are at the back of a notebook containing examples of business letters in shorthand. She is now in Bognor Regis, West Sussex, England on holiday with Rita Mellin.]

17 August Tuesday Went for a lovely sea-trip on the *Victory* with Bobby, then Father Lecourt took us to Aldwick and we had tea there. Father Lecourt's foot hurts a lot. After supper we had our usual walk on the Parade near the bandstand. No news from school. I'm not going to write to her any more till she does.

18 August Wednesday Bognor Regatta begins today on the pier. I've at last had a letter from S.S.C.; it is a nice long one; but somehow it doesn't seem like her way of speaking at all. I saw the Regatta; they had the greasy pole and no one got to the end of it. Wet evening; feel a bit homesick, had those stupid thoughts about S.S.C.

19 August Thursday Got a letter from that P. and she says she saw S.S.C. last Sunday and she spoke to P. about those letters she wrote to me. Of course that girl must be having a lovely time, now I'm gone. Had a lovely trip to Selsey Bill in the *Victory* with Father Lecourt and Bobby. We had 2 hours and a half of sea, return; we had tea there. We saw the Isle of Wight in the distance. Had a lovely bathe this morning; had my first swimming lesson, but I think I stayed in too long for I was shivering for long after.

20 August Friday Walked to Middleton aerodrome with Bobby.

21 August Saturday Walked to Aldwick with Bobby. Got a letter from Elisa and S.S.C. had written a page and a half in it. Big firework display at 9.30 p.m. on the pier, going to see it. Am beastly homesick tonight; I long to go back to S.S.C. It's no good, I don't like anybody here. The sooner I go away, the better, for when I want to answer I can't because I'm dependent on Miss Mellin. My beastly character has not changed yet, far from it; it's so horrid living with people you have to always mind what you say and do. I think Rita has changed a lot; she never used to be so particular.

22 August Sunday Lovely sky tonight; the sea is beautiful with the moon shining on it. Went to Benediction service tonight with Rita, and the blind priest, Father Gratey, preached.

23 August Monday Wet day. Went to confession to Father Coventry. After dinner Rita and I went to the Olympian Gardens. They had a very good show on. Bobby has gone back to London.

24 August Tuesday Went for a trip in the *Britannia*; it was lovely. Paddled and then I played with Stella and Ralph, two Indian children whom I see in church nearly every day. After supper I went on the pier; saw Mona De Gray do the Fire Dive again and listened to the music.

25 August Wednesday Went to the War Memorial Hospital Fête at Bersted with Rita, and shied at cocoanuts; knocked one down and brought it home. They had all kinds of races. Then I went to the X-ray room in the hospital. It is wonderful; they passed a shut handbag, a book, a bag, a rabbit, and we could see everything inside them through the X-ray. Then I saw the bones in a man's hand. After supper Rita and I went to the Olympian Gardens.

27 August Friday Went for a lovely sea-trip on the *Britannia*. They had a Carnival Dance on the pier tonight; they had fireworks too.

28 August Saturday Am longing to see S.S.C. Rita has bought two little Pekinese puppies. The weather is warmer.

29 August Sunday Got a letter from P. and a card from Elisa. Went to Low Mass and High Mass. Flew in a temper after dinner when there had been a discussion at table about something I had said. Went to Bersted Convent and chapel. The nuns are Servites and cloistered; they sing behind a railing and so we cannot see them.

30 August Monday Went shrimping with Stella and Ralph; we caught a lot of shrimps. We're going to London tomorrow by the 8.8 a.m. train; we may stay there two days and spend the night at Mrs Evans's. Did not go to Mass this morning.

31 August Tuesday Spent the day in London; we went to Mme Tussaud's, Westminster and we came back at 10 p.m.

1 September Wednesday Went to sea on the *Victory*. Had my hand read by Alma; all he said was the truth.

2 September Thursday Wet day. Went to Piertland in the afternoon and to the Olympian Gardens after dinner.

3 September Friday Went to Littlehampton with Rita; there are sand-hills there, also a river. It's a very nice place; we went in the Southdown bus.

4 September Saturday S.S.C. is going to Pesche today; God bless her. Went to Arundel; took the bus to Littlehampton and from there we walked to Arundel. We took the train to come back. Life Boat day here at Bognor.

5 September Sunday Went to Bersted and Aldwick.

7 September Tuesday Went for a trip in the *Moonbeam*; the skipper caught some fish.

8 September Wednesday Wish I were back near S.S.C. <u>She</u> only understands me. Ah! a month ago today!

10 September Friday I've been here a month today, a month since I left S.S.C.! Aunt Flo has written to invite me to spend a few days, tomorrow until Tuesday, at Bournemouth with her and Uncle Fred.

11 September Saturday Fell out of the train at Bournemouth. Uncle F. met me at the station. Aunt Flo goes out in a bath chair. Most lovely place. In the afternoon we went to Canford Cliffs, picked some heather. Then we went on the Chine.

12 September Sunday Went to Mass in a dear little chapel near the house. Lovely morning; dew very strong. After dinner Uncle and I walked on the cliffs in the Chines with all lovely views of the sea; we came back through the Gardens in which the Bourne runs.

13 September Monday After Mass I went shopping with Uncle. We all had tea on the terrace of Plummers from which we had a beautiful view of the sea and the pier. We also saw the Needles. Went through the Gardens. I pushed Aunt Flo's invalid chair.

14 September Tuesday Aunt Flo has given me a nice little gold brooch. Went to pick some heather with Uncle Fred. At 3 p.m. they both took me down to the station and I came back to Bognor. Lovely weather.

15 September Wednesday Very rough sea; no bathers, no motorboats; the waves came right over the Parade into the road. Wet day. Went to Bersted with Rita to fetch a dear little Persian kitten; it sleeps with me in my room. Letter from S.S.C.

16 September Thursday Today S.S.C. goes back to Brussels. Lucky girls who are expecting her. When shall I see her? Went to Olympian Gardens. Rough sea; waves splashing over the Parade. Went to the Olympian Gardens. Wish I were back at school, near S.S.C.

17 September Friday Daddy leaves New York today [he went to New York in June, without his wife Annie, to visit his daughter Connie, Jack and their two children]. Wrote to Cook's to find out about the boats for Antwerp. Maybe next week I shall be leaving Bognor. Tempest all night and rough sea today. S.S.C. you are in my thoughts from morning till night. Oh! the day when I shall see her again!

18 September Saturday Very windy. Went to the Farewell night at the Olympian Gardens. Jack Rickards was very funny and had a great success; they all received presents.

19 September Sunday Lovely day; wind gone down. Had a nice walk with Rita this afternoon. Feast of Our Lady's Seven Dolours; went to Benediction; they had a procession round the church, all the little boys of St Dominick's school were dressed in white, they looked so sweet.

20 September Monday Got an express letter to say I must go back to Brussels as soon as possible for I am to present myself at Nathalie's place either Friday or Saturday. What a blessing! Kathleen left today. Mr and Mrs Lucas are going to stay in the house and work. Have packed nearly all.

Coda

Amy hurries back to Brussels in September 1920 to present herself 'at Nathalie's place'. What happened next? Tucked into her last diary is a testimonial, dated a year later, 30 September 1921, from Hitchcock, Lloyd & Company, Inc., Export and Import Merchants, Boulevard Anspach, Bruxelles, stating:

> TO ALL WHOM THIS MIGHT CONCERN
> This is to state that Miss Amy Hodson has been in our office as French and English stenographer for 5 months. We are pleased to recommend her very highly, as we have been entirely satisfied with her services.

So maybe 'Nathalie's place' in 1920 was also an office job.

In a family album that has labels 'Lowestoft' and '1921' I found a photo of a young woman with the name 'Amy' written next to it: in my handwriting. I must have gone through the album some years ago with my mother. And we know from the shipping record that in that year Amy, aged twenty, was staying with her half-sister Connie in Lowestoft, Suffolk – incidentally in the same road where the young Benjamin Britten was living (Kirkley Cliff Road) – and that on 25 November 1921 she went from Liverpool to St John, New Brunswick on the *Metagama*. On the 'Declaration of Passage to Canada' she writes that her intended employment in Canada is 'housework' and that she will be staying with her married brother L.E. Hodson (Tommy) in Winnipeg. In reply to the question 'Are you or any of your family mentally defective?' She has written 'No'.

In her last diary I found also another testimonial, dated 22 March 1922, by The Canadian Power Farmer, Winnipeg:

> This is to say that Miss Amy Hodson has been an employee of the E.H. Heath Company for some time past and that her

Coda

36. Amy in Lowestoft, Suffolk, 1921, before she emigrated to Canada. In front of her: unknown boy and Doris/Dorice

work has been satisfactory in every way.

We have found her to be both industrious and trustworthy and at the same time competent. She is leaving our employ only because the work she has been doing is finished.

On 12 May 1923 Amy married Thomas Field in Winnipeg; they had a daughter, Miriam (Mimi), on 20 October 1924.

On 12 January 1967 Amy died, aged sixty-five, at Riverview Hospital, Essondale, British Columbia. I had heard a rumour while I was growing up that Amy had been in a 'lunatic asylum'. The Registration of Death implies she had been in the hospital for four years and it was indeed a mental health facility. On the form after 'Maiden name of mother' is typed 'not known'. For her mother's 'All given or Christian names' is typed: 'not known'.

We have only Amy's side of the story, but I hope she found the love she longed for with her husband and daughter.

37. Amy (right) and her daughter Mimi came over from Canada for a holiday with Connie and the family in Broadstairs, Kent, 1929

Bibliography

Note
Birth, marriage and death certificates; shipping records; wills etc. and family details, such as the testimonials for Ernest Rust Hodson, are in my personal possession or accessed via Ancestry.co.uk or Findmypast.co.uk. Unsourced quotations from newspapers are from cuttings in Jenkins albums in my possession.

City of Brussels almanacs accessed at: www.brussel.be/artdet.cfm?id=6332&PAGEID=5070&startrow=51&foldername

Archives
THE BRITISH NEWSPAPER ARCHIVE, BRITISH LIBRARY, LONDON
The Sunday Post, 1923

THE NATIONAL ARCHIVES, KEW
Belgium: Prisoners, including: Pensions ... FO 383/257
Germany: Prisoners, including: Recommendations for awards of recognition for special services rendered to British: ... FO 383/513
Medal card of Bodart, Ada WO 372/23/3807
Medal card of Hodson, L.E. WO 372/9/37403

Other sources
Beaumont, Harry, *Old Contemptible*, ed. A.E. Clark-Kennedy (London: Hutchinson, 1967).
Bodart, Madame (formerly Miss Ada Doherty) [Ada Bodart], 'My Adventures with Nurse Cavell', *The Sunday Post*, serialized 22 April–24 June 1923.
Brabant, Clothilde de, ['Ada Bodart'], essay for Université catholique de Louvain, unpublished, 2014.

Cox, Roger, *Anglicans in Brussels: A History of Anglican Worship in Brussels*, rev. edn (Brussels: Holy Trinity Brussels, rue Capitaine Crespel, 29, 1050 Brussels, 2004) [There are some errors in this booklet concerning my ancestors, the Jenkins clergymen, but Roger Cox is preparing a new edition].

Croÿ, Princess Marie de, *War Memories* (London: Macmillan, 1932).

Daunton, Claire, 'Cavell, Edith Louisa (1865–1915)', *Oxford Dictionary of National Biography*, Oxford University Press, 2004, www.oxforddnb.com/view/article/32330, accessed 6 December 2014.

Dawn (1928) dir. Herbert Wilcox (film), available to view at BFI, 21 Stephen Street, London W1T 1LN.

Debruyne, Emmanuel, *Le 'réseau Cavell': Des hommes et des femmes en résistance. France Belgique, 1914–1915* (Belgium, forthcoming).

Depauw, Liesbet, 'Reframing the Past to Change the Future: Reflections on Herbert Wilcox's *Dawn* (1928) as a Historical Documentary and War Film', in *Perspectives on European Film and History*, ed. Leen Engelen and Roel Vande Winkel (Gent: Academia Press, 2007), pp. 156–81.

Hodson, Amy Victoria, 'My Experience on the Belgian Sea-Coast During the Year 1914', typescript, and notebook containing drafts, 1915–c. 1919, donated to the Imperial War Museum, October 2014.

Hodson, Henry Clarence, 'This Is My Life', typescript, 1999, owned by Shirley Swift, Melinda Swift and Tania Swift.

House of Lords Debates, UK Parliament, HL Deb 20 Oct. 1915 (vol. 19 cc1100–4).

Jackson, B.T., 'The Surgical Case Book of Thomas Marsters Kendall FRCS', *Annals of the Royal College of Surgeons of England*, 74 (1974) [He names only two daughters and one son; Margaret Maria, Ernest's first wife, and her sister Jane Eyre are named in the 1861 and 1871 censuses.]

Kendall, Monica, 'My Grandfather Jack', *St. Bernard's School* 24 (Spring), pp. 1–2, 4 (4 East 98th Street, New York, New York 10029, 2000).

Kendall, Monica, 'Brussels, Brontë, Jenkins: My Great-great-grandparents Rev. Evan and Eliza Jenkins and the Brontës', 2014, www.brusselsbronte.blogspot.be/2014/03/brussels-bronte-jenkins-my-great-great.html.

Marks, Shula and Stanley Trapido, 'Rhodes, Cecil John (1853–1902)', *Oxford Dictionary of National Biography*, Oxford University Press; online edn, Sept. 2013, www.oxforddnb.com/view/article/35731, accessed 24 December 2014.

Riverview Health Centre, Winnipeg, Manitoba [formerly King Edward Memorial Hospital and King George Hospital], 'Our History', n.d., www.riverviewhealthcentre.com/index.php/about-us/our-history.

St Bernard's School, *Saint Bernard's School: The First Century, 1904–2004* (New York, 2004).

Souhami, Diana, *Edith Cavell* (London: Quercus, 2011).

Sparrow, Violet, *Yesterday's Stortford*, 3rd edn (Buckingham: Baron, 1997).

Villiers, Rt Hon. Sir Francis Hyde, *Who Was Who*, A & C Black, an imprint of Bloomsbury Publishing plc, 1920–2015; online edn, Oxford University Press; online edn, April 2014, www.ukwhoswho.com/view/article/oupww/whowaswho/U204161, accessed 6 December 2014.

Whitlock, Brand, *The Letters and Journal of Brand Whitlock*, ed. and chosen by Allan Nevins, 2 vols (New York and London: D. Appleton-Century, 1936).

Index

aeroplanes, 52, 72, 104, 118, 169, 172, 182, 185, 199, 204, 254, 266, 284
   Allied, 39, 41, 45–6, 50, 52, 60, 68, 70–1, 82–3, 88–9, 90–2, 95, 134–5, 137–42, 178, 201, 204
   bracelets, 224
   German, 66, 75, 150, 152, 160, 164, 167, 174–5, 181, 187, 189–90, 205 (*see also* Taube)
   see also papers thrown from aeroplanes
Africa, 251, 253, 278
   see also South Africa; Umtali, Rhodesia
Africaine, rue, xvii, 7, 20, 23, 31, *69*, 133, 153, 157
airships *see* zeppelins
Albert I, King of the Belgians (1875–1934), xxv, 10, 12, 63, 72, 101, 120, 193, *207*, 228, *228*, 233, 242, 254, 257, 261, 280
Albert, Prince (later George VI, 1895–1952), 233
Aldwick, West Sussex, 287, 289
Alimentation (foodstore run by CNSA), 108, 111–12, 119, 121–2, 131, 145, 224, 246
All Saints' Day, 97, 144, 191, 277
l'Amazone, rue de, 119, 126
America, 68, 148, 155–6, 162
Americaine, rue, Amy's fight with a girl, 54
American Consulate: Brussels, 97, 103
   Ghent, 43
American Legation, Brussels, 111, 152
American officers, 47

Americans in Brussels, 66, 122, 128–9, 142, 157
   see also tennis *and individual names*
Anaïs (schoolgirl), 166, 172, 182, 189, 192, 202, 205
'L'Angelus de la Mer' (song), 177
anniversary of start of war, 78, 81, 134, 180
Antwerp, 38, 155, 290
l'Aqueduc, rue de, 83, 154, 156
Arabians/Arabia, 130–1
'Arlequine' (musical duet), 191–2
Armistice, the, 209–10, 238, 279
arms found/looked for by Germans, 95, 99, 110
asterisks in text, xxvi, 210
Athlone, Alexander Cambridge, 1st Earl of (1874–1957), 12, 228, 233
Auntie (Esther Hamilton Irvine, 1847–1916), xvii, *xxix*, 20, 22–3, 37, 50, 54, 67, 70, 72, 74–6, 83, 90–2, 96, 103, 106–11, 113–19, 121–6, 129–31, 134, 150, 152, 164, 173, 212
   birthday, 100, 147
   crisis, 97, 120–1, 130, 153
   death/burial, 22–3, 132–3, 177
Austria/Austrians, 48, 50, 65, 90–1, 128, 140, 158
'Aux Héros de l'Yser' (poem), 100–1
'Ave Maria' (song), 153, 222, 245, 252

B./Baby *see* Hodson, Henry
B., Mrs/Mme, *see* Bodart, Ada
Back family, 131, 144
   Beppie, 122

Léopold, 104, 149, 153
  Mme, 81
  Mr, 102–3
badges as souvenirs, 39
Baes, Firmin (artist; 1874–1943), 162
  Georgette and Suzanne, 162–6
Bailly, rue du, 152
'Le Ballet de Faust' (musical piece), 256
bandits, calling Germans, 130
bands, German, 63, 79, 83, 111, 124–5, 192
Banque nationale, Brussels, 47, 139
barbed wire, 147, 265
Barrière de St Gilles (roundabout by Amy's school), 187, 212, 253
baseball, 128, 142
Bataille, Blanche (schoolgirl), 177, 187–9, 199, 262
battery, Wilhelm II, 266
Baucq, Philippe, xxi–xxii, 1, 3, 6, 9, 11–12, 93–4
Bauer, M. de, château at Boitsfort, 80, 83, 86, 109, 137
Bavaria, 175
  King, 110
  soldiers, 54
BCF (British Charitable Fund), 201
Belgian men (aged 17–65), 145
Belgian resistance, 48, 50–1, 67, 73, 79–80, 89, 107–10, 113, 131, 138–9, 146
Belgian soldiers/army, 38–9, 41–2, 45, 48, 55, 88, 140
  hats, 50
  wounded, 39, 86, 115, 260
  see also prisoners
Belleville, Comtesse Jeanne de, 93
Belle-Vue, rue de, 232
Bens, Mlle (teacher), 147–9
Berghem/Berghem St Agathe (Sint-Agatha Berchem), 43, 46, 60, 79, 86, 92, 126
Berlin, 131, 164
Bernard, Denise (schoolgirl), 148–9, 152, 154–6, 163
Bernhardt, Sarah (actress; 1844–1923), 162
Bersted, West Sussex, 288–90

Besme, avenue, 155
Bethmann Hollweg, Theobald von (German Chancellor; 1856–1921), 175
bicycles, 268, 270
  Germans ban, 57, 140
  Mr Gahan loses one, 52
  tyres requisitioned, 138, 144
Biggs, Dickie (set free), 153
Bigwood, Mr ('young'/'old'), 47, 86, 114–15, 130, 133
Bishop's Stortford, Hertfordshire, 1, 13–14, 28, 31
Bissing, General Baron Moritz von (Governor-General of occupied Belgium; 1844–1917), 11, 67, 76, 89, 94–5, 112, 118, 157, 163–5
Bivoire, Mr (crossed frontier), 185
Black Marias, 68, 70–2
Blankenberge (seaside resort), 265–6
blindman's buff, 181
Bodart, Ada (Mrs/Mme B.) (née Doherty) (1874–1936), xiv–xv, xxi, xxiii, xxvi, 1–10, *4*, 27, *53*
  Amy takes letters to, 5, 7, 52, 54
  Amy/Annie visits, 5, 59–60
  birth and nationality, xiii, 2–5
  children, xxi, 1 (*see also* Bodart, Hilda; Bodart, Philippe)
  death, xiii, 3–5
  film *Dawn*, xxi, 9
  in hiding, 79
  hiding/guiding Allied soldiers, 2, 7–9, 57, 59–60, 62, 67, 77
  honoured, 4, 9
  houses, xxiii, 2, 7, 57, 62, 67, 74
  husband, 3
  to Kommandantur, 2, 6–7, 62
  at Military Hospital, 88
  more Tommy Atkins than Miss Cavell, 1, 7, 92
  in prison, 8–9, 81–2, 100
  spied on/watched, 57, 60, 67
  trial and sentence, xxi, 3, 6, 86, 91, *92*, 93
Bodart, Hilda, 2–3, *4*, 5, 7, 59, 77, 79, 82, 92

Bodart, Philippe, 3–5, *4*, 7, 9, 78–9, 82, 92
Boer War (1899–1902), 20
Bognor Regis, West Sussex, xxiii, 287–91
Bois de la Cambre (the Bois), 51–2, 59, 65, 102, 110, 117, 120, 154, 158, 165–6, 183, 187, 189, 227–8, *228*, 244, 269, 270
Bois des Capucins, 126
Boitsfort (south of Brussels), 50, 66, 70, 77, 80, 83, 86, 108, 112, 115, 123, 131, 136–7, 139, 162–3, 169
bombs, 41–2, 66–8, 70–1, 86, 92, 111, 120, 134, 138, 141, 160
'bonbonnière' (box for sweets), 197, 199
Borelli, Lyda (actress; 1884–1959), 160
Bormans, Georgette (schoolgirl), 168, 177, 182, 188–9, 192, 194, 206, 208
Bormans, Marcel, 134, 160, 183
Botanical Gardens, 77, 276
Botha, General Louis (1862–1919), 74
Boulogne, 33, *193*, 225, 234, 236
Bourne, Cardinal Francis, Archbishop of Westminster (cousin; 1861–1935), 14, 252–3
Bournemouth, 289–90
boy scouts, 67, 225
   see also scouts
'Brabançonne' (national anthem of Belgium), 38, 81, 83, 101, 124, 206
Brabant (fine), 109
Brackie, James, Cameron Highlanders (grave), 48
Braine-l'Alleud, 73, 117
British army, 12–13, 24, 39, 45, 82, 130, 140, 146
   3rd British army corps, *234*
   55th (West Lancashire) Division, *228*
   military reviews, 12–13, 227–8, *228*, 233, *234*, 261
   numbers dead, wounded, missing (1915), 88
   Royal Army Service Corps, 33, *193*, 235
   Scots Greys, 242
   York and Lancaster Regiment, xix
   see also Lovat's Scouts; Royal Fusiliers
British/English soldiers, xxi, 39, 48, 90, 249, 252
   'The Chequers' musical troupe, 216
   Highlanders, 225
   returning home (1918), 210
   sign Amy's handkerchief, 2, 7, 11, 59–60
   wounded, 78, 116
British soldiers' canteen, 240–1
British Women (BW), 104–5, 118
Britten, Benjamin (1913–76), 292
Broadstairs, Kent, xviii, *217*, 231, *286*, *294*
bronchitis, 18, 62, 110
Brontë, Charlotte (1816–55), 16, 33
Brown, Rev. Father, *207* (centre), 280
Brown Hotel, 73
Browning, Rev. Guy Arrott (naval chaplain; 1876–1916), 129
Browning, Captain Kendall (1875–1936), 129
Brugmann, avenue, 141
Brugmann, Mr, house, 165
Brussels, *xxviii*, 37, 91, 129
   buildings damaged, 141, 167
   casualties, 141, 167
   curfews, 139, 147, 154
   review of the schools, 259, 261
   war levy/fines, 133
   see also flooding
Brussels Cricket Lawn Tennis and Football Club *see* Lawn Tennis Club
Bruyère, Jean, 128, 201
Bucharest, 149
Buckle, Frederick Ainger (1858–?), 32
Buckle, Helen Meliora (Lellie) (née Jenkins) (1866–1937), 32
Buckle, Phyllis (1891–1961), *32*
Bulgaria/Bulgarians, 79, 95
Buol's, 235
burgomasters, 146
buses/omnibuses, 39, 51, 216

Index

Butcher family, xxi, 89, 104, 150, 155, 199
   Mr Alfnoth Butcher (b. c. 1864), xxi, 46, 50–1, 92
   Bertha, xxi
   Joan, 71, 105, 110, 129, 133, 142
   Meg, 68, 71, 127, 129, 133, 142
Butler, Lieutenant General Sir Richard Harte Keatinge (1870–1935), 233
buttons, uniform, 20, 39, 67, 159, 229–30

cafés, shut, 76, 139, 146
'Caissette du soldat belge', 95
Calais, 54, 67, 213, 216
Cambridge University, xviii–xix, xxii, 13, 15–16, 18, 32
Canada/Canadians, xi, *xii*, xvii, xix, xxv, 22–4, 26–7, 29–30, 34, 93, 150, *176*, 282, 292, 294
Canadian Power Farmer, The, Winnipeg, 292
Canal Maritime, 107
candles, lack of/cost, 116, 120
cannons (guns) (noise of), 46–50, 54, 58, 62, 66, 68, 71–3, 76–7, 79, 82, 85, 89–92, 95, 97, 99–100, 102–7, 109–13, 115–18, 121–6, 128–30, 133–4, 137, 140–1, 143–9, 152–4, 157, 161–3, 165, 173, 178, 180, 183, 186, 189, 191–2, 195, 197, 200, 202–4, 207
cantinières (female canteen-keepers/sutlers), 39
Capelle Neuve *see* Neuve Chapelle
Capiau, Herman (sentence), 93
captive balloons, 47–52, 54, 57–60, 62–3, 65–8, 78, 86, 94, 104, 133, 135–7, 147
Carlton, porter at (taken), 86
Carte d'Identité *see* identity card
Carte de Ménage (ration card), 118
cartridges, 39, 41, 48
castor oil, lack of, 110
Cavell, Edith (Nurse/Miss) (1865–1915), xiii–xv, xxi–xxii, xxvi, 2–3, *4*, 5–13, 79, 96, 98, 134
   church/religious services, 215, 248–9, *249*
   'Germs' visit her clinic, 75
   grave, 215
   her denouncer, 108–10, 114
   her nurses, 100
   monument in London, 96
   in prison, 79, 81
   shot/execution, 1, 6, 92–5, *92*, 99
   trial, xxi–xxii, 91
Cécile/Cecily (cousin of Father Lecourt), xxiii, 263–5, 267–70
Celestina, Sister/Soeur, 208, 274, 282
cemeteries, 57, 244
   Beckenham, 22
   Calevoet, 192
   Forest, 191
   Ixelles, 48, 94
   Uccle, 22, 62, 80, 132–3, 144
Chaîneux, Reverend Father, 233, 279–80
Châlet du Gymnase, 123
Champs-Elysées, rue des, 33
Chanoine, M. le, 170, 172, 178, 181, 203, 233–4, 236
Charleroi, chaussée de, 78, 224, 250
Charlie *see* Hodson, Charlie
Châtelain, rue du, xviii
chauffeurs, Belgian, 129
Cheveral, Angel/Angèle (schoolgirl), 188–92, 194–9, 202–5, 207–9, 223–4
chewing-gum, 278
chocolate, xxiii, 41, 107, 122, 131, 150–1, 162, 218, 232, 244
chômeurs (the unemployed), 146, 154–5
Christ Church (Amy's church until 1917; Anglican), rue Crespel, xxii, xxvi, 51, 67, 74, 77–8, 81–3, 86, 92, 95, 97–8, 100, 102–9, 111, 113–18, 120–1, 124–6, 128, 133–4, 137–9, 143–4, 146, 149–50, 154, 157–60, 163, 239, 250
Children's Service, 10, 48, 50, 52, 54, 57–9, 70, 98, 110
   harvest festival, 89

library, 146, 214, 243, 245
service for Miss Cavell, 94
Christina, Sister/Soeur, 166–72, 174–5, 178, 180–2, 188, 190–1, 194–5, 197–8, 201, 206–7, 212–13, 215, 218, 254, 259–60, 269, 271, 279–80, 285
Christmas, 102, 105, 150, 199–200, 209, 216, 220, 222–5, 285
churches: Barnabites, ave. Brugmann, 203, 232
    Basilica de St Pierre, Koekelberg, 172
    Capucins, 260
    Carmes/Carmelite, 127, 173, 215, 219, 224, 226, 229, 233, 237, 240, 243–4, 250, 277
    chaussée de Wavre, 243
    Church of the Resurrection (Anglican), xviii, xxii, xxvi, 18–19, 32, 82, 119, 220, *221*, 274, *274*
    Rheims cathedral, 71
    rue Belliard (Anglican), 97
    rue Neuve (Notre-Dame-du-Finistère), 180
    rue Washington, 243, 252, 263
    St Alène, 191, 254, 278
    St Antoine, 262
    St Boniface, 243
    St Catherine, 182
    St Croix, 243, 270
    St Gilles, xxvi, 168, 170, 177, 184, 188, 205, 212–13, 230, 232, 237, 239, 241–3, 246, 252, 254, 256, 263, 282
    St Gudule, xxvi, 70, 166, 169–70, 177, 190, 228, 270, 272, 277
    St Jacques (St Jacques-sur-Coudenberg), xxvi, 83, 124, 167–9, 171–2, 176, 189, 198, 208
    St Joseph, 210, 219, 222, 224, 227, 230, 243, 285
    St Josse Ten Noode, 136
    St Paul's Cathedral, London, 86, 96
    St Trinité/Trinity, 120, 123, 217, 223, 232, 238, 243, 248, 250

    Servites, 264, 271
    see also Christ Church
church library, Anglican, 214, 243, 245
cinemas, 47, 76, 81, 88, 102–3, 107, 112, 115, 137, 145–6, 156, 158–60, 162, 163–5, 218, 246–7, 277
    Cigale, the, 154, 156, 162
    Cinéma Trianon, 146
    High-Life, ave. Louise, 77, 106, 108, 111, 113–14, 116, 128, 131, 146, 150, 158, 160, 162, 235, 240
    Kursaal, chaussée d'Ixelles, 149
    Majestic Cinema, rue Neuve, 151
    Modern Cinema, 161
    rue du Bailly, 99
    Scala, 152
    Select, 156, 164
    shut, 139, 147, 164
    see also films; Trocadero
circus, 246–7
Citine (schoolgirl), 181, 206, 226
Clarice, Sister/Soeur, 21, 167–8
clowns, 154, 156
club, the (Ernest's), *see* Union Club
Club of English Catholic girls/Girls' Club, 263, 270, 272, 281
Club, St George's and St Patrick's, 285
coal, shortage of, 144–5, 157, 160
    coal-carts, 108
Collart, Raymond ('the poet'), xxiv, 103, 108–9, 113–15, 119–21, 124, 128, 204, 254
Cologne, 218
Comité National de Secours d'Alimentation (CNSA), 11
Commission for Relief in Belgium (CRB), xxiii, 10–11, 116–17, 119, 128–9, 130, 157, 161, 214
Compagnie belge, 83
concerts, 177, 195, 201
Con/Connie *see* Jenkins, Constance Agnes
Connaught, Prince Arthur, Duke of (1850–1942), 225
conscience diary, Amy's, xxv, 34–5, 231, 247

Index

Conservatoire Royal de Bruxelles, rue de la Régence, 154, 187, 201, 256
Constantinople, rue de, 128
countryside, French and English banned, 59
Courrouble, Suzanne (schoolgirl), 148, 152–4, 163
Crawford, Cyril (in Ruhleben), 51
CRB *see* Commission for Relief in Belgium
cricket, 14–16, 18, 20
Crocodile (seaside resort), 37–9, 45
Croÿ, Prince Reginald de (1878–1961), xxii, 8
Croÿ, Princess Marie de (1875–1968), 1–2, 92–4
Cuissart family: Mme, 80
  Mr, 65, 123
  Georgie, 71
Culture, rue de la, Miss Cavell's clinic, 75
Curzon of Kedleston, George, Earl, 9

Daddy *see* Hodson, Ernest Rust
Dam, rue du, 80
dancing lessons, 107–8, 110–11, 113, 115–21, 124
Danly, Robert (crossed frontier), 185
Dardanelles, 30, 66, 70, 88, 108
Davidson, John R. (Amy's son-in-law), xi, *xii*, xxv, 23
'The Death of Sir John Moore' (poem; Charles Wolfe), 177
Deckers, Dymphna (schoolgirl), 202, 208, 241
Deckers, Laurence (schoolgirl), 198, 239
declarations of war, 45, 65, 90–1, 95, 117, 137, 249
Deglune, Berthe (schoolgirl), 256
De Gray, Mona (British contortionist and acrobat), 288
Delcoigne, Georges (Belgian architect, 1870–1916), 86, 125–7
Delcoigne, Georges (in Belgian uniform, 1918), 213
Delmont, Mlle Henriette (artist), 136

Delock's hôtel, 232
Deltan, Mme, 177, 220, 264, 269–70
Demeuze, Eva (schoolgirl), 195, 203–6, 240, 250, 281
Denmark, 27, 230
dentist, visits to, 49, 51, 54, 72, 76–7, 80, 102–3, 119, 126, 128, 138, 143, 151
Depage, Dr Antoine (1862–1925), 63, 260
Derveau, Georges (sentence), 94
Descamps, Germaine (schoolgirl), 187–8, 199, 259
deserters, army, 127
Deujck, Flore (becoming a nun), 183
De Wet, General Christiaan (1854–1922), 74
document to show no relations with Germans (1919), 228
Doehard, Franz (violinist), 160, 162
dogs: to be given to Germans, 190
  lost, 114
  run over, 154
  to wear muzzles, 120–1
Doyle, Miss, 133
  magic lantern, 158
  tea with, 49–50, 52, 77, 107, 123, 134
Drury, Miss, 66, 81, 95, 117, 121, 151, 205, 225, 235, 273
  turned Belgian, 111
Dupuiche, Mr (imprisoned), 130

Easter, 52, 122, 162, 244
Ecole Moyennade St Gilles, rue de Parme (Amy's school, 1916–17), 78, 141–2, 144–8, 150, 152, 154–6, 158–60, 163, 166
edelweiss, people wearing, 76
Eden theatre/Eden-Théâtre, rue Neuve, 151, 161–2
Edward VII, King (1841–1910), 16, 99
Edward, Prince of Wales (future Edward VIII; 1894–1972), 12, 226–7, 233
Ehrlich, Carl (1884–1957), xxii, 81, 114, 144, 150, 156, 160, 169, 230

303

Mrs Isabel (mother), xxii
Mrs Olga (wife), xxii, 81, 90, 123–4, 157
see also tennis: Carl Ehrlich Cup
Elisabeth, Queen of the Belgians (1876–1965), 254, 257, 261
Elisette (schoogirl), 219, 229
Ellis Island, 26
Emile Wittmann, rue, 7–8
English civilians, 104, 110, 137
  deported/sent to Germany, 62, 112
  leaving for England, 68, 71, 74, 80, 111–12
Eppeghem, 136, 263
Ernestina/Ernest, Sister/Soeur, 212–13, 232, 272, 277, 282
Errera, Mme, château at Boitsfort, 70
l'Escalier, rue de, 80
Escaut (Scheldt) river, 157
Esther (schoolgirl), 201, 206, 212, 235, 249, 256, 280
Etherington family (going to England), 68, 74
Etterbeek, 58, 67, 71–2, 74, 82, 89, 91, 134, 230
Evere, 68, 82, 92–3
exhibitions, 129, 150, 261
explosions, 109, 133, 165, 250, 252
  ammunition, 248
  boats, 266

fairs, 242, 246–7, 269
Fauconberge School, Beccles, 15
Favresse, Emilie (schoolgirl), 198, 200, 202, 204–5
Felsted School, Essex, 14–15
'Ferme Rose', 183
Fernandez (?church warden of the Church of the Resurrection), 235
fêtes, 178, 259
  Albert, King, 193, 280
  Amy, 186
  Elisabeth, Queen, 194
  Fête-Dieu, 170, 254
  Holy Ghost, 188
  national, 75–7, 133, 177, 260

Notre-Dame des Sept Douleurs, 186, 291
Notre-Dame du Mont Carmel, 260
Our Lady of Sorrows, 271
Sacré-Coeur/Sacred Heart, 171, 256
St Gilles, 184, 187
St Joseph, 239
St Michael, 187
St Thérèse, 189
Superior, Sister, 192, 197, 213–15, 256
teachers, 190–1, 195, 261–2, 278
Virgin Mary, 174, 182, 194, 197, 210–11, 214–15, 240, 257, 282
Field, Mimi (Miriam) (Amy's daughter), 294, *294*
Field, Tom (Thomas) (Amy's husband), 294
films: *Adrienne Lecouvreur*, 162
  Les Baderlans, 158
  Le Bossu, 109
  Captain Grant's Children (Jules Vernes), 111
  Dawn (Herbert Wilcox, 1928), 9, 12
  Le Fils de Lagardère (Henri Andréani), 150
  Glory and Riches (Henri Bataille), 160
  Ivanhoe, 146
  Julius Caesar, 104
  on life of Jesus Christ, 106
  Mais mon amour ne meurt pas, 150
  Mark-Antony and Cleopatra, 106
  Néron et Agrippine, 156
  Raid on Zeppelins, 240
  Roman d'un Mousse, 158
  Salâmbo, 164
  Siegfried, 116
  Les Trois Mousquetaires, 10, 106, 108
  Veronique, 152
  of the 1914–18 war, 247–8, 260, 276
  see also cinema
fines, 72, 78, 109, 130, 144, 146–7, 165, 197
fireworks, 92, 138, 227, 288
flags, 72, 83, 109, 114

Index

American/teasing Germans, 48
German, 88, 98, 107–11, 113
see also Union Jacks
Flanders, 175
Flemish girls/language, 170, 198, 203
Flo, Auntie, *see* Mourilyan, Flo
flooding, 110, 152, 155
Foch, Marshal Ferdinand (1851–1929), 261
Folsom State Prison, California, 29
food, shortages/cost, 1, 10–11, 22, 66
  beans, 119
  biscuits, 120, 128, 148–9
  bread, 43, 111–12, 126, 137, 160
  butter, 112, 114–15, 117, 128, 136, 138–9, 142–3, 149–50, 160, 163
  cakes, 142–3
  carrots, 120, 130
  caviar, 151
  cheese, 112
  choux-raves (kohlrabi), 144
  coffee, 120, 151
  eggs, 102, 123–4, 128, 138, 143, 145, 149, 151, 165
  flour, 108, 137
  fruit, 138
  geese, 151
  gingerbread, 120
  grease (lard), 108, 118
  ham, 138
  honey, 127
  macaroni, 108, 119
  meat, 120, 124, 128, 138, 146, 160
  oil, 128, 149, 160
  peas, 130
  pepper, 153
  petit-beurres, 120
  petits-fours, 151
  potatoes, 1, 102, 112–28, 143–9, 151, 160
  radishes, 161
  rice, 108, 112, 118–21
  soda, 120
  strawberries, 68, 126
  sugar, 103, 108, 112–16, 120–4, 127–9, 134–5, 142, 148, 160

  sugar-candy, 113, 120
  tea, 50, 120
  turkeys, 105, 151
  turnips, 144
  vegetables, 138
  vermicelli, 119
football matches, 149, 224, 227
Ford, Colonel (locked up), 112
Forest/Forêt, 58, 94, 152, 155, 186–8, 190
France/French army, 39, 43, 48, 70, 77, 81, 89–91, 94–5, 98, 123, 140, 149
Franchomme, 154, 187
Franz Joseph, Emperor (1830–1916), 147
Fred, Uncle, *see* Mourilyan, Frederick James
Freeling, Sir James (1825–1916), 144
frontier crossing, xxi, 104, 110, 120, 139, 154, 160, 183, 185
funerals/funeral services, 62, 68, 83, 126, 133, 191, 220, 248–9, 254

Gaeslinck, Emma (schoolgirl), 147
Gahan, Mrs Florence Buxton Muriel, xxii, 52, 113, 159, 250
Gahan, Rev. Horace Stirling Townsend (1870–1959), xxii, xxvi, 1, 13, 46, 52, 82, 113, 206, *207*, 219, 233, 249
Galicia, 51, 68, 70, 89, 140
Gallipoli, 82, 84, 109
Gare du Luxembourg, 225–6
Gare du Midi, 147, 154
Gare du Nord ('North Station'), 13, 51, 106, 190, 210, 248, *249*, 261, 265
gas, 116, 145, 161, 197
  gasmen, 156
  gas-woman, 125
  see also poison gas
George V, King (1865–1936), 70, 72, 97, 113, 215, 230
German carts of provisions/ammunition, 58–9, 62, 70, 124
German civilians, 79, 121, 158
German occupation/authorities, 91
  ban Belgian colours, 73
  ban bicycles, 57, 140

305

ban food/ban taking food, 118, 130
ban maps, 91
ban pastry cooks selling cakes, 142
ban processions, 76
bicycle tyres, 138, 144
blackout order, 197–8
boot shop displays, 190
brass, 161, 187
church bells, 207
copper, 20, 151, 156, 158, 187
cut down trees, 112, 193
deportations, 62, 103, 108, 145, 152, 154–5, 174
executions/sentence to be shot, 10, 22, 63, 77, 89, 91–3, 97–9, 106–7, 109–10, 114, 117, 120, 122, 125, 135, 139
fines, 72, 78, 109, 130, 144, 146–7, 197
gas/electricity, 145, 197
linen, 20, 158
mattresses, 11, 20, 158, 204
nickel pennies, 83
potatoes, 113, 118, 187
prisoner-of-war camps, xvii, 24, 27, 225, 230
requisition hotels, 131
school inspections, 170
search houses, 62, 91, 126
shut cinemas, 139, 147, 164
shut schools, 157
take empty houses, 98–9, 117
threaten with prison, 51, 72, 78
see also Bissing; Brussels: curfews; chômeurs; dogs; flags; horses; newspapers: banned; shops; time change
Germans/Germany, 37, 90–1
'mad letter to America', 155–6
wanting peace, 155
German soldiers/army, 47–8, 50, 67, 80, 83, 88, 100, 102, 106, 111, 140, 175
Belgian relations with, 229
in Crocodile, 40–3, 45–6
deserters, 90–1
drilling, 59
evacuating Flanders, 175

fight at cinema, 146
firing after people, 187
and German school, 145
in hospital, 156
Lancers, 40
running about mad, 196
save Amy from tram, 136
shot, 12, 77, 91
suicide, 117, 130
Uhlans, 51, 62, 77
wounded, 42–3, 51, 68
see also bands
Ghent, 43, 46, 68, 70
governor-general murdered, 112
Gifford, Miss, 131, 136, 139, 215, 217
and château at Boitsfort, 167
goat in convent garden, 173–4
'God save the King' (anthem), 70, 79, 101, 105
Goethem, Mlle M. van (tennis player), 135, 139, 141
Goffart, rue, 7
Goltz, Colmar Freiherr, Baron von der (Governor General of Brussels; 1843–1916), 122
Grace, W.G. (cricketer; 1848–1915), 15, 22
Gräffe, Willy (tennis player), 89–90, 126, 137
Graham, Mr (threatened with deportation), 152
gramophone, at convent, 174, 190, 206, 261
Grand Bazar, 154, 187, 230
Grand-Place, 214, 261
graves of soldiers, 48
Greece, 138, 149
Grimsby, 113
grippe/grip *see* influenza
Groanendael, Renée (schoolgirl), 203–4
Groenendael (south-east of Brussels), 248
guns/gunfire, 21, 40–1, 46, 50, 52, 56, 82, 134–5, 153–4, 160–1, 230
see also cannons
gymnastics, 148–9, 192, 194

Index

hail damage (1916), 124–5
Hal (Halle) (south-west of Brussels), 192–3
Haley, Mme, and walnut-trees, 112
Halles, 126, 138
Halteren, Mr Van (imprisoned), 107
Hannah, Mlle (landlady in Crocodile), 37–42
Hardinge, Sir Arthur (1859–1933), 78
hard labour (sentence), xxi, 6, 10, 93–4, 106, 116, 155
Harry (comic clown), 154
Harry Mans, The (duetists), 154
Haute, rue, 116, 201
Heineman, Mr Daniel (Dannie) (1872–1962), xxii–xxiii, 10, 130, 235
    Mrs Hettie, xxii, 107, 122, 131, 150, 162, 218, 226, 229, 244
    Jimmy, xxii, 248, 262
    Joe, xxiii, 244
    Stephen, xxii, 119, 155, 248
Heist (ruins), 266
Hélène-Maria, Sister/Soeur, 245, 248, 261
Hensmans, Jeanne (expelled), 11, 196
Hesperia (actress; 1885–1959), 162
hide-and-seek, 81, 131, 143, 177, 181
Hindenburg, Paul von (Chief of the General Staff; 1847–1934), 158
Hirsch, rue Neuve, 125
Hitchcock, Lloyd & Company, Inc., Brussels, 292
Hodson, Amy Victoria (1901–67), xvi–xvii, *xxix*, *36*, *258*
    and Africa, 233, 243, 247, 251, 253, 257, 276
    as 'aspirante' nun, 234, 236, (wishing to be a nun) 211, 213, 267
    as beggar/on charity, 262, 270–3
    birth/birthday, *19*, 20, 47, 114–15, 158, 208
    black coat, 195, 203
    blamed for taking keys, 182, 198, 203
    boarding v. day girl, 216, 219, 231, 237–8, 243, 247, 251, 253
    breakages, 197, 217, 236, 248
    called demon/following the devil, 184, 194, 214, 219, 272
    called thief/liar/hypocrite, 162, 165, 172, 235–6, 239–40, 244, 246, 254, 257, 260, 270, 281
    called/thinks she is mad, 184, 238, 253, 258, 260
    and Canada, *xii*, 26–7, 282, 292, 294
    character, 35, 172, 240, 245, 252, 273–4
    climbs onto roof, 35, 204
    death, 294
    detests herself, 212, 219, 263
    disobedient/disruptive/naughty, 34–5, 154, 169–70, 172–4, 184, 190, 192, 194, 208–9, 211–15, 219, 236, 238, 243, 245, 248, 250, 252–4, 256–7, 267, 271–4, 277–8, 280–1
    and dolls/teddy bear, 75, 187, 192, 197, 199–200, 210–11, 213
    dreams/nightmares, 34, 109, 173, 180, 207–8, 219, 231, 245, 248, 250
    and England, 127, 209–10, 215, 292, *293*, *294*
    handkerchief signed, 2, 7, 11, 59–60
    jumps/climbs out of windows, 35, 170, 282
    at Kommandantur, 36, 104–5
    loses temper, 168, 175, 288–9
    marriage, 294
    measures/weighs herself, 65, 116
    to military reviews, 12–13, 227–8, *228*, 233, *234*, 242, 261
    Mother attacks her, 20, 158, 164–5, (keeps her in) 159, 161, 165, (no/little food) 158, 161–5, (rejects her again) 253, 260, 269, 272, 280
    music, 110, 114–15, 119, 155–7, 171–2, 188, 256, 259, 273, (piano) 34–5, 132–3, 160, 186–7, 189, 191, 194, 200, 205, 213, 259, 262, (violin) 95, 172–5, 177–8, 180–3, 185–92, 194–206, 208, 227, 233, 241, 285
    'My Experience on the Belgian

Sea-Coast', xi, xxv, 37–44, 76–7
as nanny, 130–2
pitied not blamed, 262
in plays/concerts, 79–80, 82–3, 86, 88, 91, 95, 97–8, 104–5, 118, 148, 170, 177–8, 197–8, 281–2, 284
punishments, 170, 172–4, 180, 182–3, 185, 188, 190–1, 194–6, 198, 204–5, 208, 216, 248–9, 274, 276
as Roman Catholic, 171–2, 181, 195, 209, 216, 222, 224, 242, 264, 274
rude, 169, 174, 194, 196, 232, 268
school, primary (convent), 222, 224 (*see also* schools)
scrapes/practical jokes, 35, 152, 154, 162, 183, 185, 258–9
separated from friends, 154, 190, 194, 205, 254, 256 (*see also* Pauline)
shorthand, 160, 175, 282, 287
and sparrow, 193–4
as stenographer, 292, 294
swimming and the sea, 265–6, 287 (*see also* swimming baths)
takes letters to people, 5, 7, 52, 54, 163, 222–4, 246
teaching, 35, 142, 161, 171, 250, 271, 273–4, 276, 279, 282, 284
visits Mother, 191, 208
whistling, 34, 271, 276
see also St Charles, Sister
Hodson, Annie de Salis (née Mourilyan) (mother; 1870–1943), xv–xvii, xix, xxiv, *xxix*, 10, 20–2, *21*, 31, *32*, 37, 45, 60, 62, 68, 71, 76, 103–6, 109, 121, 123–4, 127, 131–3, 136, 141, 143, 152, 162–4, 167, 207–8, 211, 231, 240, 244–52, 262, 270–1, 294
ailments/ill, 21, 91, 113–16, 119, 167, 173, 177, 192, 216, 230, 236–7, 239, 244, 247
allows Amy to see her, 191, 208, 264
attacks Amy, 20, 33, 158, 163, 164–5, (keeps her in) 159, 161

birth/birthday, 69, 127–8, 170, 229, 253
death, xiii, 22
in England, 209–10, 212, 220, 224–5, 227, 229–30, 233, 236–8
letters to/from, 68, 74, 159, 173, 215–16, 219, 224, 228–9, 236–7, 253, 259, 280
to Kommandantur, 78
marriage, 20
out with Amy, 47, 50–1, 54, 59, 74, 77, 89, 91, 105, 115–16, 130, 133–4, 137–9, 142, 148, 155, 160–1, 242
people to tea, 52, 134, 136, 138, 152, 249
presents for Amy, 150, 225
rejects Amy again, 253, 260, 269, 272–3, 280, 284
staying with Miss Gifford, 167, 169
see also signing
Hodson, Sir Arnold Wienholt (cousin; 1881–1944), xvi, *xxix*
Hodson, Arthur (A.) (brother; 1904–73), xvii, xxiv, *xxix*, 24, 26, 37–45, 50, 62–3, 67, 76, 78, 83, 86, 97, 104, 122, 124–6, 132–4, 136, 142, 146–7, 159–60, 165, 169, 173, *176*, 187, 199, 268
ailments, 48, 70–2, 76, 81, 110–13, 120
in Amy's dream, 34, 173, 231
birthday/birth, 20, 22, 76, 132, 177
breakages, 225
enfant terrible, 225
in England, 209, 219, 262, 284
letters, 216, 229, 249
out with Amy, 50, 54, 60, 67, 70, 72–4, 80, 86, 99, 102, 106, 116, 121, 131, 137, 144, 148, 150, 157, 184–5, 192, 208, 231, 263–4, 269–70
and the poet, 103–4, 108–9, 114–15, 119–21, 124
school, 89, 107, 126, 192, 210, 215, 225, 249, 270, 280

Index

Hodson, Basil Ernest (half-brother; 1883–9), *xxix*, 18–19, 31
Hodson, Charles Frederick, FRCS (grandfather; 1816–1904), *xxix*, 14, 19
Hodson, Charles Rosser Kendall (half-brother; 1885–9), *xxix*, 18–19, 31
Hodson, Charlie (Charles Thomas) (brother; 1899–1925), xv, xvii, xix, *xxix*, 23–7, *25*, 94–5, 100, 111, 121, 210, 225, 242
    ailments/injuries, 24, 225, 230, 246, (TB) 27
    to Antwerp, 254
    attached to a gun as punishment, 228
    birthday/birth, 20, 31, 66, 127, 169, 252
    broken down, 228
    in Brussels, 254, 277, 280–2, 285
    to Canada/USA, 24–7
    disappears (1915), 24, 47, 112
    in England, 24, *64*, 72, 74–5, *75*, 86–8, *87*, 111, 127, 134, *211*, 229–30, *255*, 277, 285
    Germans looking for him, 36, 48, 58, 104–5
    in hospital, 225, 229–30, 246
    letters by/about, 72, 74–5, 111, 115, 228, 230
    no news, xv, 47–8, 66–7, 91, 104, 119, 124, 214, 216–18, 220
    in Royal Fusiliers, 24, 76, 108, 111
    takes Amy home/out, 277, 280, 284
    to the Yser, 88
Hodson, Ernest Rust (father; 1853–1934), xvi, xviii–xix, xxiii–xxiv, *xxix*, 1, 13–20, *14*, 24, *32*, 47, 51–2, 62, 66, 68, 71, 73, 93, 95, 103–4, 109, 111, 113, 118, 121, 132–3, 139, 141, 155, 159–60, 165, 187, 194, 207–10, *207*, 212, 214–16, 220, 222–3, 236, 241–3, 251–3, *264*, 270–1
    ailments, 59, 63, 152, 211, 284
    birthday, 99, 146, 280

    death, xiv, 22
    in England, *217*, *241*, 242, 246–7, 263, 267
    invitations, official, 11, 13, 215–16, 226–7, 233, 248–9
    to Kommandantur, 104–5
    letters to/from, 49, 94, 115, 134, 136, 191, 204, 210, 215–16, 219, 224–5, 228–9, 233, 236–7, 246, 251, 259, 273–4, 276, 279
    money, 159, 161
    out with/meets Amy, 36, 52, 57–8, 62–3, 65–6, 70, 73, 79–80, 82, 86, 97, 99, 103, 106, 108, 116, 132–5, 146, 160–1, 166–7, 169, 171, 174, 182, 184–5, 187, 191–2, 199–200, 204, 224, 227–8, 230, 240, 252, 262, 268, 270, 273
    protects Amy from Mother, 163–4
    pupils, 63, 245
    and son Tommy, 31, 217–18
    tennis, 63, 65, 70, 81, 169, 173, 177, 180, 248–9, 252–3
    see also signing; Union Club
Hodson, Henry Algernon (Uncle Algie) (1852–1915), xvi, *xxix*, 75
Hodson, Henry Clarence (Baby/B.) (brother; 1906–99), xiii, xvii–xix, xxiv, *xxix*, 22, 35, 37–45, 50, 70, 78, 105, 108, 110, 120, 129–30, 132–4, 136, 142, 147, 159–60, 162, 165, 169, 199, 219, 239, 247–8, 250–2, 256, 259, 262, 285
    ailments, 59–61, 63, 65–6, 70, 76, 102, 104, 110–12, 122, 152–3, 241–2, 244–5, 252
    birthday/birth, 20, 71, 129, 172
    to cinema, 76, 99, 102–3, 106, 115, 146, 152, 158–60, 162–5, 240
    in England, 209–10, 225, 233, 238, *241*, 284, *286*
    memoirs, 2, 20, 22–3, 26–7, 209
    out with Amy, 13, 51–2, 54, 57, 59, 67–8, 71, 77, 79–81, 83, 86, 89, 97, 102, 104, 106, 110–11, 115–17, 120–1, 124, 128, 131,

309

133–7, 145, 155–6, 160–1, 184–5, 208, 242–3, 246–8, 262, 265, 269–70
  school, 77, 89, 107, 113, 126, 210, 215, 231, 233, 237, 246, 270
  tennis, 73–4, 76, 78, 80, 82, 86, 89, 122, 128, 133, 141, 173, 246, 253
  wishes Mother was a fairy, 161
Hodson, Margaret Maria (née Kendall) (1857–93), xvi, xix, *xxix*, 16, *17*, 18–19, 31, 129
Hodson, Tommy (Lionel Ernest) (half-brother; 1890–1964), xiii, xix–xx, *xxix*, 27–31, 91, 94, 124, 214
  birth, 19, 28
  in Brussels, 31, 217–19, 232
  in Canada, 27, 282, 292
  in England, 30, *64*, *75*, 86–8, *87*, 111, *211*, 242, *283*
  in Germany, 215, 218, 237, 242
  in hospital, 30, 215, 240, 242
  Lovat's Scouts, 24, 27, 30, 76, 108, 210, (officer) 115, 210, 213–14
  marriages, 27–30, 282, *283*
  in prison, 29
  takes Amy out, 218–19
  in Turkey/Dardanelles, 30, 88
  wounded, 215–16, 242
Holland, 68, 71, 73–4, 82, 110, 112, 114, 265
'Home sweet Home' (song), 105
Honoré, Germaine (schoolgirl), 190, 238, 258
Hood, Rear-Admiral, the Hon. Horace L.A. (1870–1916), 55–7
Hoover, Herbert (later President; 1874–1964), xxiii, 11, 214
horses, taken by Germans, 100, 103, 108–9, 153, 156
l'Hôtel des Monnaies, 139
  rue de, 219
Hôtels de Ville (town halls), 146, 226, 261
Hougoumont, 73, 184
Howard, Ernest (grave), 94
Hugo, Victor (1802–85), 174

Hulse, John (grave), 48
Hungary, 90–1, 144
Huns, Germans as, 39, 40, 265

identity card (Carte d'Identité), 95, 98, 115–16, 141, 147, 166, 169, 223
India/Indians, xvii, 23, 63
influenza (*la grippe*), 119, 230, 234, 276, 284
Institut des Filles de Marie, 6 rue Théodore Verhaegen (Amy's school, 1917–19), xiv, xxiv, 33, 166, *179*, 186, 189, 191, 246, 252, *258*
  chapel, xiv, 166, 171, 185, 190–1, 197, 200, 222, 257
  Comité, 212–13, 261, 270
  Patronage, 181, 184, 188, 196, 282
Institut du Docteur Depage, La Panne, 213
  see also Depage, Dr Antoine
internment, 112–15
  see also Ruhleben
Iron Crosses, 77
Irvine, Esther Hamilton, *see* Auntie
Italy/Italians, 10, 50, 58, 65, 78, 82, 91, 106, 137, 140, 191
ivy-leaf worn by Belgians, 73
Ixelles, 152, 162

J. *see* Joséphine
Jack *see* Jenkins, John Card
Jarvis, Mr C.E., 47, 65, 78, 252, 268, 273, 280
  Mrs, 54, 57, 60–1, 65, 80
Jay, John (1770–1838), xiii
Jeffes family, 51, 249
Jeffes, Thomas (British Vice-Consul in Brussels), 20
Jenkins, Rev. Charles Edward (Edward) (1826–73), 32, *221*, *275*
Jenkins, Rev. Charles Edward (Edward) (1873–1931), xviii, *xxix*, 32, *32*, 274–6, *274*
Jenkins, Constance Agnes (Con/Connie) (née Hodson) (half-sister; 1881–1963), xvii–xix, *xxix*, 16, 18,

Index

20, 22, *25*, 28, 31, *32*, 33, 76, 94, 98, *135*, 210, *217*, 225, 242, 248, 276, *283*, *286*, 290, 292, *294*
   birth of children, 63, *64*, 264, *264*
   letters to father, 94, 136, 210, 214, 216, 224–5, 229, 233
   looks for/sees Charlie, 75, 220, 229
   sends money/presents, 219, 229, 246
Jenkins, Desmond Ernest (nephew; 1915–92), 33, 63, *64*, *75*, 76, 98, 225, *241*, 248, *264*, 276
Jenkins, Eliza (née Jay) (1797–1864), xiii, 33
Jenkins, Rev. Evan (1794–1849), *xxix*, 33
Jenkins, Helen Eliza (1827–1911), 33
Jenkins, Rev. John Card (1834–94), 18, 32, *221*, 274
Jenkins, John Card (Jack) (brother-in-law; 1874–1958), xi, xviii–xix, *xxix*, 20, 31–3, *32*, 86, 127, 216, *264*, *275*, 290
   in Boulogne, 225, 236
   in Brussels, 234–6
   demobbed, 33, 242
   in England, 75, *75*, *211*, 242, 248, *286*
   letters from, 49, 76, 86, 115
   lieutenant in RASC (1917–19), 192, *193*, 210, *235*
   out with Amy, 234–5
   sees Charlie, 75, *75*, 76
   in Tourcoing, France, 216
Jenkins, John Chevalier (Jack) (1920–2000), 33, *241*, *286*
Jenkins, Rosa Mary (Rosie) (1869–1951), *32*
Jerusalem, 198
Jeudwine, General Hugh Sandham (1862–1942), 228, *228*
Joffre, General Joseph (1852–1931), 97, 102
Joséphine (J.) (Hodsons' cook), xxiii, 52, 66, 98, 118–19, 121–2, 125, 128, 133, 138, 144–5, 147, 150, 152–3, 161–4, 211, 214, 216, 224, 226, 236, 246, 264

Kaiser, the (Wilhelm II) (1859–1941), 66, 72, 76, 97, 109, 111, 149, 153, 155, 158, 204
Kendall, Dorice/Doris Margaret (née Jenkins) (niece) (b. 1919), xi, 22–3, 31, 33, *241*, 264, *264*, 276, *283*, *286*, *293*
Kendall, Jane Eyre (b. 1855), 16
Kendall, Thomas Marsters (1820–71), *xxix*, 16
King Edward Memorial Hospital, Winnipeg, 26–7
King Edward VI Grammar School, Louth, 15
King George's Hospital, London, 230
King's Lynn, Norfolk, 16
Kirkpatrick, Jim (died of wounds), 52
Kirkpatrick, Mr, 62, 124
   Miss, 67
Kitchener, Horatio Herbert, Lord (1850–1916), 127–8
kites, 72, 81
   black, 58
   white, 63, 65
Knocke, 264–6, 270
Koekelberg (north-west of Brussels), 142, 172, 257
Kommandantur (German headquarters, 6 rue de la Loi), 1–2, 6–7, 35–6, 73, 78–80, 82, 86, 92–3, 104, 109, 114
Kovno, 81

Laeken, 18, 107
   fair, 242
   Grotto, 169
   provisions burnt, 187
Laiterie du Bois, 250
Landau, Captain, 9
Lannoy brewery, 108
Lansdowne, Henry Petty-Fitzmaurice, 5th Marquess of (1845–1927), 96–7
La Panne, 63, 213
Larking, Captain/Major, 83
Lavelaye, Baron de, 120, 236
   Emile (death), 121
   Mlle (marriage), 104
Lawn Tennis Club ('the tennis'), 294

311

ave. Brugmann, 19–20, 52, 57, 59, 66–8, 70–8, 80–3, 85–6, 89–92, 94–5, 113, 118–19, 121–30, 133–43, *135*, 165, 173, 177, 180, 182, 252–3, 268, 273
  see also tennis (playing)
Le Coq (ruins), 266
Lecourt, Father, xxiii, 33, 73–4, 110, 201, 251, 263–4, 287
  Amy at his church, 186
  helps/visits Amy, 159, 166–7, 169, 174, 253
  Italian priest taken, 50, 58
  leaving Brussels, 267
  taken by Germans, 50
Ledrut, Renée (schoolgirl), 193, 213
Leicester, xviii, 30–1, *32*, 284
Léopold I, King (1790–1865), 33
Léopold of Belgium, Prince (1901–83), 113, 242, 261
Léopold Club, Parc Brugmann, 128, 142, 182, 224, 227, 262
Léopold, St (1073–1136), 99, 146
'Les Yeux' (song), 153
Leval, Gaston de (Belgian legal adviser to American Legation), 93, 98
Libiez, Albert (sentence), 94
Liège, 38, 49, 144, 148, 260
Lille, 90, 93, 109
  famine, 138
Linkebeek (south of Brussels), 109, 256
'The Little Girl Milking her Cow' (song), 105
Littlehampton, West Sussex, 289
Loi, rue de la, 7, 124, 254
Longchamps, avenue, 68, 134
Loo, Angèle Van (Belgian soprano; 1881–1960), 152
Loretto School, Musselburgh, 15
Louise, avenue, xxiii, 50, 62, 68, 102, 116, 204, 223
Louis Morichar, place, 103, 156
Louis, St, 171–2
Louvain, 71, 111, 187, 254
Louvain, chaussée de, 51
Lovat's Scouts, 24, 27, 30, 108, 210

Lowestoft, Suffolk, 292
Lyon, General, 8
Lyon, Hon. E.B., and Mrs Lyon, *135*

Madama Butterfly (Puccini), 170, 177
mad woman/man in street, 178, 278
Maes, General (funeral), 83
magic lantern, 158
Maison Beethoven, 114
Maison Communale (town hall), 95, 116, 133, 192, 229, 245
Malines, 66–7, 254
maps of the war, banned, 91
Marchal's, 177
Marché aux Herbes, rue du, 167–8
Margate, Kent, 160
  College, 249, 270
Maria-Cécile, Sister/Soeur, 169, 183, 195
Mariakerke, 42
Marie-Christina, Sister/Soeur, 177–8, 190, 261–3, 268
Marie-Clarice/Clarisse, Sister/Soeur, 170, 173, 180, 183, 200, 213, 215, 241, 244, 249, 254
Marie José, Princess (1906–2001), 261
Marie-Paula, Sister/Soeur, 169, 178, 183, 198, 219, 232–6, 238, 258, 276
Marist Fathers, 168
Marolles, 201
'Marseillaise, La' (national anthem of France), 38, 101
Martyrs, place des, 77
'Massues' hymn, 192
Mauroy, Martha (schoolgirl mouse killer), 195
Max, Adolphe (Mayor of Brussels; 1869–1929), 220, 261
May, Mrs, 50, 109, 150
  and château at Boitsfort, 130
  Georgie, 97, 106, 123, 222
  Jules, 97
measles, 60, 104, 150–1, 155, 208
Meert, Mr (at CRB), 130
  Mrs and Frida, 139
Melina, Louise de (Amy's rival), 170

Index

Mellin, Ethel, 74, 219, 223, 244, 256, 280–1
Mellin, Lassen (Mr) (c. 1841–1918), xi, xxiii–xxiv, 19, 109, 128–9, 133, 168, 213, 216, 219–20, 244
Mellin, Rita (Miss) (1870–1956), xi, xxiii–xxiv, 33, 60, 62, 67, 107–8, 110, 120, 122, 132–3, 171, 173, 180, 190–1, 198, 202, 208, 220, 222, 231, 251, 253, 272, 280, 284
    ailments, 50, 116, 236
    Amy at her house, 47, 76, 94, 107, 110, 119, 129, 200, 206, 208, 210, 216, 219–20, 223, 227, 229, 235–7, 239–41, 244, 246, 250, 252–4, 256, 259–61, 268–70, 272, 280–1
    becomes Roman Catholic, 262, 276
    to church with Amy, 264, 269–70
    gives Amy presents, 119, 146, 165, 187, 190, 263–4, 266, 285
    holidays with Amy, 264–6, 287–91
    organizing play/concert, 79–80, 82–3, 86, 88, 91, 104–5, 118
    takes Amy out, 48, 52, 54, 57–9, 72, 77, 79–80, 95, 107, 109, 112, 117, 119, 123, 134, 136, 142, 146, 165, 167–70, 175, 177, 186–7, 190, 195, 201, 203, 205, 213, 226, 232, 247, 250, 254, 257, 262–4, 267, 282
'Mensonges des Allemands', 65
Menton, Alix (schoolgirl), 192, 194, 197, 205, 232, 256
Mercier, Cardinal Désirée-Joseph (1851–1926), 70, 118, 228, 257
Meredith, Mr (soldier, dying), 80
Méridien, rue du (École Militaire), 92
    see also signing/registration at rue du Méridien
Metz, bombardment at, 91
Mexico, 156
Meyer family (leave Brussels), 66
Michaux, Mr, 159
Michot, Mr and Mme (rescue Amy), 46
Middelkerke, 37, 41, 45, 54–5, 76, 97, 159

Mignon, Laurette (expelled), 195
Mimi (schoolgirl), 185, 190–2, 254
mines, 109, 116, 120, 127, 157, 247
'Minuit, Chrétiens' (carol), 190, 285
mitrailleuses (machine-guns, or machine-gunners), 10, 48, 50, 68, 70, 86, 106
Molière, avenue, 161–2
Molinari, Laure de (schoolgirl then assistant teacher), 172–3, 175, 178, 183, 185, 189, 192, 198, 208, 239
Molinari, Marie-Lucie de (schoolgirl), 175, 178, 189, 194–5
money, German, 83, 223
Mons, 93, 117
Montenegro, 90, 109
Morgan, J.P., Jr (1867–1943), 74
Moris, rue, 83
Mother *see* Hodson, Annie
motorcar accidents, 231, 249–50
motorcycles, 214, 231
Mourilyan, Amy (née Irvine) (1844–72), xvii, *xxix*, 20, 23
Mourilyan, Caroline Florence (Auntie Flo) (née Gardiner) (1841–1922), xviii, *xxix*, 19, 47, 117, 119, 122, 220, 238, 242, 289–90
Mourilyan, Frederick James (Uncle Fred) (1846–1927), xvii–xviii, *xxix*, 18–20, 23–4, 47, 68, 72, 74–5, 111, 119, 134, 225, 228, 233, 250–4, 256, 289–90
Mourilyan, Thomas Burton (1843–79), xviii–xix, *xxix*, 20
Movaux, Olga (expelled), 156
museums: Scientific, 274
    Wiertz, 270
musical chairs, 186

Namur (south of Brussels), 214, 216, 218
national fête, Belgian, *see under* fêtes
network, the secret, 5–6, 9
Neuve Chapelle (1915), 49, 61
Neuve, rue, 125, 195
Newry, Co. Down, 4–5, 10
newspapers, 81, 113, 122

313

banned, 58, 68, 128
La Belgique, 51, 76–7, 93–4
Dutch, 68
English, 215, 227
La Libre Belgique, 5, 66, 78–9, 100–1, 126
New York Herald, 99
sellers, 59, 72, 91
The Times, 54–7, 60–1, 65, 72, 74, 79, 84–5, 100, 108
Wochenschau, 65
New York, 22, 26, 28, 32–3, 94, 98, 290
Nicholas II, Tsar of Russia (1868–1918), 160
Nicolas, St (Santa Claus), 148, 197, 211–13
Nicolet, Dr, 70
Jean, 80, 104
Mrs, 134
Nieslet, Mrs, and David (going to Switzerland), 164
Nieuport, 39, 45, 55–7
Nieuport, chaussée de, Crocodile, 38, 43
Noblet, Mr (dead), 152
Noblet, Robert (caught), 154
notices, German, 59, 72, 74, 99, 118, 146
  condemned to death, 107
  no sign of mourning, 78
  red, 107, 114, 117, 125
nuns *see under* Roman Catholicism; *and individual teachers*

Oedecie, Mother, 224
oil, 118
Ollibaere, Henri (artist), 165
Orphelinat of Uccle, Jubilee of, 97
Ostend, 10, 13, 39, 42–3, 45–6, 55, 266, 270
d'Oultremont, Comte, 174
Comtesse, 139
'Outward Bound' (poem by officer fallen in Gallipoli), 84

P. *see* Pauline
'Paillaisse' (musical piece), 195
painting studios/paintings, 116, 148, 162, 165
Palais d'Été, 282
Palais de Glace, 52, 285
Palais de Justice, 88, 98, 107–10, 113, 134, 204
Palais de l'Injustice, 114
Palais des Académies, 101, 115–16, 126
Palais des Sports, Schaerbeek, 145, 148
Palais Royal *see* Royal Palace
Palmer, Edward John (1911–86), xix, *xxix*, *32*, 235, 274–6
Palmer, Major Frederick Edmund Corbett (Paddy) (1872–1915), xix, *xxix*, *32*, 86, 88
Palmer, Janet Henrietta (née Jenkins) (1870–1954), *xxix*, *32*
papers thrown from aeroplanes, 88–90, 140, 254
Papeterie de l'Espérance, rue de l'Amazone, 126
Paquet, Mme/Mlle, 95, 97–8, 100, 102, 104–5, 109
Parc, avenue du, 170, 188
Parc Duden, 175, 180, 183, 185, 188
Parc Rouge, 169
Parc Royal/Royal Park, 77, 257
Paris, 71, 111, 140, 278
Parme, place de, 89, 103
Parme, rue de, 141
parrot singing 'Nous sommes foutus', 63
Pascale, rue de, 4
passports, 43, 68, 73–4, 112, 229, 237
Pass-Zentrale/Centrale, place Royale, 127
pastry cooks, 142
Pauline/P. (schoolgirl), 212, 232, 250, 254–7, 259–60, 262–3, 265, 268, 272–4, 277–82, 284–5, 287–8
peace: hoping for, 108, 175
  praying for, 237–8
  see also Armistice
Peace, procession of, 259
Peace Treaty, Versailles, 257

Pêches (Pesche) and nuns, 183, 239, 264, 266–7, 289
Pégoud, Adolphe (aviator; 1889–1915), 83
Peiser, Mrs, 73, 114, 138, 208
pensionnat *see* Institut des Filles de Marie, rue Théodore Verhaegen (Amy's school 1917–19)
Perche, rue de la, 281
Père Fouettard ('Father Whipper', accompanies Santa Claus), 197, 282
Persians, 88
Petit, Abbé (in prison), 100, 107
'Petit Dictionnaire de Boche', 66
Phipps, Lady, 152, 180
photographs, 76, 83, 86, 94, 107, 116, 172, 175–6, 192, 202, 206–7, 223, 225, 258
Picture Exhibition by Belgian prisoners, 150
'Pigs', Germans as, 70, 118, 126, 131
Plaine de Berkendael, 81, 260
Plaine des Manoeuvres, Etterbeek, 58, 89, 230
plays/sketches, 159, 172
　A Hero, 91
　La Jalouse, 148
　Red Riding Hood, 170, 172
　Rumpelstiltskin, 95, 98, 104–7
　'Voyage à Paris', 178
pneumonia, xviii, 62, 125, 132
poet, the, *see* Collart, Raymond
Poincaré, Raymond, President of France (1860–1934), 261–2
Poinçon, rue du, murder in, 284
poison gas, 60–1, 66, 123
Poland, 76, 249
policemen, 45, 47, 119, 141, 214, 227, 249
　police station, 47
Polly, Aunt, *see* Robinson, Mary Anna
pony carriage/cart, 50, 70, 83
poor, the, 116, 145, 201, 211, 213
Porte de Halles, 235
Porte de Namur, 147
Porte Louise, 247

Portuguese, 116–17
priests: murdered, 284
　'tortured', 63
Prince d'Orange, 66, 134
Printemps, Paule and Renée (orphaned schoolgirls), 256
prison: St Gilles, 5–6, 80, 82, 95, 146
　threatened with, 51
prisoners, 80
　Austrian, 95
　Belgian, 50, 83, 95, 118, 150, 154, 183
　Canadian, 62–3
　English, 50, 62, 118, 132, 210
　French, 43
　German, 51, 78, 90, 94, 118
　'Hohenzollern' Dautzenbergh, 68
　rumours: burnt alive/crucified, 62–3
　see also individual people
Prower, Colonel, 51
Przemyśl, Galicia, 51, 68
public taps, 156–7

Quatre-Bras (south-east of Brussels), 54, 82, 86, 167
Queen Elizabeth's Grammar School, Barnet, 16
Queen Victoria Institute, Brussels, xxi

Racing Club/the Racing, Uccle, 142–3, 145, 147–9
Ramsgate, Kent, 20, 67
Recour, Robert, 5
Red Cross, 42, 45, 51, 67
refugees, 39, 111, 121
Régence, rue de la, 154
resistance, Belgian, *see* Belgian resistance
restaurants (shut), 147
Reuters, 95
Reverend Mother/Mother Superior *see* Superior/Supérieure, Sister/Soeur
reviews, military (1919), 242, 261
　see also under British army
Rhodes, Cecil (1853–1902), 14
Richards, Albert, 9th R.L.V., 48
Rickards, Jack, 290

Rita *see* Mellin, Rita
Riverview Hospital, Essondale, British Columbia, 294
Rixensart, château at, 233
Robinson island, Bois de la Cambre, 269
Robinson, Mary Anna (Aunt Polly) (née Mourilyan) (1845–after 1915), xviii–xix, *xxix*, 68, 74
Roest, Baron (uncle condemned), 155
Roger de Grimbergen hospital, Middelkerke, 41–2, 46
Roman Catholicism, 172
　'aspirantes' nuns, 205–6, 234, 236
　Carmelites, 205, 237
　Communion, Holy, 193, 195, 213, 223, 249–50, 252, 257, 261, 272, 279–80, 284
　confession, 171, 193, 210–13, 239, 241
　'congréganistes' nuns, 205–6, 236
　conversions, xxiv, 195, 262–3
　indulgences, 180
　Mass, 186, 191, 193, 197, 214, 219, 237, 239, 242, 244, 271, 278, (Midnight) 222–3, 285
　novena, 230, 282
　Office of darkness, 243
　retreats, 181, 184, 192–3, 264, 266–7, 279–80
　rosary, 220, 268
　Sacred Heart of Jesus, 213, 228, 256–7
　'salut' (Benediction of the Blessed Sacrament), 203, 215, 220, 222–5, 228, 232, 237, 239, 242, 263
　sermons, 127, 170, 172, 184, 279
　Way of the Cross, 243, 245
　see also under churches; fêtes
Romania *see* Roumania
rose, red, worn by the English, 73
Rothschild, Nathan, 1st Baron (1840–1915), 52
Rouge-Cloître (south-east of Brussels), 136–7, 168
Roumania/Roumanians, xviii, 137, 140, 144, 147, 149, 154–5
　and war-boots, 68
Royale, place, xxvi, 127
Royale, rue, 148, 150, 261
Royal Fusiliers, xvii, xix, 24, 76, 108, 111, 119
Royal Palace, 80, 101, 233, *234*
Ruhleben internment camp (near Berlin), 50–1, 77, 97–8, 129
Russia/Russian army, 51, 70, 86, 89–91, 95, 105, 114, 122, 128, 140, 154, 160, 200, 249

Sablon, place du, 90
Sainderichin, Costia, 130–1
　Elsie/Elsa, 130–1
　Mme, 130–2
St Alphonse, Sister/Soeur, 169, 172, 174, 190, 195, 262
St André, Sister/Soeur, 183, 186
Saint-Bernard, rue, 18, *19*, 20, 32–3
St Bernard's School: Brussels, 1, 18, *19*, 20, 31–3
　New York, xi, xiii, xix, 32
St Catherine, place, 133
St Charles, Sister/Soeur (S.S.C.), xv, xxiv, 33–4, 167, 169–71, 173–6, 178, 181–4, 186, 189–94, 198, 218–19, 222–3, 248, 250, 253, 256–7, 259–61, 263–7, 273, 278, 281, 284, 287–8, 290
　ailments, 176–7, 181, 194, 197, 201, 205, 210, 213–15, 234, 237–8, 240, 244, 252–4, 259, 261–2, 270, 276–7, 282, 284
　Amy rude to her, 169, 174, 196, 232, 239, 241
　Amy to her dormitory, 170–4, 176–7, 180–1, 186, 188, 199, 201, 204
　Amy tries not to like/see her, 177–8, 185, 206–7, 229–30, 234, 246–7, 252, 273, 276, 281
　angry with Amy, 169, 183–4, 191, 208, 212, 214–17, 219–20, 222, 229, 232, 237, 240, 244–5, 254,

258, 271–2, 277, 280
  away from/leaving convent, 188,
    223–7, 229, 237–8, 244–5, 248,
    262, 268–70, 289
  blesses Amy, 213, 217, 220, 230, 238,
    243–4
  and books, 170–4, 178, 180, 188,
    195, 199, 209, 239–42, 244–6,
    268
  church with Amy/others, 168, 173,
    177, 180–2, 187
  death of brother, 198
  death of father, 218
  indifferent to/ignores Amy, 172,
    190, 203, 232
  kind/nice to Amy, 169, 177, 189–91,
    195–7, 200, 202, 204, 208, 217,
    230, 246, 250, 263–5, 268, 272,
    285, 289
  out with Amy/others, 169, 172–4,
    181, 183, 185, 196, 198, 235,
    260–1, 267
  punishes Amy, 170, 172, 174, 180,
    182, 185, 188, 190–2, 194–6,
    198, 204–5, 243, 248, 274
  smacks Amy, 194
  verbally abuses Amy, 191, 194, 236,
    239, 246, 256, 260, 262
St Croix, place, 163
St Gilles (commune), 1, 7, 19–20, 32,
  166, 196, 259
St Gilles park, 181
St Josse (commune), 136, 139
St Nicolas day (6 December), 103,
  147–8
  see also Nicolas, St
St Petersburg, Russia, 80–1
St Quentin State Prison, California, 29
Salle Mercelis, 172
Salle Patria, 201
San Diego, California, 28–9
Santa Claus, 105, 150, 212–13, 282
  see also Nicolas, St
'sausages', 52, 54, 57, 66, 71–4, 76, 109,
  122, 135, 141–2
scarlet fever, 122, 150

Schaerbeek, xxii, 89, 107, 109, 145
Scheppers, Mme (headmistress), 11,
  154, 156–7, 159
Schoenmaekers, Yvonne (schoolgirl),
  166, 169
Schöller, Miss (dancing teacher), 91,
  107–8, 111, 114, 116, 118–19, 126
schools: cleaning, 178, 242, 262
  exams, 156, 170–1, 175, 177, 182–3,
    192, 198, 242, 260
  fête, 70
  German, 145
  Gratuite (free), 170, 178
  inspections, 170
  place de Parme, 89, 141
  reports, 147, 154, 167, 178, 199, 239,
    285
  reviews, 259, 261
  shut, 157, (by Germans) 11, 145, 157
  yellow cards, 189, 192
  see also Ecole Moyennade St Gilles;
    Institut des Filles de Marie
scouts, 70, 77, 95, 215
  see also boy scouts
Secleppe, Rosa (schoolgirl), 183, 199
Seeldrayers family, 142–7, 150–1, 153
  Germaine, 142–3, 148, 150
  Manette, 142–53, 158
  Mme, 142–3, 145, 148, 150, 152–3
Selby, Milly (died of wounds), 94
Senne River, Brussels, 152
Seraphina/Séraphine, Sister/Soeur, 190,
  194–5, 220, 279
Serbia, 90, 259
Seret, Henri (prisoner), 183
Séverin, Louis (sentence), 1, 92–3
shells, 40, 42, 45–6, 82, 138–9, 141
Sherbrooke, Quebec, 26
ships, 46, 54–7, 135, 156, 161, 292
  Allied, 40, 43, 49, 66–7, 70, 109, 114,
    116, 127, 129, 137, 155, 161, 247,
    265–6
  American, 66, 82, 157, (SS *Eastland*)
    78
  Dutch, 67, 120, 158
  German, 50, 82, 116, 127, 143, 156

Lusitania, 59–60, 63
P&O, 107
shops (shut), 76, 78–80, 147, 150, 154
shot, people, 10, 22, 74, 77, 89, 91–2, 97–9, 106, 108–10, 114, 117, 120, 122, 125, 135, 139
shrapnel, 90, 92, 240
Siasconset, Nantucket Island, *264*
signals: Belgian, 139
    German, 52, 58–9, 65, 70, 72, 74, 77–8, 92, 95, 103, 106, 118, 123, 127, 129, 137, 141, 147, 149, 168–9, 183, 198
signing/registration at rue du Méridien (École Militaire), 104
    Amy, 115–24, 126–7, 129–32, 134–41, 145, 148, 152, 156, 159, 161, 165–6, 169, 174, (certificate) 142, 181
    parents/father, 48, 58, 66, 72, 78, 83, 90, 97, 102, 105–8, 110–11, 113–15, 132, 134–6, 156, 165–6, 169, 174, 181
Simmons, Captain Gordon, 83, 133
Simms, Mr Montgomery, 97, 99, 153, *207* (centre back)
    Mrs Simms, 52, 57, 68, 128, 132–3, 152, 165, 199
skating, 155, 157, 282, 285
sledging, 154–5
Smet, Mlle de (tennis player), 79, 124, 135
Smyth, Lieutenant J.G., VC (1893–1983), 79
snowballing, 154, 196, 233–4
soap, 98, 108, 112, 115, 118, 128, 143–4, 149
soldiers *see* British army; Tommies; *and under individual nations*
'Soldiers in the Park' (song), 105
Someville, Reverend Père/Father, 192–3, 195, 212, 215, 257, 276
Somme, 140, 155
South Africa, xvii, 74, 233, 247, 276
souvenirs/relics, 20, 39, 72
    see also buttons, uniform

Spanish flu *see* influenza
Spanish Minister *see* Villalobar, Marquis de
sparrow, dead, as 'Kaiser's chicken', 66
spies, 1, 50, 68, 89, 106, 109, 112, 162
Spoelberch, Vicomte de, 233
Spong, Mr, 97–8, 273
Staeten, Mlle Van (tennis champion), 182
Stanger, Miss, 110, 133
Stassart, rue de, xxvi, 32, 220, *221*
Stockel, 117–18
Stokes, Mabel (English nurse), 213, 216
strike, tram, 233, 273, 276
submarines, 48, 56, 59, 88, 122, 135, 143, 155–6, 161
Superior/Supérieure, Sister/Soeur, 170–1, 182–3, 192, 194, 196–9, 202, 213–15, 248, 256, 262, 271, 278–9, 282
sweets/bonbons, 52, 73, 150, 167, 197, 199
swimming-baths, 166, 180, 190, 198, 274
Switzerland, 68, 152, 164

Tadini, Mme, 10, 106
    Raymond, 10, 106
    Rosine, 10, 106
Taube (Germain aircraft), 111, 143, 165–7, 169
Taverne Royal (fined), 146
Te Deum (1919), 261
temps libre (free time), 240
tennis (playing), xviii, 58–60, 63, 65, 74, 80–2, 124, 129, 137, 165–6, 187, 248–9, 262
    and Americans, 79, 86, 129
    bumple-puppy, 121
    Carl Ehrlich Cup (C.E. Cup), xxii, 89–90, 126, 128–9, 136–7, 139
    Sperry Cup, 135, 139, 141
    tournaments, 79, 81–2, 86, 129
    see also Lawn Tennis Club
Termonde (north-west of Brussels), 58
Tervueren, avenue de, 86
Tervuren (south-east of Brussels), 54
Théâtre de la Gaîté, 216

Théâtre de la Monnaie, 227, 229
Théodore Verhaegen, rue, 33, 166
  see also Institut des Filles de Marie
Thesiger, Wilfred (1910–2003), xvi
thieves, 152–3, 156, 166, 199, 216
  Germans as, 144
Thorndike, Sybil (1882–1976), xxi, 9
Thuliez, Louise (1881–1966), 93
time change, 123
Tir National, Schaerbeek (rifle range), xxii, 9, 11–12, 93, 215, *249*
Toison-d'Or, avenue de la, *see* Union Club
Tommies/Tommy Atkins (British soldiers), 1, 39, 92, 210, 233
  see also British army
'To Our Fallen' (poem by R.E. Verniede), 61–2
tortoise at school, 147
Tosca (Puccini), xxiii, 227, 229
toys: diabolo (juggling prop), 168
  revolvers and 'pink things', 192
trains, 10, 65, 83, 89, 97–100, 104, 106, 116, 121, 123, 137, 152, 154, 164
  to England, 71, 106, 111, 127
  with German troops, 139
  with wounded, 91, 113
traitors, 74, 108–9, 114
trams, 54, 59, 66, 73, 109, 131, 136, 147, 163, 172, 182, 192, 210, 225, 265
  and spies, 80–1, 95
  on strike, 233, 273, 276
  tram-lines, 67, 139
trenches, 39, 111, 265
  digging, 38
  at Ixelles, 48
trench foot ('poisoned feet'), 24, 225
Trocadero, 97, 106, 109, 112, 192
Trois-Couleurs (south-east of Brussels), 54, 59, 123, 169
Turks/Turkey, 68, 82, 91, 109, 114, 131, 140
  see also Dardanelles; Gallipoli
typewriter/typing, 271, 273–4, 280, 282, 285

Uccle, 62, 86, 89, 97, 109, 121, 135, 141–2, 152, 161–3
  Observatoire, 137, 147
  see also cemeteries
Umtali, Rhodesia, 251
unemployed, the, *see* chômeurs
Union Club (Ernest's club, 52 ave. de la Toison-d'Or), 21, 50–1, 66, 72–3, 104, 108, 131, 167, 171, 215, 218–19, 227, 235, 259, 261, 276
Union Jacks, 39, 41, 45
d'Ursel, Leo, 7th Duc (1873–1955), 174
USA *see* America

Vallée, rue de la, 130, 141
Vanderkindere, rue, 141
Vaucleroy, Dr, 131–2
Verbeckhoven, Marguerite, 252, 254, 265–6
Verdun, 115–17, 140
'Vers l'Avenir' (patriotic song), 81, 83
Veydt, Mr (violin teacher), 178, 181, 187, 194–5
Victoria Cross (VC), 70, 77, 79
victories reported, 51, 59, 63, 65, 70, 78, 95, 122, 128, 144, 146
Vieux Marché, 54, 137
Villalobar, Rodrigo de Saavedra y Vinent, Marquis de (1864–1926) (Spanish Minister), 6, 8, 12, 89, 93, 96, 106, 215, 233
Villiers, Sir Francis Hyde (1852–1925) (British Minister), xxiv, 8–9, 12, 199, 215, 220, 227–8, *228*
Vilvorde (north-east of Brussels), 57, 136, 252
Virgin Mary/Blessed Virgin, xv, 184, 211–13, 224, 227, 229, 231–2, 234, 236, 244, 246–7, 250–2, 269, 273
  Consecration to, 206
  Purification, 205, 215
  see also under fetes
Vivian, 3rd Baron, Hussey Crespigny (1834–93), *134*
Vivian, 4th Baron, George Crespigny Brabazon (1878–1940) (aide-de-

camp to King Albert), 12, 233
Viviers D'Oies (near Uccle), 109

Waelhem, 210
Walker, John Mortimer Brownlee (Morty) (1881–1942), xviii, 251
Walker, Kathleen (1915–c. 1993), xviii, 94
Walker, Margaret Doris (Doris) (née Hodson) (half-sister) (1886–1970), xiii, xvii–xix, *xxix*, 18, 22, 31, 49, *49*, 94, *176*, 233, 243, 251, 271, 276
war funds, 100, 139
Warneford, Flight Sub-Lieutenant R.A.J., VC (1891–1915), 70–2
Warsaw, 79
Washington, rue, 7, 243, 252, 263
water: none, 156–7
  taps/pipes frozen, 155–6
Waterloo: anniversary of battle (1815), 128
  trips to, 73, 121, 184–5
Waterloo, chaussée de, 54, 141
Watson, Marcia, xi–xv, 3–4, 27–9
Watt, Miss, 132–3, 136, 163, 200, 203, 206
Watts, Ethelbert (American Consul-General) (1845–1919), xxiv, 43–4, 46, 76, 106, 146, 152
Wauters, Germaine (schoolgirl), 181, 184, 187–8, 268
weather, freezing, 155–7, 161, 199
Weir family, 52, 68, 74
Wemmel, 175, 185
Werthy's (tea room), 205
Westend(e) (on Belgian seacoast), 37, 43, 55, 111
Whitlock, Brand (American Minister) (1869–1934), xxii, xxiv, 10–13, 46, 93, 96, 98, 111, 215, 261
Whitlock, Mrs Nell, 12, 114
Wielemans Ceuppens (brewery), 153
Wilcox, Herbert (1890–1977), xxi, 9
Wilhelm II, Emperor, *see* Kaiser, the
Wilhelm, German Crown Prince (1882–1951), 153
Williams, Hubert, Welsh Regiment (grave), 48
Williquet, Mariette (schoolgirl, dying), 278, 280
Wilson, (Mrs) Edith (1872–1961), 254
Wilson, President Woodrow (1856–1924), 254
Wiltcher's Hotel, 111, 121
Wiltcher, Sydney (dead), 204
Winnipeg, Manitoba, 23, 26–8, 30, 292, 294
Woluwe (east of Brussels), 86, 165
Wynne, Colonel, 112, 114–15, 126, 237

X-rays, 288

Ypres, 40, 119, 131
Yser, 52, 58, 104

Zeebrugge, 265–6
Zeppelin, Count Ferdinand von (1838–1917), 160
zeppelins, 1, 48–50, 54, 66–8, 70, 73, 86, 94–5, 111, 120, 122–3, 137–8, 141, 143, 147–50, 189, 197
  L 19: 112–13
  LZ 38: 58–9, 63
  No. 37: 67
  No. 39: 67
  sheds, 68, 72, 134
  super, 137
Zuyder Zee, 110

www.ingramcontent.com/pod-product-compliance
Lightning Source LLC
Chambersburg PA
CBHW032147080426
42735CB00008B/614